By
Eric Silver

Dateline:
Jerusalem

Reporting the Middle East 1967-2008

First published in 2011 by Revel Barker Publishing
Copyright © The Estate of Eric Silver 2011

By the same author:
Victor Feather TUC, Gollancz 1973
Begin - A Biography, Weidenfeld and Nicholson 1984
The Book of the Just, Weidenfeld and Nicholson 1992

By Eric Silver
Dateline: Jerusalem
ISBN: 978-1-907841-06-4

Revel Barker Publishing
66 Florence Road, Brighton, England BN1 6DJ
revelbarker@gmail.com

'For me Jerusalem stood alone among the cities of the world. There are many positions of greater authority and renown within and without the British Empire, but in a sense I cannot explain there is no promotion after Jerusalem.'

Orientations by Ronald Storrs, British Military Governor of Jerusalem, 1917-20

Contents

Appreciation by Sir Martin Gilbert

I was fortunate to have known Eric Silver, and to have enjoyed his thoughtful and amusing company. This volume of his articles gives a powerful picture of the quality of his mind, and his capacity to express his knowledge and thoughts in clear, incisive prose. This was of importance because what he wrote reached a wide audience, including those in many lands who needed to have a clear view of Israeli life and politics, and of the wider Arab-Israeli dimension.

These articles span forty-two years, more than two-thirds of the existence of the State of Israel. They tell us not only about its history, but about its soul.

Each article published here is worth reading, and each article has lessons that can be pondered. Even the articles of several decades ago have relevance today. No one will finish reading this book without having gained much information, much wisdom, and a sense of the qualities and character of a perceptive and remarkable man. He and his writings will be much missed.

Introduction by Donald Macintyre

There are two kinds of journalists: those who are generous with their knowledge, contacts and advice to others in the same trade, and those who are grudging with it all, perhaps because of some unspoken insecurity. I am glad I never worked against Eric in his *Guardian* heyday, or at any other time. Many of the pieces in this book from that *Guardian* period, starting from his visit just after the Six-Day War, and then during his time as the resident full-time correspondent which ran from the Lod Airport massacre and the Yom Kippur War up to the first Lebanon War and its aftermath, are a reminder, with their political insight, their eye for the telling detail, their freshness and their humanity, of what a daunting rival he would have been. But even if I had been forced to compete with him, I suspect I would have put him as unreservedly in the first of those two categories, that of the generous colleague, as I did when we worked together on the same paper.

For a newly arrived Jerusalem staff correspondent on the *Independent*, as I was in March 2004, Eric, by now long installed as the paper's resident part-timer (though that hardly does justice to the depth and breadth of his role) was the Platonic ideal of a mentor/workmate. Never pushy, interfering or didactic; always available to give counsel, share telephone numbers from his unrivalled list of contacts, dispense Johnny Walker Black Label and sympathy (though never too much of the second when it came to the vagaries of dealing with the office; he had seen it all before and always wanted to move on from the boring subject of yesterday's atrocity committed by the sub-editors). There were countless times when he saved me from embarrassment but one was when, early in my time in Jerusalem, the nuclear whistleblower Mordechai Vanunu was released. The office asked me to sum up the differences between what Israel was like when he went into gaol and when he came out of it. I rang Eric of course, and said, as I so often did: 'help'. At something like dictation speed, he constructed without pausing from his formidable memory a perfect list of the ways, from restaurant cuisine to settlement growth, in which the country had changed in those 18 years. When it appeared under my name I felt a shameful fraud; but of course Eric didn't mind that.

He was much, much, too big a man to begrudge a wholly undeserved by-line. And if he spotted you making a serious error, he told you – in private – in a firm but gentle way that ensured you would never do it again.

We didn't always agree of course; life would have been less interesting if we had. After his journalistically highly rewarding *Guardian* tour in Delhi, which followed the one in Jerusalem, he decided not to return to London. Instead he 'made aliyah'. Israel was therefore his adopted country, and as an Israeli he was probably less impatient than a few of his fellow correspondents, including me, at what we saw as its chronic disinclination to take dramatic steps needed for the region's lasting peace and security. But his Zionism was also that of a deep-dyed Labour Party man (which he had also been in Britain) who believed that division of the land was necessary for peace; that, as he wrote in his moving obituary of Yitzhak Rabin – which incidentally is an absolute masterpiece of that art – 'Israel could not go on ruling a large and hostile Arab minority if it wanted to remain a Jewish and a democratic state.' It's notable, too, reading this book, how early he saw the importance, reflected in his June 1972 piece on Mohammed Abou Shilbayih, of the first stirrings of Palestinian interest in the two-state solution. He was moreover unflinchingly objective when he saw failings of Israeli policy or conduct, as he often did. When on one occasion the *Independent* splashed on its front page a story about abuses by Israeli troops of Palestinians in Hebron under a dramatic headline referring to the soldiers' 'reign of terror' I was nervous that he would think the presentation too lurid, too over-the-top. 'Serve the buggers right,' was his succinct and only comment on the telephone the following morning.

If you asked him for advice, as I repeatedly did on all sorts of matters, historical, cultural, religious, in the hideously confusing maelstrom that engulfs the Jerusalem correspondent, Eric almost always knew the answers but on the rare occasions he didn't he would know someone who did. 'And you can mention my name, if you like,' he would say modestly. And of course it invariably helped if you did. He had a voracious appetite for work right until his last – and in terms of having to go to hospital pretty well first – illness; 'available for selection' he would say in crisp parlance of cricket, his favourite sport, if you asked him to cover at short notice. Many of us would often coast on an easy day by rewriting the news agency wires. This Eric never liked to do; right into his seventies he always wanted to add value, to make his calls; go out on the story if he could; two fine examples for the *Independent*, both happily included in this book, are the superb review cover story he did at an age when most reporters have long retired, on neo-Nazis in Petah Tikva and the 'worst of Israel, best of Israel' piece written under massive time pressure (pressure which, as always with Eric, was never visible between the lines of his invariably elegant, unhurried prose) from the Alyn Hospital in Jerusalem where the little Palestinian girl Maria Amin had been brilliantly treated after being crippled in an IDF air strike on Gaza.

A drink or a meal with Eric was always notable for what the Irish call the *craic*, the wit, and for the curiosity about the world which had animated him throughout his career. He was a gentleman in the best of senses, whether it was making sure that our Palestinian fixer in Gaza was adequately paid for his time, or displaying his great hospitality as a host. As Phil Reeves, the *Independent* correspondent from 2000-2003, wrote when he died: 'Eric was a man of great decency and kindness who never allowed our grubby business to compromise his dignity.' He was a social animal; he loved parties and gave great ones; there are not many people who would have fused his Israeliness with his irrepressible Yorkshire roots by teaching a bunch of Russian-Jewish musicians to play *On Ilkley Moor Baht 'at* at his 70th birthday. My impression was always that his family were the source of his great inner strength. The only time he really fought to protect from the inroads of work was time with his grandchildren. And it was impossible not to be aware how much he appreciated and reciprocated the love of the four women closest to him: his daughters Dinah, Sharon, Rachel and of course

Bridget, his beloved mainstay over so many years and in so many places. Bridget Silver has now performed an invaluable service by putting together this wonderfully rich collection of Eric's work; a fitting tribute to his memory, but something of lasting value, not only to those who know about, but also to all those who want to know about, the region he covered with such style and distinction over 40 years.

Acknowledgements by Bridget Silver

Soon after we met in 1958, Eric, as a young reporter on the *Harrogate Advertiser*, confessed to me that his ambition was to be a foreign correspondent, ideally on the *Manchester Guardian*. He said that it was a jungle out there and he couldn't expect me to share it. 'Shall I leave now?' I asked…

During his many years as a correspondent, he was often asked what he actually wrote about. 'War and peace' he always replied. He thrived on writing for newspapers and dreaded retirement. It was fortunate that he was able to freelance until the end, still dodging rockets in Haifa in the second Lebanese war.

Eric sadly died on July 15, 2008, aged 73, after a short and aggressive attack of cancer. This book is in memory of Eric the journalist, who was also a very kind and loving husband, father and grandfather. The book is intended to give not only an account of the events of the period but also a real sense of how it was for both Israelis and Palestinians living through the conflict.

Regretfully I had to leave out many pieces when putting this book together. There were thousands to choose from, many also from Cyprus, from when our family was caught in the coup of 1974, and others from India where Eric was the *Guardian* correspondent in the mid-eighties. I would like to thank the *Guardian* for permission to use the articles when Eric was on their staff and also Sir Martin Gilbert, Donald Macintyre and Martin Woollacott for their much appreciated contributions.

Thanks to all my family for their support; to daughter Sharon Barnett for her help and expertise with getting many of the articles onto the computer; daughter Dinah Black for her encouragement; grandson Jose Silver, who was a patient teacher with his computer knowledge and help with scanning, as were granddaughters Hannah and Libby Black. Many good friends gave advice and encouragement; in particular Jill and Victor Hoffbrand, David Fields and Henry and Judy Foner in the early stages, and Hella Pick, who also gave me the name of my publisher. Revel Barker has been a thorough and enthusiastic editor and I thank him. Many thanks too, to Jeremy Scholl for his generosity and professional advice and Minna Cowper-Coles for her help and encouragement.

Most of all, I thank my daughter, Rachel Silver, who has been with me throughout, given advice and help with the book proposal, publisher and her public relations skills.

Chapter 1 – 1966, 1967, 1972, 1973

An Israel notebook

Guardian, October 31, 1966

Jerusalem is an intensely subjective city. It catches you unawares, whether your roots are in Judaism, Christianity, or Islam, drawing out latent, inarticulate commitments. My moment of surrender was at Yad Vashem, the memorial to Hitler's six million Jewish victims. The central shrine is a building of absolute simplicity, yet it is as evocative as a cathedral. Its Hebrew name, Ohel Yiskor, The Tent of Remembrance, expresses it perfectly, a low, broad roof irregular concrete triangles, a dry wall on two sides of resilient Jerusalem stone that might have been hewn from the bare Judean hills outside, an eternal flame flicking amid welded iron in the far corner of a paved floor studded in Hebrew and Roman lettering with the names of concentration camps – an austere litany of 'a world which is no more'.

Israel is still surfing through a golden age of cinema-going. Films compete with football and archaeology as the national sport. But a cloud no bigger than a man's handout is rising on the horizon. Television is coming – not, of course, that it isn't there already. Some 30,000 Israeli citizens have TV sets, heavily taxed and costing the equivalent of 250 pounds sterling. They even pay licence fees. Yet by a philanthropic anomaly, the only service provided by the government is for schools. What happens is that, like Irishmen tuning in to the BBC, Israelis preen their aerials to the surrounding Arab states. Cowboys and Indians are the same whatever the subtitles.

In any case, many new immigrants come from Arabic speaking countries. But, most significantly, the greatest viewers are Israeli Arabs. Nazareth bristles with aerials. If every Bedouin has a transistor, every sheikh has a TV set. Which is why Israel is now being forced to start its own service. The Egyptians in particular have recognised the propaganda potential of TV, and have exploited it to stir up hostility to the Jewish State. So next year Israel will be the only country in the world screening Dr Kildare in the cause of national security.

The loneliest man in Jerusalem (rivalled only by poor, dead Mr Mandelbaum, whose shattered house still straddles the armistice line) is General Odd Bull, the Norwegian commander of the United Nations truce supervisors. He is a tall lean professional officer in his late fifties, a dry, wrinkled Scandinavian Eisenhower who served his apprenticeship in the peace business in the Lebanon in 1958. With his wife and son he has lived for three years now in the eerie isolation of no man's land. They have a small flat in the colonnaded British residence still referred to as Government House. The rest of the general's staff of 130 officers and 180 civilians from 12 countries live beyond the checkpoints in one or other half of the divided city.

Odd Bull is the man of impregnable discretion, insisting that I quote nothing he said during the half hour I spent in his office. The only fragment of our conversation I might smuggle on to the record was his welcoming question, 'What's going to happen to the *Guardian* now that Thomson has taken over *The Times*?'

Israeli folk music is at once among the most synthetic in the world and the most natural. Synthetic because it draws on no specifically Hebrew folk tradition. Natural because it sprung, long before the folk revival elsewhere, from the need of people living in difficult circumstances to provide their own entertainment. Nehama Hendel, who is coming to London for a fortnight at the Arts next month, has done as much as anyone to extend its range and deepen its hold. If she's not quite the blonde, blue-eyed Sabra we're always hearing about, she might as well be – with a husky, uncomplicated voice somewhere between Dietrich and Felix to match.

Over the grapefruit juice in a Tel Aviv café, she confessed to a normal bourgeois childhood ('I played the piano'). She learnt her trade in the Israeli equivalent of Ensa – spending a month during the Sinai campaign singing barefoot in the sand – and in the United States, where she was an Ed Sullivan discovery.

A curiosity – two Israeli getaway girls, lissome, elegant, fair hair streaming from Triumph Herald coupé, each with bandage and

15

plaster over her nose. They are, it seems, recuperating at our hotel outside Jerusalem after cosmetic operations. Even in Israel, a Jewish profile is a disadvantage. Unless, of course, they've been having them bent instead of straightened.

Tempted by the atom

Guardian, June 24, 1967

To understand Israeli attitudes towards a peace one must begin with the war. I have met no one in Israel in the past week who did not believe that the Arabs meant what they said; that they would annihilate the Jews. Seen from Britain through eyes blinkered by the cold war, this could be dismissed as so much bluster, a tactical gesture with no more intent than Khrushchev's threat to crush America. In Israel there are plenty of people with memories of an earlier final solution, plenty who resisted an earlier Arab campaign to drive the Jews into the sea. Through Israeli eyes Nasser threatened a very old-fashioned kind of war, the kind which Great Power strategists regard as obsolete – a war for national and personal survival, a war for limited attainable ends.

It was, too, a war in which the prospective victim was deserted in her time of need by all her friends. Few Israelis were sure of victory in advance. None expected it would be over so quickly. Israeli triumphs left a widespread feeling that something special, something almost Messianic, had happened in those four days of battle. An experience religious in quality, though not necessarily in content – like an atheist savouring Beethoven's mass – explains the continuing day-long pilgrimages to the wall; hundreds walking slowly along the hot, winding two miles from the main road, families, school groups, old men dressed to face the rigours of Stoke Newington in autumn, pregnant women, and soldiers dressed in camouflaged battledress. Only a tiny minority are zealots. Many do not bother to pray. Although Israeli casualties were 'small', they have left an imprint of personal tragedy. Jewish Israel is still like a big village. Most people know of somebody dead or wounded.

For all these reasons, so much said at the United Nations – not least by George Brown – seems to Israelis at best irrelevant and at worst hypocritical. Advice about 'magnanimity' falls on deaf ears. Appeals to principle that there should be no forcible aggrandisement are received as an empty affront – especially when made at the United Nations, a body widely despised for precipitating the war by withdrawing at the first Egyptian challenge. Spokesmen still insist that they do not want any expansion, but experience in the past month has left Israelis more than ever convinced that they can depend on no one but themselves. They will withdraw only on terms guaranteeing that there will be no repetition, terms public and unambiguous, leaving Israel with the strategic advantages of victory. This means negotiations with individual Arab states, recognition of Israel's national entity, tactical adjustment of the Syrian border, possibly neutralisation of the West Bank and Gaza.

The future of Jerusalem is a problem of a different dimension. The Old City has gained such symbolic significance for the Israelis that it is hard to conceive giving it up. The bulldozing of houses before the Wall is one of the few signs of arrogance. Emotions are controlled but strong. When I visited the Wall all was very calm till one woman suddenly cried, 'Let there be peace in the land and the whole world.' Universal amens were released like pressure from a vacuum.

The United Nations has emerged from the war discredited. It is difficult to envisage any positive role acceptable to the Israelis. Israelis have always doubted its impartiality. Rightly or wrongly, bias and incompetence is now taken as finally confirmed. U Thant`s standing is at rock bottom.

The military lessons of the war are still being digested. Much depends on the final political and territorial equilibrium. Israeli spokesmen are reluctant to speculate at this stage. A wary eye is being kept on Soviet rearmament of Egypt; one published suggestion here is that Egypt might be ready to fight again in six months. Seasoned diplomatic observers are less reticent. They recognise the temptation for creating an Israeli nuclear deterrent. This could easily be camouflaged in silos, and it would probably survive any Egyptian emulation at the first Israeli strike against the

Arab air bases. It would not need to be bigger than the Hiroshima-type bomb. It could be deployed without testing and delivered relatively unsophisticatedly over a short distance. The Egyptians are less capable of following suit. They are known to be having trouble with rocket guidance. Their nuclear technology is well behind that of Israel.

It must be emphasised that there is no indication that Israel is actually contemplating going nuclear and risking a spiralling arms race, but it would be surprising if it were not being examined as a long-term possibility.

Two states projected for co-existence in Palestine
Guardian, June 29, 1972

Mohammed Abou Shilbayih is a dreamer. But then, as he disarmingly reminds you, so was Theodor Herzl. Last year Shilbayih`s Arabic testament, 'No peace without a Palestine Free State,' sold out in four days. This week, like the founder of political Zionism 76 years ago, Shilbayih has followed it with a manifesto.

His theme is still that Jews and Arabs must stop brandishing guns and slogans and learn to live together in a land where they both have roots. 'We are the Jews of the second half of the twentieth century,' he says. 'The world and the Israelis must help us. We demand the right to live in a Palestinian state of our own.'

Shilbayih is 45, a refugee from the abandoned village of Abasiyah, two and a half miles north of Lydda. He studied at Cairo University, teaches literature at a college near Jerusalem and writes a column for an Arabic newspaper.

No one can be sure how much support he commands among the Arabs of Jerusalem and the West Bank. Some of King Hussein's admirers were sufficiently worried about his first book to try and guy it up wholesale with false promises of a wider market in Egypt.

Shilbayih`s first political test will come within the next month when he applies to the Israeli minister of the interior for a permit to found a party. Jews as well as Arabs will be watching to see what response he draws and then whether the Palestinians rally to his banner.

The new book *The Way to Peace* argues that there must be two states in what used to be Palestine. The Jewish State would have its capital in Jewish Jerusalem, the Arab State its capital in Arab Jerusalem. The Gaza Strip would be part of the Arab State linked to the West Bank by an access corridor.

Jerusalem would have two municipal councils possibly supervised by an Arab-Jewish coordinating authority on the lines of Greater London Council. The border would be the border of June 4, 1967. The police in each half of the city would be linked to the police of their own state.

Any Jew would be free to come to Jerusalem as would any Arab. But Jews would be forbidden to buy land or houses in the Arab sector and vice-versa. They could live across the line as tenants but not as owners.

'I do not want an Arab island in a Jewish ocean,' Shilbayih says. Arab Jerusalem must not become a ghetto. But where do the Israeli Arabs fit into his scheme, the Arabs who have been citizens since 1948?

They are, he insists, part of the Palestinian people. They would vote in the elections to the Arab Parliament but would continue to pay taxes to, and receive services from, Israel. An odd case of taxation without representation and representation without taxation.

The new partition, he adds, would have to be supervised by the United Nations, though he takes that to mean all or some of the bigger Western Powers. 'We must negotiate for everything in order to get peace; I do not care about one kilometre here or there. To get a secure border we must convince Jews and Palestinians that each is taking his legal rights.'

The Arab refugees should be compensated for their lost homes – unless their lands are still uninhabited in which case they should be free to return. 'We must make it clear that there is no question of driving out the Jews. We want our nationalism; the Jews must have their nationalism.'

Equally the Jews expelled from Iraq and other Arab States must be compensated too – but by the Iraqis, not by the Palestinians.

19

The long memory

Guardian, September 7, 1972

The Israeli man in the street is more angry than shocked, more frustrated than diplomatic at the slaughter of 11 of his country's Olympic sportsmen and officials. The latest engagement in his long war with the Arab guerrillas had to be fought by proxy and it was lost.

Israeli professionals are reluctant to fault the German police tactics at the airfield until they know all the facts. The Arabs dictated the pattern of the final confrontation. It was up to the security forces to improvise and seize the upper hand. The line between success and failure is inevitably fine. Either way, the outcome is spectacular.

In similar circumstances the Israelis would almost certainly have adopted close-combat tactics rather than rely on sharpshooters. That was what they did when Arabs hijacked a Sabena airliner to Lydda this spring. The question raised, however, is whether German troops could have been expected to feel the same motivation for such a dangerous operation.

If they had risked their lives in that way to save Jews the impact in Israel would have been deep and abiding. Memories are long and Munich is Munich. Instead Willy Brandt scores a more muted plus for his approach to president Sadat of Egypt and for making public its inconsequential ending.

Criticism of Bonn focuses more coherently on the inadequacy of the security measures taken at the Olympic village. How was it possible for the Arabs to penetrate the compound with arms and reach the Israeli pavilion without challenge? Were the Germans really warned the night before and did they really do nothing effective about it?

The censure rubs off on the Israeli security services too. The military spokesman turned away questions with the soporific line that the Israeli competitors were in Munich as guests of Germany. Guests don't go around with guns over their shoulders.

Perhaps not, but it is generally assumed here that there must have been some security men among the Israeli baggage carriers. The political correspondent of the independent *Ha'aretz* wrote this morning that Israeli security men had been active in Munich. 'This was roundabout activity,' he said, 'not direct. They were in action in Munich. It was not clear what had happened to the Israeli security elements at the time of the attack.'

The question will be asked and asked again in the next few weeks. Today's cabinet statement on the massacre put it explicitly: 'It was decided to concentrate detailed and accurate information on the security measures taken in Munich – both by the authorities of the Federal German Republic and by the Israeli bodies responsible.'

My own experience of security surveillance, covering the two recent hijacking trials at Sarafand, suggests that it tends to go slack with time. Checks become more routine, alertness fades. I suspect that it would have been harder to carry off the coup in the first week of the Games than in the second.

The sharpest thrust of Israeli popular anger, however, is directed at the Arab commandos. The cabinet resolution has its own resources, but the evening *Ma'ariv* catches the public mood in an extreme form:

> We have to think very seriously about settling the account between Israel and the terrorists and the people who have sent them. We do not want to adopt their methods. We are not going to meet them in faraway places. We must hit them in their own homes… We are now in a new period. We are not going to talk any more. It will not be enough for countries in the world to share our sorrow. We need action. The period for annihilating the terrorists has begun.

In all the beating of breasts and searching of hearts, though, one argument is missing. No public or private voice has been raised questioning the government's decision not to bargain convicted Arab prisoners for Jewish hostages. Israel is probably unique as a nation whose citizens accept that they are in a state of chronic warfare with their neighbors.

Every Israeli is a soldier – literally in that he does his national and reserve service. And psychologically in that, as one veteran put it to me today: 'we are all potential hostages'.

War and the hazards of war are part of the fabric of Israeli life, and have been for at least three generations. People have no urge to martyrdom, but the government does not have to spell out its contention that once you make concessions to blackmail you will never stop.

Twice in the past four years Israel has done deals with Arab kidnappers. An El-Al jet-load hijacked to Algeria was ransomed; so were two Israeli civilians taken from an airliner and held in Damascus. But on both occasions they were out of range of Israeli intervention or of the efforts of a friendly foreign power.

People here are conditioned to drama. They have too much at stake to succumb to threats, however persistent.

The general's will

Guardian, October 19, 1972

Moshe Dayan is the Garbo of Israel. You see him sitting alone in the members' dining room at the Knesset. No one approaches his table by the window. Cabinet colleagues, whether ally or foe, keep their distance. So do the political journalists.

It is the same at official cocktail parties. Dayan, thickening now at the base like one of those weighted dolls that bounce upright whenever you push them over, stays for five beaming, awkward minutes, then takes his leave.

Shabtai Teveth, an Israeli columnist whose Dayan biography is published in London today, attributes this beleaguered quality to Dayan's 'sovereign' personality. I am what I am, take me or leave me. It is a philosophy that endears him more to the public than to the machine politicians, who will choose and have to work with the next prime minister.

Teveth brings out, too, an unexpected sensitivity. Dayan's eye patch, the defence minister's international trademark, remains an embarrassment 30 years after a Vichy French bullet shattered his field glasses during an allied advance into Syria. Dayan has tried three times to have a glass eye installed in the empty socket, but the damage was too drastic and the results were grotesque.

Dayan is the mixture of the peculiarly Israeli aristocrat and of the self-made man. He was the first child born on the first kibbutz. His parents left five years later to found the first Moshav (a smallholders` cooperative). Shmuel, his father, soon became an absentee pioneer and full-time political organiser, a man with easy access to the leaders of the Zionist labour movement in Palestine.

Moshe's marriage complemented his own connections. His wife was the daughter of a rich and influential Jewish lawyer. Other doors opened. Chaim Weizmann, with the aid of Harold Laski, found him a place at the London School of Economics and a chance to study agriculture at Cambridge.

In the event, Dayan pursued neither course. He felt uneasy in England just as he was out of his element when he read Middle East studies at the Hebrew University after the Suez war.

His mind is searching and original, but without formal discipline. Even as minister of defence, he likes to think in public. At the end of one of his speeches, you have a sense of insight. Dayan has few preconceptions. He says real things about real issues, yet you come away still uncertain of his position.

The minister is always travelling, seldom arriving. Today's policy may be spurned next week – sometimes because Dayan is a wily, ambitious man. Frequently because he has explored new arguments and is not afraid to admit that he was wrong.

He has to work things out for himself. Nothing is taken on trust. As a soldier, this made Dayan a superb partisan fighter, but an occasionally disastrous field commander. As minister of agriculture in the early sixties, he switched Israel's entire tomato crop overnight, then found no one would buy the new variety. But by the end of his five-year stint, he had put the country`s farmers on their feet for the first time in local and foreign markets.

Dayan is an improviser. He admires audacity and courage. Shabtai Teveth quotes one of his boyhood friends as saying that Dayan's own fearlessness was a physical trait. Just as someone may have a physical deficiency, such as one leg shorter than the other. Moshe Dayan was simply deficient in fear… it always felt good to go out to fight with Moshe. He was very daring. He never looked twice. He simply ran forward. We all noticed that nothing seemed to frighten him, nor did he care a whit what might happen to him.

Yigal Yadin, Israel's second chief-of-staff, transformed the Haganah into an army of a sovereign state. Moshe Dayan, its fourth chief-of-staff, gave that army its distinctive stamp. The doctrine was offensive and unconventional. The officers led from the front, the mission had to be 'exhausted'. Bull was kept to a minimum, rules were made to be broken (in his younger days, Dayan himself was twice demoted for insubordination). The key to Dayan's popularity, as to his capacity to draw the right response at the moments of crisis, is that he is an Israeli and nothing other than an Israeli. Unlike his parents or his seniors in the present government, he is not a cosmopolitan Jew. His roots and fate are in the Middle East.

The Arabs are integral to his world. Shmuel Dayan regarded them as part of the flora and fauna of the Promised Land. Moshe's perception was never so remote. He played as a boy with Arab boys, and he speaks the Arabic language. His friendships with individual Arabs are more than mere public relations.

The young Dayan differed bitterly in the thirties with his father about the 'bearded sheikhs', an Arab terror organisation led by As-El-Din El-Kassam, a Moslem zealot dedicated to 'fighting for our religion and homeland, murdering Englishmen and Jews because they are taking over our land'.

To Shmuel, they were simply ungrateful criminals who deserved no mercy. Moshe, according to his biographer, tried to see the Arabs as they saw themselves, and not through the eyes of a Russian Jew.

'I understand that they do have a national motivation,' Moshe Dayan explained. 'Until that time I had been raised on the stories of the Hashomer guards about the most famous thief of all – an Arab named Abu Julda – and other Arab bandits. The case of El-Kassam was the first time I began to regard the gangs as a part of a national structure with nationalistic motivation. Individually, the Kassama'in were virtuous men, exceptional idealists.'

Yet none of this stopped Dayan leading reprisal raids in the Jordan Valley, or ordering them on a vaster scale as general and minister. His dilemma is a Middle Eastern dilemma. So is his response. The justice is as harsh as the terrain. Precisely because he was not of the settler generation he had to fight to survive.

The private conflict persists. The open-bridges policy, with all its security risks, is Dayan's policy. The Arabs of the occupied territories, he argues, must not be amputated from their people. More than 150,000 Arabs came west of the Jordan on summer visits this year. Even though some of them, on Dayan's own testimony, were saboteurs, he defends the scheme and talks of extending it.

Yet at the same time, his soldier's sense of battles fought and still to be fought is driving Dayan to the conclusion that Israel's frontiers must be on the Jordan River. He is a hawk without chauvinism, a dove who cannot make peace.

Sad son of Zion

Guardian, April 24, 1972

Amos Oz left Jerusalem as a rebellious 15-year-old to join Kibbutz Hulda, one of Israel's oldest communes, at the foot of the Judean hills. Eighteen years, two novels, a collection of short stories and an Oxford sabbatical later, he is still there. When he can, he teaches. When he wants, he writes. The kibbutz is generous with time and paper. In return, Oz signs the publishers' cheques and hands them to the treasurer.

He affects neither to know nor care how much his books earn, but if he is not careful he will soon be competing with cotton and fruit as Hulda's money-spinner. His latest novel, *My Michael*, has sold 45,000 in Hebrew paperback.

My Michael charts a middle-class marriage of incomprehension. It is written in the first person feminine. Below the surface of its calculation and understatement, it challenges the pioneering simplicities and immigrant aspirations (My son, Herr Doktor) that underpin Israeli society.

The novel can hardly have sold exclusively to captive wives, though there are enough painfully perceptive echoes to see them through a month of ironing. Oz, in London for its publication, is still puzzled by its success.

'It has no sex, no murders, no direct political attacks, nothing to do with any description of fighting, yet in one way or another it touched an open nerve. I think that the implications of the Israel-Arab conflict, indirect as they are, enraged some readers and at the same time legitimised certain attitudes which were around, but were not expressed before – anyway, not in literature.'

Oz deliberately set *My Michael* in the fifties, a period of Jewish anti-climax after the tragedies, struggles and achievements of the forties ('the most dramatic period in Jewish history since the destruction of the Temple.')

The book too, he says, is an anti-climax in the context of modern Hebrew literature. 'Whereas Hebrew writers of previous periods tended to describe the heights of fighting, struggling, suffering, this book deliberately deals with petty bourgeois everyday life. It shows the vengeance of the petty bourgeois instincts which were hiding even in the most heated pioneers, the most revolutionary socialists.

'After all, these people, the founders, they all came from small towns in Eastern Europe. They wanted to revolutionise the world in such a way that their sons and daughters would be able to come back to a petty bourgeois existence. So what is there? We have revolutionised Jewish history in order to carry it on in a different way under different circumstances, apparently without immediate threat.'

Like other Israeli writers published in Britain in the last couple of years – Aharon Megged, A B Yehoshua and Amos Elon – Oz picks at Israel's particular generation gap. He goes further than Elon's argument (in *The Israelis: Founders and Sons*) that the pioneers simply ignored the Arabs.

'It was in a way even worse. They confronted the Arabs with Tolstoian attitudes, missionary attitudes, Kipling's attitudes. We shall cure the Arabs, we shall educate them, we'll build for them, we'll show them what modern life is. We embrace them with a loving embrace and they must love us.'

Yet, *My Michael* is not only a novel without sex, it is a novel without Arabs. Except fantasy Arabs; the Arab at the fringe of Jew's consciousness, the Arab – in the case of Oz's heroine Hannah – as the noble savage at the gate.

The trauma is a trauma of Fortress Israel, and especially of divided Jerusalem, the city that dominates Oz's book as completely as Alexandria broods over Lawrence Durrell's quartet.

'The Jerusalem of my own childhood,' Oz says, 'was a small town of some 80,000 inhabitants. Still, it was one of the most cosmopolitan places in the world – Moslem Arabs and Christian Arabs, Armenians and Greeks, and madmen from all over the world who came to Jerusalem to establish the new redemption or to become new messiahs.

'Modern Zionists were just one of the figments, one of these many messianic movements. But for a short period, between 1948 and 1967, Jerusalem became for once a Jewish city, which is just the opposite of what Jerusalem used to be.

'Hannah sensed that this was an episode that this was artificial, that this was a besieged enclave which could not last. For her the War of Liberation, which practically separated Jews and Arabs everywhere in Palestine and especially in Jerusalem, was a personal disaster. She expects a vengeance, she is longing for a vengeance. In a way the Arab threat for Hannah is the only chance. Something must happen; this is not the end of it.'

But if the Zionist city of Jerusalem was an episode between the first and third Israeli-Arab wars, what has happened to the open city of Jerusalem since 1967? 'Well it's still happening. It's a volcano in action. It's very hard to say what's going to come of it, but I believe it's not going to become a pure Zionist town once again.

'Jerusalem never has been a city. It has been a vague federation of small villages, quarters and suburbs, each of them with an entirely different style of building, style of life and entirely different periods. There was no centre.

'During the fifties there was an ideological attempt to turn West Jerusalem into one unified city. Thank God it failed. Some of the beauty of Jerusalem was saved. Jerusalem was stronger than the obsession with knocking down walls. The attack is now being repeated on a much more energetic scale. But Jerusalem is a stubborn city. She won't give in easily.'

What Amos Oz challenges – more explicitly in his political excursions than in his novels – is Israeli pragmatism. Statehood is not enough. The country, he says, has lost the capacity to dream. 'What have we done? Established another Rumania or Bulgaria? Was that the meaning of the Zionist dream?'

Yet Oz, like his heroine, is neither suicidal nor weighed down with guilt. Oz himself left Jerusalem for the kibbutz, a reversion to one part of the pioneering ideology. He served in the tank corps in the Six-Day War and still does his 40 days a year reserve duty.

'I am a Zionist but a sad Zionist. I am a Zionist in the elementary sense that, although I regard nationhood as an archaic and murderous concept, I cannot risk personally, being a father, I cannot risk being the eternal Cape Kennedy of internationalism. To quote Ivan Karamazov in a very different context, I cannot afford it any more.

'Let someone else have a try for once. I'm not going to be the first one to give up nationhood and the attributes of national states, an army and defensive systems. Not the first one in the world and certainly not the first one in the Middle East. I shall be happy to be the second or third for once. In this sense I don't want to be a pioneer any more, not after Auschwitz.'

Harold Wilson in the Holy Land at Christmas

Guardian, December 27, 1972

Harold Wilson has waded through three Christmas dinners this year, and the most strenuous holiday of a political lifetime. On Christmas Eve he ate and talked turkey with the mayor of Bethlehem – Arab-style but with a 'kosher' guarantee on the top table. On Christmas Day Abba Eban gave him veal and two veg at the King David Hotel, Jerusalem. The new British ambassador, Bernard Ledwidge, a slimmed down Robert Morley whose wife writes best-selling French novels, offered turkey, trimmings and plum pud on Boxing Day.

The Labour leader is visiting the Holy Land on what was first presented as a family holiday, his wife Mary and his sister Marjorie, now retired as headmistress of a Cornish primary school, are in the party. Giles, his bearded younger son, has taken a seasonal break from the Galilean kibbutz where he has been learning Hebrew (well enough to be interviewed for Israeli television) and picking lemons. The Westminster entourage stayed at home.

But Harold's host is Golda Meir. The trip has taken in Nazareth, Bethlehem and Jerusalem. There have been talks with the prime minister, as well as with Yigal Allon, Moshe Dayan, the speaker of the Knesset and the secretary of the Labour Party. 'We hope you are having a good rest here,' Eban teased him, 'and that you'll find somewhere to recuperate afterwards.'

On Christmas morning the Wilsons were shown the holy places in Jerusalem. At the Garden Tomb, which competes with the Holy Sepulchre as the site of the crucifixion and burial of Jesus, Harold chanced upon the Norwegian prime minister. Lars Korvald, who really is here on a private pilgrimage. 'Didn't see you in Bethlehem last night,' quoth Harold, who attended midnight mass in the Roman Catholic church of St Catherine. 'No,' said Lars. 'You see I'm a prime minister, so I can't enter the occupied territories.' Wilson shook his head. He didn't care whether he was leader of the opposition or prime minister next time round, nothing would stop him going to Bethlehem.

It was not always thus. When Labour was last in office a posse of MPs came here on a 'fact-finding mission'. Two of them happened to be junior ministers in H Wilson's administration. Before leaving London they were forbidden to tread occupied soil. The Israelis took the group to see the West Bank. The two ministers stayed in their bus, on the principle that whoever the ground belonged to the charabanc was forever Israel.

Church rivalries have survived the ecumenical movement and even the opening of a new and opulent ecumenical institute on the Jerusalem-Bethlehem road. It is less than a decade since the Greek Orthodox and the Roman Catholics settled their long struggle for their right to clean the windows of the Church of the Nativity; one denomination feathers the outside, the other the inside.

Peace and goodwill have come still less swiftly to the several fields where the shepherds did, or did not, watch their flocks. Luke, the source of the story, neglected alas to pinpoint the site. The Greeks have one field, the Romans its neighbour, and the Protestants a third, complete with YMCA. Like Zionist apologists in another conflict, the Greek Orthodox always assert that they were here first. Now they have found archaeology to prove it.

Vassilios Tzeferis, a Greek archaeologist working for the Israeli department of antiquities, has excavated a fifth-century underground church in the orthodox field, within sight of Bethlehem, and surrounded by thick, gnarled olive trees that could easily be two thousand years old. The church is almost completely preserved with roof, windows and pavement – a small dank hangar that must have grown out of a cave.

But the showpiece is a lower mosaic pavement. The pattern includes crosses, which were prohibited on floors from 427AD. Ergo this site was venerated as early as the fifth and probably the fourth centuries. Since the whole tradition of an actual shepherds' field dates only from the fourth century, this must be it, or as near as anyone will ever get to it.

The trouble with Bethlehem itself is not so much that it is commercialised as that its commerce is limited and naïve. The souvenir shops, with names like 'Holy Manger' and 'Shepherds' Field', are good for a snigger, but they give value. So do the pilgrims' cafes. Then what? People come, see the Church of the Nativity, and go back to Jerusalem. There is no inn.

The Christian Arab mayor, Elias Freij, is determined to change all this. His ambition is to transform Manger Square from a wide-open car park into a piazza, with fountains and seats, open-air cafes and beautiful corners, 'where people can sit and glory in the thought that they are in Bethlehem'.

Mayor Freij's problem is that Bethlehem entertains 400,000 tourists a year, but has a population of only 20,000. 'From the small amount we collect in rates, how can we possibly develop the town as it should be developed?'

Instead, he has taken Teddy Kollek, the Jewish mayor of Jerusalem, as model and mentor. He wants to set up a Bethlehem Foundation, like Kollek's lucrative Jerusalem Foundation. Freij hopes to visit America to raise money. In the past few months he has buttonholed Nelson Rockefeller, the governor of New York State, John Lindsay, the mayor of New York City, and Lester Maddox, the lieutenant-governor of Georgia. All were reported 'enthusiastic'.

Rockefeller has arranged for two American architects to come to Bethlehem and study Freij's plans. It is a start, but as the Jerusalem mayor could tell him, foreign architects have a habit of melting into the horizon.

Spotted during midnight mass in St Catherine's, hard by the Church of the Nativity an Israeli plain clothes man singing *Come All Ye Faithful* in Latin. What was that about the Lion and the Lamb?

Even more self-dependent
Guardian Weekly, December 31, 1972
Israel will remember 1972 as a year of two massacres. Terror turned to drama, the front stretched to Europe and beyond. The Jewish sense of being able to depend on no one but themselves was reinforced.

At the end of May three Japanese revolutionaries, demonstrating their solidarity with the Palestinian cause, killed 26 airline passengers at Lydda. It was the first successful airborne coup against a target inside Israel. Most of the victims, and of the 70 wounded, were Christian pilgrims from Puerto Rico.

Early in September Arab kidnappers murdered 11 Israeli sportsmen during the Munich Olympics. The national anger and frustration were heightened by the premature announcement that nine of the Israelis had been rescued by the German marksmen. All Israel stayed by its radio. The 12.30 bulletin brought news of a miracle, and everyone went to bed content.

The morning brought pain and dismay. The Israelis had had to leave their fight with Arab guerillas in German hands, and the Germans had failed. The feeling of isolation was completed when, within two months, Willy Brandt's government released the three surviving murderers in response to the hijacking of a Lufthansa airliner. In the same week, the Dutch set free an 'Algerian diplomat' caught in transit through Schipol airport with a suitcase full of guns, grenades, and detonators.

It was, nonetheless, a year of more peace than war. The ceasefire across the Suez Canal marched into its third year, with the Israeli and Egyptian soldiers shouting genial abuse from either side of the waterway. King Hussein and General Dayan between them kept the eastern front quiet. By the end of the year, after one land attack and a string of air raids by the Israelis, the Lebanese government seemed to have taken the hint. For a while at least, the fedayeen drew back from the frontier.

Only the border with Syria remained hot. Bands of Sa`ika guerillas, sponsored and controlled by the Syrian Government, continued to provoke Israeli settlers and soldiers on the occupied Golan Heights with the pinpricks of mines in the road and bazookas at dawn.

After a two-year interval, the Israeli forces took the battle to the Syrian army. It was a calculated risk. The Israelis were aware of the dangers of luring Egypt into action in support of their federation partners. They knew, too, that Syria was receiving fresh supplies of arms and equipment from the Soviet Union (though they were less impressed than some observers with the scale of the airlift).

The risk, however, was taken. The ceasefire, Israel's chief-of-staff, General Elazar, said, could exist either on both sides of the border or none. But the Israelis insisted on choosing their own way and their own time for retaliation. After one Syrian bombardment, they asked for a meeting with the chief of the United Nations truce observers and sent a cool warning to Cairo not to be dragged into war.

Egypt was in less condition than ever to renew hostilities. President Sadat expelled most of his 20,000 Soviet military advisers in August, but spent the rest of the year failing to find the arms or diplomatic support he needed elsewhere. Israel, by contrast, continued to receive American equipment and political sustenance – before and after the presidential election.

Within the area controlled by Israel since the 1967 war, the twin processes of 'normalisation' and entrenchment continued. The Arabs of the West Bank held municipal elections – under Jordanian electoral laws that restricted the vote to property owners and alienated the younger Palestinian activists.

More than 150,000 Arabs crossed the river for a summer holiday on the West Bank, on the Gaza Strip and in Israel proper. Trade and pro-Hashemite notables trekked steadily eastwards to Amman. The King proposed a federal solution, but was not yet ready to do the sort of deal that Israel would contemplate. The Jewish presence grew, meanwhile, in Hebron, a city holy to Moslems and to Jews. The township of Kiryat Arba expanded to 250 homes (and another 200 approved by the cabinet), and Jewish praying rights were gradually extended at the shrine of Abraham, the father of Isaac and Ishmael. Elsewhere in the occupied territories, the number of paramilitary settlements rose to 44. Development began of a resort at Sharm-el-Sheikh, which commands the entrance from the Red Sea to Israel's southern port of Eilat. Time prints its own map.

Gaza found an uneasy peace. As many as 40,000 Arab refugees were crossing daily from the camps to work in Israel. The economy of the strip was boosted by orders from Israeli industry, grappling with its own problem of over-full employment. The Arab mayor, Rashid e-Shawa, for one saw the dangers. He was dismissed for refusing to comply with an Israeli order to provide municipal services for the huge Shati refugee camp. He feared an Israeli solution to the refugee problem that would remove Gaza from the international agenda and leave it permanently under Israeli jurisdiction.

Within the pre-1967 borders, Israel's claim to give equality of treatment to its Arab minority was challenged by the affair of Berem and Ikrit. The Christian Arabs of these two villages near the Lebanese border had been asked to leave for security reasons in

1948, but had been promised that they could return within a fortnight. After 24 years they were still waiting in the other Galilean community in which they had settled.

Prompted by a hint from General Dayan that regulations establishing security areas along the frontier might soon be relaxed, the Arabs renewed their campaign to go back. Against the wishes of the deputy premier, Mr Allon, and of Mrs Meir's chief Arab affairs advisor, the cabinet refused yet again. The government was worried about creating precedents for other dispossessed Arabs, though it did quietly allow the villagers to return to Wadi Fukin, a valley near Bethlehem, which had been a launching pad for guerilla attacks from just inside the old Jordanian border.

The second half of 1972 witnessed an extraordinary debate between ministers on the future of the West Bank. General Dayan and the minister of transport, Mr Peres, argued for annexation as the only available option. Mr Allon, backed among others by the powerful finance minister, Mr Sapir, and the foreign minister, Mr Eban, argued that annexation would be sowing disaster.

Internally, Israel seemed to be allowing itself a little more of the luxury of conflict between Jews. The combative secretary-general of the trade union federation, Mr Ben-Aharon, declared war on the employers (including the predominantly Labour government, and with a fair backwash for his own Histadrut, the biggest capitalist in the land). The muted conflict of synagogue and state threatened cabinet unity, but was put on ice by the new Ashkenazi chief rabbi, Shlomo Goren, who ruled like Humpty Dumpty that marriage laws meant what he chose them to mean, no more and no less.

But perhaps the most important story of the year was the arrival of 31,000 Jewish immigrants from the Soviet Union, more than double the figure for 1971. The Soviet Union with a Jewish population of up to 3,000,000 is probably the last source of mass migration for Israel. The survival there of Jewish sentiment half a century after the revolution is regarded here as little less than miraculous. The immigration has, however, already produced its crop of teething troubles (not very different from those of other immigrants). They are minuscule compared with the imponderables, recognised but accepted, of absorbing so many newcomers from a mature communist society.

Lines towards a lasting peace

Guardian, February 5, 1973

Nearly six years after Israel stretched its eastern border to the Jordan River, Golda Meir's cabinet remains corporately content with a policy of the highest common factor: here Israel stays until the Arabs are ready for 'real' negotiation and a contractual peace. Till then there is no sense in shaking the unity of the coalition, or indeed of the less than united Labour Party.

So there is no White Paper. The government, you are told ad nauseam, has drawn no maps. Mrs Meir's ministers are less reticent. The debates, which resumed last week in the Labour secretariat, flushed out the differences and established a majority against annexation. Even the premier, however insensitive to Palestinian aspirations, has recognised the weight of the demographic argument (she says she does not want to wake every morning and worry how many Arab babies have been born during the night).

But the real contest is still being fought backstage. It is a conflict of personality, ambition, and temperament as well as of ideas. In the long and often petty war of Golda's succession, the future of the occupied territories is snared in the competing futures of two military heroes turned politician: Moshe Dayan and Yigal Allon.

Both have their 'plans' for the West Bank, though coalition discipline stops them spelling it out on the record. The Allon plan is logical and precise, befitting a man who presents himself as a disciple of Liddell Hart, and was the most consistently successful staff officer of the 1948 war; Dayan's plan is more pragmatic, the thinking of a partisan leader. The principles are no less solid, but the policy built on them is flexible and open to improvisation.

In the Allon plan it is the principles which determine the map. The deputy premier starts with the argument that the Jews had a historic right to establish a state in Palestine. Changes in the de facto border are proposed not because Israel does not have a right to the territories, but because there are advantages to be gained from giving up some of them.

Allon then argues that Israel must be a Jewish state with an Arab minority. It must be a democracy. And it must be willing to compromise, taking into account the aspirations of the Palestinian Arabs.

On these assumptions, the key to the Allon plan is 'defensible' borders, which he defines as borders that Israel can defend for itself. The conception is strategic, but brittle. On the West Bank he insists that the old green line, determined by the tug-of-war of 1948, is not defensible.

Instead, Allon proposes minimal changes in the Latrun area, securing the main road between Tel Aviv and Jerusalem, which was closed to Israeli traffic from 1948 to 1967. He would be content to leave Qalqilya and Tulkarm under Arab rule, though they were always regarded as a danger to the narrow coastal strip between Tel Aviv and Haifa.

The deputy premier's distinctive proposition is that Israel should keep the thinly populated areas to the east of hill towns in the wilderness and the Jordan valley. Israel, he claims, would not annex Arabs, but it would sterilise their military potential. The area is bordered by the river, a useful but limited barrier. Moving westwards there are hills of different heights with a few passes. It would be an uncrossable defensive line and wide enough for Israel to prepare a counter attack.

Allon would be prepared to cede the Arabs a corridor running west to east creating territorial continuity between Ramallah, Jericho (the only substantial Arab town in the valley west of the river) and Amman. There is, though, no question in the Allon plan of Israel simply leasing the coveted area for say 10 or 20 years. It would become sovereign Israel territory.

Which leaves, as ever, the holy cities of Jerusalem and Hebron. Allon postulated a religious solution to the former. Hussein would have a special status here as a representative of the Moslem world, but there would be no political concessions. Jerusalem would stay united as the capital of Israel.

Originally, Allon advocated annexing Hebron. He is now proposing partition of the occupied land stretching south from Jerusalem to the Negev desert. The Arab slice would be linked to Ramallah and the other West Bank towns.

Almost too conveniently, the dividing line would pass between Hebron, which would stay under Arab rule, and the Jewish suburb of Kiryat Arba, which would fall in Israel. The supposed tomb of Abraham, holy to Muslims and Jews, would be in the Arab part, but Jewish access rights would be secured by the terms of the agreement.

General Dayan does not reject the Allon plan out of hand. He would be happy to see it tried on King Hussein if it had a real chance of opening the door to peace. On the other hand, Dayan resists it as a blueprint precluding Jewish settlements in specified areas of the West Bank.

His own ideas are less schematic, applying Dayan's Middle Eastern instincts to the immediate problems of administration and coexistence for which his ministry of defence is responsible.

Dayan regards peace as the dominant object of Israeli policy, but he is not prepared to buy peace at any price. 'We are not annexationist,' he said at a recent private meeting. 'Annexation does not further coexistence, and peace will eventually come about only through coexistence.'

Till then, Israel should make conditions in the occupied territories more and more livable. Although the present situation is not permanent, Dayan prefers it to what he considers unrealistic peace plans that would mean a return to conditions before 1967. It is not permanent, but nor is it temporary: it is likely to last for years.

Dayan argues that the nature of the conflict between Jews and Arabs is such that borders can no longer be drawn with a ruler. He would oppose political borders which entailed the Israeli army's withdrawal from the Jordan River. He would also insist on a continuing Israeli right to intervene against Arab guerrilla activity in, say, Nablus or any other part of the West Bank returned to Arab rule.

The defence minister rejects the view sometimes heard here that the army could easily move back in case of trouble. Israel, he says, would be creating new Fatah lands. Armed action across frontiers is no small matter, and each operation inside Lebanon of even Syria is preceded by much search of head and hearts.

Dayan also wants Jews to have a right to settle on the West Bank. At present he would not encourage settlement in the more military nationalist Nablus area, but he sees no objection to settlements near Jenin, further north, or Nebi Samwill, near Jerusalem. Both of these areas have territorial continuity with Israel.

The policy of ruthlessly suppressing actual terrorism coupled with a low profile occupation, economic advance, and open bridges, adopted by Dayan immediately after the Six-Day War, has been a remarkable and unpredicted success. It required audacity and imagination.

Dayan insists, almost certainly with sincerity, that his is not a policy of creeping annexation. The danger is, however, that because of his concentration on the short term – and his unreflective definition of the 'Jewish people's historic affinity to its land' – it will have just that effect.

Israel's 25 years: the kind of society that has grown out of the dreams of the Zionist pioneers

Observer, May 6, 1973

Israel is an act of will. Its founding fathers landed at Jaffa with a manifesto in their bundles. They were returning to a strange and arid Palestine not just to make a new life, but to create a Jewish homeland.

After 18 centuries of exile, the Jews would again be masters of their own fate. They would be beholden to no one but themselves. They would become a normal people, freed from the complexes and contortions of an inveterate minority.

Zionist migration was inspired by a nationalist and socialist vision, twin legacies of nineteenth-century Europe and Jewish Messianism. It was an exercise in emancipation, which would at once perpetuate and refine the Jew's identity, whether or not he settled in the land of Israel.

But the Jewish State – and Theodor Herzl was always clear that it would be that, even if Balfour was not – was never merely a solution to the Jewish problem. The law would go forth once again from Zion, the word of the (preferably secular) Lord from Jerusalem. The message would be one of equality, justice and peace.

Twenty-five years after David Ben-Gurion proclaimed the State in the Tel Aviv museum, Israel can withstand many tests. It is a developing country that has attained rare prosperity. The annual per capita income is about 800 pounds. The economy is growing at an average of nine per cent a year.

It is a post-colonial with a vigorous multi-party democracy, nationally, locally and in the trade unions. Thirteen factions are represented in the current parliament, including two species of communist and the nearest Israel has to the editor of *Private Eye*.

Its Jewish majority of 2,600,000 is as diverse as the United Nations General Assembly, yet for all the tensions, it has avoided communal strife.

Israelis are a literate people. Hebrew is neither an artificial imposition nor simply a lingua franca. The language had to be learnt, but now it is spoken. Forty-five thousand students are enrolled this year in seven universities.

Technological skills are so advanced that Israel is selling sophisticated modern weapons on the world market. It is the only country outside the big five making its own air-to-air missiles. It buys guns from America and planes from France; it captures Soviet tanks by the hundred, then presumes to improve them beyond recognition.

In 25 years, Israel has three times demolished the collective might of its Arab neighbours. In 1948 the world was astonished. By 1967 even the Pentagon computer could sit back and take Israeli victory for granted.

Yet for all these entries on the credit side of the ledger, Israel expects to be assessed by its own aspirations, the articulate prospectus of its pioneers. By this test, the record is conflicting and inconclusive. Its leaders acknowledge the gap.

The Prime Minister, Mrs Golda Meir, was asked in a radio interview a week ago what she would like to see in the future. She answered defensively: 'I should like to see the society in our country that we have always wanted, and always shall. I refuse to accept that when we were young we only dreamed of a just and decent society. I still want that.'

Earlier this year, foreign secretary Abba Eban felt it necessary to lecture the nation on its 'defects of style'. He argued, in an address at Haifa University, that the question being asked about Israel was not how courageous or how resourceful it was, but what was its human quality.

'A strong nation,' he insisted, 'does not have to shout or to beat drums in nervous agitation in order to make its voice heard… The problem is how to put the emphasis on freedom, tolerance, equality, social justice, spiritual and intellectual creativity and human brotherhood as the salient characteristics of a strong and confident Israeli society.'

If Israel has not evolved as its prophets assumed, the main reasons are the pattern of migration and the absence of peace. The mass of western Jews, the natural heirs to the Zionist tradition, stayed in Europe and the United States. Only now are the Jews of the Soviet Union being allowed to come, and their contributions to the texture of Israeli life is still uncertain.

Instead, within two years of the establishment of the state, Jews began arriving by the tens of thousands from the Arabic speaking countries of Asia and North Africa. The Jewish population of Israel doubled between 1948 and 1951. Almost half of the newcomers were oriental Jews. Most of those from the west were survivors of the holocaust.

Western migration never again reached the same proportion, whereas fresh waves of oriental Jews arrived in the mid-fifties and the early sixties. Between 1948 and 1970 more than 700,000 Jews of African or Asian origin had to be absorbed.

They came neither as pioneers nor ideologues. Many were refugees who had to leave their property and money behind. Israel's resources were overwhelmed. The immigrants were shunted into tenements and development towns that were branded from the start as instant slums. The egalitarian society of peasants, workers and intelligentsia had acquired an involuntary proletariat.

The inequality persists, sustained by big families, bad housing, limited educational opportunities. The result is that a classical immigrant society, reminiscent of the nineteenth-century US, has been superimposed on the warm familiarities of a ghetto community. It has the strengths and weaknesses of both the drives and the neuroses.

The new Israeli, by now into a second generation, is determined to prove himself. He is assertive, acquisitive and ambitious. He wants to pass his examinations; he wants to make money. If that means cutting corners, he will cut them. If it means trampling on the competition he will trample.

Jews steal from Jews, Jews sell their bodies to Jews, Jews extort from Jews. It took a detachment of tough border policemen, transferred from the Gaza Strip, to stem the crime wave in Tel Aviv.

More mundanely, the level of everyday competence is low and uneven; every craftsman wants to be his own boss. He improvises, he learns at his customers' expense. The economy, and consumer expectations, are growing so rapidly that he has more work than he can handle. He turns nothing away, he just doesn't come.

Israel's leaders worry about 'Levantinism', but in one sense at least they have no cause for anxiety. Israel is a hardworking society. The minister of labour, Mr Yosef Almogi, said recently that 100,000 adult males had two full-time jobs. Nor is there any taboo on married women taking part-time work. In a situation of very full employment, the law encourages it. Women workers must have generous maternity leave. They even have one extra day off a month for menstrual stress.

The incentive is strong. Israelis want middle-class standards, conspicuously and quickly. Housing in the main towns reaches London prices. Rented flats are almost unknown. Loans come at 18 per cent interest and have to be repaid over ten years. Duty of 100 per cent is levied on imported goods. High taxation starts at a low level of income. A professional man earns about half the salary of his British counterpart.

All this in a chronic state of war. Israel's domestic development is hamstrung by the need to spend 30 per cent of its budget on defence. Young men still go straight from school to three years' military service, young women to 20 months. Fathers of families are still summoned to a month's reserve duty a year.

Israel is not a militaristic society. It has no military caste. Haim Bar-Lev, who went from chief of staff into Mrs Meir's cabinet, behaves more like a politician than most of the politicians. But the marks of a military culture are everywhere – the ubiquity of guns, the intrusion into civilian life of the peculiarly Israeli military virtues ('exhaust the mission,' in General Dayan's phrase for aggressive persistence).

People here are living on their nerves. They are hypersensitive. They flex their muscles. Willy or nilly, they still have to placate the gentile, if only because he makes the kind of fighter-bombers no small state can make for itself. But no one will be invited to make their sacrifices for them, or to choose what concessions Israelis will make.

Israel remains nonetheless an intimate place. People at opposite ends of the land know one another. They talk to their neighbours. They are eager to help or to mourn. Eighty-two per cent of the population lives in towns, but they teach their children to know and love the countryside.

Only four per cent of Israelis live the kibbutz ideal, but the imprint bites deeper. You find little deference. Ministers, employers, officers and teachers are all called by their first name. A local chauffeur, hired to drive Gregory Peck while he was making a film here, took his famous charge home for Friday night dinner. Politicians sit in the Knesset wearing neither ties nor jackets.

The pervasiveness of 'protektsia' (knowing the right man, having access to the right strings) is the dark side of this spirit of community. So, on a grander scale, is the spectacular inefficiency and occasional corruption revealed by the state comptroller in recent reports on public enterprises.

In the end, however, Israel's achievement is that it is there. Persecuted Jews have a champion, whether they are in Iraq or the Soviet Union. Drifting Jews have an anchor, though Israelis seem more interested now in their money and their influence than in any real dialogue. After 25 years, even its enemies acquiesce in the existence of a Jewish state. The act of will has imposed itself, if not yet its dreams, on an unfriendly world.

Chapter 2 – 1973-74

Arafat in the firing line

Guardian, August 23, 1973

'Sooner or later the Lebanese Government will have to decide whom they prefer in Beirut – us or the terrorists.' That, in so many words, is the message the Israelis meant to convey by their commando raid on Beirut in April, the attempted abduction of Dr George Habash two weeks ago, and the public statements made since by the prime minister, the defence minister, and the chief of staff.

Israel's overt campaign against the Palestinian guerrillas is changing focus. Its first objective was to deny the Fedayeen the opportunity to fight a furtive war within the borders of Israel and the occupied territories. Its second was to push them back from the frontier zones of Jordan, Lebanon and Syria. Both aims have been substantially achieved.

For want of a choice the guerrillas then turned to spectacular terror outside the Middle East. Israel has its own way of meeting the challenge, actively and passively, on this new battlefield. More than a dozen Palestinian leaders or agents have come to a sticky end in the past year. Overseas commentators are more and more convinced that they were assassinated by the Israelis.

But the military planners in Tel Aviv have never lost sight of the fact that most of the Fedayeen operations are directed from the Lebanese capital. The old doctrine that Arab governments must accept responsibility for what goes on under their sovereignty remains central to Israeli strategy.

Much depends in the short term on how successful Palestinian attacks prove to be. Israel did not conceive the commando raid of April 10, in which three Fatah leaders were shot dead in their flats, as an isolated blow. The seizure of the Middle East Airlines Caravelle was a reminder that it is provocative enough for Lebanon to give the Fedayeen chieftains shelter and freedom of movement.

An Arab coup outside the Middle East could easily bring Beirut back into the front line.

The Arabs will have to make their own calculation of how much Israeli warnings are psychological, exploiting latent enmities between Lebanese and Fedayeen. The Israelis are aware of the dangers of destroying the subtle balances of Lebanese society. They constantly remake their accounting. But on recent experience Beirut can scarcely dismiss Israeli threats lightly.

The Israelis believe that the war against terror, which they launched a year ago after the slaughter of their sportsmen at the Munich Olympics, has been effective. It has disrupted the work of the Palestinian organisations.

The guerrilla groups were founded and are led by a small corps of fighters and ideologists. In theory, if Israel could eliminate as few as five men it could deal the Palestinians a very severe, if not quite lethal, blow. Tel Aviv does not demur at the list paraded only this week by the Lebanese press – Yasser Arafat, commander of Al Fatah, his deputy Abu Iyad, Dr Habash of the Popular Front for the Liberation of Palestine and his number two, Dr Wadieh Haddad, and Ahmed Jabril, who has broken at one time or another with both of these organisations and now leads a third, the 'Popular Front for the Liberation of Palestine – General Command.'

The Israelis do not delude themselves that they could destroy the Fedayeen if only they could catch all five at the same cocktail party. A new generation of leaders would eventually step up. As one officer put it, 'I doubt if we can extinguish the fire, but we can keep it at a low temperature.'

Israel is also keeping a watchful eye on development of a more conventional kind across the ceasefire lines. The Soviet Union is believed to have been delivering advanced equipment to Egypt and Syria steadily since the beginning of this year. They include jet aircraft (probably the MIG 21-J multi-purpose fighter), the latest T-62 tank, and SAM-6 surface-to-air missiles. What worries the Israelis is not so much that these deliveries will tilt the strategic balance, as that they will foster Arab illusions. The United States, after all, has not stopped supplying Israel with even better weapons. There has been no dramatic change in the will and capacity to fight on either side of the conflict. Egypt still lacks ground-to-ground missiles that would bring Israeli towns into range.

A further new factor is the presence of between 10 and 20 North Korean pilots flying with the Egyptian Air Force. For the time being the North Korean contingent is not taken too seriously. The North Koreans do, however, have a respectable record as combat pilots, even if they are by now a little rusty and have only limited experience with the later MIGs. A big increase in their number would force the Israelis to think afresh.

Arabs shatter myth of Israel

Guardian, October 10, 1973

However victory and defeat are finally assessed, the fourth Israeli-Arab war has already changed irreversibly the psychological balance of the Middle East.

Reality, which for a quarter of a century has confirmed the myth, does so no longer. Israel is seen at last to be something less than invincible.

The Arabs – on both the Egyptian and Syrian fronts – are fighting like soldiers. They are disciplined, combative, and intelligently commanded. There are no trails of abandoned tanks this time, no straggle of boots left behind by fleeing El Fellahin.

After four days of heavy battle, it looks increasingly as if Israel underestimated the military cost of the political decision not to strike first.

It is openly acknowledged, too, that the timing of the Arab attacks did take the Israelis by surprise. A retired general, Mattityahu Peled, said as much in a military commentary on Israeli radio.

The cabinet's reticence, when it knew that the Egyptians and Syrians were massing on the ceasefire lines, allowed the Arabs a chance to fight the war from strength.

They have been able to exploit their numerical superiority, in men and armour. On the southern front particularly, the Egyptian bridgeheads on the east (Israeli–held) bank of the Suez Canal have kept open a channel for reinforcements for the heavy toll the Israelis have exacted.

General Aharon Yariv, the chief-of-staff's special assistant, claimed last night that Egypt was having a hard time keeping up the pressure. At the same time, however, he accepted a figure of 400 Egyptian tanks east of the canal as a 'fair estimate'.

This is about the same total as the day before, so that for every tank destroyed Cairo is putting another into battle.

The Egyptian air defence system, as comprehensive as that protecting the Kremlin, is also proving more daunting than observers expected in the absence of the Russian technicians and advisers expelled by President Sadat 15 months ago.

General Yariv admitted that the ground-to-air missiles are taking their toll. On the northern front the concern is more about the Frog ground-to-ground missiles which the Syrians have been firing into the Jezreel valley – a fertile and populated area well inside the pre-1967 frontier.

General Yariv showed how gravely Israelis take the use of Frogs when he explicitly linked this development with the decision to bomb strategic sites inside Damascus.

The difference between the two fronts is that in the south Israel has defensive depth; in the north it has none. Once the Bar-Lev line of fortified bunkers had held the first Egyptian thrust, it had done its job and could be abandoned.

The Sinai Desert is like a huge Wembley Stadium for tank warfare. The minister of defence, General Dayan, has often said that Israel could afford a tactical withdrawal from the canal to fight at a place of its own choosing. The Egyptian army was no longer at the gates of Ashkelon.

This, to a limited degree, is what we are now seeing. Israeli strategy is evidently to check the depth of the Egyptian armoured penetration and to fight a battle of attrition away from the waterway. Ultimately the aim must be to drive the Arab tanks back across the canal, but it is now clear that the cost of such an operation will be high. The timing, therefore, is critical.

There is more urgency in the north. Israel cannot afford to leave its own heartland exposed. Modern technology has reduced the value of the Golan Heights as a buffer. Equally, a successful military campaign by Syria more than anything would tempt Jordan into the war. Israel's resources would be stretched across three fronts.

The war has not yet reached such a point. If we were not conditioned by the swift drama of the 1956 and 1967 wars, we would recognise Israel's achievements more readily. The army has been mobilised in record time, it has fought a successful defensive action, civilian life is on an emergency footing, but morale is steady.

On the Arab side, the Egyptians and Syrians have made a significant point. Israel has been obliged to fight a war more like that of 1948 (though with all the differences of equipment, terrain, and national maturity) than those of 1956 and 1967.

But the Arab armies have not been able to build on their initial attacks. In Sinai they have been contained to a narrow strip. In the north the Syrians have been pushed back to the 1967 line.

For the Israelis, a key question now is how long a war their society can sustain. For President Sadat, it must be how limited a 'victory' he will settle for. Ought Egypt to lobby for a ceasefire, giving it Nasser's ambition of a foothold east of Suez? Even if one were achieved – and Israel would be a very reluctant partner – would Cairo's appetite be satisfied for long?

The generals turn to post-war politics

Letter from Jerusalem

Guardian, November 13, 1973

Israel is a small country, and its public life is often small-minded. Personality intrudes constantly, even between supposed allies. A man's views are often less important than whether he is a Dayan man, let us say, or an Allon man, whether he is bidden to Golda's kitchen or Sapir's parlour. Every minister has his 'friends' who have the ear of their 'friends' in the local press. Decisions are taken haphazardly; the bureaucracy is tangled and inefficient. Israel muddles through, more Levantine already than most of its admirers care to notice.

Until this autumn, however, one strand of the national life had seemed immune to the national malaise. The army was different. Its leadership was able, refreshed by the principal of rotation and early retirement. Its structure was taut, its equipment all that technology could bestow. It won its battles with audacity and speed.

The real trauma of the Yom Kippur War is that the army was shown to be no different from the rest of Israel. It bungled and improvised, it was caught in a complacent doze. Its supposedly superlative intelligence might as well have been the research department of the ministry of immigration and absorption.

And now the generals are beginning to behave like the politicians – especially those who really are politicians. Lieutenant-General Haim-Bar-Lev, former chief-of-staff and now minister of commerce in the Labour government, was drafted to supervise Southern Command for much of the fighting war. Within 10 days of being sent back to his ministry, he published a newspaper article that was both a vindication of his own strategic thinking as chief of staff and a thinly veiled assault on his successor, David Elazar. Israel, he wrote, must never be caught in 'such a terrible posture again'.

At the same time Major-General Arik Sharon was having his fling in the *New York Times*. Sharon, who was recalled to the service only three months after retiring in anger when it became clear that he was not going to be the next chief-of-staff, is one of the undoubted military heroes of this as of previous wars.

He led the commando force that first struck across the Suez Canal. In doing so, he undoubtedly gave Israel the upper hand and cut several days off the end of the war. As also reported, however, he stretched his orders and cost more lives than the general staff had intended.

Sharon is still in the army, commanding a key sector west of Suez. But his thoughts are already turning to the general election on December 31 in which he is a leading candidate for the new right-wing Likud alliance (he can indeed claim to be if not its father then certainly its obstetrician).

The slowness of the High Command in reinforcing his breakthrough, Sharon said in his American interview, had cost Israel a decisive victory. The Egyptian Third Army had been spared. A similar slowness had dogged Israeli commanders' decisions from the beginning of the war.

General Elazar has tried to reimpose discipline and restraint, condemning 'biased and one-sided descriptions and interviews' which serve only for 'personal enhancement'. Sharon's friends replied by saying that he was the victim of a whispering campaign. Elazar has now announced an 'unflinching' inquiry into the conduct of the war. His intervention, alas, would be more effective if his own authority were not in question.

The whole deviously informal Israeli power structure is perceptively and entertainingly analysed in a book, *Who Rules Israel?* just released in London. Its journalist authors, Yuval Elitzur (whose *Washington Post* dispatches sometimes appear in the *Guardian*) and Eliahu Saltpeter, come through most instant and acid tests.

Their chapter on the generals has solid paragraphs on Arik Sharon and the other unblemished success of the war, Sharon Yariv, the man who signed the ceasefire and negotiates with the Egyptians at kilometer 101. Yariv is another would-be politician, with the prospect of a safe Labour seat and office in Mrs Meir's next government. He has, as the book indicates, the rare advantage of being a protégé of Moshe Dayan and a man trusted by Mrs Meir. Worth watching.

The war and its influx of foreign correspondents (900 at the peak) gave the Israeli military censors much trouble. Israel, as every guidebook testifies, has as many languages as the United Nations, but it doesn't quite cover everything.

The Taiwan Chinese, painting fastidious ideograms with a red felt-tipped pen, seemed to have an easier time of it than most of us. The Italians had to read their reports to a censor who could understand the language, but could not decipher it on the page. I stood next to one elderly baritone who declaimed six closely typed foolscap sheets for the *Corriera Della Serra* as if it were an aria from Verdi.

But the ultimate prize must go to the diffident man in the long tweed overcoat who presented the Jerusalem censors with a handwritten dispatch in Welsh. He brought a dictionary, but they let him through on the nod. Within minutes he was booking a collect call to Bangor – in Hebrew. He turned out to be Malcolm Lowe, who was doing his bit for the BBC Welsh Service. Lowe teaches philosophy at the Hebrew University and learnt Welsh at school in South Wales.

He didn't seem to be exploiting his loophole in the censorship, though the word 'Kissinger' did crop up with disturbing frequency in his sombre ballad.

Disaster for the generals and the diplomats

Guardian Weekly, December 29, 1973

Political Zionism set out to change the quality of the Jewish experience. The founding fathers of Israel wanted to free the Jews from the inhibitions and distortions of an exiled minority. They were to be a normal people, no longer dependent, no longer ingratiating, no longer having to look constantly over their shoulders.

The ultimate irony of 1973 is that Israel ends its silver jubilee year feeling more 'Jewish' in the old Diaspora sense than ever before. The October War was Israel's most desperate crisis since the War of Independence in 1948. Egypt crossed the Suez Canal and might have penetrated much further towards the Israeli heartland, given more nerve and flexibility on the part of its generals. Syrian tanks reached the edge of the Golan Heights, bringing most of Galilee within range of their artillery.

Mrs Meir's cabinet knew in advance that an attack was imminent, though it was not sure when it would come. Ministers decided that this time, unlike 1967, Israel would not strike the first blow. In the words of General Dayan they 'sacrificed the military advantage to the political advantage of letting the Arabs be seen to have broken the ceasefire.'

It was soon clear that they had underestimated the implications. The Egyptian and Syrian invasions were bigger, more calculated, and more effective than the Israelis had imagined possible. The Bar-Lev line was overrun, its chain of Canal-side strongpoints demolished or captured within hours. The Golan Heights proved too narrow a strategic buffer.

Yet the immediate diplomatic results were almost as disastrous as the military ones. At the first splutter of an oil tap, Britain, France, and most of Western Europe proclaimed their neutrality. A score of African states, whose friendship had been so assiduously cultivated by Israel, broke off relations as a gesture of third-world solidarity.

This reaction hit Israelis like a slap in the face. The world, they argued, was making no distinction between the attacker and the attacked. The British arms embargo was particularly resented for its 'one-sided' impact. Israel had transport aircraft standing by on the first weekend of the war, waiting for tank shells already ordered and paid for. They were urgently needed to drive back the Syrians. Alternative supplies could not be obtained from America with anything like the same dispatch. Britain refused to allow the planes to be loaded.

Israelis who understood what was happening will neither forgive nor forget. One senior government official quoted a passage from Dante: 'The hottest place in Hell is reserved for those who, in moments of moral crisis, choose neutrality.' But the dismay runs deeper, Britain and France were seen to be acting out of fear and self-interest. Israel was isolated not because she had done wrong, but because the Arabs were threatening the oil flow.

Sir Alec Douglas-Home's high-minded rhetoric only increased the feeling that the world had given way to cynicism. Racial memories are long here, stoked by experience and education. Whatever the British and French may have claimed for their motives, it looked to Israelis as if the Jews were once more expendable.

No one here doubts that Israel will have to make concessions. The dominant Labour Party has rewritten its election programme, dropping its specific plans for Jewish settlement and investment in the occupied West Bank and northern Sinai. General Dayan and his supporters – expansionists because they believed peace was impossible and did not see why the Arabs should dictate the terms of the occupation – are now on the defensive.

The basic assumptions of Israeli policy since the 1967 war have been discredited. Israel cannot take it for granted that she could defeat any combination of Arab armies. The deterrent has been called. Oil blackmail has proved itself. The super-powers are engaged and busy. It is neither possible nor adequate to sit tight and wait for the Arabs to sue for peace.

The question for Geneva is not just what Israel is prepared to give back, but also what kind of peace the Arabs contemplate. It is a major step – even a concession – that they are ready to sit down at a peace conference with Israel. But the Israelis have to be convinced that the Arabs are not simply seeking a better springboard for another war. It is less a matter of pious declarations than of dispositions emerging during the negotiations. Israel will read the signs and measure its own risks accordingly.

Israelis pin their hopes on another general

Guardian, March 16, 1974

Like Harold Wilson in Britain, Mrs Golda Meir has formed a government but solved no problems. The Israeli prime minister has bought time, but she cannot be sure whether it will be enough.

The October war has provoked more questioning of fundamentals than any of the Arab-Israeli conflicts in the past quarter of a century. The illusion that Israel could behave like a Middle Eastern great power has been shattered, and with it the credibility of the leaders that fostered that dream between 1967 and 1973.

The prolonged general election campaign, and the two months of coalition bargaining that followed it, deepened the disenchantment. Israelis wanted a sense of direction, a redefining of priorities. They were groping towards change, but needed to be shown the way.

Instead, they got the mixture as before. Mrs Meir's coalition broker, the finance minister Pinhas Sapir, traded posts and patronage. The National Religious Party created a crisis over what most people regarded as an irrelevance – the Jewish bona fides of new immigrants who had been converted by reform rabbis. Moshe Dayan returned to the fold in a seemingly cynical manipulation of an emergency on the Syrian front.

Mrs Meir has bought time, above all, to arrange her own succession. The conflicts of the old contenders are no nearer resolution than they were last spring, when the 75-year-old premier was forced to soldier on. General Dayan is discredited and knows it. Yigal Allon continues to disappoint his admirers. The dovish Sapir and Abba Eban have won an intellectual case, but failed to convince the voters. Haim Bar-Lev is marked by the post-war politico-military wrangle with Ariel Sharon. The Agranat commission into the Yom Kippur failures hangs over them all, not just the defence minister.

In private conversation and in the press, one name is chipping its way through the shell. Without the stimulus of a lobby, more and more Israelis are nailing their hopes on Yitzhak Rabin, who won a Knesset seat in December and took office this week as minister of labour.

General Rabin has a double appeal. His record is perceived as one of success, and he is untainted by faction-fighting. He is a Sabra and identifiably so, sceptical, surly and self-sufficient. At 51 he is mature without being stale. He has an analytical mind still open to fresh ideas.

As a young soldier, Rabin commanded the Palmach Brigade that lifted the 1948 siege of Jerusalem. As chief-of-staff two decades later, he is credited with the planning that won the Six-Day War. Curiously, Israelis either do not know or do not believe the published reports that he broke down for a couple of days at the beginning of that crisis.

His five years as ambassador in Washington coincided with the closest ties between the Israeli and American governments. General Rabin became an intimate of Henry Kissinger, whose aphorisms on statecraft he still quotes with a disciple's enthusiasm ('a diplomat is a man who thinks conflicts result from misunderstandings. A statesman sees that they derive from differences of interest, which have to be changed.')

Whether through General Rabin's efforts, or his political masters', his tenure brought Israel more American support – in money and arms – than ever before. It also taught Rabin the platform manner that has already impressed party audiences.

The new minister has his drawbacks. He does little to conceal his disdain for many of his cabinet colleagues. When he was in Washington, he communicated directly with Mrs Meir, by-passing the despised diplomats of the foreign ministry.

General Rabin is not the most tactful of people. His ambassadorial gaffe of hinting to American Jews that they should vote for Nixon in the 1972 American election was not an isolated aberration. By temperament, he is not suited to government by committee.

But, in their present general depression, few Israelis are worried by such considerations. General Rabin invokes a nostalgia for happier, less complicated days. The clarity, if not the ideology, of Ben-Gurion.

The land that Arafat may rule

Guardian, November 23, 1974

Talking your way around Jerusalem and the West Bank this week has been like rereading Lawrence Durrell's *Alexandria Quartet* without the purple patches. The new Palestine of teenage riots, Arafat placards and Israeli batons is a land of multiple perceptions: many dogmas and few certainties.

'The students,' said a sociology lecturer at Bir Zeit College, a few hours after his principal had been expelled to Lebanon, 'have the least to lose. There is nothing surprising in an outburst of student activity. But when the merchants move – as they did the other day – it is very significant. The merchants have the most to lose. It is a measure of how deep sentiment runs.'

An hour later, I was sipping Turkish coffee above a shop in the East Jerusalem pilgrimage belt. My host was an educated, reflective Palestinian, a power in the chamber of commerce.

'The Israelis,' he mused, 'don't understand us. When the schoolgirls started throwing stones at the police, I ran my shutters down. The police forced me to reopen the shop. They said they would not tolerate a strike. But if my window gets broken it costs me £70 to replace it.'

So, have the merchants joined the revolution? The Israelis took the locked shops of Ramallah seriously enough to impose sanctions. Local traders were barred from crossing the Jordan bridges to Amman or sending their produce to the East Bank.

'The West Bank people,' said the Bir Zeit sociologist, 'know that these are very decisive days in Palestinian history. They know Rabin's contention that the Palestinian Liberation Organisation does not speak for the West Bank population has provoked its own reply. They know the whole world is looking at them. They will play a crucial part.'

A second Jerusalem shopkeeper put it less analytically, 'You will find,' he predicted, 'that 99 per cent of the people on the West Bank support Yasser Arafat.'

Certainly, the PLO's opponents are hard to find and harder still to winkle into the open. Time and again, the least revolutionary of Arabs remind you that Arafat is one of their own, an authentic national leader. What is still not clear is how much stomach the adult West Bankers have for more than a walking-on part in the drama.

The feudal mayor of Hebron, Sheikh Muhammad Ali Ja'abari, was almost alone this week in publicly appealing to the students to stop needling the Israelis. Sheikh Ja'abari has less to fear and more to lose than most. His authority in his own domain is absolute.

The Israelis interpret his statement as one of several signs that the West Bankers have not yet burnt their bridges – either to Israel or to Amman. Professional Arab-watchers note that what most disturbed them in King Hussein's television broadcast after the Rabat summit was his pledge to give all the privileges of Jordanian citizenship to Palestinians who stayed on the East Bank.

Simple West Bankers, preparing to leave for the pilgrimage to Mecca, flocked to the Israeli interior ministry to ask whether this meant Hussein would confiscate their Jordanian passports on their way back through Amman. The Israelis told them to ask Hussein.

The passport does matter to West Bankers and to the Palestinians of the Gaza Strip. So does the chance to sell their goods east of the river and their labour west of the green line that used to separate them from Israel. The West Bank cannot absorb all the grapes of Hebron, the citrus of Qalqiliya, or the olives of Nablus. Nor can it offer the kind of wages paid by Israeli employers.

Nonetheless, Arafat's diplomatic triumph has generated expectations. The West Bankers are convinced that change is coming. The Arabic press of East Jerusalem continues its campaign of defiance.

Israeli policy is to hold the line. What comes after that, nobody will predict, but the more optimistic government experts believe Israel is still strong enough to resist the PLO. 'Israel will not commit suicide,' one official put it, 'nor will Jordan. The West Bankers recognise that.'

The prospect of an imposed solution is increasingly attractive to the Palestinians here, not least because it removes the hazards of choice.

'The difference between now and the period before the October War,' the Bir Zeit sociologist argued again, 'is that then the Americans would have imposed a solution on the Palestinians. Now they will impose it on the Israelis.' Many Israelis fear he may prove right.

Back to the frontier – without imagination

Guardian, January 4, 1975

This was the year that Israel learnt to live as a frontier society. The Yom Kippur War of October 1973 was the first since the 1948 War of Independence not to have brought the country a truce, a convalescence of rest and tranquility in the long conflict of Jew and Arab.

The pinprick warfare that accompanied Henry Kissinger's search for disengagement across the Suez Canal ended with the Israeli-Egyptian agreement of January 18. It was soon succeeded by the daily rumble of shells over the Golan Heights, which persisted till the end of May when the secretary of state contrived a separation of forces between Israel and Syria.

The Canal Zone settled into desert torpor, but the peace of the Golan could never be taken on trust. Nor could the security of northern Israel, harassed by guerrilla raids on Kiryat Shmona, Ma'alot, Shamir, Nahariya, Beit She`an and finally the Circassian village of Rihanyia.

Israel could not afford to relax. Border settlements were fenced and patrolled day and night. Volunteers guarded every school. The army of young conscripts and not-so-young reservists had to learn never again to be caught off-balance, as it had been on October 6, 1973.

Soldiers had to be trained to use the new weapons poured in by the Americans. Maintenance standards were raised, mobilisation times streamlined. All this meant months in uniform for family men in their thirties and forties.

At the same time Israel had to stop living beyond its means. In 1974 nearly 40 per cent of the gross national product was devoted to defence. This compared to less than 5 per cent in Britain and barely 6 per cent in the United States. In 1974 the benevolent uncles of world Jewry began to feel the pinch of inflation and uncertainty. The gap between what they had promised Israel in donations and investment and what they actually paid was $400 million. Their commitment to the Jewish state was as firm as ever, but they simply did not have the spare cash.

Emergency budget followed emergency budget. By the end of the year, the cost of living had risen by nearly 50 per cent and the Israeli pound had been devalued by 43 per cent. Austerity became a way of life – and after the first shocked days following the November measures was accepted as such.

The seven families in the building where I live agreed to restrict the collective central heating to six hours a night this winter. This was partly because some of the neighbours could not afford more, but also, as one of them put it at the house committee meeting, 'to help the country'. Israelis are sharing car journeys or turning to public transport for the same complex of reasons. Necessity has rekindled some of the old corporate idealism.

But if 1974 has restored much of Israel's military confidence and its citizens' acceptance of sacrifice, it has only increased the sense of isolation, anxiety, and a fatalistic conviction that another war is inevitable. In December 1973 the Geneva peace conference was savoured as the first occasion Arab governments had been prepared to sit and talk recognition with Israel. In December 1974 the prospect of its resumption was depicted by the Prime Minister, Mr Yitzhak Rabin, as a sign that the Arabs were girding for war.

The intervening year was one of disenchantment and political attrition. The Egyptian and Syrian agreements did not change the quality of the Israeli-Arab relationship. As an Israeli diplomat reflected, 'We stuck our necks out in the hope that Egypt was changing course. We hoped that Sadat was seeking an end to the conflict. Now we have been forced to the sad conclusion that nothing has really changed. Israel gave back something tangible, territory. We hoped for something in return from Cairo: a diminution of hostility, of what they might tell their own people. Instead we have seen a crescendo of political warfare against Israel.'

The automatic pro-Arab majority in most international forums became a bitter national joke. 'If Arab states proposed in the UN General Assembly that Israel could only play football if the ball was painted red,' the information minister, Mr Aharon Yariv, mocked, 'it would go through on the nod.'

For many Western countries, Israel was an embarrassing friend. Abstention became a heroic gesture. Although the energy and related monetary crises outgrew the Middle East conflict, few were ready to risk Arab displeasure. One day there would be an Alaskan pipeline, one day there would be a North Sea bonanza. Till then…

But, crucially for Israel, American support held up. Dr Kissinger did not appease the Arabs at Israel's expense. Dire predictions of another Munich were not fulfilled. The arms came, so did much of the money to pay for them. Senator Henry Jackson's success in forcing the Russians to pay for trade privileges with freer emigration for Jews reaffirmed the influence of Israel's friends on Capitol Hill.

Dr Kissinger and his new boss, President Ford, remained nonetheless on probation. Jerusalem weighed every word and demanded reassurance for every false syllable. How many slips of the tongue make a change of policy?

Within Israel itself, 1974 was the year of the long-awaited change from the generation of pioneers to the generation of Sabras. Mrs Golda Meir (Kiev and Milwaukee) gave way to Mr Yitzhak Rabin (Jerusalem and the Palmah). The natural leaders of the intermediate generation, Mr Moshe Dayan and Mr Yigal Allon, who had wasted years disputing the succession, were passed over. After the Yom Kippur War, the country had had its fill of them.

Mr Rabin won the premiership by acclamation. The people wanted a new face, a man with a record of success. The former chief-of-staff was perceived as both. He was the architect of Israel's victory in the Six-Day War of 1967. He had been a highly productive ambassador to Washington. The machine politicians were compelled to listen.

In his first six months, Mr Rabin has won more respect than enthusiasm. He has recast the style of Israeli government. His team has shown itself industrious and unspectacular. Ministers got on with the job. At moments of crisis they kept their heads.

Mr Rabin will do nothing on impulse or by default. His administration is equally unlikely, however, to do anything out of imagination or flair. The danger for 1975 is that his very sobriety, his stubborn sense of fundamentals (particularly over the Palestinian options) will trap Israel into dogmatism, and from dogmatism into war.

Chapter 3 – 1975-77

The Arabs in the middle
Nazareth

Guardian, January 25, 1975

'Twenty-six years,' sighed an Arab café owner here this week, 'is a long time to wait for a solution.' The 450,000 Israeli Arabs, the ultimate schizophrenics of the Middle East, are weary of marking time, yet apprehensive of the Palestinian challenge.

'After all these years,' Atallah Mansour, an Arab reporter for a Hebrew newspaper, explained, 'we have a certain identity, certain vested interests here. But we are reminded every minute that we are not Israelis, we are Arabs.

'Israel decided that there should be a kind of tribal division. An old anachronism was imposed on the machinery of a modern state. Every institution – the labour exchange, the health centre, the trade unions – has its Arab department.'

Although the Arabs have equal rights as citizens, they feel discriminated against. The schools in the Arab town of Nazareth are shabby and neglected. Hardly any were built for the purpose.

Their pupils find it harder than their Jewish contemporaries to get a place at an Israeli university. Ex-soldiers have first claim, and Arab school-leavers are not conscripted.

Nonetheless, there are about 1,500 Arabs studying in Israeli universities. But, once there, they meet a different kind of barrier. Where will they live? The problem is not so bad in Jerusalem and Haifa, where they can lodge in local Arab communities, but in Tel Aviv, which has two universities, it is almost insoluble.

The prime minister's adviser on Arab affairs, Shmuel Toledano, recently persuaded one of them, the religious university of Bar-Ilan, to take 10 Arab students. The Jewish students demonstrated against giving them room on the campus.

They argued that the Arab students would be a security risk.

Arab businessmen here complained this week that the Government had let their economy stagnate. No factories of any size had been brought to Nazareth. The men had to go out to work in Jewish enterprises. The contrast is pointed up by the presence of a Jewish development town – Upper Nazareth – on the ridge above the Arab town.

The discrimination is less a matter of policy than of negligence. In a society of many pressures, it is easier to ignore the demands of Nazareth than those of a new immigrant town. Resources are scarce, and there are considerations of security.

All would be different, comes the invariable answer, if Israel were not in a condition of perpetual warfare with its Arab neighbours.

Here in the city of Jesus, patience is running out. An Arab wholesaler, a Nazarene born and bred, told me he was emigrating to the United States. He saw no prospect of a change. Meanwhile, his money was losing its value, and his children could not get into university to study the subjects they wanted.

If they went to college abroad – to the Soviet bloc, as an increasing number are doing, or to the west – they would either come back troublemakers or be lost to their parents. 'I want to keep my family together,' the wholesaler said, 'they are my future.'

Yet, for most Israeli Arabs, emigration is no solution. They insist that they belong here in Galilee, and they recognise that Galilee is going to stay part of Israel. The recent success of the Palestine Liberation Organisation, in the Arab world and in the United Nations, has given another twist to their dilemma.

It has tended to separate the generations. The instinctive response of the middle-class middle-aged was to protest their loyalty to Israel, and to cultivate their gardens. Over and over again, they bring the question back to local issues: the inadequacy of the municipal leadership, the deafness of central government.

But they buy the East Jerusalem Arabic newspapers, they listen to Arab radio stations, they read Egyptian books. They want to know what is happening in the Arab world beyond Israel's borders, but they prefer not to talk about it.

'If Arafat gets his Palestinian state on the West Bank and the Gaza Strip,' the cafe owner said, 'it won't do anything for us. We are in the middle of Israel.'

The younger Arabs are less inhibited than their elders, but just as troubled. 'I see myself first of all as an Arab, then as an Israeli Arab,' a woman student explained in flawless Hebrew. 'I also see myself as a Palestinian, now more so than ever.'

Would a Palestinian State help? 'I feel a Palestinian, and I want to stay here. This is my home. Most Israeli Arabs know how Palestinian they are and how Israeli they are. If they say anything to the contrary, it's a matter of expediency. If someone says he is a Palestinian, he knows he'll get it on the head.'

The PLO, she added, did represent the Palestinian people. King Hussein had no right to speak for them.

But did the PLO represent the Israeli Arabs, too? 'For the time being, no.'

Another student thought a Palestinian state would make things easier. 'I would cease to be an Israeli Arab living in a state which is at war with my people.' Would he go and live there? 'No, I shall never leave my place, unless they send a bulldozer and shift me.'

Rootless in an occupied Gaza

Guardian, May 13, 1975

This is the time of the readers. As you drive along the shore near the Shati refugee camp you see them by the dozen: teenage boys walking one by one along the road, heads bent over open textbooks. Matriculation comes with the summer, competition is fierce, and it is easier to learn alfresco than cooped in the mud-brick, crowded, hovels of the camp.

A few years ago Ahmed and Salim would have been among the roadside students. In Israel or in Britain they would by now have passed on to university. In Gaza, after spells in industry across the green line, they have found work in the social services.

They are intelligent and articulate, with fluent English, and – though they were reluctant to admit it – Hebrew too. They had not done quite well enough in their exams to earn one of the 500 free places offered to Gaza students at universities in Egypt and Lebanon.

Ahmed and Salim are not their real names. It was one condition for meeting a reporter that I should not even ask, let alone identify them, in print. It was enough that I know where they work and that we have an acquaintance in common. Another condition was that I pick them up outside, not in their office. Then we must drive to somewhere discreet, a beach innocent with mothers and children.

'They're a little afraid to talk to you,' my contact had warned me. 'If the Israelis knew about the things they have to tell it would be very bad.

'A month ago a student we know was arrested because the army had caught a terrorist who gave them his name. This student didn't know that his friend was a commando. My friends think that if the Israelis read what you write and know who you talked to they will arrest us.'

How well founded these fears are I cannot be sure. What they had to tell me was not all that different from the editorials printed regularly by the three Arabic daily papers in East Jerusalem, with the acquiescence of the military censor. Perhaps things are more touchy in Gaza. Ahmed told me that he heard every day on Israel radio that suspects had been arrested in the strip.

Before they would talk I had to prove my credentials, declare my interest. When would I be going back to England? In a few weeks. Was I Jewish? Yes (I learnt afterwards that they knew this all along). What did I think of their problem? I was against occupations, whoever was the occupier. Could they see my press card? Done.

Slowly I turned the interrogation. The younger man, Ahmed, did most of the talking: Salim was more suspicious. Even after an hour's animated conversation, he was still not totally convinced I was a journalist.

I told them I had been looking at some of the new Israeli workshops on the northern edge of the Gaza Strip and at some of the housing projects for refugees willing to leave the camps. An Israeli officer had insisted that they were not trying to solve the refugee problem. But I wondered whether they might be moving that way. Once a man had bought a plot of land and built a house, wouldn't he begin to feel a sense of permanence?

'It's true some things are better,' was Ahmed's answer, 'But having a television set and enough money is not very important. You have to think about the future. The Israelis will not stay here for ever. If they do, then I for one shan't stay.

'Freedom is not to have a television or enough money. I want the freedom to see all the people I want to see, to go to the countries I want to go to. I must have the freedom to speak. I have two brothers in Egypt and one in Saudi Arabia. I haven't been able to see them for 10 years.'

If people felt like that, I asked, why was the Gaza Strip so quiet these days?

'There is a good opportunity for work. Some people neglect to remember that they are still under occupation. Even if I can't carry a gun, I still reject the Israeli occupation.

'I appreciate any effort to get rid of this occupation, whether military or peaceful. It would be better if it could be peaceful. King Hussein has made resistance harder by stopping the fedayeen crossing the Jordan. You need someone to support you.'

Ahmed and Salim were both born in the camps. Their parents fled in 1948 from villages near Ashkelon, within easy reach of Gaza now that the border is again open. Like all the refugees, they give you the name of their old homes when you ask where they are from.

My two young men had a simple, almost stylised view of the origins of the Israeli-Arab conflict. Jews and Arabs had lived contentedly together in Palestine until grasping Zionists like Mcnahem Begin had come from Europe and decided they wanted the whole country for themselves, and driven out the Arabs. To Ahmed and Salim, Yasser Arafat's programme for a secular, democratic, Palestine meant a return to this idyllic, fraternal past.

They agreed that it was not going to come in a hurry.

As we drove back into town Ahmed was a little overcome by his own loquacity. 'I hadn't meant to say so much to you.' he said.

Salim had another preoccupation. 'Why did my friend stop writing?' he suddenly asked.

Which friend? An English girl, he explained, who had advertised for a pen pal. 'As soon as I began telling her about our problem, she stopped writing.'

Rabin: Egypt must make first move

Observer, June 1, 1975

Mr Rabin, Israeli prime minister, approaches his first anniversary convinced that his stewardship has been vindicated and that there is no more need for a radical change of strategy now, on the eve of a new American diplomatic initiative, than there was on March 22, when Dr Henry Kissinger's last shuttle ran out of steam.

In an interview with *The Observer*, Mr Rabin insisted that Egypt would have to make the first change of position on an interim agreement. He indicated three key issues on which Cairo could have to move.

'The first,' he said, 'is the duration of the agreement, and we measure it not just by beautiful words. We have learnt, over the last year, that the real factor that decides the duration of the agreement is for how long the mandates of the United Nations forces, that are in the buffer zones and really supervise the thinning-out part of the disengagement agreements, would last. The only way to measure the attitude of either Syria or Egypt towards maintaining their obligations is: are they ready to have the UN forces in the buffer zones?

'The second issue is whether, in such an interim agreement, there is any change in the state of war. If the state of war is unchanged, and Egypt can claim all the rights of a belligerent power, we cannot give up basing our defence line on the Mitla and Gidi Passes.

'The third point is that if it is a step towards peace, even if a small one, there must be some symbolic acts that show that we are the beginning of a movement towards peace.

'Unless there is readiness on the part of Egypt on these issues, I doubt if Israel can change its position. Once there was a change of the Egyptian position, we would be ready to reconsider our former position.'

An Israeli newspaper columnist suggested recently that the most surprising thing about Mr Rabin's anniversary was that he was still there as prime minister to celebrate it. A year ago, no one here would have risked his money on it, though when I reminded him of this last week Mr Rabin was both unmoved and unamused.

What consolidated the premier's command was his refusal to be railroaded by Dr Kissinger into conceding more than he believed his country could live with. Events since March, as Mr Rabin reads them, have proved that he was right in keeping his head.

'There were many people in Israel, maybe not only in Israel, who believed that the suspension of Dr Kissinger's talks would create a very dangerous situation,' Mr Rabin said. 'First, that the dangers of an immediate war would be increased. Nothing of this has happened.

'Then there were fears that the United States would lose its dominant role in controlling the political process in the Middle East. Nothing has been changed. There were fears that Egypt would turn immediately to the Soviet Union. It did not happen. The visit of Mr Gromyko that was planned for the middle of May was cancelled.

'There were fears that the Soviet Union would press hard to convene immediately the Geneva Conference. Even the Russians said that the Geneva Conference had to be well prepared. And there were fears that there would be a real change in relations between the United States and Israel, which also did not happen.

'I am not saying that there are no differences of opinion between the United States and Israel, but what is much more important to me is that the political process continues. President Ford's decision to meet President Sadat and to meet me is the proof that the political process goes on.'

But did the political process lead anywhere? Did Mr Rabin believe that the recent signs from the Arab world – the decision to reopen the Suez Canal, the renewal of the United Nations mandate on the Golan Heights, and last week's statement by the new King Khaled of Saudi Arabia that he was prepared to recognise Israel within the pre-1967 boundaries – point to a real possibility of progress?

'It is too early to make any judgment,' the prime minister replied. 'I would not like to judge the position except by what would be proposed in a real, meaningful process of negotiation.'

Mr Rabin is systematically suspicious because he considers the risks strictly limited. 'The foreign policy of Israel,' he argued, 'has to bear in mind that we are still struggling to secure the existence of Israel. The real problem why peace has not been achieved is because of the lack of readiness on the part of the Arab countries to reconcile themselves to the existence of Israel as a Jewish viable state. This is still the issue.'

Did Mr Rabin, therefore, share the view of one of his ministers that Israel could not afford a foreign policy, but only a policy of survival. Did this mean his government was tied to looking months ahead rather than years?

'One has to look at the long term and to see also the problems that we have to face in the shorter term,' the prime minister replied. 'When it comes to the present situation, we have to realise that the coming months, three to six months, might be crucial for developments in the long term.'

Mr Rabin denied charges – by the former foreign minister, Mr Abba Eban, and other critics – that the government had failed to spell out its ultimate objectives: what it saw as Israel's final boundaries and what price it would expect the Arabs to pay for withdrawal to them.

But his exposition pointed more to another interim stage, probably with Egypt, than to the chances of an overall agreement. It is hard to see the Syrians settling for a small further withdrawal on the Golan, or any Arab leader accepting Israeli sovereignty in perpetuity over the whole of Jerusalem. Yet these were all Mr Rabin was offering on two of the critical points of contention.

'When we talk about an overall settlement,' the prime minster said, for us it is a peace treaty. But the kind of a peace that the man in the street will call a peace, not just peace in terms of an end of the state of war. We have to have what the Americans call building a structure of peace. To add to the end of the use of force in the most formal, legal way, you must also create conditions in which relations of peace will be developed between the peoples.

'For that we have said that we are ready to withdraw practically from all Sinai, except a presence in Sharm-el-Sheikh. We did not say sovereignty, we say presence.'

Sharm-el-Sheikh, at the southern tip of the Sinai peninsula, controls the entrance to the Gulf of Aqaba and thus to Israel's Red Sea port of Eilat. Although the experience of the Yom Kippur war suggests that the Arabs can blockade Eilat further down the Red Sea at Bab-el-Mandeb, some Israeli strategists have underlined the value of Sharm-el-Sheikh as a base for an Israeli counter-blockade of the Gulf of Suez.

Mr Rabin did not spell this out in our interview, but he did insist that Israel must have 'land continuity' between Sharm and Israel proper. He also talked of 'adjustments to the international boundary,' which usually means the Rafah approaches, southeast of the Gaza Strip, guarding the invasion route from Egypt to Israel.

On the Syrian front, the prime minister reiterated that even for the kind of peace he was seeking, 'we would not go down from the Golan Heights.'

Was there, I pressed him, some kind of Allon plan for the Golan, parallel to the Allon plan for the West Bank, which attempts to give Israel maximum security but a minimum of occupied Arabs?

'No, there is no Allon plan,' Mr Rabin snapped back. 'And I would not like to draw any exact lines, but I believe that the Syrians can get back something beyond the present line.'

Something which they might reasonably think was worth having? 'That I cannot promise either you or them.'

On the Jordanian-Palestinian question, Mr Rabin was as adamant as ever that he would not negotiate with Yasser Arafat. He would not dictate to the Jordanians about whom they should include in their delegation to Geneva, even if it meant accepting an identifiable representative of the Palestine Liberation Organisation. But the delegation would have to represent Jordan, and the negotiations and any agreement would have to be with Jordan. This proffers a very slim compromise for the PLO, if that is what they and the Arab governments want.

In an overall peace settlement, Mr Rabin said, Israel would expect to keep the Jordan river as its security, though not necessarily its political, border, and Jerusalem would have to remain 'united and the capital of Israel.'

The Muslim and Christian communities would be allowed control over their holy places in the city.

What, I asked, about the 100,000 Arabs, at present citizens of Jordan, who lived in Jerusalem?

'Let us distinguish between the nationality of the people and sovereign control over the area,' Mr Rabin answered. 'When it comes to the area, no question about it, it should be part of Israel. When it comes to their nationality, it is negotiable.'

Over to you, Mr Ford.

Changing patterns in Israel

Guardian Weekly, January 20, 1977

If it had ended with the fiscal year in April, 1976 would have been the year of the West Bank. If it had expired with the lunar calendar in September, it would have been the year of Entebbe. But by December both the Arab riots and the Israeli rescue have sunk into history, and the year ends for Israel under the shadow of the unpredictable.

The preliminary rounds of the general election have already begun. Two national heroes of contrasting style and appeal – Yigael Yadin, the archaeologist of Masada, and Ariel Sharon, the retired general who led the strike across the Suez Canal that turned the course of the Yom Kippur war – are challenging the established political parties.

No one can predict at this stage how well either will fare, though Yadin's supporters suggest that he may win as many as 15 of the 120 Knesset seats. The professor is expected to attract votes from the dominant Labour Party and others to the left of centre. Sharon's campaign will probably hurt the right-wing Likud opposition, which he himself moulded out of four parties in 1973.

The 1977 election is more likely than any of its predecessors to break the remarkably consistent voting pattern of Israel's 28 years of statehood. The philosophical 1973 slogan: 'for all that, it has to be Labour', has not been replaced by anything more dynamic. Yitzhak Rabin has still to establish his authority as prime minister and as party leader, while Menahem Begin's command of the Likud seems the same anachronism that prevented him unseating Golda Meir's discredited administration after the October war.

The prospect of an early appeal to the country is expected to strengthen Mr Rabin's hold on the Labour Party, which will close ranks around him and eclipse the threatened challenge of the defence minister, Shimon Peres, and the former foreign minister, Abba Eban.

It may also make it harder for Professor Yadin and General Sharon to mobilise their forces. Both of the new revivalist movements have still to build electoral machinery and to consolidate their programmes. On the other hand, Mr Rabin can by no means be sure of winning a more stable base for a new coalition.

The uncertainty is mirrored abroad. If 1976 turned out to be the year in which the heat was off Israel, with elections in the United States and the Lebanese civil war at last receiving the attention Israelis thought it deserved, 1977 promises to be a year of diplomatic activism.

The new American administration is eager for movement, and the Arabs – united and refreshed by the restoration of an uneasy balance in Lebanon – are already pitching for peace.

Both sides were shadow boxing, playing above all to the Washington gallery. But at least the lines had been marked out. Israeli and Arab recognised the central role of the United States as the only super-power that could coerce the one and coax the other. Each was ready for a resumption of the Geneva peace conference, but each insisted on his own terms.

The old year spawned no solution to the conundrum of who shall speak for the Palestinians. The lesson of divided Lebanon reinforced by the Palestine Liberation Organisation's continued assertion that its ultimate aim was the 'replacement' of Israel by a 'democratic state in the whole of Palestine', hardened Israeli resistance to negotiating with Yasser Arafat.

The Arab governments, for their part, salvaged the PLO from the debacle of Lebanon, preserving it as a symbol of Palestinian military and political struggle. They – like the Israelis, the Americans, and anyone else interested in making 1977 a year of progress and not just propaganda – are stuck with consequences, the classic diplomatic labour of reconciling the irreconcilable.

Such are the issues for 1977, but what of the history of 1976? The West Bank troubles that preoccupied the international media for the first half of the year were not, after all, the Palestinian revolution they sometimes seemed. They were a sustained act of defiance, costing the lives of ten Arab civilians. But eventually the Israeli military administration recovered its nerve and its control, while the West Bankers acknowledged their own isolation in the wake of Tel-el-za'ata. Sporadic demonstrations rumbled on to the end of the year, but never regained their intensity of conviction.

On the other hand, Israel remained resentful of the world's interest, which seemed intrusive and disproportionate. To most foreign observers, however sympathetic, the Israeli occupation of one million Arabs outside the old 'green line' frontier for nearly a decade was abnormal, especially for a country projecting itself as a social democracy. To most Israelis, even of doveish inclination, the West Bank felt more and more like a province of the Promised Land, which Israel was generously willing to exchange for peace. The result – mutual incomprehension.

The paranoia was dispersed by Entebbe. Israel rediscovered the panache of the 1967 war. Only the mean, the prejudiced and the craven forbore to cheer. International terror has been put in its place; Idi Amin had received his comeuppance.

Surprisingly, however, Entebbe did not consolidate Yitzhak Rabin's political grip. Dispassionate witnesses gave the prime minister high marks for a cool head and precise calculation of the risks involved in the mission. But old rivalries blurred the public judgement, so that the cabinet won little abiding credit. Tomorrow is another year.

In the Valley of the Moon

Guardian, March 2, 1977

We met Anaizan, one of the last of the smuggler-poets of Sinai, in the Valley of the Moon, high above Eilat. He led us from the wide plateau of compacted sand, big and even enough to land a medium-sized airliner, through its coronet of jagged peaks to his encampment at Ras Rida'abi.

It was late afternoon. At the far end of the plain a mirage was draining with the sunlight. In the encampment the women and boys were driving home the sheep and goats from the pasture. Anaizan's youngest, a tiny, handsome child with mature black eyebrows and a serious mouth, padded over the hill with the last stray camel.

Later, around the campfire, where the boy but not the women joined us, we asked how old he was. Anaizan reflected. Well, he was born after the conquest (the war of 1967). When the next war came, he was just finishing nursing. Since the Bedouin women nurse their babies for two years that made him about six.

We had come as travelling companions of Clinton Bailey, a lecturer at Tel Aviv University who has been studying the Bedouin at close quarters for the past eight years. We were honoured guests. A windbreak had been erected and blankets spread on the ground. We were bidden to make ourselves comfortable while Anaizan and his family busied themselves with the demands of hospitality.

Twigs of the white, desert broom were gathered for tinder. Slim trunks of trees, ready felled and trimmed, were dragged to the fire and pushed gradually to the centre as they were consumed. A big brass kettle was filled and put on the flames. Then to a mixture of bleating and incantation, Anaizan slaughtered a sheep. The blood was drained, as required of good Moslems, and Anaizan smeared some of it on our Land Rover, a sign to other Bedouin we would meet later in the desert that our host had done his duty.

The nomads save their sheep, worth £30 or £40 each, for special occasions. The meat is eaten fresh, which means it has to be cooked slowly. Anaizan's, womenfolk, with their black veils and embroidered dresses, boiled the mutton in a distant tent.

For the three hours it took to become tender, we huddled around the fire, sipping innumerable small cups of sweet tea and bitter coffee. Anaizan or one of the older boys fastidiously rinsed the cups after each round.

The Bedouin talked endlessly in the loud, declamatory Arabic that is their everyday speech. Bailey joined in, interpreted, and added his share of stories, lore, and history. He had been to a Bedouin trial near El Arish, and had a tale to tell of double-dealing by a young ambitious drug-smuggler, of assaults, revenge, and reconciliations made and broken. Anaizan, his face burned almost negro by the sun and wind, his beard a stubbly steel grey, listened rapt to Bailey's English, guffawing with recognition every time one of the litigants was named.

He tossed in an anecdote of his own about saving two Englishwomen on runaway horses near El Arish long ago. They were the wife and daughter of 'Mister Jarvis', Claude Jarvis, who governed Sinai for the British in the twenties and thirties. Jarvis gave Anaizan £5 reward.

The Bedouin relish a good story, however familiar it may be. Our driver, Alfonso, a Swiss with an Israeli wife, recalled a night he once spent in another encampment. The sky was black and clear, the stars brilliant and the moon full. They attended in fascination, marveling among themselves, interjecting with scepticism when he said the astronauts had brought back moon rocks. 'Go on,' they mocked, 'they must have taken them from here.'

When Alfonso came to explaining how they had made the journey, his Arabic ran out. He did not know the word for rocket. He tried aeroplanes, which the Bedouin see every day, and mumbled about aeroplanes without wings. As his embarrassment deepened, Alfonso's host took him gently by the arm and whispered: 'Tell them Apollo 15.'

Around Anaizan's fire, the conversation turned naturally to smuggling and to poetry. Until the Israelis and the Egyptians sealed the borders, running hashish from the Arabian Peninsula to the Mediterranean was a major trade among the Sinai nomads. The smugglers, who traveled farther and mixed in more diverse

74

company than most, were welcome raconteurs, news bearers, and above all, poets.

The poetry has declined with the smuggling and with the trickle of younger Bedouin into urban jobs to which they commute from their goat-hair tents. Clinton Bailey estimated that among the 70,000 Sinai Bedouin there were now only twenty poets, most of them, like Anaizan, men in their sixties or older.

The acknowledged laureate of these desert troubadours is Anaizan's elder brother, Anaiz, a poet-over-the-water whose exile and dishonour dominated the night's conversation at Ras Rida'abi with the weight of legend. Fifteen years ago he was caught and imprisoned in Egypt for smuggling. Although he is now a free man, he has never been allowed back. His brother and his sons, 'brought up to be men' by Anaizan, listen to his voice and his poetry on Cairo Radio's *Voice of Sinai*.

'My brother is in prison,' Anaizan said in one of his poems, 'but that is no blight. Looking after your interests is no reason for shame.' The real dishonour was that two of Anaiz's three wives let themselves be enticed by their husband's cousins instead of waiting for his return.

The twin themes of faith betrayed, and fortune overturned pervade Anaiz's poetry, subtly rhymed and rich in desert imagery. His cousins, he says in one poem, have become 'like a pack of hateful hyenas, crouching low beside fetid pools to drink when no wind blows, conveying our stench to others'.

In a more lyrical passage of the same composition, the exile dreams of a feast in the oasis of Wadi Wateer: 'How sweet to sip the cup down among the palms and hear the peal of the Mauser where the wadi bends, smelling the embers of broom with lamb upon them. To see friends reclining in the shade of the shelter beside girls with even teeth, darkened eyes, and tattoos as green as the pasture of spring.'

As men who can neither read nor write, the Bedouin poets compose in their head, moulding their sinuous Arabic to the rhythmic pattern of the one-stringed fiddle. They draw on a data bank of lines and metaphors, remembered and reworked.

To demonstrate his facility, Anaizan improvised a *Ballad of Dr Bailey* the day after we left his camp. The song, rhymed and formed, described the mountains and valleys we were driving through, the questions asked, the answers given, the sights and the stories.

The temperature was down towards freezing at Ras Rida'abi when the first meat was brought to Anaizan's guests. We began with tender cubes of liver, grilled on skewers, followed by mugs of mutton broth. The meat itself was served with big dishes of greasy rice, which we took as instructed in the right hand and squeezed into dumplings.

Mercifully, no one offered us sheep's eyes. We ate and were satisfied. Only then did Anaizan and his family tuck into the rest. The hospitality, like the poetry, conformed to its convention.

Hawk with a sharp eye for the main chance
Guardian, April 11, 1977

The two candidates for leadership of the Israeli Labour Party were each allotted one hour to address the three thousand convention delegates in Tel Aviv on February 23. The incumbent, Yitzhak Rabin, lost the toss and was put in to bat first.

Rabin was gawky and emotional, though he managed to start with an impromptu joke at the chairman's expense. He said what he had to say, recalling his 27 years as a soldier, his service as ambassador and prime minister, and warning his audience that if they repudiated him they would be repudiating their party in the eyes of the electorate. After 20 minutes he sat down.

The challenger, Shimon Peres, delivered an elaborately structured speech, setting out his record and the policies he and the party stood for. It was fluent, and articulate, presented without visible notes, the kind of oration Harold Wilson or Jim Callaghan would have polished for a similar occasion. With no change of pace or trimming of overmatter, he spoke for 60 minutes, almost to the second.

The contrast could not have been starker. Rabin was the general-turned-politician applying the yardstick of cost-effectiveness, impatient of parliamentary trimmings, untroubled by his sepulchral delivery. Peres was the professional, a man who had lived in and for politics since he was 18. The party conference was his home ground. On the night this familiarity was not quite enough. The delegates had other reasons for casting 41 more votes for Rabin. But Peres had consolidated his position once and for all as his co-equal, a deputy who could dictate terms.

Until April 1974, when he first stood against Rabin, the establishment candidate, Peres had always been someone else's prop. First it was his mentor, David Ben-Gurion, whom he served as deputy defence minister when Israel's founding prime minister combined his post with the defence portfolio. Then it was Moshe Dayan, the standard-bearer for the rebellious Rafi faction, once Ben-Gurion had retired to the Negev to reminisce.

By contesting the leadership after the Yom Kippur War, which discredited Dayan, Peres emerged from the shadows. He showed a sharp politician's eye for an opening, something the former foreign minister, Abba Eban, lacked, along with the audacity to risk his career. Peres, in consequence, has never looked back. Eban has spent three years in the wilderness, waiting, as it turns out, for Peres to restore him to his accustomed place at the cabinet table (provided, of course, the defence minister has such gifts at his disposal after May 17).

The votes Peres won in the party central committee fuelled his ambition. He seemed to sense that Rabin was accident-prone, that the verdict could still be reversed. Peres, who was born in 1923, one year after Rabin, retained his independence. His policies were not always the cabinet's. He sniped at his leader, sustained his own coterie, and cultivated friends in the Labour movement and among its potential coalition partners.

In the process, Peres reinforced his reputation as a hawk. He flirted with the religious expansionists of Gush Emunim (the Faith Block), spoke up for the Jewish 'right' to settle in Samaria, the mountainous northern half of the occupied West Bank and noticeably slow in stopping the latter-day zealots establishing themselves first at Sebastia then at Kadum, near the Arab town of Nablus.

Yet the impression is deceptive. Peres is a pragmatist, even an opportunist. His position on the West Bank was political, not doctrinal. Unlike Dayan, he did not fight the party convention's overwhelming decision to write a pledge of withdrawal in exchange for peace into the 1977 election platform.

Peres, who was born in Poland the son of a grain and timber merchant and came to Palestine in 1934, has a flexible, cosmopolitan mind, broader but less penetrating than Rabin's. He likes to tell people that he learnt two priceless pieces of wisdom from his early bosses in the defence ministry, Levi Eshkol and Ben-Gurion. From Eshkol, later the Six-Day War prime minister, he learnt how to distinguish between daring and adventurism, from Ben-Gurion that what is important is what you do and not what you say.

What Shimon Peres does, if he becomes prime minister next month, may well prove different from what he has sometimes said on this way there. He has a well-adjusted sense of the possible and a wholesome respect for American power.

He is the only member of the outgoing leadership who dissociated himself from the 'Allon Plan' the prevailing doctrine for the future disposition of the West Bank. Although he has never been a soldier, he was sceptical of the plan's strategic basis. He seems also to have recognised that no Arab government, even one so 'moderate' as King Hussein's, would buy the idea of a permanent Israeli presence along the Jordan valley security frontier, behind the populated hill area returned to Arab rule.

Peres was in trouble last month because he was suspected of having spoken out of turn when he met the American secretary of state, Cyrus Vance, privately in Jerusalem. He was accused of the kind of 'loose thinking' that encouraged President Carter to come up with the alternative of substantial Israeli evacuation, backed by temporary defence positions and various international guarantees across the line. A prime minister with no intellectual commitment to an outworn policy may be invaluable, either to resist or adapt to the new American diplomacy.

Peres's pet preference has for long been a Jewish-Arab federation west of the River Jordan, with Jerusalem as a Middle Eastern Washington DC. But he has never found any takers, either in Israel or among the Arabs, and he is unlikely to press his case until or unless all else has failed.

The new Labour leader projects himself as a writer and thinker, a man of wide interests who reads half the night after a long day's work. Saul Bellow put him down with a neatly concealed barb in his recent book on Jerusalem. Other politicians, he wrote, came to see him as national leaders. Peres came as a fellow author.

His record, however, is as a man who gets things done. As a young kibbutznik, he led the Labour Party's youth organisation and managed to stop it breaking away along with much of the communal settlement movement. While barely in his thirties he negotiated Israel's highly productive arms purchasing relationship with France, as well as laying the foundations of a domestic arms industry that is now capable of manufacturing a sophisticated modern fighter like the Kfir.

Peres was one of the moving forces behind Israel's development of a second nuclear reactor at Dimona. In company with Moshe Dayan, he was at Ben-Gurion's elbow in Paris when the Suez war was hatching. He suffered later for following Ben-Gurion into Rafi, whose campaign in the 1965 election he directed.

Last summer, when a planeload of Israeli and other passengers was hijacked to Entebbe, Peres was more persistently eager than Rabin for a military rescue operation.

The difference was not one of nerve, but of temperament and experience. Rabin, a former chief-of-staff, insisted on knowing the risks before he would commit his commandos to action. Peres, a civilian defence minister, was demanding that the military find a viable way.

Decade of disillusion

Guardian, June 4, 1977

A writer friend of mine, an Israeli of the reflective Left, a son of the Middle East and a Zionist by fate rather than by conviction, argues that the Six-Day War that broke out 10 years ago this weekend was as disastrous for the Jewish State as it was for Egypt, Syria and Jordan. The triumph of arms was an illusion, for which Israel is still paying.

At times, especially when the West Bank is in turmoil, it is a seductive thesis. Relations between Jew and Arab in the disputed land are reduced to the elemental: riot sticks and stones, tear-gas and flaming tyres, repression and revolt. The middle-aged reservists and teenage conscripts who garrison the occupied towns are corrupted by the power of the sub-machinegun. The facile charge of racialism and imperialism seems confirmed by the newsreels.

Yet the balance sheet is not all one way. My first working visit to Israel was in 1966, nine months before the war. With unwitting prophecy, I wrote that after 10 years of tranquility, Israel's slogan remained: 'Praise the Lord and pass the ammunition'.

Jerusalem had two cul-de-sacs, back to back in embattled hostility. The Jewish mayor, Teddy Kollek, took us to the roof of his town hall to look across to the old city. Jordanian sentries watched from behind the sandbags on the wall opposite. At the Mandelbaum Gate crossing point, we witnessed the pathetic reunion of an Arab family divided by the 1948 Armistice line. From the border kibbutz of Ramat Rachel, you could spy on Bethlehem. Israeli gunners nested on church roofs on Mount Zion.

Three weeks after the June War of 1967, I drove to Qalqiliya, an Arab town pounded by Israeli cannon, then partly flattened by bulldozers. It was an ugly sight, but so was the plateau above it. An area as big as a football pitch had been dug out and fortified, planted with a forest of artillery by the Jordanian army. The guns pointed across the fertile Sharon Plain towards Tel Aviv. Not far from Qalqiliya, the waist of Israel from the border to the Mediterranean was no more than nine miles wide.

Further north, in upper Galilee, I rode with a truckload of kibbutzniks from Kfar Hanassi on to the Golan Heights. The burnt-out Syrian tanks were still crippled at the roadside. The artillery bunkers covered acre upon acre. My companions were astonished, and not a little sobered, to see just how visible their settlement was from the enemy side of the Jordan rift.

Physically at least, the claustrophobia of Israel was lifted by the war. Jerusalem is now an open city, no longer a forlorn museum piece, an evocative backwater. In the Sharon, Galilee and the Negev, the guns are out of range.

Those rampaging six days bequeathed Israelis the freedom to breathe and to explore, but not to relax. The menace of artillery was replaced by the menace of terrorism, from within and without. Parents take it in turn to guard their children's schools, armed men travel with every class trip into the countryside. Searches at the cinema, the concert hall, and the airport are routine. Volunteer watchmen prowl the suburbs through the night.

A mixture of ruthless counter-measures, good intelligence, open bridges to the Arab world and free access to the Israeli labour market have kept terrorism within manageable proportions. So has the Lebanese civil war, which sapped the Palestinian fighting organisations, and the Arab governments who police their own borders.

But the danger is constant, and recognised. Every other month, the military spokesman announces that half a dozen terrorist cells have been cracked on the West Bank or in the Gaza Strip. Some 60 or 70 young Arabs have been arrested and will be charged. It hamstrings their operations, but it does not stem the flow of recruits. There will always be another 60 or 70 somewhere.

The one million Arabs are not resigned to the occupation. They have a gift for survival, for adapting to conquest. They have waxed plump on the chance to work and trade with the Jews. But for most of them that is not enough.

They are humiliated by detentions, checkpoints, searches and the presence of alien soldiers. Moshe Dayan, when he was defence minister, wisely chose not to bottle them up west of the Jordan. But it was inherent in the gamble that the Palestinians living under Israeli rule would not be insulated from the ferment in the rest of the Arab world. They see Arab television, hear Arab radio stations, read Arab books and periodicals. Their schools teach an Arab curriculum. They come and go across the bridges. So do Arab visitors of many stripes.

Both the 'Jordanisation of Palestine' (never exactly a hit) and the 'Palestinisation of Jordan' have been suspended. The occupied Arabs are frustrated nationalists who know that their destiny is in other hands – the Palestine Liberation Organisation, King Hussein, the oil sheiks and the super-powers. All they can do is keep the pot boiling and foreclose no options.

Radical, assertive Palestinian nationalism has spread to the half million Arabs who are citizens of Israel. In last month's general election, the old guard politicians who cooperated with the Labour government were cut down from three seats to one. West Bank mayors attended a memorial assembly for Kamal Jumblatt in Nazareth, the biggest Israeli-Arab town. One Israeli commentator suggested that the 'Green Line' had been redrawn. It was now a psycho-political frontier between Jews and Arabs within Palestine as a whole.

In the occupied territories, as in Israel proper, the two peoples tend increasingly to keep their distance. There is no official apartheid, but the old Middle East convention of communal separatism has been reinforced. With rare, almost eccentric exceptions, contacts are kept at the professional, commercial or employment levels. Jews and Arabs know each other, many speak the other's language, but they seldom meet socially.

After the 1967 war, Israelis used to throng the shops of Ramallah or Nablus. Now they stay away. They still go to the souk in the old city of Jerusalem, particularly on Saturday, a family holiday when Jewish shops are closed. They still go to sub-tropical Jericho for Saturday lunch in the winter. But otherwise they avoid the populated areas. It is not worth the antagonism and the risk of a stone through the car window, or a bomb under the bonnet.

For the West Bank Arabs there is the gauntlet of checkpoints and searches if they want to visit Jewish friends in Jerusalem or Tel Aviv. 'We know they have valid reasons for stopping us,' an East Jerusalem bookseller explained. 'More often than not, the soldiers or policemen are courteous enough. But now and again you meet one who is rude and gives you a rough time. And you never know when you will run up against one like that, so you don't take the chance. You stay at home and watch television.'

On both sides, there is also a deeper inhibition. The unresolved conflict broods over any relationship between Jew and Arab. What does the other man really think? Who is he working for? What would he do if he felt he could get away with it? Will the coffee party turn into a row – or the opposite, an evening of empty phrases and long silences?

Jerusalem remains unique as the only city where Israeli Jews and non-Israeli Arabs share the same boundaries and municipal services. The walls and street corners were decked with gaudy, socialist realist murals to commemorate the tenth anniversary of reunification. Bands and strolling players performed in the streets. But the 100,000 Arabs were like ghosts at the feast.

For a long decade, they have been preserved in political aspic. Unlike the West Bank or other occupied territories, East Jerusalem was annexed to Israel. But the Arabs living there were given the choice between becoming Israelis or keeping their Jordanian passports. They have stayed Jordanian. They have been known to vote in local elections, but not to put up their own candidates.

A coloured poster on sale inside the Damascus Gate of the old city shows an ancient Arab porter, barefoot, moustached and pantalooned, bent almost horizontal, bearing the burden of Jerusalem. It is entitled: 'Carry On'. Such is the role in which the Jerusalem Arabs cast themselves. Their presence prints a question mark against the Israeli doctrine that Jerusalem is the Jewish capital and is out of bounds for bargaining.

Mayor Kollek`s aim has not been to reconcile his Arab townsmen to Israeli sovereignty. More modestly he set himself to make life endurable here for both communities, without walls and without minefields, and to keep open a range of political alternatives. To that extent he has succeeded.

The Arabs have had to watch impotently, however, while Jerusalem has been encircled by a living rampart of Jewish suburbs. They have slipped where they could under a deliberate policy of demographic engineering that restricts Arab building densities. They resent it, but they live with it.

On the West Bank, the myth of Israeli invincibility, the nemesis of June 1967, has been replaced since Yom Kippur 1973, by the equally insidious myth of historical justice. When Menachem Begin talks of the 'liberated territories', many Israelis are embarrassed. They would rather he kept quiet. But most of them, even among his political opponents, share the underlying assumption that the Jews have a right to the whole land of Israel.

Doves, like the former foreign minister, Abba Eban, argue that Israel should sacrifice some of its inheritance in the interest of peaceful coexistence. Partition gave Israel legitimacy and insured its Jewish and democratic character. To swallow the whole of western Palestine would eventually mean an Arab majority, which could only be kept in its place by authoritarian methods.

But the biblical, ethnocentric view has taken hold more and more. Even Shimon Peres, Labour's pragmatic new leader, maintains that Jews are entitled to live anywhere in the ancestral homeland, as if that had nothing to do with policy. The Likud and the young Turks of the National Religious Party present their case in moral terms. If the Jews have no right in Shechem (now the Arab town of Nablus), what right do they have in Tel Aviv?

To challenge this dogma is like embracing sin. The Gush Emunim ('Faith Block') settlement movement does not speak for the majority, but to say it is wrong comes uncomfortably close to acknowledging that Israelis have no right to be here at all.

Zionism has always been an ambivalent ideology. Its roots are in the nationalism of nineteenth century Europe. In practice, the return to Zion was planned and dominated by Jewish socialists, who conceived it as a national liberation movement and a renaissance. These were the people who drained swamps, sowed the desert, invented the kibbutz, founded trade unions, and revived the Hebrew language.

Yet for all its sense of being a child of the enlightenment, Zionism was also a romantic movement. The Jewish right was not the right of a title deed, it was the right of a dream (the distinction is still blurred). The Zionist Congress rejected Theodor Herzl`s flirtation with a national home in Uganda precisely because there was no sentimental connection. No one yearned for Kampala.

An ageing pioneer was interviewed once on Israeli television. He explained how the elders of his Russian Jewish village had sent an emissary to Palestine to spy out the land. The man reported back: 'The bride is beautiful, but she is already married.'

For the rational Labour Zionist, the dilemma has never quite been resolved. One national liberation movement negates another. The best vindication he could muster was the right bestowed by work and creativity. The Promised Land was not empty, but it was neglected. The Jews came, bought and redeemed. There was room for all.

The Six-Day War fanned the non-rational embers. Suddenly, as if by a miracle, the pressure was released, and the Jews controlled the whole of the land. There was a revival of religiosity, if not actually of faith, a rediscovery of sites and shrines. The Eban arguments of legitimacy and demography were dismissed as pale and alien, too Anglo-Saxon by half. If the world at large did not see it the same way, so much the worse for the world at large.

The Labour governments of Levi Eshkol, Golda Meir and Yitzhak Rabin tried to restrain Gush Emunim, which was an expression of this more mystical strand. Yet they were impeded by coalition politics (dependence on the National Religious Party) and by their own lack of conviction about the future of the occupied territories. They talked of peace, but built more than 70 official settlements that looked suspiciously like dictation.

Ten years and two wars ago, few of us expected that in June 1977, Israel would still be sitting on the West Bank, The Golan Heights, and most of the Sinai Peninsula. The Arabs played their cards badly. Israel failed to tempt King Hussein to the negotiating table. The Palestinians went on demanding everything and finished up with nothing.

Pat on the anniversary, the Israeli voters have at last tilted the ideological balance. They have turned out the Labour Zionists and crowned the ultimate untroubled romantics. Gush Emunim has been awarded its licence. One of its leaders, Hanan Porat, exulted a week after the elections: 'This is our opportunity. The mission of Gush Emunim now is to grab and settle.'

It is somehow a fitting end to a decade of opportunities uncontrived. It happened by accident rather than by design. But who is going to say no to Gush Emunim?

Chapter 4 – 1977-79

Begin: the top, after 30 years in the wilderness

Observer, May 22, 1977

For the first time since independence, Israel seems likely to have as its new prime minister a leader who stands for the ideal of a Greater Israel that includes the West Bank, Gaza and Jerusalem within its borders. Menachem Begin has never deviated an inch from this claim throughout his long political career, most of it in the political wilderness.

The desert imagery is irresistible. Menachem Begin would probably deem it no less than appropriate. After comforting the muscular Zionist outcasts of the Right for 30 years, he has finally led them to the Promised Land. The Labour movement, which ruled them throughout that time with a sense of divine right, has been thrust into opposition. Begin's right-wing Likud has been elected as the largest party (though without a majority in the Knesset).

Mr Begin is a patriot, a fighter, a man with conviction of destiny. His lifestyle, like his thinking, is plain, consistent, almost puritanical. The echoes again are of the desert generation. He lives simply in the same three-roomed flat on the ground floor of 1 Rosenbaum Street, Tel Aviv that he has owned for three decades. His three children were brought up in one room. Begin and his wife used to sleep in the living room. When friends drop in for tea and political chat, the door is opened onto a small backyard to make more space.

The Likud's advertising agency, which boasted of selling the party 'like Coca Cola' in last week's elections, hit on the idea of projecting the leader as a modest family man. One picture, which provoked his Labour rivals to scorn, showed Begin holding his grandson during the traditional circumcision ceremony. The Likud had discovered, Labour mocked, that Menachem Begin was a human being. Yet the admen's image is not challenged. So far as anyone knows, he is immune to scandal. He lives simply because he has never thought of living otherwise. His wife and children are private people.

Yet there is another side to Begin's public persona. He is, and always has been, a charismatic leader in the eyes of his own followers, and he cultivates it. Last July, when the rescued hijacked passengers were being welcomed back to Lydda from Entebbe, government ministers deliberately stayed on the fringes, leaving the rejoicing to the hostages and their relieved families. Begin, as leader of the opposition, came quite properly to offer his congratulations. He was immediately hoisted onto the shoulders of his fans who chanted, 'Begin, Begin,' while he waved a bottle of whisky above their heads.

The echoes are not always innocent, but Begin would vigorously dispute any suggestion that he is undemocratic in his ways or his aspirations. In the early days of the state, after the pitched battle between the extremist Irgun Zvei Leumi and the fledgling army of Israel over the arms ship Altalena, Begin fought as hard as anyone to prevent a Jewish civil war. His roots are in the Zionist movement of Poland, where he was born in 1913.

Its rivalries were fierce and doctrinaire, but the weapons were oratorical. Begin believes in debate. He is one of the three or four best speakers in the Knesset, which he reveres with the clubland extravagance of a House of Commons man. When it suits him he can still play the demagogue, but his preferred technique is that of an old-world cabaret turn. His parliamentary speeches are impeccably wrought, thoroughly rehearsed.

Begin's political philosophy has changed little since he led the Betar youth movement in pre-war Poland. Betar was the youth wing of the Zionist revisionists, founded by Vladimir Jabotinsky who, in Begin's words, 'foretold with prophetic accuracy that the Jewish people would never achieve national independence unless they were prepared to fight for it.' The lesson was sharpened for Begin by the Nazi holocaust, and his own doctrine is neatly caught in a chapter heading of his Irgun memoirs: 'We fight, therefore we are.'

His native anti-communism was heightened by a spell in a Soviet labour camp before he was released under the Stalin-Sikorski agreement and made his way to Palestine in 1942. As a soldier in the Free Polish Army, he believed that Palestine was the homeland of the Jews, and as leader of the Irgun Zvei Leumi tried to reassure the local Arabs that they had nothing to fear, so long as they were content to live as a minority in the Jewish State. Thirty years on, he remains just as deaf to the counter-yearnings of another people. After a three-year interval under Yitzhak Rabin, Israel is on the point of being governed again by a prime minister who denies that the Palestinians are a nation.

Nor would Begin dream of acknowledging any similarity between his own status in the underground and that of Yasser Arafat or the more extremist George Habash. 'The underground fighters of the Irgun,' he wrote in *The Revolt*, 'arose to overthrow and replace a regime. We used physical force because we were faced by physical force. But physical force was neither our aim nor our creed. We believed in the supremacy of moral forces. It was our enemy who mocked at them. That is why, not withstanding the enemy's tremendous preponderance in physical strength, it was he who was defeated and not we. That is the law of history.' Begin, the Zionist fundamentalist from Brest-Litovsk, has never recognised that someone else might invoke the same law.

Begin resents the label 'terrorist' and was deeply hurt by the hostile reception he received on his first visit to Britain five years ago. The Irgun`s objective, he argues, was not to instill fear and not to kill innocent civilians. It is an article of faith with him that Irgun outrages were preceded by warnings. There is independent evidence that this was so in July 1946, when his organisation blew up the King David Hotel in Jerusalem, killing or wounding more than 200 people. (Incidentally and ironically, when Begin comes to Jerusalem he invariably stays in the King David. He has even been heard to boast that he sleeps in the same room once occupied by the British commander, General Barker.)

The old Irgun commander maintains that his men hanged British sergeants or whipped British officers only as a last resort to deter the British from perpetrating the same brutalities on Jewish fighters, whom they refused to recognise as prisoners of war. Again in his book *The Revolt* he sets out the organisation's apologia:

> The arrest of British officers in order to secure the annulment of a death sentence, the arrest of more officers which did not prevent murder of our captive comrades, but which did bring about the retreat of Palestinian officials into the famous ghettoes; the frustrations of martial law, the last attempt at mass oppression, the whipping of officers in retaliation for the whipping of our young soldiers; hangings in retaliation for hangings – all these things not only shook the Government's prestige but eventually destroyed it in the Land of Israel.

Of the massacre of some 250 Arab villagers in Deir Yassin, north of Jerusalem in 1948, Begin insists that it was a legitimate military target, a staging post for Arab forces attacking Jewish forces along the only road from the capital to the coast. He argues that there were casualties on both sides in 'very severe' fighting and that the civilian population was warned by the Irgun before the battle. At the time Ben-Gurion sent a letter of apology to King Abdullah of Jordan and many Israelis still find Begin's explanation unconvincing.

It is perhaps a measure of his creative inactivity since 1948 that Begin is still tagged abroad as 'the number-one terrorist'. In fact he is the classic case of the terrorist-turned-respectable politician. In a nation of open necks and shirtsleeve order, Begin is the man in the grey Terylene suit. His shirts are white, his ties unobtrusive. He is gracious and welcoming. Ladies can always be sure of a kiss on the hand, colleagues of a formal public congratulation after a good speech. He respects the British for their civilised institutions, and bears no grudge for the past. He has been seen at the Queen's birthday parties on the embassy lawn.

Over the years, Begin's control of his party has been challenged, but never shaken. His men still addressed him as Hamefaked, the Commander. In the short run, last week's election triumph has reinforced Begin's authority within the Likud. It had no other leader with his unambiguous appeal to the kind of voters who might be tempted into the fold, and the campaign was waged on his name. The question now is whether or not Menachem Begin, the perennial leader of the opposition, can adapt his thinking to the realities of Israel, the Middle East and the world in the era of Carter, Brezhnev, Sadat and Assad.

The first signs are discouraging. In interview after interview since Wednesday morning, he has redefined the occupied territories as the 'liberated territories', insisting that there can be no withdrawal from Judea and Samaria (the West Bank) or the Gaza Strip. At Kadoum, a Jewish settlement near the Arab town of Nablus, which the Labour government had decreed would never become permanent, Begin pledged his administration to foster a new surge of settlement. He stopped short of pledging annexation because 'you don't annex your own country'.

Begin is an unreconstructed cold warrior. Like Golda Meir, but unlike many in the next generation of Israeli politicians and diplomats, he puts his trust in a community of interest between Washington and Jerusalem. Israel, he argues, is a bulwark against communist expansion in Asia and Africa, a free, democratic ally in an age of encroaching totalitarianism. There is no evidence that he appreciates the hard truth, particularly since the 1973 war and its attendant oil embargo, that the equation is no longer so simple, if it ever was.

Others in his party do. Leaders of the liberal wing are less eager to pay the price for the 'whole land of Israel'. And it is here that Begin may, after a decent interval, face an effective challenge to his supremacy. His Herut wing is now a minority in Likud and has no outstanding personality of the generation after Begin's. The future leadership must come from technocrats like Ezer Weizman, the former air force chief and a nephew of Israel's founding president (the most likely choice for defence minister), Aryeh Dulzin (a possible foreign minister), and Moshe Arens, an American-born professor of aeronautical engineering.

The continuing uncertainty about Begin's health may give them their occasion, if not their excuse. At 64 he suffered a serious heart attack at the beginning of this year; it was complicated by pneumonia.

His mind and his tongue are as spry as ever, but even for so small and lean a figure, he looks frail and skeletal. In the Knesset, on the day before polling day, he had difficulty lifting his feet. The imagery of the desert has its traps. Moses led the children of Israel for 40 years in the wilderness, but he did not himself enter the Promised Land.

A balance of blackmail

Guardian, May 23, 1977

Sharm-el-Sheikh, the casus belli of two Middle East wars, tells its own story. As you fly south from Eilat, the Gulf of Aqaba looks like some deep, wide, navigable river, an Amazon or Mississippi of the Orient.

The granite and sandstone mountains of Sinai rear to the west, their craggy twins of Saudi Arabia to the east. The Jordanian port of Aqaba, King Hussein's only outlet to the sea, is bustling with commerce, the freighters queuing for berths. The Lebanese civil war has been good for somebody. A tanker is discharging at Eilat, its Israeli neighbour at the northern tip of the gulf. A container ship is at the quay.

Half an hour's Viscount-time away, you are reminded that this is not the Red Sea at all, just one of those little ears that jut out at the top of the map. Suddenly there below is the broad, misty expanse of the sea itself, younger brother to the Indian Ocean.

At the exit from the gulf, the plane circles Tiran before coming in to land at Sharm. Between the island and the Arabian shore, the shallows and coral reefs show turquoise through the dark blue water. To the west between Tiran and the headland of Ras Nasrani, lies the deep, choppy channel in and out of the gulf, 1,300 yards across.

This is where Gamal Abdel Nasser brought his two British five-inch field guns from Alexandria in September 1955. This is where, ten years ago today, on May 23, 1967, the Egyptian president closed the Straits of Tiran to Israeli shipping.

The United Nations peace force, stationed at Ras Nasrani when Israel evacuated Sinai after the 1956 Suez war, had withdrawn at

Nasser's behest on the 19th. The blockade, as Edgar O'Ballance put it in his book, *The Third Arab-Israeli War*, 'made war inevitable'.

The guns are still there at Ras Nasrani, spiked, flaking and forlorn, worth a detour for five minutes and an ironic photograph. A couple of miles north, up the dirt road to Nabeq, a picnic site now with mangroves growing out into the sea, an Israeli Mustang squats in the desert, peppered with bullets that brought it down in 1956. The pilot bailed out and was rescued by a comrade in a Piper.

Nasser's cannon and the Israeli Mustang are exhibits in what has become an alfresco museum of war. The Straits of Tiran are little more themselves. The Arabs no longer need them to blockade Eilat. They can now seal the Red Sea at its southern entrance, Bab-el-Mandeb (the Gate of Tears) as the Egyptian navy did during and after the Yom Kippur War of 1973.

The Red Sea is an Arab lake in practice if not in law. As far as Israeli shipping is concerned, it does not matter whether the French territory of Djibouti joins the Arab camp when it gains independence later this year. It would merely complete the circle, but the Arabs do not need Djibouti to close Bab-el-Mandeb.

The navigable channel there is controlled by South Yemeni artillery, placed on Perim Island, and commanding the 16½ miles of waterway between there and the African coast.

Eilat is as critical as it ever was for Israel. It is the main port for its expanding trade with east and southern Africa, as well as South-east Asia, and Australia. Iranian oil arrives there for Israel itself, and for trans-shipment to the Mediterranean coast and on to Europe. Israel still offers a 'land bridge' alternative to the Suez Canal and there are plans for extending the railway to Eilat.

The Straits of Tiran may be turning into a museum, but their hinterland of Sharm-el-Sheikh has lost none of its strategic influence for Israel.

The military planners insist that Sharm is now indispensable if Israel is to deter the Arabs from sealing Bab-el-Mandeb. The big air and naval bases Israel maintains at Sharm create a balance of blackmail.

As my officer-guide explained: 'If the Arabs block Bab-el-Mandeb to us, we can retaliate by blocking both Suez and Aqaba. It is hard to imagine that we will sit quietly.'

Sharm-el-Sheikh, and more particularly its southern headland of Ras Muhammad, looks on both gulfs – Aqaba and Suez. Seen from an Israeli Dabur patrol boat, they stretched like the two arms of a 'Y' into the haze. Israel's Reshef missile boats, with air and logistical support, could deny the port of Aqaba and, more punitively, the Suez Canal to Arab and international shipping.

At the same time, Israel can operate as far south as Bab-el-Mandeb itself as long as it keeps the Sharm bases. The distance from Sharm to Bab-el-Mandeb is 1,020 nautical miles. That is within the range of the Reshef, a stretched and improved version of the boats Israel spirited away from Cherbourg.

The Reshef carries launchers for seven Gabriel missiles, with a range in an improved version of almost 25 miles, two 76mm anti-aircraft and sea-to-shore guns, with a high rate of fire, and a crew of 45 officers and men.

The flight from Sharm to Bab-el-Mandeb and back stretches the operational range of Israel's Phantom and Kfir fighters to their limits. 'In practice,' an officer said, 'Bab-el-Mandeb is out of range for long-term fighting, but it is not out of range for us to do something.'

The American F-15 Eagle, which Israel began to receive last December, will, however, make a significant difference. Five years ago, the Israeli government decided to establish an 'urban settlement' at Sharm. Five hundred homes were to be built at what was named Ophira. So far, about half have been finished. Ophira remains, however, a frontier town and a garrison town.

Television does not reach this far, nor for much of the day does the radio. Ophira – for all the tourist potential of the Red Sea coral diving – is not exactly booming.

Doubts behind the candyfloss – Middle East summit
What has Mr Begin to give Mr Sadat in return for his peace initiative?

Observer, November 20, 1977

Now thrive the hucksters. Everything has moved so swiftly since President Anwar Sadat proclaimed his readiness to come to Jerusalem rather than risk another Egyptian soldier on the battlefield that Israelis are still frolicking this weekend in the dreamlike improbability of it all.

The wry little jokes have suddenly turned true. Would the army band have the sheet music for the Egyptian anthem? We smirked. No, but now it has, courtesy of Mr Sadat's advance party. Egyptian flags? Those have been brought, too, along with the communications experts and the dark-suited Cairo security men.

Jerusalem's three luxury hotels competed by press release for the honour of decanting their paying guests and entertaining the Egyptians in their royal suites. The choice inevitably fell on the Levantine splendours of the King David of which Chips Channon wrote in his diary, 'Next to the Ritz in Paris, it surely is the world's best hotel'. But that was in 1941, and he wasn't so smitten with the 'officious Jews speaking Bowery English'. Menachem Begin and Henry Kissinger have since made their distinctive contributions to its reputation.

By Friday morning, four-colour posters heralding 'Peace, Shalom, Salaam' were on sale at 10 Israeli pounds (about 40p), flourishing the Israeli and Egyptian flags under the legend, 'Sadat visits Israel – November 1977'. Plastic pennants, blue and white for Israel, red, white and black for Egypt, came a touch dearer, two on the same stick for 12 Israeli pounds.

With 2,000 foreign correspondents and cameramen due by yesterday, every room in the city was let at least once. Car-hire firms called up reinforcements from Tel Aviv. And one Jerusalem estate agent capped them all by advertising 'Magnificent 14-roomed house, prestige neighbourhood, terms negotiable. Suitable for Egyptian Embassy'.

The evening paper *Ma'ariv* flashed a welcome in scarlet across its front page in Hebrew and Arabic. The *Jerusalem Post* produced a special Saturday night issue to display at the airport. The editorials were more sombre.

'Breaking down the taboo of Arab hostility is an invaluable achievement for Israel,' the influential *Ha'aretz* wrote on Friday. 'But prosaic issues will have to be discussed, and a solution found to the question of how countries that are in a state of war can maintain neighbourly and peaceful relations. It is to be hoped that the Israeli Government will display greater flexibility than in the past.'

The paper touched here on the doubts beneath the candyfloss. Mr Sadat has swallowed his pride and gambled his political life. What has Mr Begin to give him in return? The question is more acute by the vituperation the president has provoked among the Arabs, and even among the ruling elite in his own country. Old-fashioned hospitality may not be enough, and if Mr Sadat does not press for something more than fine words and a promise of jam tomorrow, the Americans may soon do so on his behalf.

The Israeli foreign minister, Mr Moshe Dayan, recognised the dilemma in a radio interview. 'Israel will not be in a situation vis-à-vis the whole world,' he said, 'in which it will be able to be satisfied only with listening and not reacting.'

Mr Sadat, the foreign minister added, would have his say, and his remarks would have wide reverberations. His basic demands would probably be withdrawal from all the occupied territories and the right of the Palestinians to establish a state. 'I think Israel will not be exempt from replying to the question he has put, even if he not only does not request, but even refuses to listen to a concrete answer which entails bilateral undertakings.'

The president, in other words, will speak only for Egypt, but he will need pan-Arab answers. Here the Begin government faces the nemesis of its election pledge to seek an overall settlement, rather than another round of interim agreements. The comprehensive approach focuses immediately on the most intractable issue, that of the Palestinians. It cannot be ducked until the climate is more propitious.

This, then, is the challenge Mr Begin will have to confront – sooner than he wanted, and on less advantageous terms. Yet there is no sign of flexibility. The prime minister still views the Middle East conflict through blue and white spectacles. The Palestinian Arabs have interests, but as refugees, as a minority in the Jewish commonwealth. Their problems must be assuaged, a way must be found to co-exist. But Mr Begin is as far away as ever from according them the equal status of a national movement.

It was an unfortunate accident that only two days before Mr Sadat was due, the Knesset finance committee approved the allocation of 87 million Israeli pounds (£3 million) for establishing and supporting at least 11 new settlements across the pre-1967 border.

Opinion among the West Bank Arabs was torn last week between hope and hostility, reflected glory and despair that the Egyptian leader was selling them short. The conservative East Jerusalem daily *Al Quds* welcomed the visit, but quietly reminded Mr Sadat that he must not ignore the Palestinian question. Its two radical competitors were more openly critical of the visit.

Among local leaders, the mayor of Hebron, Mr Fahd Kawassmeh, said: 'It will be an important dialogue, which will break the tradition of enmity between Israel and the Arab states. I believe also that this meeting will serve in resolving the Palestinian question.'

The mayor of Ramallah, Mr Karim Khalaf, an outspoken champion of the Palestinian Liberation Organisation, argued that for Mr Sadat to accept an Israeli invitation meant he was ignoring the Palestinian question, or shunting it into a corner.

The mayor of Jericho, Mr Adb el-Aziz Sawiti, went even further: 'Sadat is a person whom the Arab people neither love nor respect. He is ignoring the roots of the Arab struggle and is focusing only on what concerns him as president of Egypt. He wants to succeed at the expense of the Arab people.'

Blessed are the peacemakers, but are the banners perhaps a trifle premature?

Sadat gives Israel friendly words and old demands

Guardian, November 21, 1977

If peace is to come to the Middle East it will not be by oratory alone. So much was clear after the exchange of speeches in the Israeli parliament here last night between President Anwar Sadat and Mr Menachem Begin.

Neither leader produced anything unfamiliar enough or radical enough to change its stance: Mr Sadat was eager for peace on Egyptian terms, Mr Begin no less so on Israeli terms.

Judged on performance and as an exercise in public relations, Mr Sadat won with surprising ease. He was challenging and buoyant. Israel was thrown on the defensive. Mr Begin was tired and predictable far below his usual rhetorical standard. Not only did he offer no new ideas but he failed to find new words for expressing the old ones.

In his 55-minute Arabic address, Mr Sadat spelled out more precisely than ever before his readiness to accept Israel as a *fait accompli*. He has hinted at that in the past, but never so unequivocally and never, of course, in the Knesset. 'We welcome you,' he assured the 120 MPs, 'to live among us in peace and security.'

To avoid 'the shedding of one single drop of blood on either side,' the Egyptian president appealed for the 'bravery and boldness of men who dedicate themselves to erect a sublime edifice'. His declared object was peace and justice.

As well as the recognition that Israel was here to stay, Mr Sadat offered 'borders secure against aggression' and whatever form of international guarantees Israel might want – two-power, American, five-power, or any permutation of those – provided the same guarantees were open to Egypt.

In return he recited the entire catalogue of Arab demands – with the one notable exception that he did not promote the Palestinian Liberation Organisation as the 'only legitimate representative of the Palestinian people' the pan-Arab consensus enshrined at the Rabat summit three years ago.

He insisted on complete Israeli withdrawal from 'Arab territories occupied by force, including Arab Jerusalem'. Land was not open to argument. Mr Sadat said he was not ready to concede one inch, or the principle of bargaining over it. Jerusalem should be 'a free and open city for all believers'. It should not be cut off from 'those who made it their abode for centuries'.

For all his omission of any reference to the PLO, he identified the Palestinian problem as 'the core and the essence of the conflict. It would be a grave error,' he said, 'to brush aside the Palestinian rights of statehood and of return.'

The president summed up his package in five points:

> 1.   The ending of the occupation of territory taken in 1967 (he made attempt to reinstate the 1947 borders, as some Arab spokesmen have done);
>
> 2.   Restoration of the rights of the Palestinian people, including a state (no blurring the issue by talking of a 'homeland' or a Palestinian 'entity');
>
> 3.   The right of all states to live in peace within secure boundaries;
>
> 4.   A commitment on all sides to operate in keeping with the United Nations charter, including non-resort to force to resolve conflicts;
>
> 5.   An end to the state of belligerency.

Point four is already incorporated in the second Sinai agreement, signed in September 1975. Point five would be redundant in a full peace treaty; the only value claimed for it would be as a limited, temporary alternative.

Mr Sadat was generously received by the packed chamber, which included such former MPs as Mrs Golda Meir and the maverick editor and peace campaigner Mr Uri Avnery. Ministers sat impassively throughout the Egyptian leader's speech. The only senior Israeli figure who seemed to be responding was the former Prime Minister, Mr Yitzhak Rabin, pink-faced and furiously passing notes to everyone within reach of his back bench.

The members rose and applauded when Mr Sadat entered in company with President Ephraim Katzir of Israel, and again at the end of his address. Three army buglers sounded fanfares at the beginning and the end of the 2½ hour session. Mr Sadat's delivery was confident, if occasionally repetitive, but persistent dabbing of the sweat from his gleaming bald patch hinted at the strain it must have been.

Mr Begin resisted any temptation to negotiate at the rostrum. He read a prepared speech with little pretence at answering his Egyptian guest. A western ambassador, listening in the gallery, suggested that the Americans had warned the prime minister against a slanging match. The only exception was the Jerusalem issue, on which Mr Begin promised that 'for ever and ever access will be free to the holy places sanctified to each faith'.

The Israeli leader proclaimed his wish for 'real peace, involving full reconciliation between the Jewish and Arab nations, without being bogged down in memories of the past.'

Nonetheless, he subjected Mr Sadat to a lesson in recent Jewish history, pointing the moral of the Nazi holocaust and of the 1948 Middle East war, which he said was forced on a weak Israel by its powerful Arab neighbours. The 'generation of the annihilation,' he said, had taken an oath of loyalty never to put the Jewish people in danger again.

Mr Sadat, the Israeli prime minister said, knew that their attitudes on borders differed, but that did not mean that there could be no negotiation. He suggested that they should negotiate about every point in their contention, and that neither side should present conditions in advance: 'We shall negotiate as equals. There are no victors and no vanquished.'

Mr Begin repeated his invitation to the rulers of Syria, Jordan and Lebanon to follow Mr Sadat on the road to Jerusalem. He offered to open Israel's borders to the citizens of Egypt, and later to those of Syria, Jordan and Lebanon. That would be an extension of the 'open bridges' policy pursued by Israeli governments since 1967.

The prime minister called for a renewal of the Geneva peace conference, on the basis of resolutions 242 and 338 of the UN Security Council, the carefully balanced formulae that sprang from the 1967 and 1973 wars respectively.

On Mr Begin's initiative, the two leaders shook hands to grateful applause at the end of his 40-minute statement. The only heckling had come from two Communist MPs – one Arab, one Jewish – trying to force the Palestinian issue, which Mr Begin simply evaded.

A similar reminder was presented to President Sadat when he joined about 3,000 worshippers celebrating the Muslim Feast of the Sacrifice in the Al Aqsa mosque, the third most holy in Islam. The Imam insisted that 'the Palestinians will stay in the occupied land and hold on to it. They want justice and they want the Arab and Islamic world to know it.'

As President Sadat left the mosque, the crowd leaving it and some of those locked outside began a rhythmic chant, 'Palestine o Sadat'.

Later in the morning his visit to the Church of the Holy Sepulchre prompted the first openly hostile demonstration of his visit. Five minutes after he had left a band of about 100 Arab adolescents, boys and girls, marched on the compound shouting, 'Go home, Sadat. We don't want this visit. You are a traitor.' The demonstration was dispersed painlessly by the border police.

Mr Sadat also had a working lunch and a working dinner with Mr Begin yesterday. It is still too early to predict whether anything of substance will emerge from these meetings and a third tête-à-tête that will follow this morning.

Pilgrimage to a land in the shadow of hope
Letter from Egypt
Guardian, December 31, 1977
'I had the feeling of a man who has corresponded with a girl, who has loved her from her writing, loved her from her picture, then meets her and finds that the picture was not very recent. I asked myself whether it wouldn't have been better to keep my distance.'

Victor Nahmias, the son of an old Cairo Jewish family, returned after 20 years to his childhood neighbourhood, a reporter for Israeli television, a pilgrim with a camera crew. Nahmias, now 42 years old, left Egypt three-quarters of the way through his course at Cairo University. It was after the Suez War and Jews were being arrested and deported. Victor's family, as Egyptian citizens, could have stayed. They chose to go to Israel. 'We felt uneasy,' he says, 'as if we were being strangled.'

Nahmias came back to the honeymoon of President Sadat's peace initiative. The Israelis were graciously received. A military correspondent returned to the Suez Canal, where he had filmed during the 1973 war. Another won an interview with Mrs Jihan Sadat, the president's wife.

The Egyptian authorities, who had met Victor Nahmias during President Sadat's trip to Jerusalem, had no reservations about letting him back or allowing him to move about freely. He says now that he regrets having visited his old home.

'I was shocked by the situation there,' he said. 'It hurt me directly in the heart. The place has gone back a century. It was like Cairo at the time of Ismail, I was disappointed, ashamed of being from this neighbourhood. I thought, if I had not left could I have lived here?

'I was full of pity for these people. They were never very rich, but it was good and sound. I remembered grass and trees and gardens. Now there was not a spot of green. Everything was disintegrating. Everything which broke down stayed like that – cement, walls, windows. There was a total lack of maintenance. These were not just slums, they were more than any slums I have seen.'

To a newcomer, seeing Egypt for the first time, Cairo is a city of cumulative horror. It is not like Calcutta. No one is dying in the streets. Most of the eight million Egyptians squeezed within its borders somehow make a living. If they have no profession or trade, they subsist as doormen, street-sweepers, or peddlers. There is enough food to keep them afloat.

Cairo itself, though, cannot cope. It has given up the struggle. There are a quarter of a million cars in Egypt. Most of them seem to be thrusting their way through the capital. Driving is slow and anarchic. You stop at red lights in the city centre, but not outside. If there is a speed limit on the six-lane motorway to the pyramids, no one has heard of it.

New cars are expensive. Old ones are kept running long after their natural life span. The air, as a result, is polluted with a distinctive mixture of desert dust and Model-T fumes. A morning in the city centre feels like Leeds or Manchester before the Clean Air Act. The grit is in your throat, the grime on your fingertips.

The fine, old French and British office buildings are still there, but cracked, neglected and thick with the dirt of the decades. Groppis still make superb chocolates, but the teahouse is like a run-down Kardomah. In the grey, unpainted walls of the high-classic Cairo Museum, King Tut lies in splendid reproach to his heirs and countrymen.

Apart from the modern hotels – the Hiltons and the Sheratons that could be almost anywhere – the only proud building I visited was the 10-storey tower of Al-Ahram, what skittish Cairenes have dubbed 'Nasser's Pyramid'. It could be the Millbank Tower, or the *Daily Mirror* in Holborn. The walls are marble, scrubbed and polished. On every floor, flunkeys buff the floors as they usher you in and out of the lift.

The Egyptians are their own saving grace – charming, self-mocking and ultimately exasperating. The telephones do not work. Appointments are not kept. Time is vulgar. The national slogans are *malesh* (don't worry) and *inshallah* (if God wills it). If you complain that a call has not come through in the five minutes promised, the clerk smiles, spreads his hands and purrs: 'An Egyptian five minutes.'

An American friend of mine took a taxi. After a couple of minutes it stopped. The driver was perplexed until our man pointed out that he had run out of petrol. 'Please wait,' said driver, trotting off with a bottle. Ten minutes later he came back, poured in a couple of pints, and started again.

Another mile, another breakdown. This time the battery had gone flat. 'We push,' the driver said. They pushed. Eventually, it started sputtered, died and started again. They arrived at my friend's hotel an hour late. The passenger handed over the £2 they had agreed at the start. The driver held out his hand for more. What did he mean more? He tapped his watch. Look how long it took; the passenger took back one pound, tapped his watch; they settled on two pounds.

Mr Sadat is selling peace offensive as a key to curing Egypt's economic ills. His experts advised him that they could achieve nothing so long as Egypt was committed to war, and preparation for war. If peace comes it will call the president's bluff.

A longing for peace, but no desire for friendship
Guardian, May 21, 1979

Anwar Sadat has made an Egyptian peace in more ways than his Arab critics would allow. A Martian reporter splashing down in the Nile would be hard pressed to identify the other party to the historic reconciliation.

The president is worshipped on every street as the 'hero of peace', though my favourite banner for all seasons — 'Mohammed Ali and his workers agree with Sadat' — is no longer stretched along the corniche behind Shepheard's Hotel. Sadat in Pierre Cardin uniform competes with Sadat in peasant shirt; Sadat in his diplomatic suit with pipe-smoking Sadat, the father of the nation.

But nowhere would our interplanetary investigator find mention of Israel. There are no portraits of Menachem Begin, no blue and white beside the red, white and black of Egypt (the minimum of Stars of David required by protocol during Begin's Cairo visit were lowered before his Boeing had left the runway). The Egyptian peace stamp bears an elegant ring of doves around Sadat's signature in Arabic and the date he appended it to the Washington treaty. No Begin, no Jimmy Carter, no Hebrew, no English.

It is more than mere tactics, the urge to drive a hard bargain in the negotiations over Palestinian autonomy starting this weekend, reluctance to flaunt a bilateral deal before the Saudi Arabians (it is both of those too). Egypt has made what a Cairo political commentator described to me as a secular peace, an agreement with a strong neighbour with whom it has fought enough wars. Egypt has not come to terms with the heresy of Zionism (Begin`s fundamentalist brand or anyone else's), with the Jewish presumption of equality in a Moslem world. The old distaste, the ideological hostility, has survived most strongly among the intellectuals. They have more words to swallow. The change was easier for the man on (or more often clinging to) the Cairo omnibus. The dusty Felaheen and their urban grandsons are used to following a lead from above. The cult of the individual is as ancient here as Rameses. A member of Sadat's negotiating team dismissed Israel's biblical claim to the West Bank as so much 'crap'. The *Egyptian Gazette* still predicts Israel's 'certain self-destruction'.

The director of Egypt's leading research centre on Israeli affairs treated me to an unprovoked diatribe on the theme that Gush Emunim represents the true expansionist face of Zionism, that there is no difference between the settlement militants and their 'peace now' adversaries. A seminar with a quartet of dovish Israeli professors was conducted like a gladiatorial contest.

The foreign ministry professionals are determined to force major concessions from Israel on the West Bank and Gaza Strip. The unanimous condemnation of the Arab world, whether or not it surprised the Egyptians as much as it surprised the American state department, makes that an essential target. But one detects a relish for the task beyond the call of duty.

In an interview with the *Guardian*, Osama El Baz, the under-secretary for foreign affairs, vigorously rejected Menachem Begin's programme for Palestinian self-rule under Israeli sovereignty. 'It is utterly unacceptable to us,' he said, 'and we are not going to talk on this basis. It is contrary to the letter and spirit of Camp David. If they behave in this way, it means they don't want us to reach any agreement.'

El Baz, a short, wiry diplomat who talks like a machine gun, blamed Israel for the intensity of the Arab reaction. 'Arab hostility serves no interest but that of Israel,' he insisted. 'Most of the Israeli actions or statements before the ink was dry on the peace treaty were designed to give the message to the Arabs that nothing was going to happen on the Palestinian plane, that this was a separate agreement. Every statement by Begin and his aides was designed to increase and deepen the rift in the Arab world and to scare away all the moderate elements among the Palestinians.'

But the Egyptian negotiator was not yet writing off the chances of reaching an agreement before the twelve-month deadline set by the peace treaty. The situation he argued was dynamic not static.

'We will not allow Israel to get away with establishing a phoney municipal council for the West Bank and Gaza under the banner of self-governing authority with genuine control. The present position of the Israeli government is untenable. They cannot maintain it in negotiations.

'They know very well that no Palestinian can accept this formula. Egypt will never deliver the West Bank to Israel. We want to deliver the West Bank and Gaza to the Palestinians in an orderly manner that does not invite violence or hatred between the two sides.'

El Baz disclosed that the Egyptian team would demand a moratorium on settlement during the negotiations. 'We think,' he said, 'that the Jewish settlements should not stay after the five-year transitional phase to Palestinian self-determination. They should be evacuated like the settlements in Sinai.'

While recognising Israel's anxiety about its security, El Baz refused to contemplate continued Israeli control over the West Bank's external and internal security, as required by the Begin plan. 'These fears,' he maintained, 'are not going to be eliminated by the territorial expansion or occupation. Don't tell me that any average Israeli thinks it would not be possible to guarantee their security by such measures as limiting armament, demilitarisation and international inspection.

'Occupation is an act of violence. They are not sending the philharmonic to the occupied territories; they are sending thirteen thousand armed men. This act of violence invites counter-violence.'

For all his tough talk, El Baz acknowledged Egypt's dilemma of negotiating by proxy for unwilling Palestinians. He did not exclude the possibility that self-rule might have to be introduced piecemeal in Gaza, where Egypt had legal as well as historic and geographic connections. It governed the strip under the terms of a United Nations Security Council Resolution from 1949 to 1967, but did not annex it.

He insisted, however, that the separation of Gaza and the West Bank must apply only to the phasing of implementation.

The Egyptians do not take Israeli extremism at face value. Even if Begin is not simply adopting a tough bargaining stance, they contend that the negotiations will dictate a more flexible logic. They recall that at the start of the Sinai round Moshe Dayan proclaimed that Sharm-el-Sheikh without peace was better than peace without Sharm-el-Sheikh, Ezer Weizman called the Sinai air bases indispensable to Israel's security, and Begin was planning to retire to Yamit. All had now been sacrificed.

Like the Israelis, the Egyptians bring to the negotiations a particular sense of history. For them the racial memories are of decolonisation, in the Arab world and in Africa. The precedent most often invoked is Algeria.

Another member of Sadat's team, the deputy foreign minister Boutrus Ghali, argued that just as the French had been forced to eat their words and give up Algeria, so Israel would have to accept the creation of a Palestinian entity in the West Bank and Gaza.

Less unconvincingly, Ghali also put Arab opposition to the peace process in historic perspective: 'There have been thirty-three inter-Arab disputes since 1945. Look at what those disputes have solved. We believe that this inter-Arab dispute will be solved more easily. Now we are at the peak of the inter-Arab confrontation.'

It sounds like whistling in the dark, though the impact of Arab sanctions on the Egyptian economy has been less drastic than it might have been. Arab aid to Cairo averaged about nine hundred million dollars a year from 1973 to 1978. Income from sales of Egyptian oil (estimated at one thousand million dollars last year), Suez Canal dues (five hundred million dollars) and remittances home by the 1.2 million Egyptians working in the Arab states ($1.8 thousand million) has risen much more rapidly.

The president's first response has been to drum up a surge of Egyptian nationalism. During a week of rallies in regional centres, Sadat repeatedly scorned the Saudis as 'dwarfs'. Jerusalem, he said, would never be restored by slogans.

Sadat has tapped a vein of popular resentment. Even his critics judge his domestic base to be secure for the time being. The internal opposition – left, right, Islamic and student – is too fragmented and too cowed to pose a serious threat.

Sadat`s negotiators know, nonetheless, that they have few cards to play in the Palestinian cause. They will make Israel pay for every shuffle towards normal relations. This weekend's opening of borders and a civil aid corridor will be no more than symbolic. There are still no direct communications between Jerusalem and Cairo.

Ultimately the Egyptians are putting their money on Washington. They hope Carter has staked too much on a successful treaty to let his Israeli protégés settle for less. In an election year the equation is finely balanced. The United States president must consolidate one of his few foreign policy achievements, but dare he alienate the Jewish vote? How far can he go in putting Saudi oil supplies at risk?

On their own, the Egyptians will in the end confront Begin with the choice between territory and peace. 'They will have to give up the West Bank and Gaza,' Boutrus Ghali insisted. 'Otherwise they will have no peace.' You will, however, find well-placed skeptics in Cairo who suspect that Sadat, with or without the connivance of his foreign ministry hawks, will back down first.

Rulers change, the Bedouin stay
Southern Sinai
Guardian, November 13, 1979
'Bedouin never think about the future,' says Mohamet, the young, Jebelia tribesman in red and white checked kefiya, who runs a lucrative tourist café in the shadow of Jebel Mussa, the biblical Mount Sinai. 'If we did,' he adds, 'we would stop being Bedouin.'

It is one of those half-truths with which they comfort themselves in the granite and sandstone of Southern Sinai, rising from 5,000 to more than 7,000 feet above sea level. It is a polite rebuff to an inquisitive reporter. Mohamet, who learnt a passable English from his customers and from an Arabic-English dictionary, feels over-interviewed. Careless talk costs who-knows-what?

Just before Israel restores this next slice of desert to Egypt, the Bedouin are watching their step. Like all survivors on the margins of society and subsistence, they are taking out whatever insurance policies they can. Even if you are sponsored by an Israeli they have come to trust over the twelve years of occupation, they are wary of strangers. They relax a little over the replenished cups of sweet, spicy tea, but insist that you don't quote them too precisely by name.

In three days of travelling and talking from Jebel Mussa into the more desolate wadis to the north, I found no single Bedouin awaiting the Egyptian return with unqualified rejoicing. Although they are Egyptian citizens, the 7,000 South Sinai tribesmen regard themselves as a people apart.

'We lived under the British,' reflected one old man who works for the monks of St Catherine`s monastery at the foot of the holy mountain, 'we lived under the Egyptians, we lived under the Israelis. Now we shall live again under the Egyptians. The Bedouins will always be here.'

President Sadat is accepted as one more in the series of alien rulers. I asked a tribal elder in a remote oasis whether they would be happier under a Moslem rather than a Jewish administration.

'Look,' he answered, rolling another cigarette of green aromatic tobacco, 'if the Moslem is a good man and the Jew is a good man, I would prefer the Moslem. We can pray together; but if the Moslem is not so good, I prefer the Jew.'

The Bedouin have mixed memories of the Egyptian garrisons posted to Sinai before the 1967 war. Their job was to control the native population, to stop the nomads spying for Israel, or smuggling hashish too blatantly from Jordan to Egypt. They were men of the towns and the Nile Delta, ill at ease in the desert and the mountains. 'They would not drink tea with us,' one Bedouin herdsman complained.

Another quoted an Egyptian officer as telling him: 'The Israelis are like a thorn in the eye of Egypt. The Bedouin are like a thorn in the foot.'

Yet there were exceptions. A tribal judge recalled an Egyptian officer coming to him in tears with what he said was an order from President Nasser to finish off the Bedouin once the Israelis had been dispatched. Not all the Egyptians were hostile, and those that were could often be deceived or bribed.

On balance, the Bedouin are reassured by stories reaching Southern Sinai from the areas already given back to Egypt. There is bad news from El Arish in the north, where notables are reported to have been victimised for collaborating with Israel, but better word from Wadi Firan, the strip closest to Mount Sinai.

The Egyptians arrested a Bedouin sheikh from the Israeli side of the demarcation line during the evacuation ceremony in September after two disaffected tribesmen had accused him of spying. He was returned on the intervention of the Israeli defence minister, Mr Weizman.

The Bedouin read this as a good sign. The Egyptians were open to argument, and there have been no further arrests. They are also encouraged by reports filtering back that there has been no discrimination against men who worked for the Israeli civil administration. Jebel Mussa will come under the same governor as Wadi Firan.

But the Bedouin's ultimate concern is economic. In their own terms, they have prospered under the Israelis. Most of the men in the south have found employment – in the administration, in tourism, or in the resort towns and settlements on the Gulf of Aqaba from Sharm-el-Sheikh to Eilat. Their families eat more meat and vegetables. Among the Jebelia, the mountain tribe, there are now 150 Jeeps and tenders where previously there were none.

If you ask the Bedouin whether they expect to continue living so well once the Israelis have gone, they shrug: 'If there is a real peace, the border will stay open and the tourists will come here from both sides, Egypt and Israel.' They remind you, too, that their staple foods – flour, rice, tea and sugar – are heavily subsidised in Egypt and have become increasingly expensive under the Israelis.

Ahmed, a sharp Bedouin of about 30 in suede shoes, trousers and a Tel Aviv shirt, introduces himself as a driver, a mechanic and a 'rais', a labour contractor. 'Don't worry,' he says, 'I'll get by.' He probably will, although it may mean living in the desert and taking his ambitions into town.

The economic signs from Wadi Firan are disturbing. The Egyptian administration dismissed all the Bedouin workers, not out of vindictiveness but simply because it is not running the same operation as the Israelis. If that means an end to the elementary schools and health clinics opened by Israel, it will be a blow to the Bedouin, but one they can sustain.

What did the boys do before there were schools here, I asked one bearded veteran. 'They ran in the hills like goats,' he chuckled. And what would they do if the Egyptians closed the schools? 'They'll go back to the hills.'

The Bedouin are resigned to a fall in standards. They recognise that they can do nothing if the Egyptians no longer provide the social services they have learned to cherish. It was an interlude but they can manage without. Economically, however, they have their own ways of softening the impact.

'The Bedouin are involved in two economies,' Emanuel Marx, professor of anthropology at Tel Aviv University, explained over supper in the Mount Sinai field school. 'They make their income from wage labour, but they know there is a short-term gain. They can lose it at any time, through political upheaval or because they become old and decrepit. So they maintain the second economy too.

'They tend their orchards and flocks of sheep and goats, they retain a tribal framework and relations with kin who will look after them if times are bad. They balance the two economies very delicately. When they feel secure, they put less work into their orchards, flocks and family ties. When they feel less secure, they put more. But they never neglect the second economy altogether.'

The balance tilts with the news. The Bedouin are inveterate radio listeners, and draw their particular conclusions. Professor Marx logged a first switch back to the basic economy early in 1974, when Dr Kissinger negotiated the Israeli-Egyptian separation of forces after the Yom Kippur War. 'That frightened them,' he said, 'but then they went back to the other extreme when it seemed to be leading nowhere.' The next swing came with President Sadat's visit to Jerusalem two years ago and has gained momentum with the peace process.

The Bedouin are augmenting their flocks. They are investing more time and money in the bustans, the walled fruit and vegetable gardens, installing plastic pipes to carry water by gravitation from the wells to the pomegranates, olives, almonds and walnuts.

'Anyway', they tell you blithely, 'these are all American cars, so we should be able to buy parts in Egypt.' And just in case they can't, they are fattening their camels on the new green shrubs sprouting after the first autumn rains.

Chapter 5 – 1980-83

Faiths battle for the heart of Hebron

Hebron

Guardian, May 6, 1980

Hebron, 3,000 feet above sea level on the rocky spine of Palestine, is a natural cockpit for holy warfare between Jews and Arabs. It was here in a valley between the steep, grey-green hillsides that their common ancestor, Abraham, bought the cave of Machpela from Ephron the Hittite as a family burial place.

The first Jewish place of worship was built above the cave in Herod's reign 2,000 years ago. It was a church under the Byzantines and the crusaders, and has been a mosque ever since, decorated and enriched by the Ottoman sultans.

During the Turkish and British eras, Jews were forbidden to enter this second most holy of their shrines after the Wailing Wall in Jerusalem. They were allowed to mount the first seven steps of the stone stairway to the entrance. Even so Hebron was venerated as one of the four sacred cities of medieval Jewry. A community of Jews lived and studied there until they were driven out by Arab rioters in 1929.

Barely six months after the Israelis captured the West Bank in 1967, Rabbi Moshe Levinger and a band of zealots smuggled themselves into the town thinly disguised as Swiss tourists (staying as it happens in the Park Hotel, owned by an Arab agronomist, Fa'ad Kawassmeh, who as mayor of Hebron was deported last weekend after the murder of six Jewish worshippers leaving the tomb of the patriarchs).

By a strategy of stubborn disobedience, Rabbi Levinger, a cartoonist's dream, with a bald head, pop eyes behind thick spectacles, and a jutting, pointed beard, cajoled the Labour government into letting them stay – first in an army camp, then in the embattled suburb of Kiryat Arba, within sabbath-walking distance of the shrine.

113

The government granted the Jews praying rights inside the building, dividing time and space between them and the Muslims. Gradually, by stepping up their demands and creating new crises, Kiyat Arba settlers have increased their share.

Even under the wily mayor, Sheikh Mohammed Ali Ja'Abari, a magnate of the old, pre-revolutionary school, who served until 1976, the Arabs never acquiesced. Hebron was dedicated to Islamic fundamentalism long before it was fashionable. It is the only town on the West Bank without a cinema, the centre of a prosperous vine-growing region where no one will sell you a bottle of wine. Every Jewish encroachment was resisted, often by violence, but seldom to any purpose.

Over the past year, the Jews have switched their campaign to demanding a return to the heart of Hebron itself. About 50 women and children, led by Rabbi Levinger's American-born wife, Miriam, squatted in the Hadassah building, a former Jewish clinic used more recently as a book store by UNWRA, the international agency for Palestinian refugees. Mr Begin's government recognised the dangers of mingling Jews and occupied Arabs, but like Labour before, it slowly sanctioned their presence. The army supplied Hadassah families with food and water and set guards on the door.

Kiryat Arba became a base for the psychopathic nationalists of Rabbi Meir Kahane's Jewish Defence League (transported from New York to Israel as the 'Kach' party).

Kahane and his thugs went out to smash the windows of Arab cars and houses in Halhoul and Ramallah in revenge for the stoning of Jewish buses. Two of his followers were convicted of ransacking the homes of Arab families living in what were once Jewish houses in Hebron.

One of them, Eli Haza'ev (Hebrew for 'Eli the Wolf'), was among the six killed by Palestinian gunmen on Friday night.

Jewish intimidation begat Arab violence. Three months ago Yehoshua Sloma, a part-time soldier and part-time Talmudic student, was shot dead as he walked unarmed through the Hebron kasbah. Mr Begin's cabinet, in what was described at the time as 'an appropriate Zionist response', decided to establish two residential schools in the old Jewish quarter – a first step towards reviving a community in Hebron itself.

The local Arab leaders responded with the kind of brazen defiance that gave Mr Ezer Weizman a pretext for deporting three of their number – the mayors of Hebron and neighbouring Halhoul, Fa'ad Kawassmeh and Mohammed Hassan Milhem, and the Muslim Kadi, Sheikh Rajab Tamimi – after Friday night's massacre.

Milhem, a communist schoolmaster who attained a political influence far above his small-town base, said: 'It is time to act. What has been taken by force can only be regained by force.'

The next test is whether the Begin Government will go ahead with its plan for restoring a Jewish presence to the heart of Hebron. The deputy Prime Minister, Yigael Yadin, won a pause for reflection by appealing to the parliamentary foreign affairs and defence committee. The Knesset is back in session this week after the spring holiday.

Popular peacenik without a power base
Guardian, May 26, 1980

I once asked Ezer Weizman, who resigned yesterday as Israel's defence minister, whether he agreed with a British politician of my acquaintance that if you didn't go into politics to be prime minister, you might as well not bother. Would he feel he had failed if he did not succeed Menachem Begin?

Weizman was enough of an honest egoist to admit that he would like the job if it were offered, but he insisted that he would lose no sleep if he went down in history as an ex-defence minister instead.

'The thing I wanted more than anything in my life,' he said, 'was to be commander of the air force. Even then I wouldn't have done everything to achieve it – cut somebody's throat – but I would have gone a longer way than for anything else. To be air force commander was my piece of cake. Everything on it is a little bit of cream, a little bit of ice.'

He added that he was glad to be defence minister because it had brought him back to the world where he had grown up, a world he knew and understood. And, yes, it was a position of power. From most politicians his answer would have seemed disingenuous, if not downright deceptive. From Weizman it rang at least half true. He lacked not only the capacity to cut throats, but the patience and political finesse to make such butchery redundant.

Weizman despaired at the disintegration of the Likud coalition and at the decline of the prime minister's authority. Domestically and internationally Israel was drifting from bad to worse. The cabinet, riven by factional and personal ambitions, could do nothing to stop it. Begin was playing out the innings.

What tipped the scale, after so many threats and retractions, was Weizman's recognition of his own impotence to influence events. The defence ministry was no power base after all. Weizman was a born-again liberal in the ultra-nationalist Herut, but it was too late for him to go anywhere else. He had alienated the right by his ready flexibility in the peace negotiations with Egypt and his flamboyant resistance to indiscriminate settlement in the occupied territories, without managing to consolidate an alternative central block.

His mixture of neglect and hasty reactions on the West Bank and in southern Lebanon, bad judgments tempered by second thoughts, confirmed the doubts of his natural allies. Weizman, for all his 56 years, still seemed too much of a playboy, a gilded son of the Zionist aristocracy. Characteristically, his friends were marketing executives and businessmen.

Like Moshe Dayan, his former brother-in-law, Weizman resigned alone. No other minister went with him. On the coalition benches there was no Weizman block. The genial Ezer glad-handed everyone, but cultivated no one. Yet the defence minister had plenty to offer. His popularity rating was constantly higher than any other member of the government – up in the 60-70 per cent when the rest were struggling in the teens and twenties – and the polls showed him to be the only Likud leader with any chance of defeating the Labour challenge.

Weizman's resignation looked increasingly to be a matter of time. There were even signs that he had planned it, dates and all, long before the gaunt finance minister, Yigal Hurwitz, was demanding further cuts in defence spending. Two months ago Weizman told a fellow MP (who predictably told a reporter) that he had set himself a 'target date' of the end of May. He still had some unfinished business at the ministry. Arrangements had to be completed for producing Israel's third generation fighter, the Lavie. Then he was going to write a book, like Dayan, on the peace negotiations with Egypt. The budget dispute gave him an occasion to resign with honour, keeping faith with his security constituency.

Whatever Weizman's future, the peace treaty will remain his political monument. He, more than anyone, broke down the barriers of suspicion between Begin and Sadat. If Dayan's inventiveness and intellectual agility persuaded Begin to swallow his words, Weizman's tenacity and single-mindedness kept the Israeli negotiators on the rail. Peace was attainable he argued; it must not be allowed to squirm out of their hands.

Yet to those who knew him before the Likud came to office three years ago, Weizman was a most unlikely peacenik. He has never pretended to be anything other than a right-wing nationalist. As a young pilot freshly demobbed from the RAF, he was drawn to Begin's Irgun Zvei Leumi in the struggle against the British in Palestine.

While studying in London, he agreed to take part in the assassination of a notoriously anti-Semitic British general, but Scotland Yard nipped the operation in the bud and Weizman went home to join the fledgling Israeli air force.

Later, as a serving officer, he lectured trainee pilots on the 'over tight straightjacket of Israeli's 1948 borders'. As an apprentice politician, he resigned from Golda Meir's National Unity Coalition in 1970 along with other right-wing ministers in protest at American proposals for a compromise peace with the Arabs.

But in November, 1977, when Anwar Sadat came to Jerusalem, Weizman was ready for necessary concessions. 'I am convinced,' he told an interviewer, 'that the State of Israel, within these or other borders, must be part of the Middle East. We must find a way to live with the Arabs.'

He rejoiced at the opportunity to contribute to 'one of the most important shifts in the annals of Zionism,' and to emulate his uncle Chaim, the first president, who talked peace with the future King Feisal of Iraq. Their 1918 agreement, recognising a place for both Jews and Arabs in Palestine, might have been a historic turning point. Instead, it proved one of the great lost opportunities. It was Ezer Weizman's tragedy, and Israel's, that he left office before guaranteeing that a similar fate would not befall the 1979 treaty.

Sages play the power game in Promised Land
Observer, July 5, 1981

Two men in long, rusty gaberdines with untrimmed beards and nicotine fingers arrive first. They say little; satisfy themselves that all is in order, then slip away.

A few minutes later another appears and mutters to our host. The men present stir in expectation, the women flee to an anteroom. The Rabbi is coming! A square figure, still vigorous for all his 83 years, enters. He wears a low-crowned black felt bowler and shabby kaftans. After asking a few cursory questions, he reads in barely audible Hebrew from a book of psalms, meditates awhile, then leaves.

Last week this same dramatic, unworldly visitor became a power not only in the ultra-orthodox ghettoes of Jerusalem, but in the State of Israel, a man whose word will decide whether Menachem Begin rules for another term. It is one of the ironies of a tied general election that the religious parties emerged with fewer seats, but unprecedented influence.

Agudat Yisrael, which grants only de facto recognition to the Zionist enterprise, holds the key. Unlike the larger National Religious Party, its more relaxed attitude towards the occupied territories gives it a choice between Mr Begin's right-wing Likud, and Labour, which is committed to seeking a compromise with King Hussein of Jordan.

The Aguda politicians, spry veterans in dark suits, black trilbies, over full white whiskers, have started negotiations with the prime minister and with his challenger, Shimon Peres. But they

118

acknowledge that they do not have the final say. That rests with the Aguda's Council of Torah Sages, 18 venerable rabbis, who took the typically Talmudic decision four years ago to support the coalition, but refuse office in Mr Begin's cabinet, a delicate delimitation of their compromise with secular nationalism.

Rabbi Menachem Porush, who leads the coalition bargainers, outlined the role of the Sages: 'They have a veto on everything which touches on religion. They give the guidelines.' For the Aguda, it is clear that politics and religion are inseparable. The politicians control mundane organisational matters, but that is all.

The two dominant personalities in the Council of Sages are the man in the black felt bowler, Rabbi Simha Bunim Alter, known to his disciples at the Rabbi of Gur, a half-forgotten Jewish township in Isaac Bashevis Singer's Poland, and another octogenarian, Rabbi Eliezer Schach, who is revered for his great learning.

What, then, is the Aguda demanding? 'Our position,' said Rabbi Porush, 'is that we should be recognised in the same class of citizens as the secular Israelis. We want the possibility to live in Israel as Jews. For us, a Jew has to live according to religious law.' As an example, it wants Saturday working restricted to questions of security and life and death. No one should be forced to work on the Sabbath.

The Aguda won at least four victories in the last parliament. It forced the Begin government to make legal abortions harder to come by; to limit the pathologists' freedom to carry out post-mortem examinations (and consequently the availability of spare parts for transplant surgery, which has come almost to a halt in Israel); to allow more girls from 'traditional' homes to dodge military service; and to clip the wings of Christian missionaries. It also extracted more money from the exchequer than ever before for its private school network and other communal institutions.

Rabbi Porush is pressing now for a re-definition of 'Who is a Jew?' for the purpose of the Law of Return, which gives every Jew coming to live in Israel, an automatic right of citizenship. The Aguda wants the state to blackball any proselytes who were converted by Reform or other nonconformist rabbis.

This demand has been rejected by Israeli governments for three decades. The secular politicians of all stripes recognise that the change would divide Israel from world Jewry. In the United States, which has twice as many Jews as Israel, the Orthodox are now a minority. Nonetheless, both main religious parties will try to exploit their new leverage to get a stricter definition on to the statute book.

Where the Aguda (four or five seats in the Knesset) differs from the NRP, (probably six), is that its prime interest remains the Jewishness of the Jewish State. Security and foreign affairs do not disturb the 18 Sages.

'Our attitude,' Rabbi Porush explained, 'is that one of the greatest attachments of the religious Jew is to the Promised Land, where it is possible to fulfil all our obligations. My own family has lived here for seven generations.

'But our idea that Israel belongs to the Jewish people does not depend on whether the Arabs agree or the United Nations agree. On the other hand, if we must give it up, we must give it up. That is not a religious question.

'If we cannot live in Hebron that does not mean Hebron is not a holy city in a holy land. It means that circumstances are such that because of our sins we have been driven out of Hebron. For us, the main role is safeguarding life. If the choice is between peace and Hebron, peace must come first, so long as it is peace with security.'

The Aguda is ready to sacrifice Hebron, the burial place of Abraham, Isaac and Jacob. It would lose even less sleep over the settlements elsewhere on the West Bank. The Jewish priority is survival. The Messiah will take care of the long term.

Before the 1967 war, the NRP was no less of a one-issue party. Its 'historic alliance' with Labour was built on preservation of the status quo between synagogue and state. The NRP belonged in the mainstream of Zionist revival, but it knew its place. War, peace and diplomacy were none of its business.

The conquest of 'the whole land of Israel' ended such modesty and eventually killed the alliance, to the point where it seems inconceivable that the NRP could work with Labour in anything but a last resort. A younger, more militant generation has seized control. The genial Dr Yosef Burg, who has served in every cabinet since 1948, has been reduced to a figurehead.

Rabbi Haim Druckman, the 48-year-old guru of Gush Emunim, calls the tune. His threat to establish a separate party stampeded the old hands into giving him second place on the NRP list of candidates. The party's campaign advertising focused almost exclusively on West Bank settlement, on peopling the land with Jews. The Rabbi is a different animal from the Aguda Sages. He wears an open-necked sports shirt and the knitted skull cap of the latter-day pioneers. 'We shall demand that the government provides more money to establish settlements all over Judea and Samaria (the West Bank), the Golan Heights and the Gaza Strip,' he said. 'This must take priority over building within the green line.'

Rabbi Druckman voted against the Camp David agreement and against the peace treaty with Egypt. He is sceptical of Palestinian autonomy, which he fears will spawn a Palestinian state, and he opposes the withdrawal from Sinai, due to be completed next spring with the evacuation of 20 Jewish settlements.

'We have to do everything we can,' he insisted, 'to find ways for the settlements to remain and be part of the State of Israel.' That would, presumably, mean re-drawing the international boundary.

The Rabbi had his bread-and-butter claims too: public funds for the 15 para-military (Hesder) yeshiva seminaries, with their 2,000 soldier-students; tighter supervision of kosher food in shops and restaurants; more aid for big families ('We need a lot of children'); and power for the religious courts to enforce their rulings with the threat of prison. The NRP like the Aguda, will exact a price for keeping Mr Begin in office, even if it has nowhere else to go.

The prospect alarms the secular majority of Israelis. 'It will,' complained Shulamit Aloni of the Citizens Rights Movement, back with one Knesset seat, 'mean more religious coercion, with greater power for the Orthodox clergy and the rabbinical courts.

'In Israel we are born into an ethnic-religious group. We are already under the clergy's jurisdiction for every personal thing from the cradle to the grave. We don't have civil marriage or divorce. In many cases, we are second after Iran with religious coercion, not in violence but with using the power of the law. All these things will become even worse. The religious parties will be robbing the budget. More people will avoid serving in the army. Fewer people will man emergency services on the Sabbath. They are going to get everything they want. Dr Burg could almost become prime minister if they pressed hard enough.'

There are those who believe that there might yet be a lesser evil.

Heir to the painter's gatehouse

Guardian, April 10, 1982.

I must be the first *Guardian* man to live in the Street of the Prophets. Not, as it happens, the first foreign correspondent. Arthur Koestler lived down the hill at No 29 from 1927 to 1929 when he was covering the Middle East from Jerusalem for the *Neue Freie Presse* of Vienna. The house, he wrote in *Arrow in the Blue,* was five minutes from the Via Dolorosa and another five from the Mosque of Omar, where for a shilling you were shown the Archangel Gabriel's fingerprint on the rock. 'I have never lived at such close quarters with divinity,' he complained, 'and never further removed from it.'

Prophets was one of the first streets, as distinct from cluster suburbs, built outside the city walls in the second half of the 19th century. Today it climbs from the jumble of Arab wholesalers, watermelon stalls and taxi ranks opposite the Damascus Gate to Davidka Square, with its monument to the homemade drainpipe mortar which helped the Israelis to hold the New City in the 1948 war.

It was, and remains, a cosmopolitan street, the home of Jews, Muslims, and Christians, of consuls and bishops and doctors, a street of schools, convents and hospitals. Writers, painters and architects lived here. So, near enough, did Eliezer Ben-Yehuda, the stubborn visionary who revived Hebrew as a spoken language. Kaiser Wilhelm camped here when he visited Jerusalem in 1898, and here Theodor Herzl solicited his aid in creating a Jewish State.

Bertha Vester, who came to the city as a child with the founders of the American Colony, then a Christian missionary community, now a hotel of soporific charm, remembered the unpaved Street of the Prophets in the eighteen eighties as 'the back road' (it runs parallel to Jaffa Road, the main route to the north and, in those days, to Europe). 'The back road,' she wrote in *Our Jerusalem*, 'was muddy or dusty according to the season of the year.'

Edwin Sherman Wallace, the United States consul at the end of the century, recorded: 'Here are the finest residences. Many of the Turkish officials and families of high social and financial standing among the Muslims consider this a desirable location. The European population generally has followed them. On the highest part of the ridge stands the consulate of our own great nation and when the Stars and Stripes are floating they can be seen from nearly every point of the city.'

We live on the same cool, if less fashionable, ridge in the courtyard of a house built in 1876 by William Holman Hunt. It is less a yard than a big unruly garden, part Mediterranean, part desert, a wilderness of pines and pomegranates, of giant cactus, prickly pear, bay leaves, loquats, bitter almonds, figs, cypress and bamboo, all surrounded by an eight-foot stone wall against the ravages of Bedouin marauders.

Our house was the gatekeeper's lodge. The oldest part – a thick-walled, double-vaulted living room – was once the whole building. If you look closely at the ceiling, you can see the traces of a dividing wall. The wooden floor – a rarity in this city of stone and tiles – is printed with a shallow notch where a connecting door used to bolt. Jerusalem makes archaeologists of us all.

Holman Hunt, the most consistent if hardly the most gifted of the Pre-Raphaelites, paid three extended working visits to the Holy Land between 1854 and 1893 (as commemorated by a stone bench carved in English and Greek outside the Mar Elias monastery on the watershed between Jerusalem and Bethlehem). Most of his religious works were painted here on location (*The Scapegoat* by the Dead Sea, the Temple pictures with Sephardic Jews recruited in the Old City to serve as models).

He built the Prophets Street house, with a large room suitable for a studio, on the second of these trips, by which time his canvases were fetching four and five figures in guineas. He worked there on *The Triumph of the Innocents*, which Ruskin celebrated as 'the greatest religious picture of our time'. It was, he wrote, 'a flight into Egypt, but treated with an originality, power and artistic quality of design hitherto unapproached by him.' The Walker Gallery in Liverpool bought it for 3,500 guineas when the sovereign was still a sovereign.

Jesus and Mary were the hardest parts for Hunt to cast. The Jews, the British consul James Finn noted, were 'very sensitive on matters of religion'. They were worried that the picture would be placed in a church and become an object of prayer, a graven image. According to Finn, 'it was not possible to get a portrait of a woman for a likeness of the Virgin Mary, even for a lot of money.' Mrs Vester, however, remembered meeting 'a converted Jewish girl whose waving golden hair he had copied for the Christ.'

Hunt's biographer, A C Gissing, tells us that he took possession of the newly-built house and worked on *The Triumph of the Innocents* 'until the rainy season set in, when such was the nature of the tiled roof and such the character of the workmen, that water streamed into the room and collected in puddles all over the floor, so that his picture had to be protected by tarpaulins and work came to a standstill until the necessary steps were taken to render the chamber proof against the drenching rains.'

A century later, we all know the feeling. I typed my own first dispatches from the Street of the Prophets in sou'wester and wellington boots for much the same reason. And, by the way, when *did* the damp course come to the Promised Land?

When the *Triumph* was finished, Hunt locked the house and left it unoccupied for fifteen years. When he brought his family back in 1893, so many other buildings had mushroomed around it that, 'it was with difficulty that we could recognise our own house.' On that last visit he worked on *The Miracle of the Holy Fire*, a painting of the wild Greek Easter ceremony in the Holy Sepulchre. 'In the end,' he wrote, 'we packed up such furniture as moth and thieves had kindly left us in our house, and abandoned it and Syria (sic) for ever.'

But that was not quite his final link. In February, 1896, Hunt published an appeal for the 'resettlement of the Jews in Palestine', calling on all Englishmen to support his programme. 'The Jews,' he wrote, a week before Herzl's first English version of *The Jewish State* appeared in the *Jewish Chronicle*, 'need a proper national metropolis and a representative spokesman.'

The Arabs, Hunt suggested, would serve as the soldiers and policemen (this was later amended to 'hewers of wood and drawers of water'). Unlike Herzl, whom he denounced as 'utopian and not practical', Hunt advocated a state independent of the Turkish Sultan. Palestine, he predicted, would become 'a centre of peace, security and stability'. So much for prophecy.

After Hunt's departure the Prophets Street house passed into the hands of the Russian Orthodox Church, which had planted its flag in Jerusalem after the Crimean War with a massive compound a couple of hundred yards down the hill. 'Modern buildings,' scolded the Rev Dr J L Porter, president of Queen's College, Belfast, and pioneer travel writer, 'of questionable taste. The Russian church, and the convents and hospices look like factories.' Western criticism was tainted. The Russians exploited their confessional links with the Greek Orthodox to buy land. The Greeks were Ottoman citizens and thus enjoyed privileges denied to the Catholics and Protestants.

For sixty years, from 1918, our courtyard was governed for the church by Dr Helena Kagan, a formidable Russian Jewess who was Jerusalem's first paediatrician. She continued practising from Holman Hunt's studio until her death at ninety-two. Every child in the city seems to have been her patient. It makes directions easy. 'Dr Kagan's house,' you say. They smile and tell you anecdotes. How, for instance, she saved the children of Jerusalem by introducing cow's milk (she kept the beast in the courtyard); her musician husband who left her to found the Budapest Quartet.

After the First World War she brought a Russian friend, Rachel Bluvstein, to live in a small, undistinguished house between ours and hers. To Israelis she is known simply as Rachel, or at most Rachel the Poet. She was the laureate of the Second Aliya, the first Zionist pioneers of the 20th century, and was suffering from consumption. Rachel's exchange of love poems with Zalman Shazar, Israel's third president, is part of the national folklore. A book of her poems is laid reverently by her grave near the Sea of Galilee – and invariably stolen, one hopes just as reverently.

Rachel has put us on the tourist map. Groups of Israelis, schoolchildren, soldiers, youth clubs, kibbutzniks in sensible shoes, troop into the courtyard to see the poet's house and the pear tree, long dead and smothered in ivy, which she immortalised as the blossoming 'conspiracy of spring'.

We are still the gatehouse. The pilgrims knock on our door and ask coyly what we know about the history of the place. After twelve months here I deliver a well-rehearsed answer in my classroom Hebrew. The youngsters tick off the pear tree, the rock-hewn water cisterns (now used by the defence ministry as emergency fuel tanks in case Jewish Jerusalem ever has to relive the 1948 siege), the famous English painter's house. Their teachers and their sergeants will be reassured that the day was well spent.

The courtyard is at once private and public. We are in the centre of town, yet we turn our backs on the traffic, rejoicing in the greenery, the scent of honeysuckle and jasmine, the resin of hundred-year-old pines. But the street comes to us, unbidden and without a by-your-leave.

Anonymous scavengers pick anything worth recycling from the dustbins (moth-eaten sweaters, worn out shoes, bits of old transistor). Arab market women deposit mysterious, but so far unsinister, bundles behind the gatepost. Yeshiva students and elderly gentlemen pee discreetly in a corner. Lovers moon in the shadows. Tramps kip in the sun (one is said to have spent a whole summer here, camping benignly under an old fig tree and complaining only when somebody beat him to Mrs Braun's *Jerusalem Post* at six in the morning).

Despite the cross over the gate, we are a secular courtyard. Six families and not a skullcap or crucifix among us. But the religions of Jerusalem impinge. Ethiopian and Episcopalian churches within belfry range, the muezzins of al Aqsa audible before dawn, the ghetto of Mea Shearim a stone's throw to the east.

'The whole unholy history of the city,' Koestler lamented in his haven down the hill, 'is an illustration of the destructive power of faith, the failure of man's attempts to come to terms with God, and the resulting unpleasantness of the union of the mortal and the divine.' Amen.

Made in the image of Jabotinsky
Guardian, August 4, 1981

Menachem Begin has reverted to type. Not so much to the terrorist Begin of Arab propaganda and selective British memory, but to Begin the disciple of Vladimir Ze'ev Jabotinsky, the prophet of muscular Jewish nationalism that bred the Irgun Zvai Leumi and the Herut movement. The prime minister is schizophrenic – Begin the demagogue brandishing a mailed fist and Begin the statesman craving respectability. During the June election campaign the first Begin submerged the second in a wave of intimidation and mob oratory, ethnic resentment and personality cult.

The intoxication of victory, however narrow, has perpetuated the change. The blitz on Beirut was its first expression. It was opposed by the two ex-generals in the outgoing cabinet, Yigael Yadin and Ariel Sharon. The army could point to no strategic justification. Begin willed it, and Begin could not be denied.

This revolution has polarised Israeli society, less between western and oriental Jews, than between fundamentally different conceptions of a Jewish state. Visitors detect a degree of mutual hostility between the two camps they have never found before. Half the country feels not just that it lost an election, but that its way of life is in danger.

For all its compromises and paternalism, the Labour movement, which ruled Israel throughout its first three decades and dominated the pioneering years of the state, was rooted in the liberal socialist tradition. However reluctantly, it came to terms with a rival claim on Eretz Yisrael, the ancient homeland. David Ben-Gurion embraced the partition of the Promised Land. Menachem Begin never did. The emblem of Betar, the Herut youth organisation, to this day flaunts 'both banks of the Jordan' as the Jewish patrimony.

For Begin, Palestinian nationalism is a fraud. The Palestinians may be allowed autonomy, but never sovereignty. There is no place for accommodation. The Jew must be proud and mighty. Concession is weakness; criticism is either anti-Semitism or Jewish self-hatred. If the world must be defied, so be it.

Opposition is seen as treachery. Israel remains a democracy. Begin the statesman rejoices in that. Parliament flourishes, the press is free. But Herut's innate authoritarianism is asserting itself. Within the public sector, independent voices are being suppressed. The two deputy governors of the Bank of Israel, a counterweight to the treasury in economic policy-making, have been dismissed. The governor is expected to follow, to be replaced by a party nominee. Ministers are waging a guerrilla war against the Israel Broadcasting Authority, whose charter is modelled on that of the BBC. Yoram Aridor, whose electioneering economics was second only to Begin's mass appeal in winning the Likud a second term, refuses to be interviewed by Israel Television's financial correspondent , whom he charges with being anti-government. The director-general of the Broadcasting Authority, Josef Lapid, recognises this as an attempt to dictate a choice of specialist reporter and is resisting, fortified by the knowledge that he was appointed because of his right-wing views and can hardly be purged because of 'bias'.

Begin constantly evokes his doctrinal origins. He is a son of Betar, the commander of what Irgun veterans call the 'fighting family', the founder of Herut, which increasingly sets the tone for the Likud block of parties and factions.

'Herut,' Ezer Weizman wrote in his recently published memoirs, 'was a tiny preserve for an endangered species.' The former defence minister, who was in the movement but never of it, depicted Herut as 'Menachem Begin's sculpture park', with a statue of Jabotinsky as its largest and most imposing monument. Jabotinsky died 41 years ago, yet the more you observe Begin, the more you listen to what he says, the more you are convinced that Vladimir Ze'ev remains his inspiration.

Last week Begin paid homage at Jabotsinsky's graveside on Mount Herzl in Jerusalem. 'Western Eretz Yisrael is in our full control,' the prime minister proclaimed. 'It will not be divided again. No part of its territory will be handed over to foreign rule or sovereignty. We believe the day will come when the two parts of Eretz Yisrael will establish peacefully, in agreement and understanding, an alliance of nations, a free confederation for cooperation.'

It was not a foreign policy pronouncement, or signal to King Hussein who happens to reign over 'Eastern Eretz Yisrael'; it was a rededication to the ideals of the master, an act of appeasement to the blessed memory. The other bank of the Jordan had not been forgotten.

Jabotinsky was not simply a right-wing nationalist. His Zionism, like that of the Labour movement, grew out of European soil. But its pro-genitors were twentieth rather than nineteenth century.

Shlomo Avineri, professor of political science at the Hebrew University, analysed Jabotinsky's thought in an essay published last summer in the *Jerusalem Quarterly*. 'Jabotinsky,' he wrote, 'was a polished European gentleman towering above other Zionist leaders between the world wars in his cultural attainments, sensibilities and intellectual horizons... No Zionist leader could rival his accomplishments as poet and translator, essayist and novelist.' Begin has stayed true to his teacher, with one major exception. Jabotinsky was a secular nationalist. He would have winced at Begin's skullcap, at his frequent invocations of divine will, and above all at Begin's theocratic partnership with the religious parties, including one (Agudat Yisrael) which does not even acknowledge the legitimacy of the Jewish state.

The greatest irony is, however, that Begin has fallen victim to the same contradiction as Jabotinsky. Their dogma rests on Jewish power. In Jabotinsky's hey-day, the Jews of Eretz Yisrael were few and weak. He sought to persuade imperial Britain that its interests were identical with that of Zionist self-fulfilment.

In the 1980s Israel has the strongest army, navy and air force in the Middle East. Yet it remains dependent, not on the British but on the United States. Begin, encouraged by the campaign rhetoric of the Reagan administration, is seeking to persuade Washington that

American and Israeli interests are identical. The haste with which the prime minister accepted last month's ceasefire with the Palestinians at the crack of an American whip demonstrated that Washington, too, was not so persuaded.

Sour ending to the love affair with the desert, from Yamit, Sinai

Observer, April 25, 1982

Israel will leave Sinai this morning with no joy and little dignity. A brigadier will lower the Star of David at Sharm-el-Sheikh in a chill 10-minute ceremony at 7.30am, then lead his men north to Eilat.

By noon all Israeli forces will have evacuated the peninsula they conquered in two wars and held in a third. Two hours later, the Egyptians will advance to the new/old border. There will be no handover, no anthems, no pious re-dedications to peace.

It is a wretched end to Israel's love affair with the desert, shadowed by uncertainty and soured by the sight of Jews fighting Jews in Yamit and bulldozers grinding that model town into the sand. The peace agreement is alive and well, Egypt's President Mubarak assured the Israeli cabinet last week, but the spirit of Camp David is hard to come by.

The Gush Emunim diehards, who subjected 5,000 Israeli soldiers to unprecedented vilification before they were bundled out of Yamit, were waging war for the West Bank and Gaza. If Sinai was lost, they would make sure no government would lightly sign away the biblical homeland.

But a precedent, as the opposition Labour daily *Davar* commented, had been set. 'It is perfectly possible to overcome resistance to an authoritative policy decision to withdraw for the sake of peace.'

The anti-withdrawal campaign, *Davar* rejoiced, failed to gain mass support. The failure ran deeper than that. Television pictures of religious teenagers spitting and screaming abuse at girl soldiers, scarcely out of high school, alienated many Israelis who shared the protesters' scepticism about Egypt's long-term intentions.

Gush Emunim, which had seemed to be drawing the centre of gravity of Israeli opinion to the right, has put itself back on the fringe. To make matters worse (or better), the Yamit show was taken over by Rabbi Meir Kahana and his still more extreme Jewish Defence League, the *reductio ad absurdum* of violent fundamentalism.

The army won credit for evicting the squatters without bloodshed, but Israel's 15 years in Sinai deserved a prouder finale.

At best, the demilitarisation built into the Camp David agreement guarantees that Israel will not be caught off-guard if Mubarak changes his mind. If there is another war with Egypt, it will still be contested in Sinai and not the Negev.

When the late President Sadat came to Jerusalem in November 1977, offering 'no more war, no more bloodshed', Israelis were bowled over. They hoped for a peace of the heart. Disenchantment soon set in when they realised that Egypt was offering a mere marriage of convenience.

Sadat wanted to recover his lost lands, he wanted to remove the Palestinian irritant, he wanted to open a door to Uncle Sam. If the price was reconciliation with Israel, Sadat alone of the Arab rulers was ready to pay it. War had failed to produce results, the Yom Kippur offensive of October 1973 had made peace an honourable alternative.

Yet Egyptian compliance has been grudging from the start. In the two years since normal relations were supposed to have been established, more than 50,000 Israeli tourists have visited Egypt, but barely 2,000 have travelled the other way. The public sector, representing 85 per cent of Egyptian trade, remains closed to Israeli firms.

Prime Minister Begin's response is to hold Egypt to the peace treaty and to spin a network of relations that will deter Mubarak from a break.

Judgment in the shadow of a massacre

Guardian, February 8, 1983

The slow fuse of the Beirut massacre inquiry has almost burned itself out. Within a few hours we shall know whether Menachem Begin's government has been sitting on a bomb or a firecracker.

The three-man commission has been unusually leak proof. No one in Israel is making firm predictions about its conclusions or their consequences. But an examination of the way the two judges and a retired general went about their task points in both directions at the same time: they will not be party to a cover-up, but they will go to exceptional lengths to make sure they can justify every word of their findings.

The list of nine men who were warned that they might be harmed and were given a second chance to testify in their own cause demonstrated that the commission is pondering the responsibility and performance of the top decision-makers. It also made no distinction between the military and political echelons.

The nine included the prime minister, Mr Begin, the defence minister, Mr Ariel Sharon, and the foreign minister, Mr Yitzhak Shamir. On the military side, the list began with the chief-of-staff, Lieutenant-General Rafael Eitan, and embraced the heads of army intelligence, the Mossad security service and Northern Command, as well as the divisional commander in Beirut. The only minor actor among the nine was Mr Sharon's personal assistant, Mr Avi Dudai.

Because the law under which chief justice Yitzhak Kahan's commission was appointed makes such warnings compulsory, we can be certain that no one other than the nine will be blamed. The warnings do not, however, mean that they all will be. Their later submissions may have cleared all or any of them, or the commission may have had second thoughts after reviewing the evidence.

The terms of the warnings indicated that only two of the nine — General Eitan and the Beirut commander Brigadier-General Amos Yaron — might face criminal prosecution. They alone risked being blamed for 'breach of duty' and not just 'non-fulfilment of duty'. That was because the commission heard evidence that Generals

Eitan and Yaron had authorised the Phalangist militiamen to continue their 'operation' in the Sabra and Chatillah camps even after it was known that they were killing unarmed Palestinian refugees.

Under the 1968 Commission of Inquiry Law, Justice Kalian and his colleagues are required first of all to clarify the facts. They may also – and evidently will – draw conclusions and make the attorney general and his military counterpart have the last word on whether to prosecute. The defence minister and chief-of-staff must decide whether a serving officer should be dismissed or demoted.

On the political side, legal experts assume that the commission will not specifically recommend a minister's dismissal or resignation. It is accepted constitutional doctrine that ministers owe their positions to parliament and not to courts or commissions.

That does not exclude the possibility, however, that the Kahan Commission might criticise any of the three ministers so severely that they would have little choice but to go. The scruples with which the panel gave them a chance to defend themselves – even extending the time limit for submissions – can only enhance the moral weight of such findings.

Under a new law passed two years ago, the prime minister is now free to sack a minister. Previously, his only choice where a minister refused to resign was to submit the resignation of the cabinet as a whole. This means that if, for example, Mr Sharon is condemned by the Kahan report but will not go quietly, Mr Begin would be able to force him out. The question then would be whether he could do so without destroying his own authority. That would depend on the shading of the commission's conclusions, the thickness of the prime minister's skin, and the ardour of his grassroots supporters.

Both the open sessions, in which the panel heard 24 out of 58 testimonies, and the language of the warning notices, confirmed that the commissioners were asking fundamental questions, and were not easily deflected. The three senior ministers will be judged for evaluations, decisions and omissions that affected the lives of hundreds of people and did untold damage to Israel's reputation. The charge hovering over Mr Begin is, in the commission's words, that he 'did not appropriately consider the role to be played by the Lebanese Forces and ignored the danger of acts of revenge and bloodshed' after the assassination of their leader, Bashir Gemayel.

Mr Sharon was warned that he might be found guilty of ignoring such dangers, failing to prevent them, and failing to order the militiamen's removal from the refugee camps.

Mr Shamir is at risk because, on his own admission, he did not follow up a report from another minister, Mr Mordechai Zipori, that the Phalangists were killing civilians. Mr Zipori claimed that he used the word 'slaughter', but Mr Shamir maintained that he talked about the Phalangists 'running wild'. An Israeli defence correspondent, Mr Ze'ev Schiff, who had passed the report to Mr Zipori and was present when he telephoned the foreign minister, confirms Mr Zipori's version.

The prime minister has hinted that if the findings go against the government, he will call new elections and seek vindication from the people. It would not, however, be that easy. In Israel a prime minister cannot simply ask the president to dissolve parliament. A bill has to be passed setting a date for elections, and Mr Begin's biggest coalition partner – the National Religious Party with six MPs – is against an early poll. The prime minister might not be able to raise a majority in the finely balanced chamber.

The Labour opposition leader, Mr Shimon Peres, is hoping instead for a change of government without elections. Wishful thinking apart, political analysts here are not betting on the downfall of Menachem Begin or his Likud Party, however fierce the inquiry's findings. They recognise that the peace movement, the universities, the kibbutzim and the leader writers did not put the prime minister in power and cannot alone remove him. For the most part, Mr Begin's alliance of ultra-nationalist and oriental Jewish voters was neither shamed nor indignant over the September pogrom.

Labour's longer-term hope rests on an erosion of confidence in the Likud government of which Sabra and Chatillah would be one factor among others. The public, on this calculation, would wake up to the fact that personal prosperity at a time of economic decline is an illusion and that the stock exchange is not a national casino where the punter always wins.

Less close to home, young conscripts and middle-aged reservists would weary of long, cold and increasingly dangerous service in Lebanon. Israelis would start to ask – as my Sephardi garage mechanic did the other day – whether Mr Sharon was as good at getting his men out of Lebanon as he was at getting them in. Professor Shlomo Avineri, a Hebrew University political scientist and Labour activist, suggested recently that in the end the key would rest with King Hussein of Jordan. A poll last week indicated a greater readiness among Israelis to exchange territory for peace. Professor Avineri argued that a decision by King Hussein to negotiate would suddenly make Labour's longstanding advocacy of the 'Jordanian option' relevant.

Is Amman listening?

The blast that swept away a dream
Guardian, February 15, 1983

The peace demonstration which ended with a grenade and a martyr outside Menachem Begin's office had little advance publicity. When I heard the raucous chanting from Zion Square in the centre of Jewish West Jerusalem I took it for a rallying of the faithful behind Ariel Sharon, who was still refusing to resign as defence minister for facilitating the Beirut massacre. It was noisy and boisterous. A couple of hundred mostly young Israelis were waving 'Sharon Must Go' placards and shouting anti-government slogans. About 20 Likud supporters responded with 'Arik, King of Israel, Will Live Forever'. A short stubby man of about 40 wound himself into a fury then burst into the crowd like a Rugby League prop forward going hard for the posts. 'Shame,' he yelled in a wild amalgam of Hebrew and Arabic; 'Traitors,' and much besides. Early evening shoppers grabbed their children and ducked into doorways. A police inspector started talking into his two-way radio.

The latent violence soon became actual. Demonstrators and counter-demonstrators exchanged blows over the placards. The peace camp grew as the protest set out through the city towards the prime minister's office, where the cabinet was in session. Young men harassed the marchers, throwing stones, spitting and shouting abuse. One demonstrator, a jazz musician from New York, said the hatred reminded him of the civil rights marches 20 years ago. Knives were flashed, though not used. Some witnesses claimed afterwards that a tall thin man kept warning Emil Grunzweig, the 33-year-old reserve paratroop officer who was killed by the grenade an hour later, that this would be his last day.

Whether or not the story is true, the explosion spelled the death not only of Grunzweig, but of the illusion that what is known here as The War of the Jews had its limits. For the first time since the establishment of the state 35 years ago, one Jew calculatedly murdered another while he was taking part in a peaceful political demonstration.

Despite official condemnation of violence and intolerance, it will now take physical as well as moral courage to protest against the Begin government. The national debate is no longer restricted to policy. It has become a struggle for the soul of Israel, a conflict between two political cultures.

The children of the mass migration from Muslim countries three decades ago are feeling their strength, redressing old inherited grievances, and repudiating the declared values of the Zionist pioneers.

There is an echo of Black Power, but unlike the Israeli 'Black Panthers' of a decade ago the orientals of the Eighties are not parroting an imported ideology. And they have the numbers to back up their aspirations. In the 1981 elections about 43 per cent of registered voters were orientals. Next time Israel goes to the polls the figure will be more than 50 per cent.

'All my life I am down here and you are up there,' a young Moroccan-Israeli complained to the kibbutz novelist Amos Oz. 'Look at the shame. They gave us houses; they gave us unskilled work, gave us an education, and took away our self-respect. What did they bring my parents here for? I'll tell you. At that time you did not yet have the Arabs (of the West Bank and Gaza Strip). You needed our parents as cleaners and servants and manual workers. You brought our parents so that they would be your Arabs.

'When you were in power you hid us away in holes, in moshav settlements and development towns, so that the tourists should not see us, so that we shouldn't give you a dirty image. But now we're finished with all that, we've come out of hiding. And because of your arrogance, you still haven't understood what's happening to you.'

The charges are unfair, but not entirely unfounded. The Ashkenazi (western Jewish) establishment was guilty at the very least of paternalism, of knowing what was best for the newcomers. Its motives may have been more worthy than the young Moroccan suggested, but the men who got things done (without whom there would have been no state) were too busy to listen.

The first generation acquiesced. Their priorities were a roof, a job, and the hope of something better for their children. If they had to ingratiate themselves with the Labour party and the Histadrut trade union functionaries, that was the price of becoming Israelis.

But at home in their Moshavim and development towns, in the slums of Tel Aviv and Jerusalem, they talked and their sons heard. Those sons are not immigrants. They are Israelis who have worked and fought and remembered. Now they are getting their own back.

They are not content with power alone. They are aiming to superimpose a new Israel on the old, an Israel rooted in the Middle East rather than Europe. Their contempt for the Ashkenazim swamps the dreams as well as the insensitivities of the pioneers.

Menachem Begin has given the orientals a sense of legitimacy. He too suffered humiliation at the hands of Labour. Like the orientals, he believes in strength, in Jewish assertiveness, in paying the Arabs in their own coin, in ceremony and tradition. He has given them back their self-respect, and it is none of their concern that he is a Polish Jew and that his Likud party still has fewer oriental MPs than Labour.

Because of Begin, they feel that their Jewishness, their Zionism, is not inferior to that of the Ashkenazim. They do not have to conform. Violence is part of their Middle Eastern political culture. So is the adulation of charismatic leaders like Begin and Sharon.

They experienced little remorse over Sabra and Chatilla, they responded readily to the prime minister's taunt that 'Goyim kill goyim and they hang the Jew'. Any attack on Begin and Sharon was an act of sacrilege. The critics were not just wrong, they were treacherous.

The ultimate result was Thursday night's grenade outside the prime minister's office. The Ashkenazim of Amos Oz's generation are beginning to understand what is happening to them. Their dilemma is how to fight back without sacrificing their own Israel in the process, and without falling into a racialist trap. 'What will become of us,' Amos Oz wrote after a voyage of discovery to a neighbouring development town. 'I don't know. Anyone with a solution should get up and offer it. And he'd better not wait too long.'

New accounts of Deir Yassin

Guardian, April 9, 1983

The Arabs of Deir Yassin believed they were safe. Their village was not at war with the Jews, and the head man had reached an understanding with the neighbouring Jewish suburb of Givat Shaul on the western lip of Jerusalem.

'There was an agreement that there would be no problems between them,' explains Muhammad Sammour, a retired schools inspector, sitting in his spacious stone house near the West Bank town of Ramallah. 'If any of their young people attacked Deir Yassin, the Jews would catch them and stop them. If anyone from Deir Yassin attacked Givat Shaul, the Arabs would stop him. There were no problems between Jews and Arabs there at that time.'

On Friday April 9 1948, the villagers and the world learnt how wrong they were. Before dawn, 35 years ago today, 120 fighters from the Irgun Zvai Leumi and the Stern Gang stormed Deir Yassin from two sides. A makeshift loudspeaker van, which was supposed to call on the inhabitants to surrender and thus avoid harm, stuck in a ditch, its message unheard.

The Arabs put up what resistance they could – more, as it happened, than their assailants had bargained for – but by the end of the day Deir Yassin was deserted and in ruins. Scores of men, women, and children were slaughtered. Others were driven in triumph by their captors through the streets of Jewish Jerusalem and released in the Old City. A handful escaped through the hills to Ein Karem, the birthplace of John the Baptist. Muhammad Sammour, then a 26-year-old teacher, spending the weekend at home with his family, was one of them. By accident, or design, Jewish or Arab, Deir Yassin sounded an alarm, speeding if not provoking the flight of 700,000 Arabs from the part of Palestine that became Israel five weeks later. The name has never lost its resonance, yet the facts have remained hard to come by. There were few, if any, disinterested witnesses. By his own published account, Jacques de Reynier, of the International Red Cross, arrived on the scene two days after the massacre began.

The official Jewish leadership condemned the slaughter, while covering up its own complicity. The Haganah commander in Jerusalem, David Shaltiel, had reluctantly approved the raid (though not the massacre) – and even sent a mortar platoon to help the attacking force out of a tight corner.

The Irgun and the Stern Gang accused the Zionist establishment of dragging their names in the mud, and insisted that Deir Yassin was a conventional military operation in which some civilians got hurt, as did about 40 of their men, anyone who suggested otherwise was accused of bias, or worse.

This version, which became Israeli doctrine after the former Irgun leader, Menachem Begin, became prime minister in 1977, has recently been challenged from an unexpected source, the ranks of the perpetrators.

Yisrael Segal, a reporter on the weekly magazine *Koteret Rashit*, unearthed extracts from testimony discreetly filed in the archives at Mr Begin's party headquarters in Tel Aviv. They show that a majority of the commanders favoured a massacre to teach the Arabs a lesson, and that the fighters did not conceal the atrocities of Deir

Yassin from their own people afterwards. Benzion Cohen, who was wounded while commanding the operation, wrote:

'When it comes to prisoners, women, old people, and children, there were differences of opinion, but the majority was for liquidation of all the men in the village and of any other force that opposed us, whether it be old people, women, or children.' The wish for revenge, he added, was strong after 'the enemy smote us' at Gush Etzion and Atarot, two Jewish settlements near Jerusalem that were lost until 1967.

The Irgun deputy commander, Yehuda Lapidot, claimed that the idea of a massacre came from the Stern Gang, who contributed about a third of the attacking force. 'The clear aim,' he wrote, 'was to break the Arab morale.'

Lapidot insisted, however, that Irgun headquarters vetoed the idea. This was confirmed to me by Meir Pa'il, a left-wing politician and military historian who was a Haganah intelligence officer in Jerusalem in 1948, and was present as an observer throughout the operation.

Another Irgun officer, Yehoshua Gorodentchik, lifted a curtain on the way his men fought. 'After suffering many casualties,' he testified in the Tel Aviv archive, 'we thought of retreating. We had prisoners, and before the retreat we decided to destroy them. We destroyed the wounded too because, anyhow, we could not give them first aid... We also found Arab men who had dressed up as women and therefore decided to shoot the women who did not make their way to the assembly point for prisoners.'

The story of Arab men disguised as women is independently confirmed by Yair Tsaban, a leftwing Mapam MP who as a 17-year-old schoolboy was drafted to bury the dead after the Irgun and the Stern Gang had left the field. But he put a different gloss on it.

'What we saw,' he told me, 'were women, young children, and old men. What shocked us was at least two or three cases of old men dressed in women's clothes. I remember entering the living room of a certain house. In the far corner was a small woman with her back towards the door, sitting there dead. When we reached the body, we saw an old man with a beard. My conclusion was that what happened in the village so terrorised these old men that they knew being old men would not save them.'

Meir Pa'il's report to Haganah headquarters is still classified, but what he remembers is 'a disorganised massacre' after most of the Arab resistance had ended. 'It was a massacre in hot blood,' he said. 'It was not planned. It was an outburst from below with no one to control it. Groups of men went from house to house looting and shooting. You could hear the cries of Arab women, Arab elders, Arab kids. I tried to hold them back, but I could not find their commanders.' One question still unanswered is how many Arabs died at Deir Yassin. The generally accepted figure is 240-250, but the Irgun has sometimes put it as low as 120. I asked Muhammad Sammour, the teacher who fled to Ein Karem. To my surprise he said 93 were killed in the village and 23 prisoners were executed in Givat Shaul, a total of 116 out of a population he estimated at 800-1,000.

How had he come to that tally? 'About three days after the massacre,' he replied, 'representatives of each of the five clans in Deir Yassin met at the Muslim offices in Jerusalem and made a list of the people who had not been found. We went through the names. Nothing has happened since 1948 to make me think this figure was wrong.'

Architect of a promised land

Guardian, August 31, 1983

Mr Begin was asked not long ago how he would like to be remembered in the history books. 'As the man,' he replied, 'who set the borders of the Land of Israel for all eternity.'

For good or ill for his own perseverance and the folly of the Arabs, he looks like achieving his ambition. The eastern border has been drawn along the Jordan river. Eternity is a long time, but it is hard to see how Palestine can be repartitioned after Mr Begin. The settlements and suburbs across the old faded green line are maturing into permanence. Even the US State Department now acknowledges that the Jews are there to stay.

Mr Begin has been Israel's most single-minded prime minister. Ever since he arrived in Jerusalem as a penpushing private in the Free Polish Army in 1942, he had devoted himself to the establishment and consolidation of a Jewish state in the whole of the ancient homeland. His idea of compromise was reluctant acquiescence in the loss of the East Bank.

After Ben-Gurion's proclamation of the State of Israel in May, 1948, Begin threatened to prolong the revolt of his Irgun Zvai Leumi to fight against partition, even though he had barely 3,000 men under arms. As leader of the opposition in the late 1940s and early 1950s, he inveighed against any accommodation the government might reach with King Abdullah of Jordan – the Rhodes Armistice agreement, acceptance of Jordanian authority in the West Bank and East Jerusalem.

He accused Ben Gurion, Israel's first prime minister, of appeasement, of courting dismemberment of the Jewish state. In his Knesset speeches he referred to the West Bank as the 'eastern part of the western land of Israel'.

After serving for three years in the National Unity Government established on the eve of the 1967 war, Mr Begin led his party back into opposition rather than endorse the very idea of an Israeli withdrawal.

His first visit after winning the 1977 general election was to the Eilon Moreh settlement group, who had defied the outgoing Labour government by squatting amid the ruins of biblical Sebastia, near Nablus, the biggest Arab town on the West Bank. 'In a few weeks or months,' he assured them, 'there will be many Eilon Morehs.'

When an unschooled reporter asked him about the future of the occupied territories, the then prime minister-designate retorted: 'These are not occupied territories. You've used this expression for ten years, but from May 1977, I hope you'll use the word liberated territories. A Jew has every right to settle in these liberated territories of the Jewish land.'

Mr Begin was true to his word. By the end of his first term, the number of West Bank settlements had grown fourfold. The Labour policy of keeping them away from the uplands of Judea and Samaria, where most of the Arab population is concentrated, had been overturned. It was no longer possible to define where the Arab areas stopped and the settlements began.

In the negotiation with Egypt, Begin resisted all attempts to force him to trade Palestinian territory for Egyptian peace. The late President Sadat could have the whole of Sinai. In the last resort Israel evacuated its settlements and military airfields there. But Begin would rather have destroyed the Sadat initiative than yielded an inch of the Land of Israel.

The Camp David agreement, of September 1978, endangered the Begin doctrine. It offered the Palestinians an opportunity to lay the groundwork for independence after five years, but the Israelis wrote all manner of safeguards into the text, and Begin acted immediately to frustrate anyone who tried to exploit it. Happily for him, neither the Palestinians nor the Jordanians called his bluff.

Despite Egyptian denials, Begin negotiated as if Sadat were ready for a separate peace. In practice, that is what they achieved. The Palestinian section of the Camp David framework proved no more than the fig leaf Begin always intended it to be.

Begin is a complex, but not a mysterious, man; a paradox, but not a puzzle. He means what he says, though it is always as well to read the small print. His master, Vladimir Jabotinsky, taught him that weakness achieves nothing.

The mainstream Labour Zionist pioneers argued that the Jews would win independence only if they transformed themselves into workers, farmers, and builders. Jabotinsky would have none of that. If the Jews wanted a state, they had to learn to shoot. They had to erect an 'Iron Wall' between themselves and the hostile Arabs. This has remained the core of Begin's vision. The Jew had to be strong and proud, ready to take by force what was his due. If the Arabs wanted to talk, so be it. But they would only seek a *modus vivendi* when they recognised that they could not stifle Jewish aspirations at birth.

In that perspective, Begin's quest for peace and readiness to negotiate with Sadat was perfectly consistent. He won his Nobel

Peace Prize the hard way by taking risks. But he never renounced force as an instrument of policy. In that sense, the war in Lebanon was equally consistent. His defence minister, Mr Ariel Sharon, convinced him that it was possible to destroy the Palestine Liberation Organisation as a military threat in Lebanon (and indirectly so solve the Palestinian problem to Israel's satisfaction once that had been done).

Sharon, as Begin reflected after the war, always consulted him, 'sometimes before the event, sometimes after'. The defence minister pulled the wool over the cabinet's eyes, and sometimes over the prime minister's. But he would never have got away with it if Begin had not been excited by the whole enterprise. A strong-arm solution was in tune with his philosophy and his temperament.

It was not the first time that Begin had been carried away by his admiration for generals, a weak spot for war heroes. His first foreign minister, Moshe Dayan, had exploited it in a more benign cause at Camp David. But Sharon's war proved Begin's undoing.

It was supposed to last a week. Fourteen months later thousands of Israeli soldiers are stuck north of the border. Week by week, if not day by day; they are being killed and maimed. The death toll is now 518, and the protests are spreading. After all the cumulative strains of the past two years, Begin lacks the resilience to fight back. It is as if his battery has gone flat, and at 70 he cannot recharge it.

He has been in a state of melancholia since last summer. His colleagues complain that he is listless and apathetic. Visiting statesmen report at best that the prime minister makes no creative contribution to their discussion. One diplomat who knows him well said that Begin no longer enjoyed being prime minister of Israel. It had become an arduous chore.

The death of his wife Aliza last autumn was only part of the degenerative process. First Begin broke his thigh in a fall in his bathroom. He returned, still in acute pain, to a confrontation with the United States over the Golan annexation (a confrontation which he brought on himself). Then he went through the anguish of evicting Jewish settlers from Sinai.

Within two months, again by his own choice, Israel was at war in Lebanon. Begin had to run to keep up with Sharon, a task which proved beyond him. In September there was the massacre of Palestinian refugees by Israel's Phalangist protégés, and the remorseless pressure for the prime minister to appoint a judicial enquiry.

The Kahan Commission generated its own tensions, the uncertainty of whether Begin and his cabinet would be to blame. In the event they were, along with three senior army commanders. Begin then had to force Sharon to recognise the commission's authority and resign.

In the midst of all this, his wife of 43 years died after a protracted illness; violence blossomed in the streets of Jerusalem; and his government's much-vaunted 'proper economics' finally received its comeuppance.

On Friday a cabinet minister, Aharon Uzzan, griped on television that there was nobody in control. By Sunday, Begin seemed to have come to the conclusion that he was right. 'I feel I cannot carry on shouldering my responsibilities with things as they are the way I should,' he told a stunned cabinet. It was as convincing an explanation as any.

Chapter 6 – 1987-89

When men with beards turn liberators
Gaza
The Statesman, Calcutta, November 5, 1987

The seafront restaurant with its wide picture windows overlooking the Mediterranean and Gaza port serves excellent fish and spicy west-Asian salads. But you can no longer order a beer to wash them down. The men with beards came a couple of years ago, the waiter explains, and set the place on fire. Since then the bar has stuck to soft drinks.

The men with the beards, Muslim fundamentalists of Arab Palestine, have been active in the occupied Gaza Strip since the early eighties. Their first targets were fellow Muslims, who represent 97 per cent of the strip's crowded half-million. The Israeli military administration looked the other way on the principle of divide and rule.

More recently, however, the zealots have turned their guns on the Israelis, and their operations have spread from Gaza to Jerusalem and the West Bank of the Jordan. Since October, they have stabbed to death two Israeli taxi drivers and shot dead a military police commander in Gaza, thrown grenades at an Army passing-out parade near the Wailing Wall in Jerusalem, and plotted to blow up a lorry-load of high explosives in the Israeli capital.

In the past month, Israeli soldiers have killed at least five members of the Islamic Jihad ('holy war') movement in Gaza shoot-outs. Another 52 were arrested and an arms cache was uncovered.

'The religious awakening of the Arabs in the occupied territories is very threatening,' Major-General Amram Mitzna, chief of central command, which includes the West Bank, said recently. 'If there is something which should worry us in the future, it is the religious awakening, which has begun in Gaza and which is growing and is liable to intensify'.

The most disturbing development for the Israelis is the emergence of an informal alliance between the Muslim fundamentalists and the Palestinian Liberation Organisation, which has always claimed to be fighting for a secular Palestinian state. The Israeli defence minister, Mr Yitzhak Rabin, told foreign correspondents last week that there was no difference between Islamic Jihad and the PLO. He said that the PLO chairman, Mr Yasser Arafat, 'realised there was a growing tendency to return to Islamic fundamentalism and decided to exploit it'.

Since the Palestinian Muslims belong exclusively to the orthodox Sunni stream, unlike the Shia Hezbollah in Lebanon, they have no known links with the Iranian revolution; Mr Rabin said their operational links were with Jordan and their main source of funds was Saudi Arabia.

The Jihad has added an extra degree of fanaticism to the Palestinian armed struggle. Halad Al-Juaidi, a 22-year-old Gazan convicted of killing the two taxi drivers, told a military court: 'We, the members of the Islamic Jihad, attach greater importance to death than to life. Either we liberate our country or die in the attempt.'

Dr Elie Rekhess, a Tel Aviv University expert on Palestinian society, commented: 'Twenty years of Israeli rule over the territories and continued Jewish-Arab disputes over places sacred to both Islam and Judaism have given the Palestinian version of Islamic resurgence and its struggle against the Jewish state a unique character. The local Arab opposition to the occupation is gradually becoming more and more charged with Islamic fervour.'

In Gaza, the leading Islamic revivalist is Sheikh Ahmed Yassin, a 51-year-old teacher now paralysed in both legs, who has to be taken to the mosque in a wheelchair. In 1984 he was sentenced to 31 years in prison after an arsenal was discovered in the basement of his mosque, but he was released a year later in return for Israeli prisoners of war held by the PLO.

Sheikh Ahmed, a lean, prematurely aged figure with a grey beard trimmed to a point, sits in evident discomfort swathed in a blanket on a foam rubber mattress. His plain cement house is unheated

147

against the cold of an autumn evening. From time to time a young disciple tries to make him more comfortable, but it is a losing battle.

'I am teaching the people to return to Islam,' he says in high-pitched Arabic. 'I am also teaching them that they must reject the occupation in whatever way they can. Nationalism is part of Islam. If a person is a Muslim, he should be a nationalist.'

Does that mean armed resistance? 'Each person tries to get his rights peacefully,' Sheikh Ahmed replies. 'But if he cannot get his rights in that way then he is entitled to get his rights in another way.'

At Gaza's Islamic University, the main recruiting ground for the Jihad and the less extreme Muslim brotherhood, the president, Dr Mohammed Siam, claims that the Palestinians are turning back to religion because everything else has failed them. 'There is no other solution except Islam.'

The Nationalist Islamic revival, Dr Siam adds, is also a reaction to the increasingly religious tone of Jewish nationalism. 'The Palestinians here have noticed that. According to religious Jews, God gave them the right to Palestine; they are the chosen people of Allah. On the other side, the Koran gave this right to the Muslims as well. Therefore confrontation begets confrontation'.

Some secular nationalists are uneasy with the new alliance. They remember what happened in Iran when the Islamic revolutionaries turned on their left-wing partners after they had overthrown the Shah. A pro-PLO journalist in the West Bank town of Nablus compared the fundamentalists to a violent householder. 'He starts by beating his wife,' he said. 'Then he beats his children. After that, if we are not careful, he beats the neighbours.'

In Gaza, Dr Haider Abdul Shafi, a leading PLO supporter whose clinic was once burnt down by the fundamentalists, is content to have them on his side now. 'If any revivalist section has agreed that our first priority is fighting the occupation,' he explains, 'that is welcome. Our immediate problem is the occupation. We must hope that after that has been resolved our internal differences can be dealt with peacefully.

'If there is an alliance, I do not expect that it would be at the expense of abandoning our basic principles or our outlook on the quality of a future Palestinian state. We cannot abandon the principle of secularism, and the interests of the Christian minority among the Palestinians cannot be sacrificed.'

Mr Rashid al-Shawa, a former mayor of Gaza now in his late seventies, earns the last word.

'If you need to be religious to secure the liberation of Palestine,' he says, 'I too am ready.'

Israel divided over iron-fist tactics
The beginnings of the first intifada
Times on Sunday, Sydney, December 20, 1987

Israelis acknowledge that the latest Arab riots in the occupied West Bank and Gaza Strip and the iron-fisted army response add up to the bloodiest confrontation for a decade.

They are divided, however, in assessing how important a challenge it represents. Is it the start of a civil insurrection, or is it just another, more violent, twist to the 20-year-old cycle of defiance and repression?

The facts are not in doubt. Young Palestinian nationalists in the teeming refugee camps have taken the offensive, pelting Israeli army patrols and civilian settlers with stones, petrol bombs, iron bars and axe heads.

They show less and less fear for their own safety. Tear gas and rubber bullets, where they are used, are no longer a deterrent. And the youthful militants are mobilising their elders, including women, to join them in the firing line. The Israelis claim that these older demonstrators have been intimidated, but whether from coercion or conviction they are there, visible and vulnerable.

Israel has reacted with a show of force. Isolated patrols have shot their way out of trouble. Units of no-nonsense border police, trained in riot control, have been sent into the camps.

Their methods have been brutal and indiscriminate. Experienced television crews said they had never seen firing against civilian targets as heavy as that in the Balata refugee camp, near the West Bank town of Nablus.

Correspondents met women, old men and children who had been clubbed and shot. Cars were smashed. Cement and corrugated iron houses were vandalised.

'You have been oppressing us for 20 years now,' a 40-year-old woman with chest and leg injuries said, 'but it has never before been so bad.' Her son said: 'What is happening now in Balata is no longer demonstrations. It is full-scale war.'

The chief of central command, General Amram Mitzna, has ordered an investigation into border police conduct, but there is little doubt that the police were carrying out the spirit, if not the letter, of their assignment. In the 363 square-kilometre Gaza Strip occupied by Israel since the 1967 Middle East War, a Swedish United Nations refugee relief officer, Borje Lagerstrom, said: 'The situation is getting worse. It's building up to an explosion. There is a general feeling of hopelessness and oppression.'

Mr Lagerstrom saw Israeli soldiers grab Palestinian boys, blindfold them to the front of their jeep as a human shield. On another occasion he saw soldiers and plain-clothes security men beating three stone-throwers, hitting one of them mercilessly in the groin with a rifle butt.

The Gaza Strip is home to a 650,000 workforce who commute to Tel Aviv and other Israeli cities each day.

The right-wing evening paper, *Ma'ariv*, commented that the situation in the occupied territories had reached 'boiling point'. Its liberal-minded competitor, *Hadashot*, said life there had come more and more to resemble the South African black township of Soweto. The trade-union morning paper, *Davar*, noted that demonstrators were not deterred by daily killings. Military sources cited by the daily *Ha'aretz* were worried about 'a situation resembling South Africa'.

The Arab mayor of Bethlehem, Elias Freij, believes that the disturbances are an inevitable response to Israeli policy and that they will continue. 'No people can accept or tolerate a foreign military occupation,' said Mr Freij, who is regarded as a moderate with strong links to Jordan.

'There is no movement, one way or the other on the peace process,' the mayor complained. 'There is a consensus among our people that the only solution left is to have a negotiated peace, but for the Arabs, peace means an Israeli withdrawal from the occupied territories. There is strong opposition to this aspiration in Israel. We hear harsh, radical statements from Israeli leaders about a transfer or expulsion of the Arab population, and about non-withdrawal. These statements are very disappointing.'

The Middle East editor of the *Jerusalem Post*, Yehuda Litani, who has covered the occupied territories for most of the past 20 years, sees a connection between the riots and last month's hang-glider raid on northern Israel in which six Israeli soldiers were killed.

'The operation has encouraged Palestinians, and especially Palestinian youth, to feel that the Israelis and the Israel Defence Forces can be beaten,' he wrote. Mr Litani insisted, however, that the intensification of violence was 'still within the bounds of civil strife'. It was too early to say that it had turned from strife to rebellion.

Asked whether the Arabs were now in open revolt, the co-ordinator of activities in the occupied territories, General Shmuel Goren, said: 'Absolutely not.' Revolt, he said would mean a break with the military government, but there was no such boycott. Dialogue continued; day labourers still came to work in Israel; the bridges across the Jordan remained open to trade and travel.

'Neither side has any more lessons to learn from bloodshed,' the *Jerusalem Post* commented. 'The only lessons still to be learnt are those that will derive from the uses of political negotiation. This is the only course that can offer escape to both sides.'

Arab rioters feel backlash as Israel wields big stick

Observer, January 24, 1988

Israel is winning its campaign of attrition against the rebellious refugee camps of Gaza and the West Bank – but at a high price in terms of Palestinian limbs, Jewish conscience and international esteem.

The combination of club, boot and curfews ordered by defence minister Yitzhak Rabin is restoring the deterrent powers of the army and reminding refugees of their economic dependence on Israel.

Attacks on military patrols are petering out. Arab shopkeepers, who now fear the troops more than their own militants, are opening their shutters. And the convoys of cars and buses taking 60,000 labourers from the Gaza Strip to Israeli factories, hotels and building sites every day have resumed.

The results of Rabin's strategy of 'force, power and blows' can be seen in the crowded casualty ward of the Shifa Hospital, Gaza's biggest medical centre. An Arab doctor said last Thursday that the centre had treated 200 people since the beginning of the week, most of them suffering from broken elbows and knees. Three had fractured skulls.

The doctor, who declined to give his name because the Israelis had barred hospital staff from speaking to the press, said most of the casualties were boys and young men aged between 13 and 30. About 25 were older men and women. Three pregnant women had suffered abortions after their homes were tear-gassed.

The injuries, the doctor said, were more serious than the bullet wounds they had treated earlier, although there had been no fatalities. Many more injured Palestinians, he claimed, had been afraid to come to the hospital in case they were arrested. Medical staff were going to their homes.

The doctor, who lives in a refugee camp, said he had treated 30 injured people there in a day. He maintained that the beatings had become more severe since the curfews were imposed, although most people were staying indoors.

In the casualty ward, we were greeted by Mahajer el-Wahidi, a grey-bearded 75-year-old with a broken right hand. He said 25 soldiers had burst into his house and clubbed him. An 18-year-old youth, Ali Sha'afi, who had two broken arms, told much the same story. Troops had stormed his house while he was eating.

In the bed opposite, Muhammad Ali Massoud, 35, showed a broken arm and a broken leg. His right shoulder was purple from blows. 'The soldiers broke into my house,' he said. 'One of them asked me which hand I wrote with. I said the right. He said OK then smashed it.'

Assad Abu-Jasr, an English-speaking United Nations relief worker, brought in his brother from the Jabaliya camp while we were at the hospital. He said soldiers had attacked his house before dawn when the 20 members of his family were still asleep. They had hammered on doors and windows.

'We woke up and said: What are you doing? What's going on? What have we done?' he recounted. 'They told us to keep quiet. Then they forced the door open and threatened to shoot. They just came in and started striking everyone. My father is 80 years old. They caught him by his neck and pushed him against the wall.

'They said: Stay away, stay away. One of my brothers tried to hide in another room. A soldier broke the door down and hit him on his head and wrist. He has had 25 stitches in his head. Here is an X-ray of his broken hand. Another brother has a broken leg.

'I was beaten on the chest. After that the soldiers broke the cupboards, television, radio, everything. Everything is broken.'

Individual accounts are hard to check. Jabaliya, the biggest camp in the Gaza Strip with 65,000 refugees, is also the most militant. Sporadic rioting has continued there even during the curfews.

A senior Israeli officer showed reporters an arsenal of confiscated knives, axes and gardening tools that had been used to attack military patrols. The army admits that it is arresting alleged troublemakers during the night.

Whatever the provocation, the wounds are real. The clubs were aimed at arms and legs. 'A detainee sent to prison will be freed in 18 days unless the authorities have enough evidence to charge him,' a security source told the *Jerusalem Post*. 'He may then resume stoning soldiers. But if troops break his hand, he won't be able to throw for a month and a half.'

Rabin was frank about the objective. 'We will make it clear who is running the (occupied) territories.' After five weeks of Arab taunting, the army has recovered its power to intimidate. The Palestinians are cowed, but that does not mean they have abandoned their uprising. With Israel's fortieth anniversary barely three months away, few observers expect the territories to stay quiet for long. The riots have put the occupation back on the international agenda and the Palestinians are determined to keep it there.

So far, the Israeli conscripts and reservists are obeying orders, however brutal. But misgivings are growing – among senior officers, newspaper commentators and politicians.

Dedi Zucker, a left-of-centre Citizens' Rights MP, said after touring the Gaza camps and hospitals: 'I've been in wars, I've seen the miseries and results of wars. But I never thought our soldiers would have to carry out orders from the political leadership to harass and beat people.'

Jerusalem: the divided city

Observer News Service, February 11, 1988

Palestinian resistance, active and passive, has spread from the West Bank, setting a question mark against Israel's claim to retain Jerusalem as its 'indivisible capital'.

Young Arabs block roads with burning tyres, defy the police with rocks, stone Jews driving home to new suburbs built across the pre-1967 border. In one of them, East Talpiot, Arabs from the neighbouring village of Jebel Mukaber, waving PLO flags, pelted Jewish houses and smashed the windows of an Israeli school. For the first time in two decades the police are imposing curfews on Arab districts of the city.

Israelis avoid Arab East Jerusalem as much as possible. The Muslim and Christian quarters of the old, walled city have become no-go areas. All Arab shopkeepers have been on strike since the beginning of January (cheques are bouncing like ping-pong balls because they can't pay their Israeli suppliers). The municipality closed Arab schools after they became a rallying point for riots.

Meron Benvenisti, a former deputy mayor and disenchanted architect of Jewish-Arab coexistence terms it 'the Belfastinisation of Jerusalem' – a step towards polarisation.

'All those who believed that Jerusalem was different from the West Bank have found that they were wrong,' he said. 'Jerusalem is the heart of the West Bank. Those who tried to draw an artificial line around Jerusalem and say this is part of Israel have found that reality would not comply.'

Sari Nusseibeh, a Palestinian professor whose father was once King Hussein's defence minister, insisted: 'The fate of East Jerusalem can't be separated from the fate of the West Bank. Ours is a political problem, not a problem of who runs the municipal library.'

The mayor, Teddy Kollek, admits that the situation is 'grave', that there is a danger of redivision. He has not given up the struggle, but he is more defensive than usual.

'Coexistence in Jerusalem has existed for 1,500 years,' the 76-year-old mayor told *The Observer*, 'and it will continue to exist because we will all exist in Jerusalem. The question is whether it will be a good coexistence or a bad coexistence. I will do everything to see that it is a good coexistence.'

On the national level, Kollek recognises the weight of Palestinian aspirations. 'I am convinced that Jews shouldn't rule one million Arabs, not because we want to do the Arabs any good, but because it doesn't do us any good,' he said. The mayor is more ambivalent over the 120,000 Arabs of Jerusalem, a third of the population.

'I don't think we have to rule over them,' he argued. 'I think it's perceived that way because of the situation on the West Bank. Jerusalem is their city, it should remain their city. But there is one difference. It is also the capital of Israel.'

His administration was continuing to help the Arabs run their own affairs, even though they chose not to serve on the city council. 'Twenty years ago they had water once every six days,' the mayor recalled; 'today they have water all the time. About 1,500 Arab city employees are still coming to work. Arab clinics are functioning. At the (Israeli) Hadassah hospital on Mount Scopus a third of the patients are Arabs.

'Things are continuing, but I don't know if this will remain so. Quite true. But we have to do everything so that it should.'

Kollek, who has served as mayor for 22 years, acknowledges that Jerusalem will have to be 'an essential part' of any peace agreement between Israel and Jordan. 'You cannot make an agreement if you do not have an agreement about Jerusalem.'

But how did that square with Israel's claim to exercise sovereignty over the whole of what would remain its capital? Kollek replied that what he termed 'functional' sovereignty could be divided, as it had been already despite the fact that Israel annexed East Jerusalem in 1967.

'We have given up a lot of functional sovereignty,' he explained. 'We gave the Arabs an option. They could remain Jordanians or they could become Israelis. We did not enforce a right of sovereignty on them.

'We haven't enforced a right of sovereignty on the Temple Mount (revered by Jews and Arabs, but still controlled by the Muslim authorities). We haven't enforced a right of sovereignty on the fact that people can walk across the Allenby Bridge to Jordan and deal with enemy agents.'

Kollek contended that this practical division of sovereignty could be extended 'in many other ways'. He declined to specify what they might be. That, like much besides, would have to wait for negotiations.

A long winter of revolt in search of Palestine

The Statesman, Calcutta, April 9, 1988

Driving north from Jerusalem up the spine of Palestine at the end of a wet and eventful winter is like driving through the vale of Kashmir with olives standing in for the chinars. The fruit trees are in blossom, white and pink against the green, rocky terraces. The meadows are lush with wild flowers, pale purple cyclamen, livid red anemones, yellows and blues.

The strains of military occupation and civil unrest are seldom far below the pastoral surface. Israeli army jeeps, their soldiers equipped with helmets, plastic visors, wooden clubs and Uzi submachine guns, are constantly patrolling between the Arab towns. The jeeps are mounted with iron grappling hooks to clear the highway of the rocks, burning tyres and assorted debris that have become the trademark of Arab discontent. For once our Palestinian taxi driver, a thickset Yasser Arafat look-alike with a stubbly chin and a black and white chequered kefiyeh, is not stopped at military checkpoints.

In Ramallah and El Bireh, Christian and Muslim towns respectively straddling the main road, 80 per cent of the shops are shuttered. Whether from fear or conviction, the business strike is holding firm as the Palestinian uprising enters its fourth month. Traffic is busy but there are few pedestrians. 'Welcome to El Bireh, a city on the move,' reads the municipal signboard. Not today it isn't.

Down below to the left, the Jelouzoun refugee camp is closed to visitors. The curfew seems to have been lifted, but the Israelis are taking no chances. Jelouzoun, like most of the camps, has been at the forefront of the rebellion. Its youth has rioted, stoned and petrol-bombed. It has paid in spilled blood and broken bones. Today the only sign of defiance is a red, white, black and green Palestinian flag trapped in the wires at the top of an electricity pole. Radio Jerusalem, a Palestinian station broadcasting from Syria, had declared it the 'Day of the Flag'.

On the hilltops, the red-roofed Jewish settlements seem as deserted as the Arab villages. The settlers have gone to work in Jerusalem or are staying indoors. The builders' cranes are still. The government has offered fresh incentives, but no one is rushing to live in the eye of the hurricane.

Outside the Balata refugee camp on the approach to Nablus, the biggest West Bank town, Israeli infantrymen mount guard. They look sulky, edgy and bored. The entrance to Nablus is dominated by the local military headquarters, an ugly, cement fort built by the British half-a-century ago.

Arab parents in long, shapeless coats wait stoically for news of teenage sons standing trial in the military court or undergoing interrogation in the prison.

Nablus, 800 metres above sea level, is a city walking in its sleep. Again, most of the youths are calmed. Women keep watch from the flat roofs and balconies of their stone houses.

Our host, Ibrahim, welcomes us with sweet black tea. He studied in Europe and sells educational services and advice to the ambitious Palestinian middle class. A month ago his son, Karim, had his jaw smashed by an Israeli soldier. He was, he says, playing cards in a friend's house when the Army burst in. The friend had once served a year in gaol for membership of the Fatah guerilla organisation. Karim has just had the clamps removed from his jaw, but is still on liquid diet. He has lost 5kg.

'I used to believe that we could learn a lot from the Israelis to develop our country,' Ibrahim says. 'We have today very modern agricultural methods. We learnt it from Israel. Before 1967, when we lived under Jordan, the government didn't let us open a university on the West Bank. Now we have six or seven. The Israelis allowed us to open them.

'I have some friends in Israel, Jews who came from Iraq. I buy books and teaching cassettes from them. Even while there is an uprising, one of them phoned to ask about my health, my situation. I can't say I like the Jews, but I consider them human beings. When I was studying in Austria, I saw what the Nazis had done to the Jews. I was deeply influenced by that. I thought, why can't we live together?'

After what he had seen since December, Ibrahim is disabused. 'I am convinced now that it is impossible to live together,' he explains. 'My son did not take part in politics. He has never been questioned by the police. They had treated us with cruelty before, but never like this. I could not imagine that they would bury boys alive, as they did in a village near Nablus. They have deepened the hatred between Arabs and Jews.

'At the beginning I thought the uprising would end in three or four days, as in the past. But the Israelis were more cruel than before. The boys felt that their dignity was broken. They had to fight, with stones or whatever they could lay their hands on. It is not a matter of admiring them. I am not a fanatic. The boys are seeking our freedom. When the Israelis beat my only son, it changed my thoughts.'

Karim, a 20-year-old student, is emphatic: 'The uprising must continue to the end, until we reach a good solution for the Palestinians.'

But what will constitute a good solution? There is no love for King Hussein. One of Karim's friends says that if they have to choose between a Jordanian occupation and an Israeli occupation, they will choose the Israeli. Hussein, he says, slaughtered 20,000 Palestinians when they rebelled in Amman in 1970.

Ibrahim demurs. At least, he says, the Jordanians are Muslims and fellow Arabs. But the younger generation is adamant. What it wants is a Palestinian state, no more and no less. Alongside Israel? Yes, so long as the border is internationally guaranteed. After 21 years of occupation and a long winter of revolt, they no longer trust the Jews not to come back.

Our conversation, punctuated now with thick black Turkish coffee, is interrupted by a gunshot. Karim and his student friends lead us warily into the garden. Sheltered by a stone wall, we watch boys, no more than 12 years old, dragging stones, a discarded zinc boiler and old tyres across the road. Within minutes the rubber is blazing and the familiar cloud of acrid black smoke is staining the sky.

'Allahu Akbar,' the boys exulted. Two, middle-aged soldiers, reservists old enough to be their fathers, run towards them, shoulders hunched, firing rubber bullets and teargas. The boys flee into hills. The site, our guides explain, is too exposed for them to slog it out.

A Red Crescent ambulance appears in case it is needed. A girl in the house next door starts screaming hysterically. Her brother, she sobs, has been hit. How does she know? She doesn't and as it happened, he had not. But across the valley in the old, walled Nablus casbah the daily confrontation has taken its toll. An 18-year-old youth has been shot in the head. The Palestinian uprising has found its eighteenth shaheed.

Intifada and after – turning point in West Asia

The Statesman, Calcutta, December 12, 1988

'I am beginning to feel that the intifada constitutes a turning point in the history of the Arab-Israeli conflict,' said Dr Sari Nusseibeh, a Palestinian philosophy professor whose late father once served as King Hussein's defence minister. 'It sets a kind of dynamic in motion that was not apparent before. Nothing is inevitable, but the uprising has created a vast series of possibilities for a just settlement. A new awareness is developing among Palestinians.'

One year after the outbreak of a running insurrection that has cost more than 310 Arab lives and 11 Israeli, both sides are taking stock. Their conclusions are guarded. The recent Israeli elections, which increased the influence of the hard-line Jewish nationalists, put a break on premature optimism but neither side is without hope.

'The intifada is important in that the Palestinians showed a readiness to suffer,' said Professor Yehoshafat Harkabi, a former chief of military intelligence and Hebrew University authority on Palestinian strategy. 'There will be ups and downs,' he predicted. 'But it won't end. The solution is not military; it is political.'

On the Israeli side of the equation, Mr Dedi Zucker, an MP from the centre-left Citizens' Rights Movement, detected a transformation in assumptions about the occupation of the West Bank and Gaza Strip. Apparently contradictory opinion polls found Israelis ready, if the terms were right, to negotiate with the Palestinian Liberation Organisation, and at the same time giving increasing support to extreme solutions like mass expulsion of Arabs, Mr Zucker noted.

'There is one common denominator,' he argued, 'Israelis don't believe that Israelis and Palestinians can live together under the present circumstances. Both the advocates of talking to the PLO and the advocates of transfer believe now that we can't control the Palestinians.

'Some of Israel's fundamental beliefs have been smashed by the intifada. Under the surface, despite the result of the election, something is happening among Israelis. Most of us accept that it will prove impossible to go on ruling the Palestinians for a long time,' Mr Zucker said.

The intifada was a spontaneous, if long incubated, revolt against the status quo, belying the assumption among Jews, Arabs and the world at large that nothing was going to change. The match which lit the fuse on December 9 was a traffic accident in Gaza which was interpreted by Palestinians as an act of revenge by an army driver for the murder of an Israeli businessman. But if it had not been that, it would have been something else.

In the previous month an Arab summit conference in Amman had downgraded the Palestinian issue, giving priority to the Iran-Iraq war. The leaders of the Soviet Union and the USA had met in another summit and totally ignored the question. Israel meanwhile was consolidating its hold on the occupied territories. The 1,500,000 Palestinians of the West Bank and Gaza were not prepared to leave it at that.

The Palestinian National Council meeting in Algiers was a measure of their success in stirring their leaders in exile for the first time in 40 years. The leadership began to grapple with the practical problems of a compromise solution as the occupied Palestinians had long known that this was the only way of getting the Israelis off their backs. It is easier to fight for a maximalist solution in Tunis or Baghdad than it is in Nablus or the Jubaliya refugee camp.

Although Israel's caretaker government was reluctant to acknowledge it, the PNC declaration of independence did mark a step forward. Its recognition of Israel was still not explicit enough to satisfy either Tel Aviv or Washington. Its renunciation of armed struggle was ambivalent. (The PLO could hardly expect Israelis to rejoice at an end to terrorism abroad, so long as it continued at home). But what mattered was that the Arab side endorsed the partition of Palestine, which it had rejected ever since it was proposed by the United Nations General Assembly in November, 1947.

As Professor Harkabi pointed out, this effectively abrogated Article 19 of the Palestinian national covenant, which set the guidelines of PLO policy two decades ago. The clause dismisses partition and the establishment of a Jewish State as 'entirely illegal, regardless of the passage of time, because they are contrary to the will of the Palestinian people and to their natural right in their homeland.'

However grudgingly, the November 15 Independence declaration asserts: 'Despite the historical injustices inflicted upon the Palestinian Arab people, UN Resolution 181 of 1947, which partitioned Palestine into two states, provides conditions for an international legitimacy that guarantees the right of the Palestinian Arab people to sovereignty and national independence.' By inference it must also guarantee the right of Jewish sovereignty and independence, though Palestinian leaders do nothing to clarify their international appeal by explaining away their intentions in interview after conflicting interview in Arab capital after Arab capital.

The occupied Palestinians lay no claim to leadership. In the end the PLO must take the decisions. But the teenage boys and girls in the vanguard of the intifada do insist on setting the agenda. They will not suffer silently as hostages to ideology or expediency.

Apart from the changing balance between the diaspora and the homeland, Dr Nusseibeh pointed to three transformations in conservative Palestinian society over the past year.

'The status of the young has been revolutionised. In the long run this will have vast implications, opening up many possibilities. We are opening the door to the creativity of the young, which will increase the potential of the Palestinian nation to meet the challenge that continues to face it.

'The second is the participation of Palestinian women in the front line of the uprising. Again, we have been witnessing a revolution, which will open up new possibilities. The third is the key role of the countryside as against the traditionally political towns.'

Despite his euphoria at the upheaval wrought by the intifada, Dr Nusseibeh's prognostication remained sober: 'I will not say that

that uprising will escalate for an indefinite period, but the struggle will continue with increased potential, increased strength. Catastrophe is just as possible a scenario as a settlement, but the fact that the Palestinians have increased their potential has increased the chance of a settlement. The uprising has given us the chance to bring a settlement about.'

The intifada may have created a chance. The question is whether Israelis and Palestinians will grasp it. The Israeli, Professor Harkabi, was worried that intransigence might rather provoke the Arab states into another war. He put his faith in that of a self-styled 'Machiavellian dove', in the hope that the two superpowers would intervene to solve yet another regional conflict.

'I don't believe that Jews and Arabs left to their own devices can solve it,' he said. 'There is a need for international midwifery'.

Over to you, Sister Bush. Over to you, Sister Gorbachov.

Victory at last? An assessment of Arafat's new politics

The Statesman, Calcutta, May 27, 1989

A few days after the late President Anwar Sadat broke the ice and visited Jerusalem in November 1977 as the first Arab head of state openly to accept Israeli hospitality, I was entertained to lunch by a Palestinian politician in Nablus, the biggest and most nationalistic of the West Bank Arab towns. He was a member of the local council, a radical who had seen the inside of Arab as well as Israeli prisons, a student contemporary of George Habash, leader of the uncompromising Popular Front for the Liberation of Palestine.

As we chewed on our lamb chops and kebabs and talked of Sadat's defection from pan-Arab solidarity, my host paused. 'You know,' he mused, 'the Zionists have been saying yes for 50 years. The Palestinians have been saying no. The Zionists have finished up with the whole of Palestine, we have finished up with nothing. Perhaps it's time we started saying yes.'

After another Arab-Israeli war (Lebanon 1982), two more Palestinian expulsions (from Beirut and Damascus) and finally a revolt of the masses weary of living under Israeli occupation,

Yasser Arafat has complied. In Algiers and Geneva, Cairo and Paris, in declarations and interviews that began with the Palestinian National Council last November, the chairman of the Palestinian Liberation Organisation is at last saying 'Yes'.

It was not surprising that the first call for recognition of Israel came, however discreetly, from the occupied territories. Twenty hard years of Israeli rule taught the West Bank and Gaza Palestinians that the Jewish State was here to stay. They shed the illusion, long before their leaders in exile, that time was on the Arab side, that the Zionists, like the crusaders 800 years earlier, would one day pack their bags and go back where they came from. They could feel Israel's durability, the strength of its Army, the commitment of its people and, above all, the creeping annexation of its settlements, foreclosing Palestinian options.

It was hard to believe, as some commentators have suggested after the event, that Arafat's belated conversion to the partition of Palestine, an Arab state established alongside a Jewish State, was part of a grand design, that he planned it that way. It is true that within the Palestinian movement he fought for a strategy of the gun and the olive branch, but there was always a sense that he still dreamed of an Arab Palestine with a compliant Jewish minority, which is what a 'secular, democratic state' would have meant. At the very least, Arafat had not absorbed the key lesson of Zionist history: take what you're offered, then build on it.

His latest missed opportunity was the 1978 Camp David accord. The Palestinians, understandably enough, felt betrayed by a separate Egyptian-Israeli peace. But if they had read the text and listened to the agreement's American sponsors, they might have seen it for the opening that it was. The Israeli prime minister, Menachem Begin, was not presenting them with a state on a silver platter, but he was committing himself to a process that he would have been hard-pressed to control if the Arab side had made the most of it.

Time and again, Arafat explained to the Americans and the Europeans that he could not recognise Israel because that would be giving away his best card before negotiations had begun. Yet his interlocutors knew, if the PLO leader did not, that no Israeli government would talk voluntarily to an organisation pledged to wipe it off the face of West Asia.

It took the intifada uprising, which broke out in December 1987, to convince Arafat that the Palestinians could negotiate as equals, and that he could carry a majority of his movement with him to the bargaining table. The people of the occupied territories had asserted themselves as never before – and their target was as much their own diaspora leadership as it was the Israeli oppressor. They had had enough, and if the price of getting the Israelis off their backs was compromise, so be it.

'This was the juncture,' wrote Meron Benvenisti, a clear-eyed and often apocalyptic Israeli analyst of the Arab-Jewish conflict, 'at which Yasser Arafat found his calling as a leader.'

'Submitting to the constraints of reality, he sacrificed the maximalist formulations of the Palestinian revolution in favour of a political plan that recognised the facts of life of which the cardinal component is acknowledgement of Israel's unassailable, permanent existence... Arafat grasped that subjective will cannot overcome objective reality – and forced this realism on his movement.'

In an interview with the veteran American diplomatic correspondent, Tad Szulc, the PLO leader claimed that it took him 600 hours to convince his colleagues to go for a two-state solution. No one but Arafat could have done it. His authority is unique, though he has always had his challengers and detractors. As a co-founder of Al Fatah in the late 1950s and chairman of the PLO since 1969, it was he who restored the Palestinians' self-esteem. To the world at large, he was and remains Mr Palestine, despite the setbacks of Black September, 1970, when the PLO was expelled from Jordan, and 1982, when it suffered a similar fate in Lebanon.

'Arafat was the chief architect of a large PLO organisation,' wrote the political dictionary of the Arab world, 'and transformed it, with huge funds put at his disposal by the Arab states, mainly the rich oil countries, from a feeble association of small guerrilla bands into a wealthy, multi-branched establishment conducting military, economic, financial, social, medical and educational operations.'

Once committed to the diplomatic option, Arafat played his hand to maximum advantage. 'I am challenging Israel to peace,' he told the American journalist T D Allman, but his sights were on Washington as much as Jerusalem. 'The American administration,' he urged Tad Szulc, 'must now decide if it will support our strategic policy of peace.'

Arafat accepted the logic of the PLO decision. He was ready, step by step, to pay the American and Western European price for respectability, if not that demanded by Israel's hard-line Likud Prime Minister, Yitzhak Shamir. He was prepared to recognise Israel, to renounce terrorism, to settle for compensation instead of a comprehensive right of return for the Palestinian refugees of 1948. Prompted by Francois Mitterand, he declared the Palestine National Covenant, which sought the destruction of Israel, 'null and void'.

He played the public relations game with relish. He gave press conferences and interviews by the dozen. T D Allman flew 3,500 miles between four countries in a 40-hour jaunt in Arafat's executive jet. In Cairo the PLO chairman staged an unprecedented encounter with Israeli reporters, using them to appeal to the Jewish public over the heads of its wary government. 'We are cousins,' he told them. 'You have to treat me as an equal and a human being... I am addressing my appeal to all Israelis to work together or we will lose this historical chance.'

After four decades of warfare, declared and undeclared, the Israelis were not won over that easily, but the impact of Arafat's campaign on the hitherto sceptical West was immediate and dramatic. The American administration abandoned its self-imposed taboo and opened a dialogue with the PLO at ambassadorial level. Arafat was received in audience by the Pope. A British foreign office minister, William Waldegrave, went to meet him in Tunis. President Mitterand welcomed him to Paris. Between times Arafat was feted as head of the newly proclaimed Palestinian State in capital after capital of the Third World.

'Arafat has engineered one of the most astonishing transformations in modern Middle East history,' T D Allman commented. 'He has turned himself from a pariah into a world leader. And he has transformed the PLO from a terrorist organisation, according to official US terminology, into what the USA now officially recognises as a legitimate partner in the search for peace'.

With the intifada keeping the heat on Israel, these are heady days for the Palestinian revolution. But Arafat knows as well as anyone that victory has yet to be won. Possession is nine parts of the law and Israel, for all the buffeting it has taken at home and abroad, still controls the West Bank and Gaza Strip. In Washington the Bush administration is moving slowly and cautiously. It is sympathetic to the Palestinian cause, but it seems reluctant to twist Israeli arms. The USA, Arafat has said, has a decisive role to play. Without American arm-twisting, Shamir is unlikely to budge.

Time is ticking away. New American administrations do not have to act in their first 100 days. But if they leave West Asia initiatives beyond the first year, party managers start worrying about mid-term elections and the Jewish vote. After two years, the President's eyes turn to his re-election campaign. Incumbents prefer to play safe.

Arafat, too, has his timetable. Palestinian radicals like George Habash of the Popular Front, and above all Ahmed Jibril of the Popular Front general command, have not turned their backs on armed struggle. At best they have given Arafat one or two years to deliver, or to discredit himself.

Israel's stone-faced stonewaller
The Observer profile of Yitzhak Shamir
Observer, May 21, 1989

Like Margaret Thatcher, Yitzhak Shamir, the Israeli prime minister who arrives in London tonight on an official visit, is a conviction politician. He is as likely to lecture as be lectured, to hector as be hectored.

He will listen to what his host has to say, but he will insist on delivering a message of his own. Yes, of course, he wants peace with the Palestinians ('the Arabs of the Land of Israel', as he prefers to call them, at least when he's speaking Hebrew), but on Israel's terms, not Yasser Arafat's, not George Bush's, and certainly not Margaret Thatcher's. What he is seeking is diplomatic support for his government's peace initiative, not gratuitous advice.

If it's up to Shamir, once described in these columns as 'a small, hunched, almost frog-like man who exudes an air of deep suspicion', the walls of Number 10 will not shudder. There will be no slanging match. Decibel diplomacy is not his style.

Unlike his right-wing Likud predecessor, Menachem Begin, Shamir does not provoke. He seldom invokes either the Bible or the Holocaust, although as a Polish Jew he is acutely conscious of his people's vulnerability. If an Arab says he means to destroy Israel, Shamir takes him at his word.

He is discreet about his role in the Stern Gang, though as one of its commanders he authorised the assassinations of Lord Moyne, Churchill's minister of state in the Middle East, and Count Bernadotte, the Swedish United Nations mediator in Palestine.

Characteristically, his office responded to new revelations on the Bernadotte affair with a bland put-down. 'The Prime Minister is concentrating on the present and future problems of the State of Israel. We don't want to deal with this affair. All that can be said has been said.' The controversy soon curled up and died, as he knew it would.

A man who has worked with him in both the Mossad secret service and politics says: 'He has nerves of ice. He never makes snap decisions. He thinks that time is on his side. His adversaries usually make the first mistake while he waits.'

Two years ago, he killed an opening to Jordan, engineered by his own Labour foreign minister, Shimon Peres, by a mixture of attrition and arithmetic. He knew Peres could not command a coalition majority. King Hussein was ready to negotiate. The Americans were pushing. But Shamir sat tight, and prevailed.

The full emotion of his commitment to Eretz Yisrael, the ancestral Land of Israel, emerges most frankly when he is addressing his own, the Likud faithful. 'A foreign state will not arise here,' he promised a party rally in February. 'A Palestinian state will not arise here. Never. The world should know that Eretz Yisrael is connected by thousands of strands with one people, the people of Israel. The Jewish people. Eretz Yisrael belongs to the people of Israel, and only to the people of Israel.'

For Shamir, the Palestinians are 'foreigners and terrorists, brutal, savage, alien invaders'. It makes it harder for his right-wing critics to challenge his most recent peace initiative for they know, deep down, that he is not going to sell out. It makes it harder, too, for the Palestinians to believe he is offering anything worth trading for the sacrifices of their 17-month intifada.

Yitzhak Shamir, nee Yzernitzky, was born 73 years ago in Poland and brought up in Bialystok, a rich metropolis of Jewish life and culture. He joined the Betar youth movement, inspired by Vladimir Jabotinsky, the guru of right-wing muscular Zionism.

In 1935, at the age of 20, he dropped out of Warsaw University law school and migrated to the Promised Land, completing his studies at the Hebrew University of Jerusalem. Two years later he joined the Irgun Zvai Leumi, Betar's underground military arm, defecting under Avraham Stern in 1940 over whether to co-operate with Britain in the war against the Nazis.

The Sternists insisted that the struggle against the Palestine mandate must take precedence, even trying at one stage to make common cause with Germany and the Italian Fascists. After Stern was shot dead by the British police in 1942, Shamir was one of a collective leadership of three that took command.

The Stern Gang was the Provisional IRA of the Zionist revolt. It had none of the Irgun's scruples about assassination. It sought the spectacular. Its fighters were fanatical, but less doctrinaire than the Irgun's.

Shamir's strength was organisation: he planned and deployed. Matti Shmuelewitz, who served under him and survived a British death sentence, says that even as a 30-year-old, Shamir never showed his enthusiasm. 'What you always saw was his thinking, his caution,' Shmuelewitz says. 'People in the underground sometimes thought he was too slow taking decisions, but everybody felt you could trust him.'

On one occasion, Shamir ordered the execution of a Stern Gang fighter who had taken to drink and dangerous ideas (he advocated assassinating David Ben-Gurion and other mainstream Jewish leaders). The man was shot dead.

Shamir was twice captured by the British (once by an alert sergeant who recognised his eyebrows, although the future prime minister was disguised as a bearded Talmudic scholar), and twice escaped. His wife, Shulamit, was arrested, but went on hunger strike for 11 days and refused to divulge where he was hiding – a record she draws to the attention of any interviewer naïve enough to expect her to reveal family secrets (the only one that is known is that their son Yair, an air force colonel, does not vote Likud).

Shamir's last escape was from exile in Eritrea, crossing the desert in the secret compartment of an oil tanker before finding sanctuary in French Africa. To this day he prefers speaking French to English, but after nine years as foreign or prime minister his English is much more confident.

After a spell in private business, Shamir joined the Mossad in 1955. He is reported to have operated undercover in French-speaking Arab countries; in a moment of indiscretion, he has labeled his Mossad days 'the most exciting and often the most dangerous in my life'.

After leaving the service, he joined Begin's Herut, the forerunner of the Likud, in 1970 and was elected to the Knesset in 1974. He was appointed speaker after the Likud's maiden victory in 1977. Despite his opposition to the 1979 Israeli-Egyptian peace treaty (he feared it would create a precedent for evacuating settlements on the West Bank), Begin appointed him foreign minister a year later.

When Begin retired in the wake of the Lebanon war in 1983, Shamir succeeded him as prime minister and party leader. He rotated the premiership and foreign ministry with Peres in the 1984-88 national unity coalition, and is now prime minister for the duration of its uneasy successor.

Despite his age and crippling workload, Shamir still reads voraciously every night, political biographies for preference. 'He gives the impression of not being very well educated,' an old associate says, 'but he is self-educated, with a good, logical mind that it doesn't pay to underestimate.'

He is fallible, nonetheless. For months before the intifada uprising broke out in December 1987, Shamir dismissed warnings of mounting violence in the occupied territories. 'Nothing,' he said, 'is burning.' He knows better now.

Shamir comes to London at a time of crisis, both for Israeli diplomacy and for his own leadership. To counter the PLO peace offensive he has adopted what is as much a Labour as a Likud initiative. In particular, he has swallowed his own words and accepted the idea of Palestinian elections leading to negotiations for transitional and final settlements of the conflict.

Likud MPs, including at least three highly ambitious cabinet ministers, fear that the peace plan will launch a process Shamir cannot control. The hard-line industry minister, Ariel Sharon, has warned that it will produce 'neither peace nor security'. It would, he said, lead to a Palestinian State and the redivision of Jerusalem.

The prime minister's dilemma is how to promote the initiative in Downing Street and beyond, while satisfying the Israeli Right that he doesn't really mean it. It is made no easier by his Labour partners who do believe in territorial compromise and would like nothing better than to lure him into concessions.

In the past, Shamir has marginalised or worn down internal Likud dissenters. But in the ugly, frustrated atmosphere generated by the intifada, with Jewish settlers increasingly taking the law into their own hands, it will not be easy, even for a stubborn old steamroller.

Chapter 7 – 1989-92

The Soviet diaspora
The Statesman, Calcutta, March 7, 1990

The Russians are coming. Natan Sharansky, the human rights activist who spent nine years in Soviet prisons before leaving for Israel in 1986, hails the current migration wave as the biggest exodus of Jews since they were expelled from Spain in 1492.

According to the Jewish Agency, which is responsible for bringing them to Israel and settling them there, 3,000 Soviet Jews arrived in November, the first month after the USA closed the door on mass admissions. In December the influx had risen to 3,600 and in January to 4,700. Around 1,300 landed in the first seven days of February. These monthly figures compare with totals of 6,300 for the first ten months of 1989 and of 2,200 for the whole of 1988.

'The number is not only big,' Simha Dinitz, the Jewish Agency chairman, told me. 'It's rising every month.' No one can tell how many of the more than two million Jews in the Soviet Union will eventually leave under President Mikhail Gorbachov's liberal emigration policy, but Dinitz believes that the estimate of 100,000 in 1990 alone will prove conservative.

'The only criterion that we have for the future,' he added, 'is the number of requests that are being processed. By April we shall have close to one million requests. This potential can come in ten years: it can come in seven years, or in 11 years, but we are talking about a potential of one million.' This would mean an increase of about 25 per cent in Israel's Jewish population.

Israeli officials and Soviet Jewry campaigners acknowledge that most of the emigrants would prefer to settle in the USA but, as Sharansky argued in a meeting with foreign correspondents, once the exodus reaches six figures no country other than Israel will welcome them.

The huge increase was triggered by the negative as well as the positive side of glasnost, fear as well as opportunity. Minorities always feel vulnerable at a time of upheaval. The Jews who played a prominent role in the party are being blamed for 70 years of communism. Russian and central Asian nationalists are turning against them as outsiders.

'There is a real panic now,' Mikhail Agursky, a Soviet affairs expert at the Hebrew University of Jerusalem, explained. 'There is a socio-economic crisis. There could be civil war and anarchy. The Jews in the Muslim areas feel threatened by rising nationalism.

'At the same time the image of Israel has dramatically improved over the past two years for Soviet Jews. Many of them have been able to visit Israel as tourists. What they met was an affluent society. Israeli Russian-language broadcasts are no longer jammed. The Israeli image in the Soviet media has become much more positive. Now, with all that is going on there, Israel seems more calm than the Soviet Union.'

The influx is a boost for Israel's battered morale. The Zionist dream of 'the ingathering of the exiles' no longer rings like a hollow slogan. However reluctantly, the Soviet Jews are coming and are determined to succeed.

But the question being asked with increasing urgency is: can Israel absorb so many newcomers with unemployment running at nine per cent and inflation at more than 20 per cent a year?

Dinitz is convinced that it can. 'Israel not only can absorb them,' he insisted, 'but the more that come, the easier it will be. Israel always had difficulty in absorbing a trickle of immigrants. It never had difficulty in absorbing mass immigration.

'When you absorb mass immigration you are mobilising every muscle that exists in this land and among the Jewish people abroad. This is a tremendous force.'

Last October international Jewish fund-raisers pledged themselves to contribute an extra $100 million a year for five years towards the absorption bill. At that time it was expected that 30,000 Soviet Jews a year would settle in Israel over the next three years.

In January, when it became clear that this was a gross underestimate, the fund-raisers doubled their annual target to $200 million, initially for three years. Of the $600 million total, US Jews are aiming to raise $420 million and the rest of the Jewish diaspora $180 million.

At home, Dinitz contends that the very process of absorption will generate economic activity, which will benefit both the immigrants and established Israelis. The notoriously cautious governor of the Bank of Israel, Professor Michael Bruno, had recently predicted that an influx of 100,000 newcomers would stimulate at least six per cent growth in the gross national product.

'If you are going to spend $1 million on housing,' Dinitz argued, 'you are bound to create an economic incentive. And this will mean economic betterment for all. None of the roads we are going to build, none of the extra schools, none of the housing and none of the factories will have a sign on them saying: For Russians Only.'

Not all Israelis have taken these assurances at face value. The predominantly oriental Jewish population of the development towns, city slums and moshav cooperative villages have borne the brunt of the current recession. They fear they will be forgotten in the rush to accommodate the Russians.

One of their aspiring leaders, Yamin Suissa, the son of Moroccan immigrants of 40 years ago, wrote to President Gorbachov last autumn, urging him to restrict Jewish emigration. Eli Ben-Menachem, an Indian-born Labour MP and union organiser, made the point more tactfully: 'The absorption of new immigrants is important for all of us, but heaven forbid if we don't know how to keep the balance in our order of priorities in the allocation of resources.'

The Russians themselves, from Sharansky to the newest arrival, insist that they will not be a drag on the economy. 'The experience of the 200,000 Jews who came from the Soviet Union in the 1970s shows that they made a tremendous contribution to the economy,' Sharansky said. 'Whatever was invested in them was paid back within three or four years. Today almost 30 per cent of Israeli doctors are from the Soviet Union. So are 20 per cent of engineers, as well as almost half the teachers of mathematics and music.'

At the Mevaseret Zion absorption centre in the Jerusalem hills, Leah Cherobilsky, a 42-year-old electronics engineer who arrived from Moscow three months ago, told me she was determined to find a job. She had been barred from working in her profession for 14 years after first applying to leave for Israel. She recognised that experience was out of date.

'I'll take whatever I can get,' she said. Asked if she would do unskilled manual work, she retorted, 'Why not?'

Her husband Boris, also an electronics engineer, had turned down the offer of a refresher course. 'He wants to work,' Mrs Chernobilsky explained. 'He's 45, he spent a year and a half in prison for Zionist activities. He's in a hurry. He'll take whatever he can find, labouring, or work as an electrician.'

Jobs and housing are the two main problems confronting the immigrants once they have mastered Hebrew in intensive courses at the absorption centres. There are very few homes available for rent. Apartments in the big towns, where most of the newcomers want to live, are expensive (a modest three-bedroom flat can cost $150,000).

The Russians arrive with little or no capital. Loans are available from the government and the banks but they cover barely half the cost.

The massive immigration has provoked a fierce Arab diplomatic offensive. The Arabs are alarmed that change in the Jewish-Arab balance will consolidate Israel's hold on what they regard as Palestinian territory on either side of the pre-1967 war border.

The right-wing Likud Prime Minister, Yitzhak Shamir, fanned their fears – and their propaganda – with a statement to party supporters that 'a big immigration requires a big land of Israel'. It was interpreted as an attempt to exploit the influx to justify keeping the occupied West Bank and Gaza Strip.

In fact, hardly any of the current wave wants to live across the old 'green line' border. Money donated abroad is spent only on the Israeli side. According to official figures, a mere half of one per cent settle in the occupied areas.

'This is not an ideological immigration,' Mikhail Agursky, himself a Soviet immigrant of the 1970s vintage, argued. 'They don't settle on the West Bank.'

Yigor Khait, a 22-year-old engineer from Leningrad, was typical. 'I went to look at the settlements,' he said, 'but they didn't interest me. I lived in a big city in Russia, and I want to live in a big city here too. Also we don't know what will be the future of the territories.'

Among those I interviewed at the Mevaseret Zion centre, I did find one family determined to settle on the West Bank. But their motives were practical rather than doctrinaire.

Naum Simanovsky, a 29-year-old paediatrician with a wife and two children, hoped to get work in a Jerusalem hospital. 'We want to live in the territories,' he said. 'The main reason is economic. We want a little house of our own, not a flat in a block. We want privacy. It's impossible to find one at a price we could afford anywhere else.'

Weren't they afraid of the Palestinian intifada uprising? 'Not really,' he replied. 'We hope everything sorts itself out and there will be peace. We hope Jews and Arabs can live together, without stones. We are not religious and we are not extremists.'

Such distinctions do not impress the Arabs. King Hussein of Jordan called for an urgent Arab summit to forge a unified stand against 'the snowballing danger' of the immigration, while 85 members of the Palestinian National Council urged President Gorbachov: 'Stop this exodus, which is considered another invasion of our homeland.'

In Arab East Jerusalem, a leading supporter of the Palestinian organisation, Faisel Husseini, told me: 'I am not against Soviet Jewish emigration, but I want them to have the freedom of choice as well as the freedom to leave. The Americans have taken away their right to choose where to go by closing their borders to them.

'The only places I object to settling them in are the West Bank, Gaza and Jerusalem. Insofar as they are not going to settle in the occupied territories, it is the problem of the State of Israel. It is not my problem.'

Not surprisingly, Dinitz takes a more upbeat view of the impact on the diplomatic prospects. 'A lot of the problems behind the Arab-Israeli conflict are psychological,' he maintained. 'We don't have such a tremendous war over resources, oil or rivers, but it was over Israel's margin of existence. That is our basic battle.

'If Israel is going to be stronger in terms of the number of people, of the occupational distribution in the country, of the professional level, of the strength which comes with higher technology, a greater confidence in your ability to exist and to produce, to compete – to that extent Israel will be more willing to make compromises because the margin of its security will be enhanced. The chance for peace will be enhanced.'

Gulf War – why Palestinians supported Saddam
The Statesman, Calcutta, January 23, 1991

'Open the Jordan bridges I want to go to Iraq and fight,' cried a hen-pecked Palestinian buying tomatoes from the back of the van in the Shuafat refugee camp, north of Jerusalem, an hour after the Israelis lifted a six-day curfew.

'I support Saddam Hussein because he is going to solve the Palestinian problem,' interjected another, hawking sticky tape to seal rooms against Iraqi gas attack. 'Saddam will win,' added a third. 'His tactics are good. He has a very strong army.'

But weren't they worried about the damage the allied air strikes were inflicting on Iraq? One Palestinian admitted he was. He had a cousin in Baghdad. The rest dismissed it as so much American propaganda.

'On the first day of the war,' a young man explained, 'they said they had destroyed the Iraqis, but it was a lie. We don't believe them anymore. Yes, we watch CNN on Jordanian and Israeli television, but we know it's controlled by Americans. It's an American network. It puts out propaganda to finish the military's job. You can't trust it'.

So the refugees tune their radios to Amman and watch Jordanian television. King Hussein, once himself an enemy, gives them what they want to hear. 'We believe Jordan,' said an older man with a plastic bag full of oranges. 'They will tell us the truth.'

A week into the Gulf War, Saddam's stock is still riding high among the Palestinians of the occupied West Bank and Gaza.

'Saddam is a man who does what he says,' argued a blacksmith in Gaza town. 'Saddam is the spark that will lead to the liberation of our homeland,' added a more cautious car body repairman in Gaza's Shati refugee camp, 'but it will take years.'

The euphoria that greeted the first Iraqi missile attack on Tel Aviv has evaporated, but you have to look hard for doubts. 'I don't know what the future will bring,' conceded one of the Shuafat shoppers. 'If Saddam Hussein loses,' reflected another when no one else was listening, 'the Israelis will make us pay.'

Jonathan Kuttab, an Arab human rights lawyer still under curfew in the West Bank town of Ramallah, confessed to helplessness. 'It is hard to tell if we are nearer or farther away from a solution to our problem,' he said in a telephone interview. 'It is as if we are all under house arrest, glued to our radios. There is nothing that we can say or do that will influence events – either in the Gulf or here at home. Meanwhile we are vulnerable to attack from both sides, Iraq and Israel.'

Saddam's appeal, according to Sari Nusseibeh, a Palestinian professor, is his defiance. 'He was an Arab ruler who stood up to a super-power. Some people thought there was an element of madness in it. Some thought it was not madness, but honour. Either way, they admired him for it.'

Palestinians woke up depressed on the first morning of the war. They thought Iraq had been devastated. But as the days passed, their admiration revived.

'It continues to increase as they see his ability to withstand the onslaught against him and his ability to retaliate. People admire him as a man who can wage war. The fact that he could send missiles against Israel in fulfillment of his pledges was again a confirmation that he meant what he said. For 43 years the Israelis have been hitting us. Now what we see is missiles going the other way.'

We were talking on Tuesday, the sixth day of the war. That, too, struck an echo for the Palestinians. 'In 1967,' Nusseibeh recalled, 'Israel was able to destroy the military capability of three Arab countries in six days. This time, we've entered the sixth day and

Iraq is still standing up against the United States. Saddam has demolished the myth of the six-day war.'

Nonetheless, the intellectuals, if not the man in the Palestinian refugee camp, acknowledge that Saddam cannot win the war. At best they hope a diplomatic solution might still be found – and might provide a precedent for the Arab-Israeli conflict.

'If, in the end, Saddam is destroyed,' said Sari Nusseibeh, 'it will be extremely difficult within the foreseeable future to address and resolve the Palestinian problem. We would continue in our present state of occupation for years to come.'

He disagreed with commentators who suggested that once the Americans had dealt with Iraq, they would press for a Palestinian solution. 'The USA,' he contended, will not be in a position to do it successfully. In the Arab world, they will not be a credible peacemaker, especially in Palestinian eyes. There will be a lot of anti-American sentiment, which will hamper Washington's manoeuvrability.

'On the Israeli side, it won't be able to do that much either. The USA will be unable to put the degree or kind of pressure on Israel that will force Israel to make the minimal concession that would be acceptable to the Arabs, namely withdrawal from the territories occupied since 1967. Although the Americans may win a military victory, by doing so they will sustain a political defeat – in the Arab world at least'.

But wouldn't the Palestinians also pay a heavy price for jumping on Saddam's bandwagon? Nusseibeh, a champion of the mainstream Palestinian Liberation Organisation, would not admit that its policy was wrong. The PLO chairman, Mr Yasser Arafat, had not supported the invasion of Kuwait, he maintained, but had campaigned for a diplomatic rather than a military way of getting the Iraqis out.

Nusseibeh agreed, however, that was not how it looked to the outside world, which saw Mr Arafat rushing to embrace the Iraqi aggressor. 'The projection of the Palestinian position was badly handled,' he acknowledged.

'The best hope for us,' added the Ramallah lawyer, Mr Jonathan Kuttab, 'is a very quick end to this war so that we can again begin to address our own issue.'

From Eric Silver's Israel Diary
'To whom it may concern' – Saddam
Jewish Chronicle, January 25, 1991

To keep the kids happy last Saturday afternoon, Israel Television screened *Bedknobs and Broomsticks*. I'm not sure they meant it, but there was something decidedly eerie about the shots of the London Blitz.

The echoes in the past week have been irresistible. The rise and fall of the sirens in the night. You wake slowly and resentfully, grope for slippers and dressing gown, round up the family, scurry for shelter. Turn on the radio, obey instructions. Seal the room with sticky tape. Unpack the gas mask, screw on the filter (a refinement since 1940).

You strain your ears for the whistle of a missile, the blast of an explosion, the wail of ambulances or police cars. Wait for the all clear.

A veteran American war correspondent, who won a Pulitzer Prize in Vietnam, reflected on the fatalism of his trade. If the bullet has your name on it... 'What still worries me,' he said, 'is not the one with my name on it, but the one addressed to whom it may concern.'

I've covered wars before, here and in Cyprus. But this is the first I've reported from my spare bedroom.

On the first night, we had barely settled in our bolthole when the *Daily Mirror* phoned and asked me for a piece on our 'typical' family at war. I said I couldn't write but let's talk, then you write it. The gas mask was perched by now on my forehead, the cordless phone was at the ready.

What was my wife wearing? What was my twenty something daughter doing? Reading *Psalms* ('Brilliant,' said the man from the Mirror).

The Jerusalem family Silver was spread across two pages of the *Mirror*. If for nothing else, I shall remember this as the war in which I became a tabloid journalist.

'Why are we being attacked, Daddy?'

Natan Sharansky, Gulag hero and scourge of the Israeli authorities' mishandling of Soviet immigration, hoped nobody would think he was going soft. 'I'm going to make an uncharacteristic remark,' he confided. 'I'm going to pay some compliments to our government.'

We bumped into each other on Sunday, the day after the second raid on Tel Aviv. Sharansky has been through much, but never a war in Israel or in Europe.

'I really feel the government made a good job of preparing the population,' he said. 'They distributed the gas masks and educated us in time.'

Like all parents of small children, Natan and Avital Sharansky had some educating of their own to do. 'The difficult thing,' he said, 'was to prepare the children.' Their elder daughter, Rachel, is four; the younger, Hannah, two.

'We explained to Rachel about Saddam Hussein, why we were being attacked.' For all the preparation, the girls were hysterical when the first alarm sounded.

'Hannah was asleep when they put her in the transparent tent supplied for children too small to wear masks. When she woke up, she didn't know where she was or who these strange people were with funny masks over their faces.

'It was difficult to convince her that behind these gas masks were the same mum and dad. I sang her songs and we gave her toys. It worked so well that after the second alarm she didn't want to leave the tent.'

Flight to freedom ushers in new life

Observer, May 26, 1991

With a tip of the hat to the Queen of Sheba, who was in at the beginning 3,000 years ago, they called it Operation Solomon. Israel yesterday completed evacuation of all the remaining 16,000 Jews of

Ethiopia in a 24-hour airlift that disdained the laws of gravity and the precarious state of Colonel Mengistu's former republic.

Our antiquated Boeing 707 must have earned a place in the *Guinness Book of Records*. When it was built 25 or more years ago, it was meant to carry 190 passengers. Yesterday morning it flew 1,500 nautical miles from Addis Ababa to Tel Aviv with a payload of 450 immigrants, four pilots (just in case), two doctors, an army medic, half a dozen Amharic speaking stewards, two loaders and five journalists.

Air Force Transport Command had ripped out all the seats and replaced them with foam mattresses, covered in bright blue PVC. We sat for three and a half hours with our knees under our chins, dodging the dripping air conditioners and smiling reassurance at uncomprehending peasant children.

The captain, Major Yisrael, was confident he could carry the load without danger. 'We had no problem taking off,' he purred. 'We normally allow 200lb per passenger. These people are so skinny, and are flying without luggage, so they only amount to 100lb.' Four out of 10 passengers were children under 12.

Earlier in the night, a 747 jumbo had left Addis with 1,060 immigrants and arrived at Ben-Gurion with 1,062. One of our stewards, an Ethiopian Jew who went to Israel a decade ago, was on that flight. He reported that two pregnant women were so excited by the adventure that they went into labour. The flying doctors turned the first-class upper deck into a maternity ward. Mothers and baby girls were said to be doing well.

After flying down the politically neutral Red Sea and across the crazy-paving plateau of Ethiopia, we landed at Addis just after dawn. Another Israeli Boeing took off as soon as we cleared the runway. Two more came in after us. Two sets of steps were wheeled into place immediately we taxied to a halt. A column of five airport buses shuttled from the terminal and discharged the migrants like bottles on a conveyor belt.

They clambered up in white woollen shawls, striped headscarves and charity safari suits. Mothers carried their babies, papoose-like, on their backs. Some official had stuck numbers on the immigrants' foreheads, one for each family, so they wouldn't get lost in the post. A mother was so eager to get aboard that she stumbled and had to be picked up. With no need to refuel, we were back in the air after 40 minutes.

Our loadmaster, Benny Lapide, reported that Operation Solomon was going so well that another two planes would probably finish the job 12 hours ahead of schedule. The 25 blue and white military airliners pressed into service were unmarked. The crew, mostly reservists, wore civilian clothes, as did the Israeli security men discreetly posted round the perimeter.

Addis was quiet when we were there, with no sign of movement or sound of gunfire. Israel had paid generously for use of the airport, and an army officer claimed they had forked out a last-minute $35 million in extras to make doubly sure.

On the flight back, the Ethiopian immigrants were orderly and subdued, asking few questions, waiting to be told what to do and where to go. One of the medics, Dr Shaul Baram, said they never asked for help.

The Ethiopians clapped and ululated the safe landing. The conveyor belt swung into action again, with buses taking the immigrants straight from the tarmac to 40 special absorption centres around the country.

Tuvia Ya'alon, one of the Ethiopian stewards, had a sweet and sour tale to tell. He heard his name called by a woman passenger. It was his younger sister, whom he had not seen since he fled to Israel via Sudan in 1985. He hadn't recognised her. She asked after her mother who had escaped with Tuvia. She's fine, the steward replied. He was too busy to explain tactfully that she had died before reaching the Promised Land.

In Unknown Territory
Diplomats see opportunities – and new perils
Financial Times, December 7, 1992
The new world order of the 1990s tempts Israeli diplomacy with unprecedented opportunities. The accompanying disorder haunts it with unprecedented dangers.

The good news for Israel is that its Arab neighbours can no longer rely on the Soviet Union to back them in international forums, to supply them with advanced weapons or to bail them out if they overbid their hand. They have little choice but to ingratiate themselves with the US.

Operation Desert Storm cut President Saddam Hussein of Iraq's army, the most powerful in the Arab world, down to size and divided Israel's potential enemies. The danger of unconventional Iraqi attack, or of a coordinated eastern front, has receded.

For the first time since the 1948 war over Israel's foundation as a state, all the parties directly involved in the Arab-Israeli conflict are negotiating. And since the June elections, Israel has a government which has staked its political capital on making peace, unlike its predecessor under Mr Yitzhak Shamir which appeared interested in the process largely as an exercise in public relations.

The bad news from Israel's perspective is that the collapse of central control in the former Soviet Union has threatened an international supermarket in nuclear know-how and materials. The taboo of non-proliferation is eroding and other suppliers – China and India among them – are joining the rush. Israel's most dedicated foe, the Islamic regime in Iran, has the money and the motivation to buy into the nuclear family and break Israel's regional nuclear monopoly.

At the same time, the end of the Cold War has reduced mainstream demand for sophisticated weapons and the recession has made it very difficult for American and other western producers to turn away Arab business. If the choice is between thousands of aerospace jobs in St Louis, Missouri, and upsetting the Middle East balance, the jobs tend to win.

The peace process itself has stimulated hardliners on both sides. Islamic fundamentalists and Palestinian rejectionists have stepped up attacks, with everything from knives and Molotov cocktails to sub-machine guns and car bombs both within Israel and in the occupied territories. The Shi'ite Hezbollah, inspired actively by Iran and passively by Syria, is harassing Israel and its proxy militia in southern Lebanon and, occasionally, in Israel itself.

On the Israeli side, the Jewish settlers in the West Bank and Gaza Strip have seized on the government's readiness for at least partial withdrawal on the Golan Heights to revive their campaign against territorial compromise on any front. And the most extreme are more disposed to take the law into their own hands.

Mr Yitzhak Rabin, the prime minister, will not be put off easily. 'I believe that we are on a path of no return,' he told a Tel Aviv university audience in mid-November. He remained confident that peace would be reached, even if it took another year or two.

'The reality of the international situation, the regional situation, the genuine need of nations and countries, is to arrive at a resolution of the dispute,' he argued. 'Therefore, even if my position was not received enthusiastically, certainly not in regard to the Golan Heights, I am convinced that we must continue on our way.

'We must distinguish between dealing with terror and continuing, even as we grit our teeth, with the negotiations, and not giving those who wish to sabotage the peace process by means of terror the pleasure of stopping the negotiations.'

On a broader canvas, Mr Yossi Beilin, the deputy foreign minister, defined the object of Israeli diplomacy as 'to use the new situation in order to become a more welcome member of the international club'.

The peace process has already yielded dividends. Israel now has diplomatic relations with 120 countries, the highest number in its 44-year history. Before the 1967 war, the figure was 96. After the 1973 Yom Kippur war, it fell to a low of 62.

Mr Beilin mapped Israel's course: closer integration with the European Community; a constructive role in the rebuilding of the former Soviet republics; cooperation with the new US administration; a concerted international effort to restrict the transfer of nuclear capability, which he described as a 'cloud hanging over us all the time'.

Although the team surrounding President-elect Bill Clinton are not exactly strangers in Jerusalem, Israel is bracing for a change of emphasis on the part of its staunchest ally and most generous benefactor. Mr Binyamin Netanyahu, the former deputy foreign minister and current frontrunner to succeed Mr Shamir as leader of the opposition Likud party, has warned his countrymen to prepare for a sharp drop in US aid, now running at $3bn a year, as the focus in the US shifts to the domestic agenda.

Washington is expected nonetheless to continue working for Middle East peace, if only because the stability of a region which supplies such a large proportion of its energy needs is essential for western economic recovery. As Mr Beilin put it: 'They understand the linkage between home and foreign policy.'

Chapter 8 – 1992-93

Outcasts

Observer, December 20, 1992

The Israeli guards called them the 'Hamas government'. There were 15 Palestinian graduates in the cell in Gaza central prison: four doctors, two engineers, five schoolteachers, two university professors, one pharmacist and one journalist. All but one – the journalist, Taher Shriteh – are now across the border with another 401 deported Muslims in the bleak limbo of southern Lebanon.

The 14 included Dr Salem Salama, the principal of Gaza's Islamic University; Dr Mahmoud Zahar, a surgeon; Dr Abdel Aziz Rantisi, a paediatrician; and Dr Omar Ferwana, who trained at the Leeds University medical school. Zahar and Rantisi have been particularly outspoken champions of the Hamas Islamic Resistance Movement, whose murder of a kidnapped Israeli sergeant major provoked Yitzhak Rabin's centre-left government to banish the 415 alleged activists for two years.

Palestinian sources in Gaza estimate that at least 60 per cent of the staff of the Islamic University there have been either detained or deported. The Israelis rounded up about 1,600 Palestinians in Gaza and the West Bank after Sergeant-Major Nissim Toledano was abducted on the way to his border police station near Tel Aviv last Sunday.

Taher Shriteh, a 32-year-old father of three who freelances for a dozen international news organisations (and the ultra-Zionist *Jerusalem Post*), was the odd man out. He is the only one of the detainees to have been set free, and even that was a close call. Along with his 14 cellmates, he was sent almost to the Lebanese border before the army thought better of it.

His story confirms the impressions that the Israelis acted precipitately and with no regard for their own law, let alone the fourth Geneva Convention. At least until Shriteh was brought back to Gaza, they were never served with deportation notices or advised of their right of appeal. The security services could muster no evidence that Shriteh was linked with the Islamic fundamentalists.

Another 34 detainees (who remain in custody) were also taken off the buses at the last minute in what the army spokesman admitted were cases of mistaken identity. Thirty-two replacements were rushed north in their place.

The 15 men in Shriteh's cell were ordered at about 8pm on Wednesday to be ready to move, he told *The Observer* yesterday. A guard said they were being transferred to another prison. They assumed he meant the Ketziot camp in the Negev desert, where Israel normally holds its 'administrative detainees', security suspects jailed without trial. No one mentioned Lebanon.

'They tied my hands behind my back with three plastic cuffs and bound my ankles with three more,' Shriteh recalled. 'Then I was blindfolded. We were put on a bus, with at least six soldiers to guard us. They punched me a couple of times for talking to another prisoner. We were surprised that the journey was taking so long. Ketziot is not that far from Gaza.

'Around midnight one of the soldiers asked: Who is Taher Shrieh? I said: Me, and they took me off the bus. They added metal cuffs on both my wrists and ankles and put a hood over my head, then they bundled me into a van.

'I was made to lie down on the floor with soldiers sitting on benches on either side of me. They put their feet on me and told me not to move. Whenever I did try to ease my position, they kicked and punched me.

'When we got back to Gaza prison, they removed the handcuffs and blindfold, but kept my legs tied. I asked: Where am I? I'd been there often enough before, but after about nine hours on the road I was confused. My hands were swollen and my arms very painful.

'Then I collapsed on the floor. I didn't lose consciousness, but it took me a minute or two to regain my strength and my bearings. I was extremely tired. One of the soldiers kicked me again. I started crying. I realised what I was doing, but I couldn't control it. I never thought I would be humiliated like that when I had done nothing wrong.'

Shriteh was put in solitary confinement and questioned by two Shin Beth security service interrogators. One asked why he had come back from Lebanon. Only then, he said, did he realise that was where the buses were going. They asked him which Palestinian organisation he favoured. He replied that if he was identified with any one group, he wouldn't be able to do his job as a reporter. Eventually, they seem to have been convinced. Four days after he was detained they sent him home. It was his fifth arrest; so far the only charge ever laid against him was for owning an illegal fax machine.

By banishing 415 Palestinians, Israel was gambling with both the Washington peace talks and the international credit Yitzhak Rabin's election won last summer. Ministers were aware of the risks, but calculated that the storm would blow itself out and the Palestinian delegation would return to the table. Officials argued that Hamas was the enemy not only of Israel, but of peace and of the mainstream Palestinian nationalists who are seeking a compromise settlement.

Hamas, founded by Sheikh Ahmed Yassin after the intifada uprising broke out five years ago, opposes the existence of a Jewish state in any part of 'Muslim' Palestine, and rejects the peace negotiations root and branch. It claims the allegiance of up to 40 per cent of Gaza and West Bank Palestinians. More conservative estimates put its maximum support at a fluctuating 30 per cent.

The Israelis believe Hamas has a hard core of about 100 men under arms. According to Palestinian reports, the group receives $30 million a year from Iran, which is also said to be training 3,000 Hamas fighters in Lebanon, Sudan and Iran itself.

The peace conference is not due to resume until after President-elect Bill Clinton's inauguration. One left-wing minister said privately yesterday that they were already receiving hints from Washington that the American bark in support of a United Nations censure was worse than its bite.

Leaders of the intifada responded by calling a general strike, but Palestinian predictions are divided. Hanna Siniora, editor of the East Jerusalem daily *Al Fajr*, which backs Yasser Arafat's Fatah, insisted: 'The deportations are the end of the peace process. If we go back to the negotiations, it would mean we were accepting a policy that could end in population transfer. We are against the eviction of Palestinians from their land, whether it is wholesale or retail. This is a precedent that will be followed with other large groups. This time it is Hamas. Next time it could be the Popular Front, then the Democratic Front, and then it could be us.'

But the veteran mayor of Bethlehem, Eliaz Freij, a member of the negotiating team, was more sanguine. Surveying yet another unprofitable Christmas in Manger Square, he said: 'Christmas means joy and peace. We have no joy, we have no peace. But by next Christmas things will be much better. The peace process will continue.'

Both Labour and left-wing Meretz ministers defended the mass deportation as the best of a bad choice. One Meretz MP, Naomi Chazan, called all the options 'obscene', but she could see no acceptable alternative.

Rabin justified deportation as the least inhumane of the measures considered by his cabinet after Hamas hit squads had killed Toledano and five other Israeli soldiers since the beginning of December. 'It means the least damage in life or property,' he contended. 'Let's not forget the mood of the Israeli public and the demands for the imposition of the death penalty, for more curfews, or for relaxing the open-fire restrictions.'

It was this public anger, accompanied by a rapidly declining confidence in the prime minister's capacity to fulfil his election pledge of 'peace with security', that prompted the government to do something drastic. Its dilemma was not whether to act but how, given that the gunmen live among the civilian population and that Israel has an outspoken human rights movement, often backed by the courts.

Only one cabinet member, Labour's justice minister David Liba'i, opposed the deportation, but doveish Labour and Meretz ministers were excruciatingly embarrassed by the decision. They feared that if they resisted, Rabin would bring into his coalition two parties opposed to the peace process, the National Religious Party and Tsomet. Ran Cohen, a Meretz deputy minister, went so far yesterday as to demand that the 415 be brought back.

Ziad Abu-Zayad, an adviser to the Palestinian negotiating team, accused the Israeli Left of betrayal. 'It was a knife in my back,' he protested. 'It was a knife in the backs of all people who want peace and a two-state solution. Now people are saying only Hamas is fighting against the occupation, and we are called collaborators.'

If any good is to come out of this dismal episode, it is that the Israeli Left, in the cabinet and the Knesset, now recognises that the only way to resuscitate the peace process is to make the Palestinians an offer they cannot refuse. They know that if they fail to convince Rabin of this, they will forfeit all credibility with their own voters.

Eric Silver's Israel
Listening to the sounds of the Golan Heights
Jewish Chronicle, May 26, 1993

The first time I climbed the Golan Heights was on the back of an open lorry crammed with kibbutzniks at the beginning of July, 1967. It was barely a month after Israeli soldiers, tanks, artillery and planes had flushed the Syrian army out of the Heights. The mines had been cleared, the last stragglers rounded up, and the plateau's 452 square miles had just been opened to civilian traffic.

We drove across the flimsy Daughters of Jacob Bridge spanning the Jordan, north of the Sea of Galilee, and up a dusty, twisting road to an old customs house, fortified by the Syrians and pounded into submission by the Israelis.

We stopped in the shade of a eucalyptus grove and looked back to Kfar Hanassi, where my companions had lived for 20 years under the threat of Syrian shelling and hit-and-run sabotage raids.

They were shocked by what they saw. There was the kibbutz – which has a large British-born population – cottages, dining hall, swimming pool, the lot, five miles away and clearly visible to the most myopic of enemy artillerymen. They had always believed they were hidden behind a fold in the Galilee hills.

I went back the other day. The customs house was still standing, a shabby concrete shell, pockmarked and neglected. It has given its name to a road junction, where you turn right for the Israeli settler township of Katzrin. The only difference was that the customs house was painted with the slogan 'We're not budging from the Golan'.

The message is everywhere, on walls, hillsides, car stickers, T-shirts and baseball caps. The 12,000 Israelis who have made their homes in 32 Golan settlements since the Six-Day War are taking to the hoardings, if not yet to the barricades.

They have heard the Israeli Prime Minister, Yitzhak Rabin, talk of territorial compromise, and President Hafez al-Assad of Syria speak of 'full peace' for 'full withdrawal'. They do not like the sound of it.

I drove on to an observation point where a guide with a bus-load of German tourists was pointing across the narrow United Nations buffer zone to the black basalt ruins of Kuneitra, a former Syrian garrison town Israel evacuated under a disengagement agreement after the 1973 Yom Kippur War. Damascus promised to rebuild Kuneitra, but instead left it an empty propaganda shrine.

Merom Golan, a kibbutz affiliated to Mr Rabin's Labour Party, is less than two miles west of Kuneitra. Some of its settlers had once planned to make their homes in the town. Now they know they will be among the first evacuees if Israel yields any territory for peace.

Like all the Golan settlers, the 160 kibbutz members are divided over the prospect. Is peace worth the sacrifice? Can Assad be trusted? Should they resist? If so, how and how far? At their most optimistic, they hope, in the words of another slogan, for 'Peace *with* the Golan'.

At their most pessimistic, they suspect that Mr Rabin and Mr Assad will never reach an accord anyway.

They came here as an expression of a national consensus. The Golan, louring over the towns and villages of Upper Galilee, was viewed as a strategic asset Israel could never afford to give back. To make certain of keeping it, Jews had to sink roots. Now the rules have changed, and they are not sure the consensus is holding.

'It's not fair,' complained Uri Kerzer, a 38-year-old factory worker and father of two who has lived in Merom Golan since 1974. 'We cannot plan ahead. We live in terrible uncertainty. Nobody wants to invest in the Golan any more.

'I voted for Mr Rabin. I would still like to vote for him, but only if he assures me he won't give back the Heights. If he does give them back, I won't vote for him again.'

Diana Frankenthal, a 34-year-old technical writer in the kibbutz engine plant, was more fatalistic. 'I should like to believe we will be able to stay here,' she said. 'But if you read the map objectively, we are on the front line. I would like reality to be different, but I don't believe we shall be able to stay. If there is a referendum which endorses evacuation, I'll accept it – with a lot of pain.'

What, then, are the alternatives? Would the settlers, like their counterparts who left Sinai under the 1979 Israeli-Egyptian peace treaty, take government compensation and go?

'It's not just a matter of money,' Ms Frankenthal explained. 'In the end, people will take the money, but they have spent a good part of their lives here. They believed in something; they still believe in it. That's something no money in the world can compensate for.'

Would the settlers be prepared to stay on under Syrian rule? In Katzrin, a town of 4,500 established 16 years ago, the Likud deputy mayor, Meir Monitz, delivered an emphatic 'no'.

'Even the Syrians don't want to live under President Assad, so how can anybody expect us to live under his dictatorship? There is no chance ever that people here would agree.'

Would they leave peacefully? In Moshav Nov, a religious farming community in the southern Golan, 43-year-old Shmuel Hillman and his wife Kitty insisted they would not just pack their bags and go. Would they resist an order to evacuate? 'What we personally will do, I can't say,' Shmuel replied, 'but there's no way we'll use arms against brother Jews.'

For a last word, I drove back five miles and 26 years to Kfar Hanassi, which would once again be on the front line if Mr Rabin returned the Golan to Syria.

'We definitely wouldn't want to go back to the situation as it was before 1967,' Aryeh Wolfin, a teacher who joined the kibbutz from London more than 30 years ago, asserted. 'But if the Syrians are prepared for real peace, I can't see a reason for not compromising on the Golan, so long as it is completely demilitarised. If that means settlements can't be retained, that is the price we shall have to pay.'

Taking a chance with a Middle East peace deal

The European, September 2, 1993

Yitzhak Rabin, the most calculating of generals, most ponderous of prime ministers, is taking the gamble of a lifetime. It is far from certain that the volatile Israeli public will buy the 'Gaza-Jericho first' peace plan he sprang on an unsuspecting nation this week.

As recently as a month ago, Rabin was rejecting any idea of negotiating with the Palestine Liberation Organisation (PLO). Apparently, Shimon Peres, the foreign minister, convinced him that Israel had no alternative if it wanted to show results.

The West Bank and Gaza Arab negotiating team demonstrated in session after session that it had no authority to take decisions – on elections for a self-governing council or for the powers it would exercise.

The Israelis and the Palestinians recognised that time was running out. Rabin was elected on a platform of 'peace with security'. He predicted an agreement on Palestinian autonomy within nine months to a year. Yet after 14 months of a Labour-led coalition, committed to territorial compromise, the talks were getting nowhere.

The next Knesset elections, due in 1996, were casting a backward shadow. 'The time has come,' Rabin told coalition MPs on Monday, 'to take a chance for peace.' On the other side of the barricades, PLO chairman Yasser Arafat was rapidly losing credibility among the 1.8 million Palestinians of the occupied territories. They could see no sign of autonomy, let alone a Palestinian state. The Israelis were still sitting on their backs. And the PLO was no longer capable of buying allegiance.

Saudi Arabia and other Gulf benefactors taught the Palestinians a lesson by cutting off funds after Arafat applauded Saddam Hussein's invasion of Kuwait.

Palestinian economists estimate that PLO subsidies to the West Bank and Gaza Strip have collapsed from $350 million a year at the height of the intifada in 1988 to $40 million today. The Islamic fundamentalist Hamas, who resist any compromise with the Jewish state, are taking up the slack, exploiting the disenchantment, even though they are not pumping in cash on a comparable scale. Arafat was fighting for his political life – and for that of his movement.

So both Israeli and PLO leaders urgently needed something tangible to revive their domestic appeal. Israel had been talking for months about 'Gaza first', an opening gambit for limited self-rule that could be implemented without recourse to elections, but the Palestinians were worried that this might turn into 'Gaza last'. They needed a foothold on the West Bank too. Once that was appreciated by the Israelis, Jericho – an isolated oasis city, conquered by, but never sacred to, the ancient Israelites – was the best option. And Rabin was no doubt persuaded that, with the PLO on its knees, this was the best time to seal it.

Even Israelis who sympathise with what Rabin is doing are worried that he has not prepared the ground well enough. Although many of the Israeli taboos against talking to the PLO have been eroded since Labour's victory in the 1992 elections, the prospect of an agreement negotiated explicitly with the PLO leadership in Tunis has shocked many Israelis.

Gaza-Jericho confronts Israelis and Palestinians with a moment of truth. Since the 1978 Camp David agreement between Israel and Egypt, just over half of Israelis have supported territorial compromise, if the terms were right. But it was inevitable that the first withdrawal from the ancestral homeland would be traumatic.

More specifically, the deal has forced the Israeli right to take a stand. The Likud leader, Binjamin Netanyahu, accused Rabin of 'saving a bankrupt organisation whose goal is to destroy us'. He told a radio interviewer: 'We are witnessing the absurd sight of the Rabin-Peres government saving the PLO from breaking apart, giving it a Palestinian state instead which will endanger the very existence of Israel.' With a vulnerable majority of 67 to 53 in the 120-seat Knesset, Rabin can look forward to an autumn of unrelenting parliamentary warfare. In the West Bank settlements, a group of militant rabbis is going further and talking of real insurrection. 'We warn the government,' they said after an emergency assembly, 'about the danger of a split in the country and a civil war.'

The opposition's strength will be tested in the streets. Until then, no one can know how many of Israel's four million Jews will resist. The police have announced that they have contingency plans to deal with disturbances. They quelled a riot outside the prime minister's office on Monday night when the cabinet endorsed the peace plan.

But if Rabin is to outface his enemies, he will have to convince Israelis that he is not pre-empting the big, strategic decisions on Palestinian statehood, final borders and the disputed city of Jerusalem. Ever since Camp David, Israel has insisted on a trial period in which to assess how far it can trust the Palestinians – to manage their own affairs and to live peacefully with their Jewish neighbours.

On the Palestinian side, Arafat will have to assure the doubters that he is not selling their birthright for two paltry enclaves. He will need explicit links between the 'interim interim' stage of Gaza-Jericho, the full-blown interim self-rule for Gaza and the rest of the West Bank, and a final resolution of the conflict.

It will be a painful balancing act for two national leaders who have never met, and who are unlikely to enjoy each other's company if they ever do.

Future shock

Jerusalem Report, October 21, 1993

The little boy, a tableau glimpsed through the car window, looks about four years old. He stands alone in bare feet and ragged shirt on a street-corner garbage dump in Gaza city glumly waving a red, green, black and white Palestinian flag at no one in particular.

The forlorn image says more about Gaza in the fall of 1993 than all the speeches and slogans, the rallies and counter-rallies, that followed the reluctant handshake on the White House lawn. Yasser Arafat is inheriting a wasteland that nobody else wants – one of the world's most crowded pieces of real estate, with 2,000 people to every square kilometre, whose only resources are cheap labour and citrus plantations.

The main roads are rutted and overflowing with sewage. Most of the back lanes of the towns, villages and refugee camps are unpaved tracks through the sand. The stinking refuse on every patch of spare ground looks as if it hasn't been collected since the intifada exploded almost six years ago.

The strip's 720,000 Palestinian inhabitants, about 450,000 of them refugees from the 1948 Arab-Israeli war, are ill-prepared to rule themselves under the Gaza-Jericho agreement. They are fatalistic, apprehensive and divided, accustomed to being objects, not subjects.

'Arafat will provide,' says Muhammad Kafarna, shopping in Gaza city. He is 25 and worked in a Tel Aviv shirt factory until Israel closed the old Green Line border at the end of March. 'I trust in Allah up above and Arafat down below,' he smiles.

Outside a gas station in the Shati camp, home to more than 40,000 refugees, half a dozen men in their mid-20s are loafing on white plastic chairs. Do they expect things to get better? '*Inshallah*,' shrugs one of them, Nasser al-Shram, a 27-year-old driver; 'God willing.'

Nasser is married with four children. He lives with an extended family of 13 in a two-roomed cement house measuring 100 square meters (1,100 square feet). Does he hope to move his wife and children to a home of their own, perhaps outside the camp? 'It would be nice,' he says, without conviction.

What future do Nasser and his friends see for their families? More shrugs. What dreams do they have for themselves and their children? It's as if they don't understand the question. Pressed for an answer, one of them spits back: 'What do you want me to say? That I want to be a pilot?'

As we drive away my interpreter, Adnan Abu Hassna, a local journalist, muses: 'People here are not used to having a future. They have forgotten that they have a right to dream.'

Abu Hassna estimates that 40 percent of the Gaza Strip Palestinians belong to Arafat's Al Fatah and 20 per cent to the fundamentalist opposition of Hamas and Islamic Jihad. Other observers put total support for the Muslim extremists, active and passive, at between 30 and 40 per cent.

The hard-core Muslim fanatics are girding to resist the new Palestinian regime. For all the talk of a truce between the mainstream PLO and its rejectionist enemies, mayhem is in the air.

Hani Arhim, a black-bearded Jihad activist who has spent a total of five years in Israeli jails, spells it out: 'Anyone who gives the Jews any part of Palestine is a traitor. The conflict will go on for as long as there is a Jewish state.'

On the day Yasser Arafat and Yitzhak Rabin went to Washington, 38-year-old Hani visited the grave of his younger brother, Sami, shot dead four years ago when he tried to escape from Israeli soldiers who had come to arrest them both. Hani surrendered and survived.

'I tell my friends,' say Hani, in his home in the Zaitoun district of Gaza city, 'that those who lie under the ground condemn Arafat. This is not a peace between the people, but a peace between the leaders.'

Does he agree with those who would put a price on Arafat's head? 'Arafat and anyone who negotiates over a single speck of our Muslim soil deserve to be killed.'

If the Islamic gunmen have been restrained since the March closure, it is because Israel has taken the initiative, seeking, harassing, arresting or shooting. The proposed Palestinian security forces will have to be equally aggressive. Hamas and Islamic Jihad have the strength and the motivation to endanger the flimsy peace.

But much will also hinge on the quality of leadership Arafat deploys, the trust and confidence it engenders. The refugees have to be weaned from the fantasy that one day they will go home to the towns and villages they fled 45 years ago. And they will have to be taught patience. Their lives are not going to change overnight, whatever PLO propaganda is telling them.

Eyad Sarraj, director of the internationally funded Gaza Community Mental Health Program and a member of the Palestinian's Washington negotiating team, is not sure the leaders will be up to the task.

'People here have sustained themselves on the dream of liberating all of Palestine,' the London-trained psychiatrist explains. 'Now they have to come to terms with the fact that Palestine is going to be shared with Israel. The danger is that the grief of this realisation will be compounded by disappointment. In the short term, there won't be more money, there won't be more jobs.'

Sarraj fears a collective and individual breakdown. The six years of intifada have put everyone under chronic stress. 'The children lost their childhood through constant exposure to trauma,' he says. 'Tens of thousands of adults were detained or imprisoned. Many of them were tortured. We found that 30 percent of those who have been in prison have psychiatric disorders. The most common expression is violence in the home. They beat their wives and kids. You have a whole nation that needs rehabilitating.'

At the same time, national solidarity has fragmented in the last two years, as the uprising has waned. 'In the earlier years,' Sarraj recalls, 'people were Palestinians, first and second. Now other identities are becoming a more secure base – your family, your tribal or political faction, your religion.

'If we don't have the necessary leadership,' the psychiatrist predicts, 'these divisions will deepen. And this will lead to fighting because there is a build-up of energy and tension, which has to come out. If it doesn't come constructively, it will be destructive.'

How does Sarraj rate the changes? '50-50,' he answers. 'I can't be more hopeful than that.'

The psychiatrist's anxiety is shared by the 5,000 Israelis in the 16 settlements of Gush Katif on the southwestern flank of the Gaza

Strip – and by the veteran kibbutzniks of Yad Mordechai and other old-established communities on the Israeli side of the Green Line.

In Gan Or, a farming village barely five kilometres (three miles) from the turbulent Arab town of Khan Yunis, ex-New Yorker Susan Shaul fears a bloodbath between rival Palestinians. 'It would,' she admits, 'be too close for comfort.'

Susan's Canadian-born husband, Mike, prefers not to think about it. 'What I do,' he says, 'is just keep working. If I stop to think, I don't move ahead.' Mike has been growing cherry tomatoes in Gan Or since 1978. Last year he grossed about £115,000.

Mike, a 40-year-old father of three sons, confides that it wouldn't be a disaster if they had to move. 'I didn't come to Gaza for political reasons,' he says. 'I came to make a living as a farmer. It was a place the government wanted Jews to settle. But they would have to compensate me, and that could mean half a million dollars.'

During the interim period of Palestinian autonomy, Mike trusts the army to protect the village, though military sources say they are still working out how to do it. The general staff is expected to present a range of options – and budgets – to the government by early November. But Mike says if an Arab policeman ordered him around, he couldn't go on living there.

If Gaza became part of a Palestinian state, five years down the line, would the Shauls and their neighbours stay on? 'Nobody would stay,' Mike snorts, 'not one person.' Susan agreed: 'With all the hatred the Arabs feel for us, it wouldn't be conceivable for either side.'

Four kilometres (2.5 miles) north of the Erez crossing, Yad Mordechai is preparing to become a border kibbutz again. It was founded in 1943 by Polish pioneers from the left-wing Hashomer Hatza'ir youth movement. In May 1948, it blocked an Egyptian thrust toward Tel Aviv for six vital days before the young defenders were forced to retreat, with 26 dead and 35 wounded – having killed 300 Egyptians.

The kibbutz was retaken five months later. Army engineers have reconstructed the battlefield, complete with armoured cars and life-sized models of Egyptian soldiers in British army helmets zigzagging across the dunes toward the hilltop trenches.

Yehoshua ('Shike') Katzir was one of the 1948 heroes. Later, in the 1950s, he killed Palestinian fedayeen infiltrating from the Gaza Strip. Now aged 78, he is eager for peace, but resigned to the probability that the founders' grandsons will have to pick up the burden.

'I believe that the army, and we ourselves, will have to take more precautions,' he says. 'Maybe terrorists will try to pass through. Maybe they will lay mines here and there. But these will not be the acts of organised Palestinian authorities. It will be the opposition to those authorities. I'm more concerned that thieves may come at night – as they do even now – and steal our horses, cattle or irrigation pipes.'

But will it endanger our existence? 'No! No!' the old warrior scorns. 'We are strong enough. This is not 1948. And the 50s won't come back either. We had no real army then. Today we do. The soldiers who are in Gaza now will have to spread out along the border. They'll find it more pleasant than shooting stone-throwing children.'

Inshallah, as they say south of the old-new border.

Filling in the blanks

Los Angeles Jewish Journal, September 17-23, 1993

The interim Israeli-Palestinian accord will sink or swim on the common interest of the two sides in suppressing the extremists who will try to destroy it.

That much is agreed. The trouble is that because of the pace and secrecy of the negotiations, neither the Israelis nor the Palestinians have yet thought through what this cooperation is going to mean.

According to the draft declaration of principles, the Palestinian police will be responsible for internal security in the self-governing enclaves of Gaza and Jericho (and later of the rest of the West Bank). The Israel Defence Forces will be responsible for the safety of Israelis.

But this leaves an infinity of potential turf disputes. What if a Palestinian terrorist attacks Israelis, in a settlement or on the highway, then retreats into self-governing Palestinian territory? What, more prosaically, if an Israeli car is involved in a crash in the Arab zone? Or if a Jew goes to buy dates in the Jericho market and gets into a fight with a vendor?

Police minister Moshe Shahal confessed at a foreign press briefing last Monday that he had no final answers. 'The Palestinians,' he said, 'have an interest in peace and stability. I believe they will do their utmost to cooperate.' But he added that the level of cooperation and the details of how it will work would have to be left until the declaration of principles was signed. Only then would negotiations begin on implementing the deal.

Shahal favoured the idea of joint patrols. He has been studying the experience of English and French-speaking communities in the Pacific islands of the New Hebrides, each of whom police their own people. He was prepared to let the Palestinians import former soldiers from the Palestinian National Army, currently based in Jordan, and train them as police, but he dismissed the kind of strength – 30,000 – being cited. The whole of the Israeli police force, on both sides of the old Green Line border, he said, numbered only 20,000. At present, the Palestinians – with Israel's blessing – have 100 men in a police-training program.

The army, like the police and most of Yitzhak Rabin's cabinet, were kept in the dark. The security services may have had contingency plans, but none of them knew where the starting line would be. They are having to go back to square one.

The deputy chief-of-staff, Major General Amnon Shahak, betrayed some of their resentment when he appeared before the Knesset foreign affairs and defence committee. The IDF, he said, would have a hard time fighting terror. The security problems would be very complex.

President Ezer Weizman, who has been both a commander and a peace negotiator, bluntly reminded the army brass that it was the politicians' role to set the problems, and the generals' role to come up with solutions. If they couldn't think of solutions, he added, they should resign.

When a television interviewer chided foreign minister Shimon Peres for not consulting the security experts, he retorted: 'When Rabin and I meet behind closed doors, remember who is in the room – two former prime ministers, two former defence ministers and a former chief-of-staff.'

The incumbent army and police chiefs are not yet showing their hands but some of their retired colleagues have been thinking aloud about the criteria that would have to apply if Israelis are to be satisfied that they are not being exposed to unreasonable dangers.

Ephraim Sneh, a freshman Labour Knesset member, served as head of the West Bank administration in the mid-80s. Before that he commanded the medical team on the Entebbe rescue operation. He retired with the rank of brigadier-general.

'We have to slice it in several layers,' he told me. 'First, the good intentions of the mainstream Palestinians are very important – their readiness to cooperate, their will and capability to maintain law and order. That doesn't mean we're dependent on that, but it will be a test of how serious they are about the entire agreement.

'Then there are those within the Palestinian community who oppose the agreement. If they are not tamed by the Palestinian authorities, we shall have to deal with them – and we should have complete freedom to do so. We bear the responsibility for the overall security of Israelis, inside the territories and outside the territories.

'It will be very helpful, especially to the atmosphere that should prevail, if the Palestinian authorities diligently and seriously try to contain terrorists. But the detailed agreement, which will be signed hopefully next year, should give us the freedom to act on our own, where needed and if needed.'

Other security veterans are not sure Israel will be able to retain the freedom of operation it has enjoyed up to now. A former senior officer of the Shin Bet internal security service, who preferred not to be named, argues: 'I don't believe that Israel will be able to maintain the same control of internal security. People who think the

IDF and the Shin Bet will be able to go every day and arrest people are living in a dream world.'

He suggested that intelligence cooperation between Israel and the Palestinians would have to start straight away, during the period of the interim agreement. But Israel would still need to gather information independently, and to devise new ways of fighting terror.

'I am saying,' the former Shin Bet man explained, 'Israel has to sharpen its intelligence activity. We shall have to have higher intelligence capability and knowledge. At the same time, we shall need to fight terrorism without risking the peace agreement that has been reached. That will mean a much sharper, more clandestine, operation ability.'

And what if all this fails, if the Palestinians are incapable of maintaining order and decline to cooperate? Ephraim Sneh has a bleak, but brutal answer; 'People tend to forget who is the strongest power in this region. Allow me to remind you: it's the IDF. While talking about peace, people forget the huge military strength that lies behind it. If all else fails, we shall have to take other measures to protect our security.'

Jordan opens the door

Los Angeles Jewish Journal, October 8-14, 1993

Crown Prince Hassan's encounter last weekend with foreign minister Shimon Peres was not the first between Jordanian and Israeli leaders. But it was the first to have been openly acknowledged. The Hashemites are coming out of that particular closet.

In fact, the dialogue dates back to the partition of Palestine in 1948, when Golda Meir and other Zionist emissaries crossed the Jordan for clandestine talks with King Hussein's grandfather, King Abdullah.

Since then the Israeli media have logged dozens of 'secret' meetings – In Jordan, Israel and abroad – between King Hussein and his supposed enemies. On one occasion, the Jordanian ruler is even believed to have sat down with the former hard-line Likud

Prime Minister, Yitzhak Shamir, though he always refused to meet his right-wing predecessor, Menachem Begin.

The talks never quite bore fruit. The nearest to a successful conclusion was a meeting in London in April, 1987, with Peres, who was at that time foreign minister under Shamir in a national-unity government. The King and the minister drafted what became known as the London Agreement, a formula for implementing Peres's long-cherished ambition of starting to make peace with 'Jordan first'.

It was immediately vetoed by Shamir, who rejected – as he still does – any notion of bargaining away territory captured in the 1967 war. In his eyes, compromising with Jordan was no more acceptable than compromising with the Palestinians. The West Bank was to all intents and purposes part of the historic Land of Israel.

What was groundbreaking about last weekend's Washington talks was that the Jordanians courted the publicity of a handshake and joint press conference on the White House lawn.

The Hashemites, the most calculating of Arab rulers, wanted a share of the action. They were worried that the Palestine Liberation Organisation was going to make peace without taking Jordan's interests into account. And in effect Arafat has taken much of the limelight with the historic PLO-Israeli agreement and his meeting this week with Yitzhak Rabin in Cairo, which was taking place as we went to press.

At the Rabin-Arafat meeting, it was announced that a special liaison committee will meet next week in Cairo, and PLO delegates to that committee were named.

More controversially, Arafat named Faisal Husseini, the senior Palestinian negotiator in the Israel talks in Washington, as chairman of a committee that would deal with Jerusalem. This brought an immediate response from health minister Chaim Ramon of the Labor Party that Jerusalem was not on the agenda at the current discussions.

With regard to Jordan, Israeli commentators noted, however, that Amman was still treading cautiously. The King sent his brother to meet Peres. A first public encounter slightly lower than the summit was less likely to provoke the domestic opposition – the Islamic fundamentalists and the Palestinians living on the East Bank of the Jordan.

The cautious tone has been maintained. Prince Hassan denied that Jordan was opting out of the Arab boycott against Israel, even though he endorsed President Bill Clinton's proposal to establish a joint economic commission. Amman continues to insist that it is not looking for a separate deal.

What, then, are Jordan's objectives? First and foremost, the King wants to secure a greater measure of influence over an eventual Israeli-Palestinian settlement. He is particularly concerned about future relations between the two banks of the river.

At least half of the East Bank population of three million are of Palestinian origin. They carry Jordanian passports. About a quarter of a million still live in refugee camps, but the rest are integrated into Jordanian society. There are strong business and family links between the two banks. The Hashemites, as descendents of the Prophet Mohammed, retain a strong affinity with the Muslim holy places in Jerusalem.

The form and terms under which the Palestinians west of the river attain independence will affect the stability and the identity of the Hashemite Kingdom. The King needs to be involved. The Israel-PLO agreement, negotiated with a minimum of consultation, was both a shock and a warning.

The Jordanians want a say in whatever security arrangements are negotiated, short-term and long; specifically they would like 70,000 refugees who left the West Bank after the 1967 war to go back.

The King also does not relish being left out of the international financial arrangements being made to underwrite the Israeli-Palestinian deal. Jordan has a foreign debt of about $12 billion and a gross national product of about $5 billion a year. It has shared the cost of the Palestinians tragedy for 45 years. It feels entitled to a share of its economic resolution.

On the bilateral level, Amman is disturbed that Israel might go along with major civil-engineering projects, like a canal between the

Mediterranean and the Dead Sea, to the exclusion of its own favourite, a canal along the Arava Valley from the Gulf of Aqaba to the Dead Sea.

Jordan wants this Red-Dead canal as a source of water for the mineral-rich Dead Sea, so that it can exploit more of the sweet water that flows into it from the Jordan further north. It is also looking for joint hydroelectric schemes with Israel.

A risk for King Hussein is that he may provoke his stronger and less accommodating neighbour, President Hafez Assad of Syria.

There are, however, limits to Syria's capacity to whip Jordan into line. Assad still hopes to win back the occupied Golan Heights in a deal of his own with Rabin, even if he has to wait until the Israeli public has digested the Palestinians rapprochement. He can't afford to alienate Rabin too far.

No less to the point, he is still wooing the Clinton administration. Since the disintegration of Syria's Soviet patron, Assad needs an American umbrella, financial and military. And he knows that to earn it he has to join the 'good guys club' and persuade Washington to delete Syria from its list of countries that foster terrorism.

Sabotaging the Middle East's best chance of peace in half a century would hardly be the way to go about it.

Eric Silver's Israel

Strange encounters of the Israeli-Palestinian kind

Jewish Chronicle, December 17, 1993

Nothing better illustrates the Alice-in-Wonderland world of Israeli-Palestinian relations at the end of 1993 than last week's visit to Tunis by housing minister Binyamin Ben-Eliezer at the personal invitation of PLO leader Yasser Arafat.

Baghdad-born Mr Ben-Eliezer, known by his Arabic nickname of Fuad, is a former military governor of the West Bank. After arriving in Israel as a boy, he was a career solider for 28 years, retiring with the rank of brigadier-general. As commander of an elite cross-border reconnaissance unit, he was wounded eight times.

The PLO 'colonel' who looked after his programme in Tunis had spent 17 years in an Israeli prison for security offences and was deported at the beginning of the intifada – by General Amram Mitzna, now mayor of Haifa, to whom he sent greetings. Mr Arafat's adviser on West Bank affairs, Akram Haniya, who was deported earlier by Mr Ben-Eliezer, asked to meet him. They had a nostalgic dinner together.

The minister and his Austrian-born wife, Dolly, were entertained to lunch by Mr Arafat's spouse, Suha. She is the daughter of Raymonda Tawil, a flamboyant Palestinian publicist of the 1970s, who was put under house arrest by none other than governor Ben-Eliezer, who once told me while he was still in uniform: 'There is no such thing as a benign occupation.'

Mr Ben-Eliezer, who is close to Prime Minister Yitzhak Rabin and backs the peace process to the hilt, arrived in Tunis with an Israeli bodyguard. The Tunisian authorities refused to let him carry a gun. When their PLO hosts saw how distressed the bodyguard was about this, they offered him a choice of revolver or Kalashnikov assault rifle from their armoury – an offer he prudently declined.

The housing minister's media adviser, Ofra Preuss, flew in two days ahead of her boss to supervise arrangements. She worked with him on the West Bank 15 years ago and is still a lieutenant colonel. She took leave of absence to handle his public relations.

The Tunis trip was her first visit to an Arab country. She was greeted at the airport by a Palestinian security man, who announced: 'I'm from the PLO. I'm your bodyguard.'

'I watched Rabin and Arafat shake hands,' Ms Preuss said after returning to Jerusalem. 'It did nothing for me. But when that man said he was my PLO bodyguard, for the first time I felt that something irreversible had happened.'

Even after the disappointment of Monday the thirteenth.

The postponement of the December 13 deadline feels more like a stay of execution than a reprieve to the 35-Jewish families of Vered Yericho, the nearest settlement to the Arab oasis town.

Gershon and Sarah Richter grow grapes and dates on 10 acres of thin, irrigated soil below the Mount of the Temptation. Wherever the borders of Jericho are finally drawn, their land will be on the inside looking out.

Even if their home stays under Israeli control, they will have to cross Arab territory to their fields.

When he is not farming, Gershon runs a mobile tyre-repair business. Sarah is the headmistress of the regional primary school, 20 miles up the Jordan Valley.

Like most of their neighbours on the 13-year-old moshav, they are secular, pragmatic Israelis in their mid-30s.

At the last elections, Gershon voted Likud and Sarah, Labour. 'I want peace,' Sarah told me this week. 'I have a son and a daughter in the army. But our land here is our livelihood. No one has told us what is going to happen. We're due to start pruning the vines next Monday for next spring's grape crop.'

Would they stay, I asked, if it meant submitting to a Palestinian police checkpoint on the way to their jobs? Sarah's answer was a blunt, instinctive 'No.'

What then? If necessary, the Richters would leave Vered Yericho. 'But where', she asked, 'are we going to find work at our age?'

Eric Silver's Israel
1993 – annus mirabilis for some, horribilis for others
Jewish Chronicle, December 31, 1993

In 1992, Abie Nathan, Israel's most iconoclastic peace campaigner, was serving a prison sentence for going to Tunis and meeting the leader of the PLO. At the end of 1993, Yitzhak Rabin's ministers were beating a path to Yasser Arafat's door and the prime minister has met him three times in as many months.

In 1992, I was advised by a Tel Aviv lawyer that I had broken the law by having had lunch with the PLO's man in London, Afif Safieh, and that the last thing I should do was publish an interview with him – even though I hold British as well as Israeli citizenship.

At the end of 1993, I found myself wishing Mr Safieh, a 43-year-old Roman Catholic, Christmas greetings at his mother's house in Jerusalem – and even Israel TV was interviewing him.

Here in the Middle East, 1993 was one of those years, like 1948, 1967 and 1977, of geological change. It was as if an ice cap had melted. Things which had seemed impossible before, suddenly became practical options. Whether it turns out to be an *annus mirabilis* or an *annus horribilis* will depend on the skill and authority of Israeli and Palestinian statesmen, at the negotiating table and in the towns and villages and settlements of this contentious land.

But for Mr Safieh, the sea change has already come to pass. Israeli immigration officers, he told me, received him 'smoothly and decently' at Ben-Gurion airport when he and his family arrived for his first visit in 25 years.

More than 750 well-wishers attended a service in the Latin patriarchate, inside the Jaffa Gate of the Old City, where Mr Safieh's elder daughter, 10-year-old Diana, was confirmed by Patriarch Michel Sabah, and her sister, Randa, eight, received her first communion.

Although no invitations had been sent out, the congregation included Israel's communications minister, Shulamit Aloni; her fellow Meretz MK, Naomi Chazan; the former president of the Board of Deputies, Greville Janner, MP; and the Liberal Democrats' foreign affairs spokesman, Sir David Steel MP.

Nonetheless, Mr Safieh had mixed feelings. 'This visit has been the most moving moment of my life,' he said, 'a time of immense joy. I'm back in my home, sleeping in my own bedroom, meeting childhood friends.

'But it is also a moment of immense sadness, because I see that my society has been brutalised, its energy has been suffocated. My city, East Jerusalem, has been mutilated, its expansion restricted by a band of settlements.'

Most of all, he said, he was disappointed that the Israeli evacuation from Gaza and Jericho – due to have taken place on December 13 – had been delayed. 'I had hoped to witness a first withdrawal at Christmas,' he declared. 'Instead, I am finding increasing scepticism, even among the main body of Palestinians who enthusiastically supported the Oslo agreement.'

Scepticism, but not yet despair. 'Palestinian society,' Mr Safieh sensed, 'is in suspended animation, still awaiting the moment when it will see the triggering of the Palestinian entity.'

Meanwhile, an ambassador-in-waiting, Mr Safieh is extending his 'home leave' into January, so that he can be in Jerusalem to meet foreign secretary Douglas Hurd. Think what ructions that would have stirred a year ago.

After four years, this is the last of my 'Israel Diary' columns – although not the last time I will be appearing in the pages of the *Jewish Chronicle*.

The diary has been, among other things, a kind of serial letter to friends and relatives. I once came across a London family I hadn't seen in years. They were visiting the Tayelet promenade looking across to the Old City of Jerusalem from Government House Hill. 'I told them we had to come here,' said the father, 'because Eric Silver said we must.'

Thank you to all those *JC*-reading tourists who looked me up and down in Zion Square and asked: 'Don't I know you from somewhere? Aren't you the chappie...?'

Thanks even – perhaps above all – to the Orthodox gentleman in black hat and matching beard who said: 'I don't agree with a single word that you write... But I always read you.'

Chapter 9 – 1994-95

A tepid turnout

Los Angeles Jewish Journal, July 8-14, 1994

The lean, wiry Palestinian with the toothbrush moustache introduced himself as Abie. Queried whether he didn't mean Ibrahim, he said not, but Abie was what the staff in his Miami supermarket called him. They found it easier to remember.

His real name was Aziz Mashni, a 46-year-old father of six from the West Bank hill town of Ramallah, who had lived in the United States since 1969. We met in the crowd walking back through the sweltering streets of Jericho after witnessing Yasser Arafat's first visit to the West Bank for a quarter of a century.

Aziz had come specially from Florida for the occasion. It has cost him 'five grand', he confided, 'and worth every penny' to see the PLO leader back on his home turf.

Not everyone among the West Bank's one million Palestinians was so enthusiastic when their self-styled president dropped in Tuesday. The Jericho trip was a whimper of an end to his five-day inaugural tour of the newly autonomous enclaves.

A vast, gritty field had been fenced and levelled between the city and the Jordan River, but barely 5,000 turned out to welcome the legendary leader. Arafat, clearly embarrassed, blamed the Israelis for blocking the roads, but my own experience, driving down from Jerusalem, suggested that anyone who wanted to reach Jericho could have done so.

Taking a leaf out of the Arab intifada, Jewish settlers erected barriers of rocks and flaming tires, but the army and police quickly cleared them. As Uri Dromi, formerly of the Los Angeles consulate and now an Israeli government spokesman, put it with more truth than tact: 'Instead of looking for scapegoats, the Palestinians would do well to examine their own performance.'

Arafat had already been to Gaza. The novelty had worn out. But perhaps the best explanation for the poor turnout was either that the West Bankers had no stomach to confront the settlers, just as many Jews kept away from Arab areas during the intifada, or that there was nothing much to celebrate. Outside tiny Jericho, with a population of 14,000, the West Bank is still under the Israeli yoke. The future remains uncertain.

There had been something of the same reticence in Gaza earlier. The crowds were bigger, but not as big as the organisers had expected.

Imm Hashem, a fresh-cheeked mother of eight, was shopping last Saturday in the dusty, pot-holed street market of the Jabaliya refugee camp, where the intifada broke out six-and-a-half years ago.

Arafat was due there a few hours later. In her long embroidered peasant's dress and white headscarf, 35-year-old Imm Hashem was happy to welcome him, but with reservations.

'I am excited that he came to Gaza,' she said. 'But the excitement is not yet complete. We are waiting for more results.'

Imm Hashem, whose family lives on handouts from the United Nations Relief and Works Agency, has not seen one of her brothers since he was exiled by the Israelis for security offences 21 years ago. 'We want Arafat to bring back the deportees and get the rest of our boys out of prison,' she insisted.

Israel has released about 3,500 of the 5,000 Palestinian prisoners it promised to free under the peace agreement. The rest either murdered Jews, or have refused to sign a pledge not to engage in political violence once they are out.

Like Imm Hashem, the 750,000 Palestinians of the Gaza Strip have seen Arafat. Now they want to see what he can deliver. Each has his own agenda.

'We want jobs for the workers,' demanded Adel Saleh, a 34-year-old banana vendor. 'We don't mind if it is in Gaza or in Israel. The economic situation here is very hard. People have no money.'

Fathi, a 32-year-old father of nine who declined to give his second name, has been denied a permit to work in Israel. He was employed for 10 years in a Tel-Aviv gas station, one of 60,000 day labourers who once crossed the Green Line to jobs in Israeli factories, farms and services.

'I haven't been paid a penny for 18 months,' he protested. 'I'm looking for work, but there's nothing for me in Gaza. My brothers are supporting me from their savings. I have had to borrow from money lenders.'

The people in the Jabaliya market were bitter at the international community's reluctance to finance Palestinian autonomy without rigorous accountability. 'They have to pay up,' said Subhi el Ajez, a 70-year-old, white-bearded grocer sporting the crocheted white skullcap of the pious Muslim. 'They are making fun of us.'

Arafat and the PLO mainstream are enjoying a honeymoon, but the streets of Gaza could yet turn against them if they don't produce tangible benefits soon.

The Palestinian opposition, radical left and Muslim fundamentalist, is giving Arafat a chance – perhaps to fail. There were no anti-Arafat demonstrations, few hostile slogans on the painted and over-painted walls. But the opposition is putting down markers – and keeping its guns underground.

'The peace agreement doesn't give our people all they need,' said Rakif Abu Sa'ada, a 25-year-old greengrocer and supporter of George Habash's Popular Front for the Liberation of Palestine. 'It has brought us autonomy, but no state. Arafat has sold the Palestinians too cheaply.'

Hammad el Shurafa, who sells jeans from a stall in Gaza city, was deported to Lebanon by the Israelis two years ago. He is a member of Hamas, the Islamic resistance movement. He didn't go to cheer Arafat, but he didn't go to jeer either.

'If we had demonstrated against him,' he said, 'it would have set Palestinian against Palestinian. That would have harmed us all. But we are planning future demonstrations – not against Arafat, but for Hamas. He has his program, we have ours.'

Above all, el Surafa rejected the PLO's two-state solution, Palestinian alongside Jewish. For him, partition was not just wrong, it was blasphemous.

'This is a holy land,' the 24-year-old militant contended. 'Nobody should give it away. The struggle against Israel will continue to the end of the occupation of Palestinian land, from the Mediterranean Sea to the Jordan River.'

Shehadeh Abu-Shamla and Rami Abu-Lahiya did go to the Arafat rally. Shehadeh is 15, Rami is 16. They were the boys of the intifada, the urchin shock troops of the revolution. Shehadeh bared his leg to show four bullet scars. He was arrested four times by the Israelis, Rami was arrested six times. They put on mock khaki battledress to cheer the chairman.

'The intifada is over now,' boasted Shehada. 'We have gone back to school. But we will return to the streets if the Israelis ever come back.'

And who would they throw stones at in the meantime? we asked. 'We can always throw them at the Palestinian policemen,' they laughed. Their elders were quick to assure us they were joking. Just in case.

The PLO's man of ideas

The Statesman, July 18, 1994

Nabil Sha'ath, stately, plump, bald and twinklingly bespectacled, looks more like a business school professor or self-made tycoon than a Palestinian revolutionary.

His chin is as smooth as a Gillette razor ad. He sports tailored suits or yuppie polo shirts. He drives his own sleek Peugot 605 around the Gaza refugee camps. He has a house in Cairo and has founded the biggest management consultancy in the Arab world. If anyone handed him a gun, he probably wouldn't know which end to hold it.

Since the Israeli withdrawal from Gaza and Jericho three months ago, the 55-year-old Sha'ath has emerged from the PLO pack as Yasser Arafat's chief executive. He is donating his company's expertise to put the new Palestinian administration on a sound footing. And as an early advocate of a two-state solution, he has been appointed to head the negotiating team with the Israelis.

Last Friday he became the first returning Palestinian leader to pray at Jerusalem's Al Aqsa mosque, the third holiest shrine in Islam, with Israel's authorisation. He has recently asserted his independence by condemning a call by the PLO 'foreign minister', Farouk Kaddoumi, to destroy the Jewish State, and Arafat's banning of a pro-Jordanian Palestinian daily paper.

Sha'ath, a widower with three grown-up children, is an ideas man whose time has come. The murderous Abu Nidal once put him on his hit list for speaking out against indiscriminate violence. Yet Sha'ath persisted in preaching, and where possible practising, dialogue and compromise – but not capitulation.

'We were thrown out of our country,' he explained on the terrace of this seafront Gaza hotel. 'We were oppressed, we were occupied. We had a natural right to fight back. The struggle to be recognised as a nation justified the resort to arms, but not to terrorism. I distinguished between civilian targets, like school buses or airliners, and the legitimate target of the occupation forces.'

Sha'ath was born in the northern hill town of Safed, where his father was a headmaster. The family fled to Egypt during the 1948 Arab-Israel war. But the Sha'aths were relatively well-heeled refugees. Nabil took his BA in business administration at Alexandria University, then an MA and PhD in Philadelphia.

Exile, he admitted, was not especially traumatic. He had no horror stories to tell. But his parents bequeathed him a 'fiery dedication' to the Palestinian cause. 'From a very early age,' he recalled, 'I considered Palestine my foremost goal. The return to Palestine was my dream.'

As a finance professor at the University of Pennsylvania in the sixties, he discovered he could argue with his American Jewish students without coming to blows. As a Palestinian delegate to Arab solidarity conferences in the seventies, he found unexpected common ground with Left-wing Jews.

One of them, a French writer, told him how her mother shivered every time she heard a knock on the door. She still remembered the day the Gestapo took her husband and two children away. Sha'ath set out to 're-educate' the Palestinians. 'I told them about the suffering of the Jews in Europe,' he said.

As early as 1974, he came out for a two-state solution: 'In my mind, peace was not only reconciliation with Israelis, but the way for my people to obtain their rights... I was realistic enough to see that the only way to have peace is to have the two persecuted peoples who are destined to share this holy land living side by side in their sovereignty, in their right to do what they please.'

Sha'ath was the first of the exiled leadership to move to Gaza after the Israeli evacuation. He has watched with satisfaction as autonomy, however flawed and however incomplete, has conditioned Palestinian opinion to peaceful change.

'They feel now that negotiations can bring fruit,' he said. 'Up to the moment we came to Gaza, most people who opposed a peaceful settlement opposed it not on ideological grounds, but on the ground that it would never work. They said Israel would not withdraw an inch, that these were people who were determined to take away our country, piece by piece. The establishment of a Palestinian national authority has shown people that through negotiations one can achieve more rights, more freedom, more equality.'

Did that mean that the Palestinian refugees, who make up 60 per cent of Gaza's 800,000 people, were reconciled to never returning to the towns and villages they fled in 1948? Was Sha'ath preparing them to abandon a 46-year dream?

'Negotiation means compromise,' he replied. 'I don't think we can say that this is a foregone conclusion about how this thorny issue is going to be settled. The only thing we know is that we have to settle it by peaceful means.'

Arafat's chief executive sounded uncannily like the Israeli Prime Minister, Mr Yitzhak Rabin, fending off the inevitability of evacuating Jewish settlers from the West Bank and Gaza. Softly, Softly...

Progress? What progress?

Jerusalem Report, November 3, 1994

Gaza City is having its unlovely face lifted. With wages paid from a $4-million Japanese government grant, 1,400 council workers are languidly whitewashing over the accumulated graffiti of war and peace, struggle and dissent. Masons are patching and levelling cracked pavements.

Traffic is controlled by the Palestinian police, the streets are occasionally swept. About 30 new blocks of eight to 10 storeys are sprouting up for homes and offices in middle-class neighbourhoods.

A movie theatre is showing films for the first time since the intifada broke out seven years ago. Beach cafes stay open till midnight, shops till 6pm. The curfews and confrontations of the intifada are over.

So much for the good news. The bad news is that as Palestinian autonomy approaches the end of its first six months, few of the Gaza Strip's 800,000 Arabs have money to buy anything. Unemployment is estimated officially at 30 percent of the 130,000 labour force: unofficially at nearer 60 percent. Only 28,000 day labourers have been granted permits to work in Israel, compared with a peak of about 55,000 three years ago.

In Samir Nabhan's fashion store in downtown Palestine Square, a woman spent two hours bargaining him down from 90 shekels (about $30) to 80 shekels ($27) before buying a dress. He was so grateful for the sale that he threw in a bar of Camay toilet soap.

And whatever dividends peace may have brought do not extend to the stinking, overcrowded refugee camps where two-thirds of the Strip's Palestinians subsist. The slogans there are as livid as ever, the garbage is still uncollected, the sewage overflowing, the streets unpaved.

'Things are getting worse and worse,' complains Izak Badr, a 19-year-old student, outside a grocery store in the biggest and most militant of the camps, Jabalya, where the intifada exploded in December 1987.

'After five months of autonomy,' interjects Jamal Muhammad, 22, a fellow student with unkempt brown hair, 'we haven't seen anything on the ground. All the young people are unemployed.'

Badr blames Israel, which he accuses of using economic cooperation as a lever on the Palestinian negotiators, and foreign donors, who have been slow to come through with their promised $2.4 billion in aid.

Muhammad condemns Yasser Arafat's Palestinian National Authority for rejecting the donors' demand to see how their taxpayers' money will be spent. 'They collect taxes,' he says, 'they take license fees, but they haven't done anything yet. If things don't change soon, I foresee another intifada, this time against our own leadership – riots, stone-throwing and a lot more.'

So far, there are no signs of an anti-Arafat uprising. But neither are there signs of any fall-off in support for opponents of the peace process. And the extremists are thriving on Gaza's continuing frustration. In the second week of October alone, Gaza-based members of the Hamas Islamic fundamentalist movement staged two major anti-Israeli attacks, shooting dead two people in a late-night rampage along one of Jerusalem's most popular restaurant promenades, and kidnapping a soldier near Ben-Gurion Airport outside Tel Aviv.

Sympathy for Hamas in Gaza is being fuelled by despair at the performance of the PNA. Aown Shawa, the 60-year-old economist who took office as mayor of Gaza in July, warns: 'If people can't support their families, they'll become frustrated and start to question the whole peace process.' Yet Shawa, a supporter of Arafat's Fatah and a member of one of Gaza's richest business and land-owning families, remains optimistic. 'I know,' he says, 'that despite the delay, the international funding will come. As long as people know that the PNA is doing its utmost to get these funds, I don't think there'll be another intifada. The PNA is not taking the money and depriving the people.'

The mayor is disappointed that Palestinians who have made their fortunes abroad are still not investing in Gaza. 'But I understand,' he smiles, 'that business is business.' Sa'id Moddalal, PNA director of employment services, is less diplomatic. 'The overseas Palestinians,' he says, 'aren't prepared to gamble. They're cowards.'

Both Shawa and Moddalal acknowledge, however, that even when foreign aid and investment come on stream, Gaza will continue to depend on access for thousands of workers to jobs in Israeli building sites, farms and services.

Nonetheless, for most Gaza Palestinians, Israel remains the villain. They are not convinced by Israel's security case for restricting the flow of workers. They are impatient at the slow growth of Israeli imports of Gaza farm produce (about 3,500 tons of vegetables a week, as monitored by the agriculture ministry). They bitterly resent the continued presence of up to 6,000 Jews in 17 settlements – and the hundreds of soldiers deployed to protect them. 'We understand Israel's need for security', fumes Shawa, 'but we don't understand the misuse of this concept to the point where it affects our economic cooperation.'

Deiab al-Louh, a Fatah spokesman and former security prisoner in Israeli jails, adds: 'The presence of armed settlers offends the Palestinians. They feel the occupation is still in place.'

But what about persistent armed attacks on Israeli soldiers and settlers since the Palestinian police assumed responsibility for security in mid-May? According to Israeli army figures, five soldiers and one civilian were killed there in the first five months after the May 4 Cairo agreement, which paved the way for withdrawal; 59 soldiers and 13 civilians were wounded. And that was before the terrorist actions inside Israel in the second week of October.

The Fatah spokesman responds that the PNA stands by its commitments. It wants peace and has condemned acts of violence, but stopping operations by opposition groups has never been easy – for Israel or the Palestinians. 'The Palestinian police will try to protect Israeli civilians,' he says. 'They are working on it.'

He recognises that working on it will scarcely be enough. So what else can the Palestinians offer? 'The PLO and Israel should negotiate the removal of the army and settlements and reduce the transitional period to a minimum,' Louh suggests.

But evacuation of settlements before the final stage of negotiations will hardly appeal to Prime Minister Yitzhak Rabin. Not while the campaign to keep the settlers on the Golan Heights is rattling around his ears – and Hamas gunmen use Gaza as a base for operations as far afield as Tel Aviv and Jerusalem.

Assad's demands

Los Angeles Jewish Journal, November 4-10, 1994

On 26 March 1979 Anwar Sadat and Menachem Begin signed the Israeli-Egyptian peace treaty in Jimmy Carter's White House. Three years later the last Israeli soldier left the Sinai desert. Egypt had regained 'every inch of sacred Arab soil' captured by Israel in the 1967 war.

Ever since, that has been President Hafez Assad's model. If Israel seeks peace with Syria, he said again after talks in Damascus last Thursday with President Bill Clinton, it will have to withdraw from the Golan Heights 'to the line of 1967'.

In the peace treaty signed with Israel in the Arava desert 10 days ago, King Hussein of Jordan created a dangerous precedent for Assad. Israel agreed to restore about 300 square kilometres of disputed border territory to Jordan. In return, Jordan agreed to lease some of them back to the Israeli farmers who had encroached on them over the past three decades.

Assad condemned the treaty as a betrayal of Arab solidarity and angrily dismissed any chance of following suit. 'Our land is ours,' he said. 'We consider that it would be blasphemy for any country to speak of leasing its land. There won't be peace, even if we live tens or hundreds of years, unless the land is restored in full.'

Prime minister Yitzhak Rabin may want to test the idea through private channels, but independent experts are inclined to take Assad at his word. 'He is not likely to submit to the Jordanian model,' said Moshe Maoz, a Middle East specialist at the Hebrew University of Jerusalem and author of a biography of the Syrian leader. 'His model is Sinai, and he's going to be very adamant.'

Assad, Maoz pointed out, lost the Golan twice – as defense minister in 1967 and as president in the 1973 Yom Kippur War, when Syrian tanks overran much of the Heights, then forfeited them again to an Israeli counter-attack.

But it is not only a matter of vanity. 'Assad has to demonstrate that he can regain the Golan for the Arabs,' Maoz said. 'He cannot be less Arab than Egypt.' The Golan also has strategic importance for Syria. The stationing of Israeli troops 50 km from Damascus represents a major threat.

There are credible, but unconfirmed, reports of a secret understanding between Rabin and Assad under which Israel would return all of the Heights in exchange for full peace. Rabin has lectured the Israeli public often enough on the 'illusion' that they can have peace without relinquishing territory. But even if the reports are true, the details have still to be filled in – and the devil is in the details.

How long would Israel be given to withdraw? Five years, as Rabin has suggested, or the one year the Syrians think is enough? How would Israel's security be guaranteed, once it relinquished the strategic buffer from which it has guarded the towns and villages of Galilee 500 metres below? How would disputed water sources be divided?

On the other side of the peacemakers' equation, how does Assad define 'full relations'? He still declines to talk of 'diplomatic' relations, a hair-splitting distinction, but one that matters to the Israelis who don't want to be trapped in to a mere state of non-belligerency. Will there be an Israeli embassy in Damascus, a Syrian embassy in Tel Aviv? If so, at what stage of the withdrawal? Will Syria's borders be open to Israeli travellers and traders?

Clinton told reporters after his return to Jerusalem that he had made 'some progress', but achieved no breakthrough. All the signs are that the visit failed to kickstart the stalled negotiations. Whatever technical or tactical advances the Americans may have induced, the process looks long and grudging.

Assad knows what he wants, and is not going to settle for less, though he is eager to win the financial and diplomatic rewards of American goodwill. On the Israeli side, Rabin has to convince an uneasy public that he is not exposing them to mortal danger by evacuating the Golan without adequate safeguards.

He faces a strong, well-funded lobby supporting the 13,000 Jewish settlers in 32 Golan towns and villages. Its champion is Avigdor Kahalani, an MP in Rabin's own Labour party who as a tank commander was one of the heroes of the Yom Kippur War on the Heights.

'Anyone who thinks that territory is no longer important in an age of missiles,' he argues, 'need only remember the Gulf War to see his mistake. For six weeks the US Air Force pounded the Iraqis, and nothing happened. But when the tanks moved in, the war ended in 100 hours.'

Rabin has agreed to submit any evacuation plan to a referendum. In a country where almost all able-bodied men do military service, the humblest reserve sergeant considers himself a security expert.

Hafez Assad has few such constraints. It would be much easier for the Syrian dictator to impose an agreement on his people. 'If he could go to war in 1991 against Iraq, a brother Arab state, alongside British and American imperialism,' Moshe Maoz insisted, 'he could also make peace with Israel.'

Observers are satisfied that Assad's control over the Syrian armed forces is secure. He broke the back of the Islamic opposition in February, 1982, when his troops massacred an estimated 20,000 rebels in the provincial town of Hamma. 'The merchant class want to see peace,' said Maoz. 'The rest would need some re-educating.'

But for all Bill Clinton's airborne diplomacy, Israeli-Syrian peace is not around the corner. Israel and Jordan had been *de facto* allies for decades. Syrian antagonism towards the Jewish state remains deep and passionate. For Assad, peace with Israel is not an act of reconciliation, but the price for American investment. Now that he's seen the tab, he is not yet sure he wants to pay it.

Talking with Hamas
Los Angeles Jewish Journal, April 21-27, 1995
Emad al-Falouji, one of the few Hamas leaders to have escaped arrest by the Palestinian police since Islamic suicide bombers killed

seven Israelis and an American student in Gaza on April 9th, carries his drama with him like a mobile telephone.

He surges into his second-floor flat over a soft-drinks warehouse near the Jabalia refugee camp, wishes his guests *Salaam Aleikum*, apologises for being late, then dashes off to pray so that we won't have to interrupt our interview.

The 33-year-old publisher of the Hamas weekly paper, *Al Watan*, sports a prophetic black beard, a white, short-sleeved shirt embroidered with a pot plant that looks as if it was lifted from a Chinese watercolour, lovat pants and open sandals without socks. He served four years of a six-year sentence in an Israeli prison for Hamas activities.

As soon as he gets back, his phone rings. Police have raided his office, detained two senior editors, taken away computers and a fax machine. 'Right,' he snaps, 'let's get on with your questions while we still have time.'

Does he expect the police to come for him too? 'Everything is possible in these circumstances. They came to arrest me on the first day after the bombings, but I was not here. They searched my house, seized my personal papers. I don't sleep at home any more.' Do the Muslim fundamentalists now regret hitting a busload of Israeli soldiers and settlers inside territory controlled by Yasser Arafat's Palestinian Authority, a provocation which the Authority could hardly ignore? Previous suicide bombings were carried out inside Israel.

'We don't have any agreement with the Palestinian Authority not to operate in their territories,' al-Falouji replies. 'The settlements are still here. They will remain a target until the settlers leave. Our position is not to embarrass the Authority, but if they try to protect the settlements, they are putting themselves in an embarrassing position.'

Could this lead to armed confrontation between Hamas and the Palestinian security forces?

'If the Palestinian Authority goes on arresting our people,' he warns, 'I do expect armed conflict. But I don't think the Authority will continue with these unwise steps. What the Authority is doing now is a response to pressure from Israel and the west. [It] is showing its weakness. I think the Authority will retreat because it will face strong pressure from the Palestinian public. Hamas is a movement. We have our supporters, we have our strength. The Authority will have no choice but to negotiate with us. The arrests and undemocratic military court, which has started sentencing opponents of the regime, will be at the top of the agenda.'

But what if the police try to disarm Hamas and the smaller, more extreme, Islamic Jihad group?

'I don't think they will do it. I don't think they'll be able to do it. The military wing of Hamas is very secret. Even the Hamas leaders don't know where the arms are kept. I can't say if they will defend themselves with arms. The political decision is not to clash with the Palestinian police. Hamas has a general policy, but everyone implements his own policy.'

How worried is he at the prospect of civil war?

'Hamas is trying to calm things down. We don't want a civil war, but we are continuing our struggle against the Israeli occupation. Our ultimate goal is to liberate Arab Palestine.'

All of Palestine, including what has been Israel since 1948?

'Our minimum goal,' al-Falouji says, choosing his words with care, 'is Israeli withdrawal from the Gaza Strip, the West Bank and East Jerusalem. We want them to dismantle all the settlements in the West Bank and the Gaza Strip and release all Palestinian prisoners. Then we want elections to a Palestinian parliament.'

What about Israel?

'We don't recognise the legitimacy of Israel, but Israel is here. I said the minimum needs of the Palestinian people and Israel. That does not leave out the rest of our rights. What I'm talking about is like a cease-fire between the Palestinian people and Israel. If Israelis want peace and security, they should accept this.'

A cease-fire while the Palestinians prepare to resume their war of liberation? Or a cease-fire as a prelude to peace?

'We need a ceasefire in order to achieve a stable Palestinian society. That will need a lot of time. A 10-year ceasefire will be enough to show us what the future is going to look like. The rest will have to be left to the next generation.'

As we leave, Emad al-Falouji's Audi is waiting at the door. Soon, clutching his mobile phone, he drives away. One jump ahead of Arafat's policemen.

A tale of two cities – Palestinian elections put the shared sovereignty of Jerusalem to the test

Los Angeles Jewish Journal, November 2, 1995

Ministers and senior officials deny it, but you don't have to be an enemy of the Oslo peace process to argue that Yitzhak Rabin's negotiators have taken a first step toward shared Israeli-Palestinian sovereignty in Jerusalem.

The terms, sealed in the September 28 accord, under which tens of thousands of East Jerusalem Arabs will go to the polls next January in elections for a Palestinian national council, are a tacit acknowledgement that Israel cannot dictate a unilateral solution to the Jerusalem problem if it wants a durable peace. Negotiations on the final status of the holy city are scheduled to begin next May, but positions are already being compromised.

Danny Rubinstein, a veteran left-wing observer of Israeli-Palestinian relations, wrote in the daily *Ha'aretz* last weekend: 'There will be almost no difference between the elections in Gaza, Nablus and Hebron and the elections in East Jerusalem. The points which are in dispute between Israel and the Palestinians over elections in East Jerusalem have been resolved so that the Palestinians in essence got what they wanted.'

In the same paper two days later, the right-wing Likud mayor of Jerusalem, Ehud Olmert, denounced the government for perpetrating a 'fraud and a swindle'. He wrote: 'There is an intolerable gap between the government's pronouncements on its professed allegiance to an undivided Jerusalem, the capital of Israel forever and ever under Israeli sovereignty, and its actions and inactions on the ground.'

Perhaps the only difference between the journalist and the mayor is that the first approves of what the government is doing and the second condemns it.

Ever since Israel annexed East Jerusalem in July 1967, a month after it was conquered in the Six-Day War, successive governments have treated it as part of Israel. Even though its Arab residents were not forced to adopt Israeli nationality, they were (and are) issued with the same blue identity cards as Israelis. West Bank Arabs, occupied but not annexed, carried orange-coloured IDs. When Israeli security forces close the old border, East Jerusalemites are allowed to cross back and forth; West Bankers are barred.

Elections to a Palestinian council were first mooted in the Camp David accord signed by Menachem Begin and Anwar Sadat in 1978. The late Likud prime minister sought to separate Jerusalem Palestinians from their West Bank and Gaza brethren. The latter could vote and run for office; the Jerusalemites could not.

Since the Oslo agreement two years ago, this clear-cut maximalist position has eroded – for the very simple reason that Yasser Arafat and his team could not, and would not, buy it. For them, the 150,000 East Jerusalemites, more than a quarter of the city's total population, are an integral part of the Palestinian people. To disown them would have been political suicide.

First, the Labour-led government said that the East Jerusalemites could vote, but it insisted that they could not be candidates and that they would have to cast their ballots outside the city limits.

Uri Savir, who headed Israel's negotiating team under the foreign minister, Shimon Peres, maintained this week that they had not sold any pass. The elections, he told foreign correspondents, would not affect the status of Jerusalem. The campaign there would take place under Israeli law, and Israel would be responsible for security.

His assurance seemed a little disingenuous. Israel has agreed that Jerusalem Arabs with a residence on the West Bank can be candidates, so long as they run from this second address. Most of the Palestinian elite have such 'country cottages' – in tropical

227

Jericho for the winter or the cool Ramallah hills for the summer. Those who don't will soon acquire them.

In a desperate search for a fig leaf, Israeli negotiators agreed that the Palestinians could vote inside Jerusalem, but at five regular post offices, not polling stations. The votes will be 'mailed' outside the city to be counted.

Finally, Israel has also agreed that international observers will monitor elections in Jerusalem, just as they monitor those in the West Bank and Gaza. Mayor Olmert frothed that this took the city back to the 1950s. 'It is,' he said, 'an admission that the eastern part of the city is not under our absolute sovereignty.'

Uri Savir hotly denied the mayor's claim. 'I don't feel that our position is eroded by the fact that we shall have five international observers in Jerusalem,' he said. 'I don't see any erosion of our status or our position in Jerusalem.'

On this point, the foreign ministry director-general is on firmer ground. Jerusalem already has a corps of foreign consuls who are not accredited to the State of Israel and whose main role since 1967 has been to watch over the welfare of the Palestinians in Jerusalem, the West Bank and Gaza. The United Nations Relief and Works Agency for Palestinian Refugees and the International Committee of the Red Cross maintain quasi-diplomatic missions in the city.

If the election monitors challenge Israel's sovereignty there, it is challenged already. But the other concessions are precedent enough for the Palestinians. The earth is moving.

A nation weeps for 'father' Rabin

Yorkshire Post, November 7, 1995

Thousands of grieving Israelis climbed Mount Herzl, the highest point in Jerusalem, last night, to pay homage at the grave of murdered Prime Minister Yitzhak Rabin beside the tombs of the founders and giants of the Jewish state.

Most of them were young, in their teens and twenties. Parents brought their children. Some prayed, most just stood, bowed their heads, and then moved on. In a spontaneous, informal, Israeli way, the nation was taking its leave.

Their pilgrimage articulated a surge of national emotion, provoked by the assassination of this most taciturn of men. They began by mourning a warrior and statesman. They ended by weeping for what more and more of them called a 'father'.

It was as if Rabin had to die for Israelis to recognise how much they relied on him as an anchor in turbulent times.

Rabin, shot dead by a Jewish fanatic as he left a peace rally in Tel Aviv on Saturday, was buried yesterday afternoon in a two-hour ceremony attended by leaders of nearly 100 nations.

They included President Bill Clinton from the United States, Prince Charles and John Major from Britain, Chancellor Helmut Kohl from Germany, Prime Minister Viktor Chernomyrdin of Russia and the United Nations Secretary-General, Boutros Boutros-Ghali.

But perhaps the most eloquent testimony to Rabin's legacy was the presence of King Hussein of Jordan, President Hosni Mubarak of Egypt and senior ministers from three other Arab countries, Morocco, Oman and Qatar.

A delegation from the Palestinian Authority was led by Nabil Sha'ath, planning chief and peace negotiator. Yasser Arafat was not invited. It was said to be too early and perhaps too dangerous for him to join them.

It was President Mubarak's first visit to Israel since he succeeded Anwar Sadat, another assassinated peacemaker, 14 years ago. It was King Hussein's first visit to Jerusalem since 1967, when he lost it, along with the West Bank, to an army commanded by Yitzhak Rabin.

Despite the congregation of 2,500 guests, including 22 presidents and 25 prime ministers, the banners and guard of honour from all three of Israel's armed forces, Rabin's funeral was almost a family affair.

The prime minister's plain wooden coffin, draped in the blue and white Star of David, was addressed in the second person as if he could still hear.

President Clinton remembered the open-necked Rabin's difficulties in knotting his tie. Shimon Peres, his successor and partner in search for peace was almost conversational.

His eulogy had none of his trademark rhetorical tricks. He stressed the quality of Rabin's leadership – his vision, his courage, his tenacity – but also his essential seriousness and his caution.

Peres's farewell drew its emotion from the event itself, from the long, sometimes contentious history of their personal relations and ultimately from its very simplicity.

Like the US president, Peres pledged his government and his people to continue along the road of peace adopted by the dead leader.

Two of those closest to Rabin, his granddaughter, Noa Philosoph, and his aide and speechwriter, Etan Haber, struck a more emotional note. Both broke down before they reached the end.

Noa said she did not want to talk about peace, but about her 'sabba' (grandpa). He was, she said, like the biblical 'pillar of fire that went before the camp' to guide the children of Israel after their exodus from Egypt. 'The fire has been extinguished,' she lamented, 'and the camp is in darkness.'

Haber recalled the fateful Tel Aviv peace rally when Rabin broke the habit of a lifetime and joined the demonstrators in singing a song of peace. 'Singing was never your strong suit,' Haber reminded him. 'You were always afraid that you would stumble over the words.'

But sing the prime minister did, then folded the song sheet neatly into four and placed it in his breast pocket. Haber said he would like to read some of the words, but it was not easy. The assassin's bullet passed through the paper. The song of peace was soaked in Rabin's blood.

Yitzhak Rabin

The Independent, November 6, 1995

Yitzhak Rabin was the least predictable of peacemakers, an old soldier with an instinctive distrust of the kind of bright young intellectuals who contrived the Oslo breakthrough with the

Palestinian Liberation Organisation. He visibly cringed when President Bill Clinton coaxed him to shake hands with Yasser Arafat on the White House Lawn in September 1993.

As prime minister of Israel for the first time from 1974 to 1977, Rabin could hardly steel himself to utter the word 'Palestinian'. He and his defence minister in that administration, Shimon Peres, connived, however reluctantly, at the establishment of the first Jewish settlements planted among Palestinian towns and villages on the spine of Palestine. As defence minister in the 1984-90 national-unity government, Rabin ordered his troops to break the intifada uprising 'with might, power and beatings'.

Yet on the night of his death at the hands of a lone Israeli gunman, Rabin was singing *Shir Hashalom*, the Hebrew hymn of peace, with 100,000 supporters of Peace Now. It was, Peres said afterwards, probably the first time in his life that the croaky-voiced Rabin had sung in public.

His farewell message had a ring of Martin Luther King's 'I have a dream'. His government, he said, had decided to give peace a chance. 'I was a military man for 27 years. I waged war as long as there was no chance for peace. I believe there is now a chance for peace, a great chance, and we must make the most of it.'

What wrought the transformation was the realisation that Israel could not batter the children and mothers of the intifada into submission without compromising its own humanity and alienating the civilised world with which Israel identified itself.

As early as the 1988 election campaign, Rabin and Peres argued that Israel could not go on ruling a large and hostile Arab minority if it wanted to remain a Jewish and a democratic state. The only alternative was separation, a line on the ground with Israelis on one side and Palestinians on the other (though to the last Rabin refused to acknowledge that his policy might spawn a Palestinian state).

The 1988 electoral stalemate denied the two Labour leaders an opportunity to put 'territory for peace' to the test. But after their narrow victory in June 1992, Peres, as foreign minister under Rabin, convinced himself and his chief that Arafat was ready for a symmetrical compromise. Isolated and impoverished by the historic decision of siding with Saddam Hussein in the 1991 Gulf War, the leader of the PLO had become a partner for peace.

It was Peres, always the more imaginative and restless of the two, who selected and backed the freelance diplomats for the Oslo back channel. But without Rabin, checking every detail, reining in their enthusiasm, a deal would never have gelled. And without Rabin, elected on a platform of 'peace with security', the Israeli public would not have acquiesced.

Despite their history of bitter personal rivalry, Rabin and Peres were an extraordinary team. In their seventies, they recognised that a solution to a century-old conflict between Jew and Arab was attainable.

This was their own last chance, and they were not going to let mutual recrimination get in the way. Nor would they be deflected by the enemies of peace, Arab or Jewish. After every suicide bombing, a grim-faced Rabin announced to the television cameras that the negotiations would continue. Echoing a celebrated phrase of Israel's first Prime Minister, David Ben-Gurion, he said he would 'fight the terrorists for peace as if there was no terrorism'.

Rabin was equally stubborn in defying a campaign of unprecedented vilification by the Israeli right and its paymasters abroad. They branded him a 'traitor' and an alcoholic, portrayed him in Nazi uniform or Arafat kefiyeh headdress. To their enduring shame, leaders of the parliamentary opposition were slow to disown these excesses. Even when his Knesset majority was reduced last month to a single mercenary MP, Rabin bulldozed on. 'A majority of one is still a majority,' he insisted.

Foreign critics accused Rabin of dictating a humiliating peace to a vulnerable Arafat. But for most Israelis, Israel, too, was paying a price – not just in territory, but in personal security. By finely calculating when to accelerate the peace process and when to slow it down (by, for instance, closing the old Green Line border to workers from the West Bank and Gaza Strip), Rabin stopped the pragmatic centre of Israeli public opinion from joining the settler ideologues at the barricades.

His tenacity won Israel a peace treaty with Jordan to match that Menachem Begin signed with Egypt in 1979. It banished the kind of isolation that had dogged Israel in international forums for 47 years. Israeli commentators were quick to notice that when Rabin addressed the jubilee General Assembly of the United Nations last month, no Arab or Third World delegation walked out (the Syrians and the Libyans were not there to start with).

Yitzhak Rabin was born in Jerusalem in 1922. His life and career marched step-by-step with the struggle for, and consolidation of, a Jewish state in the biblical homeland. His father, Nehemia, a working-class Ukrainian Jew who had emigrated to the United States, arrived in Palestine in 1918 as a volunteer for the Jewish League, fighting to help the allies oust Turkey from the Levant. His Russian-born mother, Rosa, the daughter of an orthodox rabbi, immigrated with a Zionist uncle.

In the best pioneering tradition, Rabin studied at an agricultural school, then joined the Palmach, the elite professionals of the Haganah Jewish defence force, in the struggle for independence. During the 1948 Arab-Israeli war, he commanded a battalion that kept open the lifeline between Tel Aviv and Jerusalem.

He made a career in the army, reaching his peak as chief of the general staff in Israel's resoundingly victorious Six-Day War in 1967. Rabin collapsed with nervous exhaustion (excused at the time as nicotine poisoning) on the eve of war, but after two days' rest he returned to his post. Moshe Dayan, the flamboyant defence minister, seized the international limelight, but the more taciturn Rabin was credited with the planning and control that expanded Israel's borders to the Suez Canal, the Jordan river and the Golan Heights.

After retiring from the military at the end of 1967, Rabin was appointed ambassador to Washington. He scorned the frivolities of the cocktail circuit, but established a highly productive working relationship with the Nixon administration.

Rabin returned to Israel in 1973 and ran for election on the Labour ticket in the elections of December that year. Israelis welcomed him as a leader with a record of success, a man who was untainted by the almost disastrous errors that exposed Israel to invasion in the Yom Kippur War. In April 1974, he defeated Shimon Peres in their first contest for the party leadership, after Golda Meir had stepped down.

Despite his initial popularity, Rabin had a disappointing first term as prime minister. He had difficulty adjusting to the demands of political life. He found the Knesset, Israel's parliament, a bore and showed it. He lacked the patience to cultivate party allies. He failed to stem a flood of corruption scandals that started under previous leaders, but fed escalating disenchantment with his party, which had ruled since independence.

On the eve of the 1977 general election, Rabin was forced to resign after an Israeli correspondent in Washington unearthed an illegal foreign currency account in the name of Rabin's wife, Leah, who survives him with their two children. Labour lost to Menachem Begin's Likud, which prompted a West Bank settlement boom designed to prevent a repartition. The present government is finally trying to unravel this.

But Rabin stayed in politics and the Knesset, a restless subordinate to Shimon Peres, whom he accused in an autobiography, *The Rabin Memoirs* (1979), of undermining him when he was prime minister. Nonetheless, the pair remained locked together like Siamese twins through three unsuccessful attempts to regain power.

In 1992, the party concluded that Peres could never win and turned again to Rabin. It worked, but by a dizzyingly precarious margin. The peace process – and the Nobel Peace Prize that it brought to Rabin, Arafat and Peres – was the improbable outcome. In the spirit of the Palmach and the Israel Defence Forces, Rabin insisted on leading from the front. In a Tel Aviv square on Saturday night, he paid for it with his life.

Chapter 10 – 1995-96

Next stop Jerusalem, vows conquering hero Arafat

Independent on Sunday, December 24, 1995

Setting his seal on the transfer of Bethlehem from Israeli to Palestinian rule, Yasser Arafat made his historic entry into the town yesterday and told thousands of exultant Palestinians in Manger Square that it would soon be the turn of Hebron, Ramallah and 'Arab Jerusalem'.

Fathers hoisted sons onto shoulders. Young men whistled, gave the V for victory sign, and chanted that they would redeem the Land of Palestine 'by blood and soul'.

As he upstaged Christmas celebrations with his strident speech from the roof of an Armenian monastery next to the Church of the Nativity, Mr Arafat added a message to the Christian world: 'Bethlehem is a liberated city. Bethlehem is a city of peace.' But he warned 'the Muslims, the Christians and the Jews who live in this holy land' that they still faced a long road to complete the peace process.

The nearest thing to anything new in his address was his reference to 'Arab Jerusalem'. This was interpreted as an acknowledgement of an Israeli claim to at least part of the city both nations claim as their capital.

Before heading into Bethlehem, Mr Arafat flew into the village of Beit Sahour, a few miles south, in an Egyptian helicopter. Church bells tolled as it passed overhead. Several thousand people jammed into the schoolyard where the helicopter set down, cheering and shouting as the Palestinian leader waved.

Mr Arafat saluted as a marching band played the Palestinian national anthem *Biladi, Biladi* and inspected an honour guard of police and officials before getting into his car to drive the short distance to Bethlehem.

In Manger Square, thousands of ecstatic Palestinians, most of them Muslims, had gathered since the early hours yesterday. A whole seminar of young women in white headscarves filled a strategic corner beneath a huge portrait of Mr Arafat, two storeys high. They chanted, clapped, ululated and drummed in jubilation.

The square was festooned with pictures of Mr Arafat and Palestinian flags, including a 30ft one hanging down the side of the Church of the Nativity – built over the grotto where tradition says Jesus was born.

After his speech to the multitude from the roof of the Armenian monastery, Mr Arafat was to convene his cabinet in Bethlehem later in the day and to address the people again from the rooftop on Christmas Eve. He and his wife, Suha, were expected to attend Midnight Mass at the Church of the Nativity.

Mr Arafat and their five-month-old daughter Zahwa had arrived on Friday and ushered in the Christmas celebrations by switching on the Christmas tree lights just outside the church.

Across Manger Square, where Israeli barricades have been removed from the police station, the boys of the intifada, sporting T-shirts of Arafat's Fatah youth organisation, stamped and marched. They had earned their day. Without their seven-year war of stones, petrol bombs and flaming tyres, the Israeli army might have been presiding over its 29th Christmas.

A large banner in the square read: 'Congratulations to our people for the departure of the occupation. May it never return.' It was signed by the PLO's mainstream Fatah faction.

The local Scout band added a skirl of bagpipes. A popular Lebanese singer began to croon *Jingle Bells* in Arabic over the public address system, but she was quickly switched off.

Bethlehem is celebrating a double feast this weekend, but Christmas is playing a distinct second fiddle. Portraits of Mr Arafat and the red, white, green and black Palestinian colours have pushed the trees and lights and Holy Family tableaux into a corner. Hawkers were doing a roaring trade yesterday in Yasser balloons.

Foreign pilgrims arriving here in the morning found the Church of the Nativity closed for security reasons. Security for Mr Arafat's appearance, the most public test so far for the Palestinian police, was firm but courteous. The green-uniformed paramilitaries,

Kalashnikov automatic rifles at the ready, blue-uniformed police and plain-clothes secret service men were everywhere but were not throwing their weight about. The crowd was good-natured in the warm summery sunshine.

Elias Freij, the 78-year-old mayor, said: 'I have waited a long time for this day.' No one was in a mood to spoil it.

Bethlehem was the fifth of six Palestinian towns to be transferred from Israel to the Palestinian Authority by December 31 under the September agreement expanding self-rule, which began in Jericho and the Gaza Strip last year.

Israeli troops pulled out of Bethlehem on Thursday, and 850 Palestinian policemen replaced them. Another 180 arrived yesterday as policemen came out in force to control the masses upon Mr Arafat's arrival.

Just eight kilometres south of Jerusalem, Bethlehem is the closest Mr Arafat has ever come to the controversial city, a site of dispute between Israel and the PLO. Both sides want control over East Jerusalem, which Israel captured in the 1967 war, and both want Jerusalem as their capital.

Palestinians sight end of a long journey

Sunday Statesman, January 21, 1996

If campaigning in the first Palestinian legislative elections ended with a bang on Thursday night, it owed more to the weather than the 672 candidates and the one million voters in 16 districts of the West Bank and Gaza Strip.

About 100 Palestinians, muffled in woolly overcoats and chequered kefiyeh headscarves, braved thunder, lightning, torrential rain and a hint of snow to hear Dr Hanan Ashwari wind up her campaign in Al Ram, a hill village on the northern fringe of Jerusalem.

The road outside the community centre was rutted, muddy and flowing with water. The storm was washing away myriad candidates' portraits pasted on every wall and lamp post.

Almost all in the audience were men, middle-aged or older. Half a dozen well-dressed women with smart hair dos filed in towards the end.

Everybody including the candidates was chain-smoking. Volunteers distributed small glasses of sweet, black tea. Dr Ashwari, the former spokeswoman for the Palestinian peace negotiators, purred conversationally into a hand-held microphone.

She focused on the unfinished business of peacemaking: the status of Jerusalem, which both Israelis and Palestinians claim as their capital; the future of the Jewish settlement; the 4,000 Palestinian prisoners still in Israeli jails.

'Jerusalem is sovereignty', she insisted. 'Whatever was occupied in 1967 must go back to the Arabs. East Jerusalem for the Arabs, West Jerusalem for the Jews.'

Beyond that, Dr Ashwari was cautious, even defensive. She is running as an Independent, one of 52 contenders for seven Jerusalem seats. In her boxy donkey-brown coat, gold earrings and bracelets, she remains part of the urban establishment.

Questioners challenged and interrupted, animated but polite, savouring their moment in the limelight.

'We made a big mistake in postponing the big issues,' Dr Ashwari acknowledged, 'But we must learn from our mistakes. Our main role in the new Palestinian council will be to rectify these mistakes. Put the right person in the right place and you'll get results.'

Al Ram was typical of the dozens of meetings she has addressed over the past two weeks.

'I was amazed', she confided afterwards in a voice hoarse with speechmaking, 'that people were most concerned about the larger issues. They worried about what kind of state we're going to have, about civil and human rights. This is not going to be another municipal or village council.' What was missing, however, was the conflict of debate, the clash of government and opposition.

In Al Ram, no one heckled, no one argued. It has been the same everywhere. The main critics of the peace process – Islamic and radical Left – put up no candidates.

Reporters Sans Frontieres, a Paris-based media defence group, has been monitoring the election coverage. Today it criticised the public-service television and radio for giving an unfair advantage to Mr Arafat in his presidential campaign and to his Fatah candidates for the legislature.

It admitted, however, that they had tried to redress the balance in the last week. Mr Arafat's rival, Mrs Samiha Khalil, was given one hour 15 minutes on TV and radio.

The chairman's exposure was cut by half, but still amounted to four hours 30 minutes. At least one third of the legislative candidates took up an offer of two minutes to state their case on Radio Palestine.

But the Arabic newspapers chickened out. 'There were almost no interviews with candidates, or other opportunities for them to address the voters directly,' complained Mr Thierry Cruvellier, the chief of the Reporters Sans Frontieres mission.

'This timid coverage was based on threats, following the arrest by Palestinian police of a leading editor and a human rights campaigner. Other editors didn't want to be arrested. They didn't know how far they could go. So they played safe.'

Another constraint, for Ms Hanan Ashwari, who was campaigning in Jerusalem but lives outside, was interference by Israel, which continues to rule the whole of the disputed city.

'The siege is still on. Palestinians cannot go in and out freely. If you have a poster on your car it's not allowed. Posters can only be put up in specific places. The municipal council tore others down. Very few venues were approved for campaign meetings. You had to give five days' notice, but they announced this only seven days before.'

The Palestinian election must be the world's most intensively monitored, with more than 600 international observers here to see fair play.

They have not yet had their final say, but most of them agree that, as an exercise in democracy, it has been flawed.

For the Palestinians, what matters is that it is happening at all.

'It`s a beginning,' suggested Dr Ashwari, 'I don't think it can effect a miraculous change, but it will be the beginning of a change, the start of an institutionalised democratic system, a framework of law, a pattern of accountability.

'But in the end it will depend on the nature of legislative council, the people who get elected.'

Israel needs tougher Arafat to crush terrorism

The Statesman, Calcutta, March 7, 1996

The first priority after Monday's Tel Aviv bombing is to regain the initiative.

The Israeli Prime Minister, Mr Shimon Peres, established an emergency headquarters to fight terrorism, but it – and he – will be judged by the grim test of results.

On Sunday, Mr Peres declared 'all-out-war' on Hamas members, Islamic revolutionaries who had blown up a second Jerusalem bus in eight days.

Hundreds of soldiers and police were deployed on Monday in the streets of the holy city, but once again Hamas got in first. It chose where and how to strike the blow.

This is not how Israel is used to fighting its wars. The style, inspired by the late Moshe Dayan, was to catch the enemy from the rear, to wage innovative battles – to surprise, not to be surprised.

Ministers have acknowledged that it is almost impossible to stop a human bomb once he has reached his target. If he is challenged he will press the button. The focus they argued had to be on the infrastructure of terror – the commanders and preachers who recruit, train, arm and dispatch the naïve young suicides.

The question is how they are going to do it, and how complete a job they can make of it. 'From today onwards,' one Israeli minister said after Sunday's declaration of war, 'they will not be able to sleep quietly in their beds, whether we are talking about the Gaza Strip, Nablus, or anywhere else in the world.'

It was no idle boast. In the two years since it evacuated the Gaza Strip, Israel has carried out pinpoint assassinations of two Islamic

Jihad strategists (one in Gaza and one in Malta) and the Hamas master bomb-maker, Yihya Ayyash, in Gaza.

After the latest wave of bombings, these are unlikely to be the last. Israel's will and ingenuity have not dried up. But the Israelis recognise that they cannot dismantle the Hamas infrastructure on their own. They no longer occupy the towns, villages and refugee camps which are the breeding ground of Islamic fanaticism.

It is much harder for their own agents, let alone their busted network of Arab informers, to operate.

They cannot routinely send in the Army at 3am to kick down doors and flush out suspects, though Israel is reserving an option of selective raids into areas under Palestinian control.

Israel needs the active co-operation of Mr Yasser Arafat's Palestinian authority and Palestinian police. Mr Peres has demanded repeatedly that the PLO leader honour his commitments under the Oslo peace agreements and disarm the bombers. Otherwise there will be no peace process.

What, then, can Mr Arafat do?

'He's not going to get anywhere by being nice to them,' said Mr Barry Rubin, a Tel Aviv based Harvard historian of the Palestinian Liberation Organisation. 'What he needs is intimidation. I don't expect him to put everybody in prison and throw away the key. But he can harass them.'

The first thing Mr Arafat can do is to make an example of Hamas military leaders by jailing them for long terms. Since the February 25 bus bombing, Israel has presented him with a list of 43 key Hamas planners.

A week later only two of the 43 had been picked up, though he has since arrested the alleged planners of the Jerusalem bombings.

Israeli security experts are convinced that Palestinian intelligence would have no difficulty locating at least 80 per cent of the top brass.

Mr Arafat could stop letting fugitive Hamas murderers use the self-ruled areas as safe havens. Two Palestinians, who killed a pair of Israeli hikers in the Judean wilderness, are moving freely and openly in Jericho despite Israeli requests for their extradition.

Palestinian police could also ban street celebrations of terrorist attacks and wakes for the 'martyrs'. One, last month in the West Bank town of Kalkiliya, drew thousands of demonstrators, including two senior Palestinian policemen.

As for Hamas's middle-aged, middle-class political leaders, Mr Arafat could expose them to what Mr Barry Rubin called non-violent guerrilla warfare.

'The leaders,' he contended, 'should know that they cannot function politically, or enjoy secure and normal personal lives, as long as they engage in organising terrorism against Israel. They would not know if their businesses would be closed, if their property would be confiscated, their homes raided.'

Mr Arafat could also restrict the flow of money, donated by Palestinian exiles in the West, for the Hamas youth programmes from which the teenage suicide bombers are recruited with promises of instant ascent to the joys of paradise. These programmes, widespread throughout the West Bank and Gaza, are nominally sporting and educational, but are a transparent cover for brainwashing.

Palestinian spokesmen have protested that the Israeli demands humiliate Mr Arafat before his own people.

They maintain that if he confronted Hamas, which enjoys the support of at least 20 per cent of the West Bank and Gaza population, he would be inviting a civil war. Hamas, they say, is not just a movement. It's an idea.

But every new suicide bombing makes it an even greater risk for him to let Hamas bombers rove Jerusalem and Tel Aviv. The Palestinian elections in January gave Mr Arafat and his Fatah organisation an unprecedented legitimacy.

Hamas and other rejectionist groups failed to persuade the voters to boycott the polls. Mr Arafat has the authority – and the support – of the street, as a massive Palestinian peace rally in Gaza demonstrated on Monday.

And Hamas has shown in the past that it has no more taste than Arafat for a civil war. Even when the Palestinian police opened fire on a crowd leaving a Gaza city mosque last year, Hamas did not retaliate. Its leaders knew they would be crushed.

Not all of them are seeking instant martyrdom.

Rattling sabre for sabre in a mini-war

Maclean's, Canada, April 22, 1996

Rivka Jacobs was not budging. The fifty-year-old primary school teacher has lived in Metulla on the Lebanese border almost since she and her late husband emigrated from the United States to Israel 25 years ago. When the Katyusha ground-to-ground rockets started flying in during the Passover holiday, her daughter Yael drove up from Tel Aviv to take her out of range.

'I'm not going,' Jacobs told *Maclean's*. 'I prefer to sleep in my own bed. This is my home. I'm not going to let Hezbollah push me out.' By Friday afternoon last week, four of her neighbours had been injured by the latest barrage of Katyushas fired on nearby Kiryat Shmonah, raising the tally of Israeli wounded to more than 40 in five days. By then, half of Kiryat Shmonah's 23,000 residents had moved south and the rest were sitting out the latest mini Arab-Israeli war in bomb shelters.

From her steel-reinforced 'security room' in Metulla, Rivka Jacobs could hear Israeli artillery pounding Shia Moslem villages on the other side of the border from where the militant Islamic group Hezbollah (Party of God) had launched its rocket attacks. There, thousands of panicky villagers were streaming northward, their cars packed with mattresses and supplies, after Israeli army broadcasts gave them four hours to leave 44 villages just outside the enclave Israel controls in South Lebanon. Earlier in the day, Israeli warplanes had attacked Beirut, a city that is finally beginning to rebuild after a decade and a half of civil war. It was the second air strike in two days – the first Israeli bombings of the capital in 14 years. Witnesses said two Syrian army posts were hit, killing at least one Syrian soldier and further injuring chances Syria will join the Middle East peace process. In an effort to head off a dangerous escalation, Israel announced that the Syrians were not a deliberate target. Officials said that a helicopter had been attacked from the ground and returned fire.

The retaliatory strikes came seven weeks before Israel votes in an election that could determine the fate of the peace process. Initially prime minister, Shimon Peres responded with restraint and diplomacy, but the political heat from Israelis in the north prompted him to unleash the warplanes, laser-guided missiles and heavy artillery. His right-wing challenger, Binyamin Netanyahu, had been received like a conquering hero when he visited Kiryat Shmonah and called for action. Although Rivka Jacobs planned to vote for Peres in the May 29 elections, she was angry he waited so long before hitting back. 'We've sat in shelters often enough, but we always felt the army was taking care of us. This time we felt the government was tying the army's hands,' she said. 'Hezbollah was calling the shots, and we were sitting here like hostages. Now, we're satisfied that finally Peres is doing something.'

But Beirut observers dismissed early Israeli boasts about 'surgical' strikes.' It was zero. They wanted to annihilate the brain and failed,' said one European diplomat. 'What they did in the Beirut suburbs was nothing,' added a Lebanese political analyst who asked not to be identified. 'There was no significant target damaged.' Peres, though, vowed to hang tough. 'If Hezbollah think they can impose a change upon us, they will learn quickly that they don't stand a chance,' he told a news conference. 'We have to remind them that we have missiles that are better than the Katyusha.' In Beirut, the Hezbollah leader, Sheikh Hassan Nasrallah, rattled sabre for sabre. 'We shall choose the time and place to retaliate for the bombing of Beirut,' he told Hezbollah's television station. 'We shall stun Peres.' Hezbollah's top commander in southern Lebanon, Sheik Nabil Kaouk, swore to 'blow up the ground under [the Israeli's] feet.'

Hezbollah's first response on Friday was more Katyushas, but Israel was braced for a more varied and far-flung reaction. 'As well as Katyushas,' wrote military commentator Alex Fishman in the mass-circulation daily *Yediot Aharonot*, 'there may be suicide bombers and attacks on Israeli targets abroad. Endurance will be important. Who will be the first to break?' Ministers and generals were preparing the people of northern Israel for an extended haul. Major-General Amiram Levine, chief of Northern Command, told local leaders: 'You will have to organise for the possibility that our activity will continue for some time.'

It may sound like wartime talk. Yet Israeli spokesmen insist they do not seek confrontation with either Syria or Lebanon, but just want to persuade them to reign in Hezbollah. Israeli leaders say they are not trying to repeat the 1982 invasion that carried Israeli tanks to the gates of Beirut. But as Levine acknowledged: 'It is in the nature of military actions that it is known where they begin and where they are meant to go, but you can't guarantee how they will work out.'

Washington, meanwhile, appeared to support the Israeli action even as it called for a stop to the cycle of violence. 'The best way for that to happen is for the unnecessary provocations by Hezbollah to cease,' said White House press secretary Mike McCurry. For Rivka Jacobs and other civilians on both sides of the Israeli-Lebanon border, that couldn't happen soon enough.

The cold shoulder

Los Angeles Jewish Journal, July 12-18, 1996

Yasser Arafat is worried that Israel's new right-wing Prime Minister, Binyamin Netanyahu, is downgrading the Palestinians on his agenda for peace.

The Palestinian Authority president has complained to US diplomats that while Netanyahu has addressed King Hussein of Jordan, President Hosni Mubarak of Egypt and sundry gulf sheiks, he has yet to send anyone of weight to talk to Palestinian leaders.

Arafat is insulted by the grudging way the prime minister speaks about him, as if he were still a pariah, as if the Oslo accords, the handshake on the White House lawn, all the face-to-face meetings in the Gaza buffer zone had never happened.

He dismisses his June 27 session with Dore Gold, Netanyahu's foreign-policy advisor, as a waste of time. Gold, Arafat told the Americans, read out a list of five points that the prime minister wanted to convey, but had no mandate to discuss them or to explore alternatives. He was a messenger not a negotiator.

The Palestinians are disturbed that in the five weeks between Netanyahu's election victory and his departure from Washington, he announced no substantive decisions on such outstanding issues as the closure of the green-line border to Palestinian workers, the delayed redeployment in Hebron and a negotiating timetable.

On at least one of these points, Arafat has sent an unequivocal message of his own to the Clinton administration – the Palestinian leader is not prepared to renegotiate Hebron.

The previous Israeli government signed an agreement to withdraw from most of the Arab sections of the holy city, while keeping troops in place to protect the 450 Jewish settlers who live alongside the 150,000 Palestinians. The redeployment was scheduled for March 28 but was postponed (with Arafat's acquiescence) after the Jerusalem, Ashkelon and Tel Aviv suicide bombings.

Netanyahu's aides have indicated that the prime minister is ready, in principle, to honour the commitment – but not on terms endorsed by his Labour predecessor, Shimon Peres. There is talk of widening the corridor between the settler enclave around the Tomb of the Patriarchs (which the Arabs call the Ibrahimi Mosque) and the Jewish suburb of Kiryat Arba. Netanyahu, it is reported, wants to look again at the numbers of Palestinian police and Israeli soldiers deployed, and perhaps to stretch the implementation period.

Arafat insists that the deal is closed. The Palestinians accepted some things they didn't like, the Israelis accepted some things they didn't like. Then they signed on the dotted line, with the blessing of the United States and the world community. Now, the Palestinians say, it's time to pull out of the only West Bank city still under occupation and then move on to the unfinished business of peace.

In Hebron, the local Palestinian leadership is equally adamant. 'We reject any change in what was agreed,' Mayor Mustafa Natshe said last week. 'They must redeploy according to the agreement. If they don't redeploy, the peace process will stagnate. The new

Israeli government will lose credibility with the international community. And Arab governments will freeze relations. Jordan may keep its embassy in Tel Aviv, but commerce with Israel will come to a halt. Half the population of Jordan are Palestinians. They won't stand for it.'

In the neighbouring township of Halhoul, mayor Muhammad Hassan Milhem has just returned, some 16 years after Israel deported him to Jordan.

Although Halhoul is administered separately, its 20,000 inhabitants share Hebron's fate. If the Israelis pull out of Hebron, they will pull out of Halhoul along its northern fringe astride the road to Bethlehem and Jerusalem.

'Mr Netanyahu and Mr Arafat must see to it that the peace process goes on,' the mayor said, 'if they are concerned about the security of their people. Pessimism is contrary to all the feelings I've had since I came back. But I cannot convince the people here to support the peace process if they are not getting something in return.

'My homecoming gives me an impetus to see that nobody will be deported in the future. But I cannot fold my hands and say, Let's not talk about any plans to fatten Jewish settlement in Hebron.'

Milhem, one of the most thoughtful of Palestinian spokesmen, is enough of a politician to appreciate that Netanyahu cannot say one thing during the election campaign, then say the opposite only a few weeks later. Nonetheless, he contends, the Likud prime minister cannot go on offering the Palestinians nothing beyond autonomy.

'Land for peace is the only option,' he said, 'Even if we say, Let's give him a chance; let's wait and see, you have to remember that Mr Arafat and Mr Netanyahu are not the only players in the politics of the Middle East. What Mr Netanyahu is saying will affect the kind of people who blew up the American barracks in Saudi Arabia. President Clinton cannot offer a $2 million reward every week. The Israelis faced the assassination of Yitzhak Rabin. These are indicators of what may be expected to happen if peace collapses.'

The irony is that, to all intents and purposes, the Israelis have already abandoned Arab Hebron. The only soldiers you see as you drive around town are manning roadblocks on the approach to the Jewish enclave or making sure that no one gets too close to the Tomb of the Patriarchs, now 'closed for repairs', a sure sign that the authorities are expecting trouble.

In the Palestinian shopping areas, cars with West Bank licence plates are triple-parked. Drivers go the wrong way down one-way streets with impunity. Mayor Natshe confirms that there are no regular police (the Palestinian cops resigned from the Israeli-run force soon after the intifada broke out in December 1987).

But Yasser Arafat's notorious Preventive Security Force has 200 agents working undercover in Hebron despite the fact that the city remains under Israeli rule. Israel is not complaining, because the Palestinians are cooperating with the Shin Bet security service against the common enemy of Islamic extremism.

Walking through the crowded Arab meat market, I was accosted by a wizened old Palestinian porter trundling a barrow. *'Wie gehts?'* he asked in Yiddish – How goes it? Perhaps he remembered it from before the last Jewish community was expelled from Hebron, in 1929. I didn't stop to ask him who he was working for.

Israel's best salesman sells himself

New Statesman, August 30, 1996

The last time Binyamin Netanyahu earned his living outside politics was as marketing manager of Rim, Israel's biggest manufacturer of fitted kitchens, in the early eighties. By all accounts he was rather good at it.

'I was very unhappy that he left,' says his old boss, Ronaldo Eisen. 'I had been negotiating to promote him to run the company, with a seat on the board.'

In the first three months of his premiership Netanyahu has exercised his salesman skills. What he has been selling is himself: a man of peace and a man of war; a champion of Jewish settlers who can deal with the Arabs; a free market zealot who won't abandon the poor; 'Bibi' in Israel, 'Ben' on Larry King's talk show.

For now President Hosni Mubarak of Egypt and King Hussein of Jordan have decided to give him the benefit of the doubt, but the forbearance is wearing thin. Bill Clinton has little choice until after the November presidential elections if he wants to keep his Jewish voters and contributors sweet. Yasser Arafat says he made an agreement with a country, not one particular leader. His people, disaffected by the diplomatic stagnation, by unemployment as high as 60 per cent in Gaza and by the heavy hand of the multiple Palestinian security services, are proving less patient.

Mustafa Natshe, the mayor of Hebron, warns: 'If the peace process does not move forward the people will return to the struggle. It won't come by order from above, it will come from the people, as it did in the intifada.'

Yet nothing Netanyahu has spread before the punters suggests that his 'pragmatism' goes beyond tactics. He has said openly that the 1993 Oslo agreement with the Palestine Liberation Organisation was a disaster. At the beginning of the spring election campaign he swore he would 'never' meet Arafat. Under the influence of his American spin-doctor, he qualified that at the hustings. If shaking Arafat's hand would serve Israel's interest, he would 'consider' it.

That remains his position. He sent his foreign minister, David Levy, to chat up the chairman after Arafat had refused to receive an underling. The defence minister, Yitzhak Mordechai, and the finance minister, Dan Meridor, are next in line. If Netanyahu is preparing to bite the bullet, it is only because President Ezer Weizman shamed him into it by inviting the Palestinian leader to his seaside villa. Weizman at 72 the most populist, interventionist of Israel's presidents, sensed a growing national fear that Netanyahu was leading Israel back to war.

Another old soldier in that conflict, Gideon Ezra, a Likud backbencher and former deputy chief of the Shin Bet internal security service, warned his party leader: 'We have to allow the Palestinian Authority to survive. We must give honour to the head of that Authority. To do what we want from him, Arafat must have the necessary public support – and we are taking this support away from him.'

Netanyahu seems to have received the message, but he will embrace Arafat with barely concealed revulsion. For the Likud prime minister, Arafat is still an unreconstructed terrorist who would destroy the Jewish state if he were given half a chance. He speaks of him at best with condescension, at worst with contempt.

Netanyahu employs the language of reason. Unlike his Polish-born predecessors Menachem Begin and Yitzhak Shamir, he quotes neither the Old Testament nor Vladimir Jabotinsky, the ideological mentor of the muscular Zionist right. After his July 10 address to the United States Congress, an admiring Republican hailed him as 'one of us'. His media friendly rhetoric was forged in the US, where he went to high school and university, then served as number two in Israel's Washington embassy and later as ambassador to the United Nations.

Yet he is not simply a by-product of Reaganite neo-conservatism. Everyone who knows him agrees that the core of his hard-right nationalism – the siege mentality of the Jew as eternal victim, the Jabotinskyite conviction that only an 'iron wall' of Jewish bayonets will sustain the Zionist venture – was learnt at his father's knee. Benzion Netanyahu, a historian whose politics cost him a chair at an Israeli university in the days of Labour hegemony, was a disciple of Jabotinsky, who preached the Jewish 'right' to both banks of the Jordan. He taught his three sons an apocalyptic truth. The oldest of them, Yonatan, died fighting for it at Entebbe airport in 1976.

But three years after Yitzhak Rabin reluctantly clasped Yasser Arafat's hand on the White House lawn, Netanyahu has no option but to accept Oslo as a fact of life. He is not going to send an Israeli army of occupation back into Gaza or the six West Bank towns the Labour government ceded to the Palestinian Authority. In its unfocused way, the Israeli electorate still wants peace. But the name of the game is damage control. Netanyahu's strategy is to avoid provocation, of the Arabs, or the Americans, or the Europeans, but to salvage as much as possible of the 'Greater Israel' dream. No Palestinian state, no sharing of sovereignty in Jerusalem. But softly, softly.

Netanyahu insists that Jews have the same right to live anywhere in their ancient homeland as they have to live in New York or London. Settlement, he reminded Arafat this month, was not restricted by the Oslo accords. It was 'an internal Israeli affair'. So his government has cancelled Labour's settlement freeze, but is not yet seizing Arab land or establishing new colonies. The emphasis is on 'natural growth'. A settler delegation went home happy, but with no promises. 'We did not stipulate what our policy would be in the future,' Netanyahu reassured Hussein during his August 5 visit to Amman, 'when and if we shall build new settlements.'

Nonetheless, the first caravans, heralds of expansion, have begun to roll again. Whatever can be put off will be put off. 'Reciprocity' is presented as the key to further advances, though Israel has committed as many breaches of the Oslo agreement as the Palestinians. Netanyahu says he wants to make peace with democracies, though he can hardly contend that Egypt and Jordan are models of representative government. He would like to sign a treaty with Syria's Hafez Assad (another democrat?), but without sacrificing the Golan Heights. Assad is not buying, but don't shoot the salesman.

The previous government sealed an agreement with the Palestinian Authority to redeploy Israeli troops in the West Bank town of Hebron, where 450 Jewish settlers live among 150,000 Arabs. As Arafat pointed out at the end of his July 23 meeting with David Levy, the deal took care of the Israelis' security needs. The generals who negotiated it concur. The Labour Prime Minister Shimon Peres postponed the redeployment, scheduled for March 28, because of the suicide bombings in late February and early March. Although Netanyahu and his ministers constantly hint that the troops will pull out of the Arab neighbourhoods, they now insist on renegotiating.

'If Bibi's clever,' says Noam Arnon, the Hebron settlers' spokesman, 'he will try to find ways to get out of the agreement. I don't think he can do it as planned. We and our supporters are the people who fought for him and voted for him.'

On the cardinal issues of war and peace, Netanyahu is not a prisoner of his chauvinist partners in the six-party governing coalition. He is their standard-bearer. But unlike Begin and Shamir, he has a socio-economic as well as a Zionist vision. He learnt Friedmanite monetarism and preaches it with missionary fervour. He is determined to privatise the Israeli economy, to deregulate, to set the people free (though not to cut their taxes).

Netanyahu is savvy enough to recognise that if he is going to transform Israel into a Mediterranean tiger, he will need foreign investment, as well as a business foothold in the Arab Middle East. Foreigners are impressed by stability. Arab rulers have to calculate the political risks. That, above all, is why Netanyahu is rattling no sabres. It may make a pragmatist of him yet. 'His opponents always underestimate him,' says his old boss, Rolando Eisen.

Maybe, but don't bet on it.

The patronising last straw

The Statesman, Calcutta, September 28, 1996

Like most things in West Asia, the latest crises endangering the Israeli-Palestinian peace process is not what it seems. It is not over an archaeological tunnel in the Old City of Jerusalem, though that is what both sides would like us to think.

Nor, for that matter, is the 500-yard tunnel either new or a threat to Muslim holy places. And to crown the negatives, it is not, whatever Binyamin Netanyahu may instruct us, the most exciting ancient Jewish site in a much-excavated city.

To see what all the fuss was about I took a guided tour along the full length of the tunnel, from the plaza of the Jewish Wailing Wall, passing under the schools and houses of the Muslim Quarter and coming out through the contentious new turnstile opposite the Second Station of the Cross ('The Flagellation') in the Christian Via Dolorosa, Jerusalem is nothing if not a multi-faith city.

It is a romantic and instructive trip. The Israeli ministry of tourism calls it a 'time tunnel' taking visitors back through 2,500 years of history. As public relations hype goes, that's not bad. But it is a condensed, highly selective slice of Jerusalem's history.

You trace the buried extension of the Wailing Wall, built by Herod 2,000 years ago. You walk through huge vaults, raised by the Muslim Mamluks 12 centuries later. You tramp over paving stones that Jesus may, or may not, have trodden. And finally you squeeze through the newly opened tunnel along which the Jewish Hasmonean rulers piped water 200 years BC.

It will not bring thousands more tourists to Jerusalem. It will add to the pleasure and interest of those who would have come anyway. But, from the political point of view, any open-minded visitor can see that the tunnel does not burrow under the Herodian platform, which the Jews call the Temple Mount and the Muslims revere as the Haram al Sharif (Noble Sanctuary). Nor has the tunnel undermined any of the Arab building standing over it – in the 20 years in which the dig was going on, or the 11 years since it was completed.

Why, then, has the opening of the Via Dolorosa exit before dawn on Tuesday hurled Jerusalem and its two contending masters into the most severe crisis since Yitzhak Rabin and Yasser Arafat shook hands on the White House lawn three years ago this month?

The answer is that the Israeli initiative was both an insensitive reassertion of Jewish sovereignty over part of Jerusalem the Palestinians hope will one day be their capital, and a catalyst for all the hurt and frustration the Palestinians feel at the stagnation in the peace process since Mr Netanyahu came to power 100 days ago.

The exit could have been opened any time in the last three years. The previous Labour government chose to keep it closed for fear of provoking Palestinian violence just when it was making and consolidating a historic peace. 'We've waited 2,000 years,' Mr Rabin said, 'We'll wait a bit longer.'

A deal was agreed with the Palestinian Authority last January. Muslims were granted additional rights on the Temple Mount, the site of the Al Aqsa Mosque, the third most holy in Islam; Israel could open the tunnel. But, again, after the wave of suicide bombings in February and March and the harsh Israeli counter-measures, Mr Rabin's successor, Shimon Peres, postponed the opening.

Mr Netanyahu felt Israel had waited long enough. He overrode the continuing reservations of the security services and opened the exit door. 'The process of decision-making,' Ze'ev Schiff, the dean of Israeli defence commentators, wrote in the daily *Ha'aretz* on Thursday, 'was short, incomplete and, in the opinion of many, faulty. The astounding fact is that the decision was made on the assumption that after the first spate of reactions things would calm down and the Palestinians would accept the inevitable.'

The government underestimated the strength of the Palestinian humiliation. It was a patronising last straw. The prime minister was treating them as pawns. 'The policy of this government is the *fait accompli*,' complained Saeb Arakat, the chief Palestinian peace negotiator. 'Mr Netanyahu thinks the peace process is peace for the Israelis, not peace for the Palestinians. It undermines the fact that we are partners. He is saying that we can go to hell.'

The Hebrew novelist, David Grossman, who wrote a best-selling memoir of the West Bank occupation, said this week: 'If you try to build a partnership with someone, even if he is your enemy, you cannot knock him down. The steps taken by the Israeli government are not directed at building a peace of equality and mutuality, but rather at freezing the Palestinians into a situation in which they are subordinate to us and dependent on our goodwill.'

The opening of the tunnel struck a religious spark in an already explosive environment. Even though they may know that the Al Aqsa is not at risk, the Palestinians in the street are easily persuaded that it is. They want to believe it and their leaders are eager to encourage them. Nothing unites Muslims – or frightens Israelis – more than the holy war or 'jihad'.

What Mr Netanyahu and the Palestinian president, Yasser Arafat, forgot is that once you saddle the tiger you can't always stop him running away with you. Both of them lost control in the suburbs of Ramallah on Wednesday. Both have a vested interest in getting back on the road to peace. The question, amid Wednesday's continuing carnage, is whether they have the time and the wisdom to do it. The tiger was still running amok.

The political columnist, Hemi Shalev, wrote in the mass-circulation *Ma'ariv*: 'One way of repairing the damage is a quick agreement on rapid removal of Israeli forces from Hebron (the last West Bank city still under occupation) as initial proof that the peace process indeed exists. A continuation of the current situation will quickly drag everyone back to the era of blood, intifada, terror and mourning, this time with 30,000 armed and vengeful Palestinian policemen lined up against the Israeli army.'

Jew against Jew

Jewish Chronicle, November 1, 1996

On a chill, rainy Friday morning, six days after Yitzhak Rabin's assassination, I visited his grave on Mount Herzl, high above Jerusalem. Hundreds of Israelis, singly, in families and in groups, were trudging up the hill to place flowers, light candles, recite psalms or simply to stand in mute incomprehension.

Among the mourners – a busload of kibbutzniks who had left the Galilee at five in the morning, a man with a knitted kippah, walking crablike on crutches – was a class of teenagers from a Jerusalem vocational high school.

Twenty months earlier, boys from the same school, cocky and unabashed, had boasted on a local television chat show of standing in tribute to Baruch Goldstein, the settler physician who mowed down 29 Muslim worshippers in the Ibrahimi Mosque, the Cave of the Patriarchs, in Hebron.

What, I asked one of the boys, were they doing at Rabin's grave?

'Look,' he answered, 'I was against his policies. But he was a warrior, he was our prime minister. He didn't deserve to die like this.'

A man on crutches, who had driven his handicapped motorist's car specially from Bnei Brak, near Tel Aviv, said much the same: 'I remember Rabin as he once was. I had to come here.'

It was these encounters, more perhaps than the 'children of the candles' keeping vigil in the Tel Aviv square where Yigal Amir gunned down the gruff, reluctant-peacenik prime minister, that convinced me that a change was taking place in Israel's divided society.

A silent majority, especially among the young, was speaking out. The messianic right was thrown on the defensive, if not marginalised.

Twelve months and one election later, I have to confess that I was wrong. Israel is as polarised as ever. The silent majority is still in good voice, but the dark fanaticism that inspired Rabin's murderer still haunts the land.

A class of boys at a state religious high school in the northern resort of Netanya boycotted a Rabin memorial service. At a national young people's anniversary rally, members of Betar and Bnei Akiva, the Likud and National Religious Party youth movements, declined to join in the *Song of Peace*, which Rabin sang just before his murder, because its anti-war sentiments 'were against their principles'.

In Hebron, Moshe Levinger, the single-minded rabbi who led the first settler nucleus there in 1968, is warning of violence as Binyamin Netanyahu's government prepares to pull Israeli troops out of 85 per cent of the disputed holy city, where 450 Jewish militants live in the midst of 150,000 equally zealous Muslims.

After Prime Minister Netanyahu and his military commanders had briefed settlement leaders on the proposed agreement, Levinger told Major-General Oren Shahor, the government's West Bank coordinator: 'This agreement strangles us. Baruch Goldstein and Yigal Amir did what they did because they felt strangled. We maintained restraint for years among the Hebron settlers, but I cannot promise you that we will be able to control our public in the future.'

This was no pulpit rhetoric.

Levinger himself has served jail terms for harassing Hebron Arabs, in one case shooting dead an innocent shopkeeper who happened to get in the way.

Pilgrims still read psalms at Goldstein's grave in the neighbouring Jewish suburb of Kiryat Arba. A public park there is named in memory of Rabbi Meir Kahana, whose Kach party was excluded from the Knesset because of its racist programme.

Last week, a middle-aged admirer of Kahana's flung a cup of scalding tea in the face of Yael Dayan, an outspoken left-wing Labour Knesset member, during a visit to Hebron. She suffered second-degree burns. Back in Jerusalem, an anonymous caller left a message on her answering machine: 'Thank God someone chucked a cup of tea in your face. Next time they'll kill you.'

When Mr Netanyahu phoned to express his regret, Dayan warned him: 'The same forces on the extreme right that are after me will be after you, too, because you are advancing the peace process. Please protect yourself and your family.' No one accused her of hysteria. Half-a-dozen Labour and left-liberal Meretz MK's have been given police protection after receiving hate mail.

Rabbi Benny Eilon, a far-right Moledet MK, was confronted in a Rabin memorial television special last week with old newsreel footage showing him among a mob storming the car of a Labour cabinet minister, Binyamin Ben-Eliezer. They were protesting at the second Oslo agreement with the Palestinians. Eilon said he would not hesitate to join a similar demonstration again.

Rabbi Levinger and Eilon remain on the fringe of Israeli politics. Moledet won only two seats in the last Knesset elections. When Levinger ran alone in the 1992 campaign, he failed to win a seat. But they set the tone and the agenda for a much wider religious Zionist and secular right-wing constituency.

Binyamin Netanyahu, a most secular Israeli, justified opening a door to a controversial tunnel alongside the Temple Mount in September with the argument that it touched 'the very core' of his being.

In the subsequent carnage, no Likud MK questioned whether six brave young soldiers need have died to defend the right of an ultra-nationalist yeshivah to study in what may or may not be the tomb of Joseph in Palestinian-controlled Nablus.

Back in Hebron, Rechavam Ze'evi, a retired general who now leads Moledet, shoved his way through an army barrier, brandishing his private Uzi sub-machinegun, so that he could visit the tomb of Othniel ben Kenaz, an Israelite judge and military commander of the 13th century BCE. Ze'evi is a non-observant Jew.

'The rift in Israeli society,' the novelist and peace campaigner Amos Oz said in a yahrzeit eulogy, 'is not a rift about the future of the territories, but about our very identity. Are we here to renew by force of arms the kingdom of David, perhaps the kingdom of the wicked Ahab? Or are we here to establish a home for the people of Israel? Yitzhak Rabin had deeper roots in the Jewish heritage than the worshippers of caves and tunnels.'

When Netanyahu defeated Shimon Peres, albeit by the narrowest of margins, in the May elections, the 'worshippers of caves and tunnels' believed they had won. The new government would not re-occupy the West Bank Arab cities, would not send the tanks back into Gaza, but it would draw a line. Thus far and no farther.

They have been painfully disappointed. Netanyahu shook hands with Yasser Arafat, even after the Palestinian leader's police had shot dead 16 Israeli soldiers. He is negotiating to redeploy in Hebron.

'We paved their way to power,' reflected Yisrael Harel, a former chairman of the Council of Jewish Communities in Judea, Samaria and Gaza. 'Soon we shall have to be in opposition against them.'

Mainstream settler leaders, like Harel, may be content to demonstrate and to lobby. But the heirs of the 1970s 'Jewish underground,' who killed and maimed Arab politicians and students, are stockpiling stolen arms and ammunition.

They are meant for self-defence against the Palestinians, but self-defence can quickly shade into provocation, if not worse. The idea of civil war is still remote but, after the Rabin assassination, we cannot dismiss the spectre of Jew against Jew.

Running out of chances

Los Angeles Jewish Journal, December 6-12, 1996

Binyamin Netanyahu has always been a great believer in the 'realism' of Arab leaders. Once they saw the way the wind was blowing in Israel, the right-wing prime minister was confident that they would trim their sails accordingly.

A Likud government was not bound by Yitzhak Rabin's unwritten offer to return most, if not all, of the Golan Heights to Syria in exchange for peace and security. Ergo, Syrian President Hafez al-Assad, who had a well-known interest in peace and no longer had a big brother in the Kremlin, would go back to square one and the 1991 Madrid Conference framework – 'peace for peace, no pre-conditions', however sterile that framework had proved.

A Likud government would honour the Oslo agreements with the Palestine Authority to the letter. Yasser Arafat had only the one partner for peace. Therefore he would settle for what Netanyahu was ready to yield, a semi-sovereign entity such as Puerto Rico.

Six months since he came to power, Netanyahu is learning, reluctantly and painfully, that his 'realism' and Arab 'realism' are not the same animal. Assad and Arafat, not to mention Hosni Mubarak of Egypt and King Hussein of Jordan, have their own visions, their own imperatives, their own leverage. They have been at the controls of Middle East diplomacy much longer than he has – and they have survived.

So, for all Netanyahu's complacent assurances that Damascus is coming round, Assad is rattling his Scud missiles, complete with chemical warheads; reinforcing the Syrian garrison on the eastern flank of the Golan; moving troops across the checkerboard of Lebanon; and tipping the wink to Hezbollah to step up its harassment of Israeli patrols and their South Lebanese Army allies.

Despite almost daily ministerial predictions that Israeli redeployment in Hebron, the last West Bank Arab city still under occupation, is just around the corner, Arafat is making Netanyahu sweat.

'Arafat,' the political columnist Yoel Marcus wrote in *Ha'aretz* last weekend, 'is simply more experienced than Netanyahu. He has outlasted eight Israeli prime ministers. He has been buried and resurrected several times. He is the most devious of negotiators.'

Netanyahu's government is left with little choice but to cry 'foul' – and to restore the arms stocks that Rabin's Labour team could risk running down when war was receding from anyone's agenda.

In the end, war on the Golan remains remote, but Israel cannot write off a limited Syrian invasion designed to force Netanyahu to the negotiating table on Assad's terms. The generals, who leaked their anxieties to *Time* magazine this week, dare not be caught napping, as their predecessors were on Yom Kippur 1973 by the same Syrian president.

'I think Assad's still interested in an agreement,' says professor Moshe Maoz, one of Israel's most assiduous Assad watchers. 'He knows he has to pay a price if he wants to get the Golan back. But I don't think he will wait another four years. If his present strategy doesn't work, I wouldn't rule out a blitzkrieg to grab part of the Golan and try and break the stalemate.'

In the end, Israeli troops probably will withdraw from 85 per cent of Hebron. As Marcus reminded us, 'Arafat knows that there is a limit to how tight he can pull the rope.'

Netanyahu has charged Arafat with wilfully delaying an agreement, but the Palestinians insist that there is more at stake than a residual right for Israeli troops to pursue suspected terrorists in the Arab part of town, or the depth of the buffer zone around the enclave where 450 militant Jewish settlers live amid 150,000 hostile Palestinians. They are worried that once he has redeployed in Hebron, Netanyahu will sit back and allow the rest of the Oslo accords to wither.

'We're saying we want this government to show, not just by words but by deeds, that it is committed to the Oslo agreements,' says Saeb Erakat, the chief Palestinian negotiator. 'Why is that so difficult? We're asking when they will implement things that were agreed on months ago, or that require very little further negotiation.

'We want them to give us a date for redeployment from other parts of the West Bank, which was supposed to have started in September. We want a date for the release of the Palestinian prisoners, especially female prisoners. We want a date for the free movement of Palestinians travelling between Gaza and the West Bank. We want a date to start negotiations for building a Palestinian airport and a Palestinian harbour.'

With right-wing critics, in and out of the Netanyahu cabinet, watching every move, it is easier to blame the Arab world for ganging up on poor little Israel. In an interview with the mass-circulation *Yediot Aharonot* this week, foreign minister David Levy accused the Arab leaders of taking a strategic decision to isolate Israel and cut it down to what they call its correct size.

That is not how it looks from across the river. King Hussein, the second Arab ruler to sign a peace treaty with the Zionist enemy, told David Frost in a BBC television interview last weekend that he was becoming 'a little impatient and a little concerned' with the pace of the peace process.

Jordan's Prime Minister, Abdel Karim Kabariti, was more explicit. 'We wanted so much to believe in Netanyahu,' he said to the Tel-Aviv daily *Ma'ariv*. 'We gave him the fullest possible opportunity. We gave him the benefit of the doubt. But, as time passes, we are very frustrated. You hear positive things from Netanyahu, but on the ground, the results are negative.

'When we met him before the elections, he was adamant that only the Likud could attain peace. So we thought he had everything planned in his head, that he had a well-formulated strategy. But now we are asking ourselves whether he has any strategy at all.'

In Cairo, President Mubarak has been even cooler, refusing to meet Netanyahu, pointedly telling Israeli questioners that he cannot force Egyptian businessmen to trade with Israel, with which a peace treaty was signed 17 years ago, or order the Egyptian media to stop being nasty to its leaders.

All is not lost, however. An emergency conference of the Arab League, meeting in Cairo on Sunday, condemned the Netanyahu government's planned expansion of Jewish settlements on the West Bank and the Golan Heights, which it warned could destroy the entire peace process. But the Arab states also rejected a Syrian proposal to put normalisation with Israel on hold.

Frustrated or not, the more moderate Arab regimes are giving Netanyahu another, perhaps a last, chance.

Chapter 11 – 1997-99

Good guys too thin on the ground

The Statesman, Calcutta, January 4, 1997

Wednesday's orgy of gunfire by a 19-year-old off-duty Israeli soldier underscored with the shock of revelation just how volatile relations between Jews and Arabs are in Hebron, a biblical holy city which pits fanatics of both faiths at each others' throats.

The imminent Israeli troop redeployment, dividing the city between 150,000 Palestinians and 450 Jewish settlers, looks increasingly like a fragile stopgap. Roni Shaked, who covers the West Bank for the Tel Aviv tabloid *Yediot Aharonot*, predicts that the new line will be a 'wall of hatred'. Ya'acov Perry, a former chief of the Shin Bet agency, argues that Israel will have to evacuate the settlers whether it likes it or not, after a first, inevitable, violent confrontation.

As so often in the West Asia conflict, in Hebron good guys are thin on the ground. The mutual hostility, the historic fears, the refusal to acknowledge any reciprocal claim, surfaced immediately after the shooting, which wounded seven Arab civilians in a fruit and vegetable market.

Huddled in a shop doorway, a 17-year-old youth who escaped the barrage of automatic fire blamed the Palestinian leader, Yasser Arafat, for acquiescing in a continued Jewish presence. 'That dog Arafat,' he screamed, 'has sold out the Palestinians of this city. The people of Hebron are Muslims. We don't want Jews here. We don't want the settlers. We don't even want peaceful Jews. We don't want Jews, full stop!'

When an older man in traditional Jalabiyeh tunic and Kefiyeh headscarf demurred – he was against the settlers, but said he would entertain a peaceable Jew in his home – a man in his twenties interrupted: 'Don't say that. This is a war between Muslims and infidels. What we have to do is slaughter all the Jews. Only then will there be peace here.'

On the other side of the barricade, David Wilder, a settler spokesman, distanced his community from the gunman, Noam Friedman, who came to Hebron to undermine the peace process. 'We have no control over who comes here,' he said. But no regrets, no condemnation, it was just a reinforcement of settler demands.

'After the shooting,' the American-born Wilder contended, 'there was sheer chaos in the street. The Israeli Army couldn't enforce a curfew. When Arafat's people take over the city, thousands of Palestinians can descend on the area in minutes and overwhelm us. The only solution is to keep the Israeli Army as the sole military authority in Hebron.'

When Noam Friedman was being taken to an Israeli prison, he told reporters that he had fired to prevent the redeployment of troops. His purpose, he said had been to kill the enemies of the Jewish people. It didn't matter whether they were men, women or children. Abraham, he explained, had bought Hebron for the Jews. No one had a right to give it away.

Hebron's history is more chequered than the embattled antagonists are prepared to admit. According to the book of Genesis, Abraham, the common ancestor of Jews and Arabs, bought the Cave of Machpela as a family burial vault. King David reigned in Hebron for seven years before moving to Jerusalem. His son, Absalom, raised the banner of revolt there.

King Herod built a magnificent sanctuary, whose walls still stand, on the site. It served as a church under the Byzantines and the Crusaders till the 14th century when the conquering Mamelukes transformed it into a mosque.

Pious Jews lived in Hebron, as a minority alongside Arabs, for four centuries till 1929, when an Arab mob massacred 67 and injured 60. The British authority then governing Palestine evacuated the remaining 500 to Jerusalem. The first of the current settlers came back after Israel captured the West Bank in the 1967 Six-Day War.

Avraham Burg, a dovish Labour politician whose mother was among dozens of Hebron Jews saved by their Arab neighbours, maintains, like most of the survivors' descendants, that the settlers have no claim to their inheritance.

'These people do not represent me,' he said. 'They are trying to appropriate the massacre. Jews were living in Hebron for 400 years before the massacre. To say that relations between Jews and Arabs in Hebron started in 1929 is just self-serving.'

Burg argues that, despite Jewish ties to the city, the settlers should be removed. But even his own party, when in office, shrank from the prospect. The settlers are armed and would not go quietly. The current coalition of right wing and religious parties would not even contemplate it.

The Likud Prime Minister, Binyamin Netanyahu, did, however, agree to honour Labour's commitment to redeployment, even though it went against the grain of everything he had ever stood for. 'There's no logical reason,' complained the settlers' spokesman, David Wilder, 'but he's going to implement it anyway.'

Yigal Amir, who assassinated the former Prime Minister, Yitzhak Rabin, 14 months ago, believed he would demolish the peace process with one burst of gunfire, so did Noam Friedman.

Both, it seems, got it wrong. If anything, their coups only strengthened Israel and Palestinian determination to see it through. But how many more blows must this fragile peace absorb?

Peace in jeopardy as deadlock deepens
The European, March 27, 1997
Yasser Arafat and Binyamin Netanyahu looked over the brink this week and recoiled. Rather than let the Israeli-Palestinian peace process collapse, both leaders announced that they were ready to talk.

It was a beginning, but nothing more. The Palestinian president was in no hurry to return from an overseas tour, drumming up support in the Muslim world. He was due back on March 28. Perhaps he wanted to make the Israelis fret. Neither Israeli nor Palestinian spokesmen displayed readiness for compromise.

Israel still accused the Palestinian Authority of giving a 'green light' to the kind of suicide bombings which killed three Israeli women and wounded 50 others in a Tel Aviv café. The Palestinians charged Netanyahu with provoking a crisis of trust by dictating terms, rather than negotiating.

Ahmed Qurei, chairman of the Palestinian parliament and an architect of the Oslo peace agreement, told *The European*: 'If Netanyahu wants to restore confidence, he has to freeze all settlement activity until the end of negotiations on the permanent relationship between us.'

That would include work on Har Homa, where Israeli bulldozers began excavating this month to build homes for 6,500 Jewish families in Arab East Jerusalem. Har Homa, Qurei contended, was at the heart of the current confrontation.

Prime Minister Netanyahu insisted on Israel's 'right' to build anywhere in Jerusalem, which Israel annexed after the 1967 Six-Day War, but which both nations claim as their capital. Israel rejected an EU suggestion that it suspend construction in exchange for a Palestinian pledge to fight terror.

The Palestinians were committed to doing that, the Israelis said. The Europeans couldn't expect them to buy the same goods twice.

The Palestinians denied giving a green light to Hamas, the Islamist group that opposes the peace process. Israel maintained the signal had been given, in Gaza, at a meeting between Arafat and opposition leaders on March 9. And the Tel Aviv daily *Ha'aretz* said Israeli intelligence had acquired a transcript.

Jibril Rajoub, the Palestinians' West Bank security chief, said the gathering was only a 'meeting of national reconciliation'. But the Israelis could also interpret visible signs. For within hours of the Gaza meeting, Arafat released more than 100 Hamas militants from preventive detention, among them Ibrahim Makadmeh, a commander of its military wing, according to Israel.

At almost the same time as Mussa Ghanimat, the Hamas suicide bomber, blew himself up in Tel Aviv's Apropos café, Makadmeh swore at a Gaza rally to 'continue on the path of *jihad* [holy war] until we die as martyrs, or until we achieve victory.'

To exultant applause, he added: 'The bulldozers will not be stopped by slogans. Only the *mujaheddin* [warriors] who carry the bombs on their bodies and blow up the enemies of God can do it.' Arafat had him rearrested two days later.

Whether Hamas received the go-ahead from Arafat or not, the Palestinian security services openly acknowledged that they had scaled down co-operation with their Israeli opposite numbers in the war against terror.

Mohammed Dahalan, the head of Palestinian preventive security, told a Gaza press conference that it was impossible to stop every aspiring suicide bomber, adding: 'Up to today we have made efforts to prevent this, but today we will not do so.' And one well-placed US diplomat said: 'The Palestinians see withholding security co-operation as the only card they have to play.' Israel has become dependent on such co-operation for the safety of its citizens as it withdraws its forces from Arab towns and villages in the formerly occupied West Bank and Gaza.

On March 24, leaders of Arafat's Fatah organisation said they were returning to the 'struggle' against Israel. After an emergency session in Bethlehem, they called on Palestinians to fight against settlers and settlements, using 'all means and methods'.

Israel accused Fatah of fomenting riots that saw Palestinian students in Bethlehem and Hebron hurling stones and Molotov cocktails at Israeli troops, who responded with tear gas and rubber bullets.

Israelis are convinced that the Palestinian security forces can restrain the bombers and the gunmen. 'Nothing happens in the Palestinian territories without Arafat's knowledge or acquiescence,' the influential columnist Yoel Marcus wrote in *Ha'aretz*.

'His security men are less gentle than ours, and when they want and receive the right orders, they operate forcefully.' They proved their mettle by bottling up the terrorists for 12 months after last year's winter of suicide bombings.

But if Netanyahu wants to stop the spiralling violence and get the peace process back on track, short of halting the Har Homa construction, what could he do? The US diplomat suggested two immediate measures: the restoration of Jerusalem identity cards to more than 1,000 Palestinians who forfeited their right to live in the city; and a moratorium on land confiscations for roads and settlements on the West Bank.

But these responses will only satisfy in the short term. To create a future for the peace process, the Israeli prime minister must persuade the Palestinians that he wants to talk, not just impose his will.

He could start to do that by showing that he meant what he said when he promised housing for Arabs as well as Jews. He could conclude the long-delayed deals for Palestinian sea and airports in Gaza, and agree to a 'safe passage' Palestinian land route between the West Bank and Gaza.

Time is on the side of war. As the US diplomat warned: 'The longer the situation is deadlocked, the more it becomes possible that a terrorist will set off another bomb – or that Israeli troops will shoot Palestinian demonstrators. The longer the situation goes on, without being defused, the greater the risk of an explosion.'

A brave show of business as usual

Los Angeles Jewish Journal, September 12, 1997

'When's our luck going to run out?' my wife asked after last week's triple suicide bombing on Jerusalem's Ben-Yehuda shopping street. 'They're getting nearer every time.' It was one of those days when people phone around to count their friends.

We live downtown. In March 1996, one of the No 18 bus bombings took place barely a quarter of a mile from us. This summer, on 30 July, two bombs went off in the Mahane Yehuda market, a short walk away, and where we do our weekend shopping. My wife's fish man, Nissim, still has not re-opened his store. His arm was smashed. He's only just come out of the hospital.

The Ben-Yehuda Street explosions were so close, perhaps 300 yards, that they shook the pictures on our walls. Yehudit, the manager of our favourite coffeehouse, Café Atara, was talking to a couple with a baby at an outside table when the first blast hit them. Her leg was wounded; the baby and mother were burned.

Another friend, Natan, who runs a *bureau de change*, saw it all from his office just off Ben-Yehuda, and was the first to help Abe Mendelson, the wounded Los Angeles student who called his father from a hospital bed on prime minister Binyamin Netanyahu's mobile phone.

By next morning, city workers had scrubbed the pavement. Most of the shattered shop windows had been replaced. Café Atara had a new stock of chairs and tables. The crowds started coming back. It was a brave show of business as usual.

But it was a show. No one is running away. The bombers, we tell each other, will not dictate how we lead our lives. Yet we do feel less safe. We are savvy enough in such things to recognise that all the police in the world cannot guarantee that the Hamas kamikaze boys won't get through again.

Jerusalemites, perhaps Israelis everywhere, are worried by the bombings, but they are not in despair. They know that the security forces can reduce the risks. They also know that the job has been made harder by the army's evacuation of major Palestinian population centres – whether they liked or disliked the 1993 Oslo accords that brought it about.

What, then, can Israel do to fight the terror? I turned to Gideon Ezra for a professional answer. Ezra, now one of Netanyahu's Likud legislators, is a former deputy chief of the Shin Bet internal security service. His last assignment, in the early 1990s, was to supervise operations in the West Bank and Jerusalem.

The key, he said, is intelligence. 'You have to collect information,' he said. 'Israel should invest all its efforts with all its best people to collect information on Hamas. But that depends on sources, and, afterward, you have to be able to arrest the suspects and shake the tree until the apples fall down.'

Ezra agreed that Israel cannot do it alone now that the whole of Gaza and much of the West Bank is under Palestinian rule. Recruiting and handling informers is infinitely more difficult. So is interrogating Hamas activists. Cooperation with the Palestinian security services, he said, is essential.

The question remains how effective cooperation can be. Even at the best of times, the experience has not been encouraging. 'We can give names to the Palestinians,' Ezra said, 'but they will only give us what they want us to know. If somebody in an area under our control is involved, they won't tell us because they don't want to hand Palestinians over to us.'

Another problem has been that the Palestinian security services have been too busy extorting bribes from their own citizens to fight terrorism. 'Arafat's people are not interested in collecting information,' Ezra said. 'They are interested in collecting money. They try for one week, then they stop for six months.'

Israel, he argued, has to put pressure on Yasser Arafat to stick to his Oslo commitments. 'The minute we impose a closure, the minute we don't give him money, the minute the Americans don't give him money, he's in trouble. Hamas is a problem for him too. If he doesn't act, he might as well go back and live abroad.'

But Israel, too, can do more. 'We have to see that explosives don't enter the West Bank and Gaza from abroad. The explosives used in recent bombings, TNT and RDX [a plastic explosive], aren't available here. They must have come from outside. They smuggle them with small boats into Gaza and through tunnels under the Egyptian border at Rafah. We have to stop them coming in, and we have to make sure nobody brings explosives through Eilat or across the Dead Sea.'

Israel has also to wage war on Palestinians who slipped into Jerusalem through side routes without permission – usually to work. 'The minute they enter Jerusalem,' he said, 'a car picks them up. We have to arrest the drivers. We have to make people afraid to pick up such people.'

All this will help, but it won't solve the problem once and for all. Yossi Beilin, one of the architects of Oslo, still believes that Israel has to offer a carrot as well as a stick. 'Arafat,' he said, 'cannot fight terrorism if the street is with Hamas. And the street is with Hamas if Israeli policy does not give any hope to the Palestinian people.'

Over to you, Secretary Albright.

Israel pays tribute to King Hussein

Los Angeles Jewish Journal, February 12, 1999

Israel mourned King Hussein this week as one of its own. The government ordered flags flown at half-mast on all public buildings. Flower children lit memorial candles in Tel Aviv's Rabin Square. In a conscious echo of Bill Clinton's valediction to Yitzhak Rabin, the two mass-circulation daily papers headlined their lead stories 'Shalom, Friend' and 'Shalom, King'.

Ruhama Cohen, whose daughter was one of seven Beit Shemesh schoolgirls shot dead two years ago by a Jordanian soldier during a trip to the 'border of peace', gave birth to another daughter on Saturday just as Hussein was losing his last battle. She named her 'Jordan' in the king's honour.

'He was a good man,' Ruhama told reporters from her bed in Jerusalem's Hadassah hospital. 'I remember how he came to our house after the tragedy, knelt and wept. He helped us, our families, and also the peace. Even when he was ill, he kept in touch with us.'

It was that visit of condolence and contrition that convinced grassroots Israelis that the peace with Jordan was for real. A crowned monarch went from house to house, knelt beside mothers and fathers, sitting shivah on shabby mattresses, and begged forgiveness for the 'shame' brought on his nation by one of its soldiers.

Israelis have not erased the down side of their common inheritance. It was precisely because Jordan's army had fought against Israel in the 1948 and 1967 wars, and sundry skirmishes in between, that Israelis cherished the 'warm' peace Hussein offered them in 1994 – and sustained despite the scepticism of many of his own citizens.

Chief Rabbi Yisrael Meir Lau, who visited Hussein in the Mayo Clinic six months ago, celebrated him this week as 'a hero of heroes'. The Jewish sages, he explained, defined a hero of heroes as 'he who makes his enemy into his beloved'.

Eitan Haber, Rabin's advisor, speechwriter and confidant, recalled his own first private conversation with Hussein. Addressing the dead king through his column in *Yediot Aharonot*, Haber wrote:

I started by telling you that I would never forget that you had been our enemy. Friends of mine, many of them, I told you, were killed on your orders.

'The Israelis also killed us, many of us,' you answered. How many from Jordan and how many from Israel were killed in the various wars? You said a number, I said mine, and then, while still amicably disagreeing, you said, 'People are not numbers. Every dead person is 100 per cent dead for his family. Every one dead is one too many.'

In mourning Hussein as one of its own, Israel may have crossed a Middle Eastern Rubicon. 'There are cynical people among us,' Hemi Shalev commented in *Ma'ariv* on the morning of the King's funeral, 'who are impatient with the collective sadness that has descended upon us, but Israel's mourning of Hussein and identification with the Jordanian people's sadness is a ray of hope, after a long period of darkness and despair.

'The public in Israel never loved an Arab leader as it loved Hussein, and never felt so close to its neighbours as it will feel today. Like the historic visit of the late Egyptian President Anwar Sadat, and Hussein's noble gesture when he visited Beit Shemesh, this is something which breaks down barriers. It is an emotional and psychological experience which, in the future, might seem like a turning point, maybe even a momentous one.'

The British actress, Sian Phillips, currently touring Israel, opens her one-woman show by telling the audience she nearly caused an international incident in 1962 when her husband, Peter O'Toole, was filming *Lawrence of Arabia* near Aqaba. Jordanian extras hoisted her on a racing camel, slapped its rump and sent it speeding towards Eilat. One of them managed to halt it just short of the mines and the barbed wire.

This week a vast Israeli delegation, led by President Ezer Weizman and Prime Minister Binyamin Netanyahu, not only mingled with Arab and world leaders at Hussein's funeral, they drove there across the Allenby Bridge and back. The party openly included Ephraim Halevy, the head of the Mossad secret service. And no one marvelled. The transformation had become routine.

Yet anxiety sits on the shoulder of Israel's grief. Is it all too good to be true now that Hussein has gone and his 37-year-old son, Abdullah, an unknown quantity, has succeeded to the throne?

The transition is expected to be smooth – at least for the short term. Despite ex-Crown Prince Hassan's disappointment at losing the prize for which he had been groomed for 34 years, the royal family is closing ranks. The new king, a career soldier, can rely on the army. Uncle Sam and the Gulf oil states are shoring up the shaky dinar.

But the succession raises disturbing questions. Abdullah had no time to prepare himself. He has acknowledged that he was as surprised as the rest of us when the dying king named him his heir. He learnt of it only 24 hours before the official announcement. Abdullah's international links are limited. In Israel, for instance, he has contacts in the military, but none among politicians.

In the condolence line after Hussein's interment, Netanyahu shook hands with Abdullah, but embraced Hassan as an old friend. For Israel, Hassan would have been a more comfortable choice. He learnt Hebrew at Oxford, he reads Maimonides, and he works for Muslim-Jewish reconciliation.

Abdullah, by contrast, not only knows no Hebrew. The new, British-educated, king is having to brush up his spoken Arabic. He will have to learn quickly. And not only his native language.

Chapter 12 – 1999-2001

A profile of Ehud Barak

Los Angeles Jewish Journal, May 31, 1999

Two decades ago, after hearing the then Colonel Ehud Barak deliver a eulogy for a fallen comrade, Haim Guri, a popular Israeli poet, predicted: 'One day this man will be prime minister.' On May 17, Israel's voters proved him right. Barak was elected by a landslide, 56 per cent to 44 per cent for the right-wing incumbent, Binyamin Netanyahu – the younger brother of the man he eulogised in 1976, Yonatan Netanyahu, killed rescuing a planeload of hijacked passengers at Entebbe airport.

His countrymen have been prophesying great things for Barak since he launched his military career nearly 40 years ago. When he passed out of his first officers' course with distinction, the chief-of-staff, Yitzhak Rabin, said: 'If this boy doesn't make chief-of-staff, there's something wrong with the system.' Moshe Dayan, the sceptical, eye-patched hero of the 1967 Six-Day War, added: 'He's too good to be true.'

When Barak hung up his uniform in 1995 after four years in the army's top job, Rabin brought him into his cabinet and tapped him as heir apparent. He served briefly as minister of the interior, then foreign minister (after Rabin's assassination in November that year). Following Netanyahu's defeat of Rabin's successor, Shimon Peres, in 1996, Barak was elected leader of the Labour Party.

In this spring's election, he fought like a general. His campaign was focused. He selected his targets – the Russian immigrant voters, as well as the disenchanted blue-collar Sephardim, who had voted Netanyahu in 1996, then found themselves on the dole – and stuck to them. 'He was at the heart of every decision,' testified one of his American spin-doctors, Robert Shrum. 'Once he makes up his mind,' said an old friend, Ron Ben-Yishai, 'he goes at it like a missile.'

Like Rabin and Dayan, the 57-year-old Barak will always be seen as a soldier turned politician. But he brings a broader, more trained intellect to the premiership. After the 1967 war, he took a BSc in mathematics and physics at Jerusalem's Hebrew University and a master's in systems analysis at Stanford in California. He is an accomplished classical pianist. Acquaintances say he can talk as knowledgeably about the novels of Dostoyevsky and Proust as about those of the modern Israeli masters Amos Oz and A B Yeshoshua. He jogs, likes a good cigar and an occasional drink. The eulogy he delivered for Yonatan Netanyahu is taught in Israeli high schools for the richness of its Hebrew language. His wife, Navah, teaches English. They have three grown-up daughters.

Barak was born of pioneering, kibbutz stock in Mishmar Hasharon, where his parents still live. In the army, he commanded the top special operations unit. As Israel's most decorated soldier – a record his television campaign spots highlighted remorselessly – he won the Distinguished Service Medal and four citations.

In May, 1972, he led a squad, disguised as white-overalled maintenance men, who stormed a hijacked Belgian airliner at Tel Aviv airport. A month later, he and his commandos snatched five Syrian intelligence officers, on a tour of inspection in Southern Lebanon, as a bargaining counter for Israeli prisoners of war. The following spring, dressed as a buxom woman tourist with a brunette wig, Barak led a hit team that landed in Lebanon from the sea and killed three Palestinian leaders in their Beirut apartments.

After graduating from Special Forces, he went on to command an armoured division and the intelligence corps. Subordinates dubbed him 'Napoleon', a reference not just to his stocky build, but to his supreme self-confidence and intolerance of those who failed to measure up to his standards.

Amos Gilboa, Barak's deputy at military intelligence, said: 'He is very demanding. Freedom to do things without his permission is a privilege for those he trusts. You have to get it right. If he sees that people handle things loosely or against his directives, he will come down on them without mercy.'

Ron Ben-Yishai, a military commentator who served with Barak as a young officer and studied with him at university, added: 'He's very determined, very ambitious. He's a man of his word. He thinks very fast and tends to rely on himself. But he reacts slowly. He's a calculator, a tough guy. It is very difficult to pressure him.'

As a civilian politician, he has learnt to seek advice. 'He listens,' said Ben-Yishai. 'He respects different opinions. He's open-minded. He grasps things very quickly. The downside is that he gets bored very easily, then he neglects things he ought not to neglect.'

On the campaign trail, he learnt to glad-hand the voters, if not quite to kiss their babies. 'He was never an emotional person,' Ben-Yishai explained, 'but once he saw that it was important to hug people if he wanted to win, he became one.'

Similarly, the strictly secular Barak has started quoting Jewish texts, something his friends say he never did before. He is courting religious parties in an attempt to build a government of national reconciliation. 'He quotes the Bible, and quotes it fluently, because he thinks he needs it,' said Ben-Yishai. 'It's an instrument, but he's not a liar. He wasn't anti-religious before. He's always respected the Jewish tradition.'

Like Dayan and Rabin, Ehud Barak is a Labour hawk destined to make peace. He starts with a huge fund of goodwill, at home and abroad. Israeli analysts are warning him not to squander it. 'The real test of his leadership,' Sima Karmon wrote in the mass-circulation *Yediot Aharonot* in the heady dawn of May 18, 'starts this morning.'

A Barak diary

Los Angeles Jewish Journal, November 19, 1999

Ehud Barak stomps down the aisle of the old white Boeing 707 that doubles as Israel's Air Force One. He has come to shmooze with the travelling press corps. Close up, he is shorter than expected. He clenches his shoulders like a muscle-bound wrestler. His pudgy face looks as if it was moulded from children's modelling dough, his hair as if he still has it trimmed by his old army barber. No $200 stylist at the airport for him.

Barak's brisk, efficient media adviser, David Ziso, describes himself as 'the prime minister's personal spokesman and producer'. There is indeed an element of performance about all his boss's appearances, even off the record and 30,000 feet over the Mediterranean.

The prime minister is genial and informal, but never totally relaxed. He listens to himself speak. He teases political reporters by their first names, flirts with the women among us, but inoffensively. You won't catch him calling them *meidele* as Ezer Weizman, another macho general turned politician, might. He asks to be introduced to the half dozen foreign correspondents in the party.

Ziso confides that Barak has taken a conscious decision not to emulate you-know-who and spout sound bites as a substitute for policy. If anything, the Labour leader has gone too far the other way. Like Golda Meir and Menachem Begin – and for all I know David Ben-Gurion – he belongs to the didactic school of prime minister.

He mocks that he reads the Hebrew press to find out what's going on in his government, but on the plane there is little dialogue. Barak educates. He is determined to be understood, without any room for doubt or confusion. Politics being politics, media being media, he won't always succeed, but it won't be for want of trying.

Standing between the seats, with the journalists craning our necks to hear him above the engine noise and air conditioners, Barak spells out his strategy for the final-status negotiations just starting with the Palestinians.

A nervous press officer, Gadi Baltiansky, late of the Washington embassy, reminds us that it's all 'background', attributable to senior officials etc. In fact, at least 90 per cent of what Barak said was on the record in his own speeches, stakeouts and press conferences within 24 hours.

His contention that United Nations Security Council Resolution 242, which calls for Israel to withdraw from territory captured in the 1967 war, didn't apply equally to the Palestinian track as it did to the Egyptian, Jordanian and even Syrian was less surprising for its content than for the provocative way it was presented.

We – and the Palestinians – know that he does not intend to pull back to the old 'Green Line' armistice border, but Barak sounded as if he was repudiating the sacred resolution, the template for all Middle East peace efforts for three decades, root and branch. Once the wire services filed, he was quick to limit the damage. Of course, Israel was committed to 242, but...

The nearest to an indiscretion was a mildly sexy description of the way Barak is wooing Syria's Hafez Assad. It remains 'not for quoting', even by those anonymous officials. But my own impression, from airborne and terrestrial briefings during the prime minister's visit to Paris in early November, is that he knows no more than us about Assad's readiness to make a compromise peace.

Barak says flattering, optimistic things about the ailing Syrian president. Like a girl dropping her handkerchief in an old-fashioned romantic movie, he hopes Assad will pick it up. Maybe yes, maybe no. Assad's son and heir, Bashar, met French President Jacques Chirac the day before Barak. The verdict in the Israeli camp, after Chirac had privately briefed Barak, was that Basher's mission hadn't made a breakthrough any less likely. Don't hold the front page.

In his public appearances, Barak was confident and assertive – a man with a mission to complete the circle of peace, but not at the cost of Israel's security. Dare I suggest that he ease off on his military past? We've all read that he was Israel's most decorated warrior. As the world gets to know him, he doesn't have to keep reminding us. The law of diminishing returns soon takes its toll. At one point, he actually said: 'Having spent most of my adult life as a general.'

On the flight back to Tel Aviv, the prime minister sent his aides to talk to the travelling press corps. We had, it seems, had our ration of quality Barak time. In any case, we were strapped to our seats for most of the four hours. An electric storm was raging over the Mediterranean. The pilot, a veteran air force colonel, turned off the lights and took us way above the clouds and put his foot on the gas.

I watched the lightning flash from my window seat. No one else seemed worried, but I kept wondering if I was going to have the story of a lifetime - and never be able to write it.

The Palestinian Authority in Abu Dis

Los Angeles Jewish Journal, May 19, 2000

'Palestinian Authority: Economics Studies Centre,' reads the grimy Arabic sign high on the wall of the imposing new building rising on a rocky, ragged hillside in the West Bank village of Abu Dis.

As we pick our way inside, through the rubble and raw cement, planks and ladders, the only economics lesson taught by the genial young site engineer, Hussam Mousa, is that Yasser Arafat's government-in-the-making doesn't have enough money to finish the job. A couple of labourers are languidly plastering a concrete beam, but no one is hurrying to fill the dusty, completed shell.

Yet even if its reputation had not gone before it, this doesn't look like a business school. The main, two-storey building is a vast chamber; the adjacent seven stories an office block. The architect is Jaffer Touqan, the man who designed the Jordanian parliament two hours' drive away in Amman. The choice was no accident.

Like an enigma from *A Thousand and One Nights* the building, with its narrow, vertical windows and mellow limestone cladding, is a parliament that is not a parliament for a capital that is not a capital in a state that is not a state. Not yet, anyway.

Abu Dis, on the eastern fringe of Jerusalem, is currently under Palestinian civil administration, but Israeli security supervision (though the only police in sight were directing traffic at the entrance to the village). Part of it falls within the negligent jurisdiction of the Israeli Jerusalem municipality, which acquired it when the victors expanded the city limits after the 1967 Six-Day War. Although they are not Israeli citizens, about 20 per cent of its 14,000 Arab inhabitants hold Israeli Jerusalem identity cards, which makes it easier for them to work or shop across the border that is not a border.

The new building's assembly hall is in 'Palestine', but the office block is in 'Israeli' Jerusalem. This may yet prove more than a bureaucratic curiosity. Abu Dis is one of three neighbouring Arab villages the Israeli Prime Minister, Ehud Barak, is planning to deliver to full Palestinian self-rule as a 'down payment' towards a Palestinian state.

Optimistic Israelis suggest that Arafat could call it Al Quds (Arabic for Jerusalem) and establish his capital there. From the yard outside the new parliament building, you can see the slim pencil-like tower on the Mount of Olives that marks the spot from which Christians believe Jesus ascended to Heaven. Al Aqsa, Islam's third holiest mosque, is barely a mile away as the crow flies (the same distance as the Knesset from the Western Wall).

So, the spin goes, Palestine would have its capital in Al Quds, as Arafat promises his people daily, and Israel would retain Jerusalem as the 'eternal, undivided capital of the Jewish people'. Bingo! Except that, as Ali Johar, an elderly gent sunning himself outside an auto accessories shop, insists, 'Jerusalem is Jerusalem, Abu Dis is Abu Dis.'

Othman Muhamad Qurei, the 72-year-old *mukhtar* (village headman), concurs. 'We are proud,' he says, 'that we are going to have a parliament here, but we are not proud that they say this is Jerusalem.' The mukhtar, who happens to be an uncle of Abu Ala, the speaker of the Palestinian legislative council, is a study in white. White hair, trim white beard, white eyebrows, Persil-white head scarf, ankle-length white shirt. Abu Dis is a suburban village, he explains. Jerusalem is where you go if you want to buy shoes.

So, do they want to be under full Palestinian rule? In the Jerusalem Internet cafe, Samer Saman, an electronics student, says: 'I am Palestinian, and I want my government to be Palestinian. At the moment we have no proper government here. It has to be better. I hope so.'

Yet not everyone in Abu Dis shares even such qualified enthusiasm. 'Many people don't want the Palestinian Authority,' says Nasser Arar, a 30-year-old labourer who works on Israeli construction sites. 'It's going to be difficult. We are afraid we'll lose our ID cards, along with the health and national insurance benefits that go with them. The PA gives us nothing.'

Yousef Idais, a fruit and vegetable vendor, is worried about the abuses for which the Palestinian security services have become notorious. Idais, 28, moved to Abu Dis from Hebron. 'They arrested five of my brothers and cousins there,' he says. 'They said they'd made passes at girls in the street. The police shaved their heads and beat them, then threw them out in the street.'

Like the best enigmas, Abu Dis remains hard to read. Not least because no one is sure Barak really will hand it over. And if so, when. 'The problem with Abu Dis,' advises Rami Mahmoud, a savvy, 16-year-old schoolboy, 'is that people are afraid of both Israel and the Palestinian Authority. Don't believe a word anyone says.'

A bold gamble at Camp David

Los Angeles Jewish Journal, July 14, 2000

The Camp David summit looks like the boldest gamble by an Israeli leader since the founding father, David Ben-Gurion, declared the Jewish state in May, 1948, to the rumble of invading Arab guns and the chattering teeth of his own querulous associates. Ehud Barak flew to the United States this week determined to make peace with the Palestinians, but with his coalition government and parliamentary support in tatters.

Three of Barak's coalition partners – the Sephardi Orthodox Shas, the pro-settler National Religious Party and the Russian immigrants' Yisrael B'aliyah – resigned at the very prospect of a peace agreement that would require Israel to yield more territory in the occupied West Bank and Gaza Strip. The foreign minister, David Levy, declined to accompany Barak to the Maryland retreat, where Menachem Begin set a pattern for peace with Egypt's Anwar Sadat in September, 1978.

Commenting in the mass-circulation Yediot Aharonot, the novelist Meir Shalev called the coalition defectors rats of a very special kind. 'These rats,' he wrote, 'are not deserting the ship when it is sinking, but when it sets sail.' In the up-market *Ha'aretz*, Yoel Marcus compared the prime minister's embarrassment to Haydn's *Farewell* symphony, which ends with each musician rising in turn to put out a candle and leave the stage until the conductor stands alone in the darkness.

Barak is celebrated as Israel's most decorated soldier, a veteran of some of the most daring commando operations behind enemy lines. He is also the least experienced politician among the 10 men and women who have served as the country's prime minister over the past 52 years. In the current crisis, he is showing both sides of his record.

He is going for broke at the summit. Peace, he believes rightly or wrongly, is attainable. And peace is worth the risks. In a governing culture tainted with faction, interest and compromise that takes rare courage. 'I need to stand above all these political differences and all these party considerations,' a beleaguered Barak said, 'and to make every possible effort in the search for a peace agreement which will end the bloodshed between us and our neighbours.'

Yet he cannot blame anyone else for the humiliation of his disintegrating base. His ambition to be 'everybody's prime minister', the head of a government embracing left and right, religious and secular, eastern and western, Jews and Arabs, was doomed from the start.

You can, as he had, serve as everybody's chief-of-staff. The army is, by definition and consensus, everybody's army. But democratic politics is about the clash of conflicting ideals, conflicting interests and conflicting claims on national resources. In a society like Israel's, still defining its identity and its place in a hostile geographical environment, such conflicts cannot be wished away. Rivals are not silenced with jobs, handouts and sweet talk. Not for long anyway. The voters elect leaders, who then have to make hard choices that won't please all the people all the time.

The three parties that have now bailed out of Barak's coalition all served in the Likud administration headed by Binyamin Netanyahu. By instinct and ideology, they were more at home with the nationalist right. They never pretended to support the kind of territorial compromise that even the most 'moderate' Palestinian might swallow. As soon as Barak put them to the test, they jumped ship.

Foreign minister Levy was another shortsighted import. A former construction worker, he was a product of the Likud, a protégé of Menachem Begin, who fostered him as a rallying point for the large, disaffected North African Jewish minority. Barak bought him over with a top place on his One Israel list for the 1999 elections – as a symbol of ethnic reconciliation – then flattered him with the foreign ministry.

Yet as soon as he needed some serious diplomatic spadework, Barak assigned it to other confidants, whom he evidently judged to be better qualified. Levy may have been genuinely uneasy with the emerging Palestinian deal. But he was also hurt and insulted. As he demonstrated in his break with Netanyahu in the previous government, he knows how to take his revenge. He did so this week by rejecting Barak's invitation to join him in Maryland, though he remains at the foreign ministry and is serving as acting prime minister in Barak's absence.

With or without his foreign minister, with or without a government, with or without a parliamentary majority, the prime minister persisted in going to the summit. He is putting his faith in the 56 per cent of the population who gave him a mandate for peace and for change a year ago under Israel's two-tier electoral system, where citizens vote separately for prime minister and parliament.

'In the coming days at Camp David,' Barak told them, 'I will need to take my strength from you, the people. I will know that I am there on your behalf.' Speaking at Ben-Gurion airport after suffering a moral 54-52 defeat in the Knesset, he promised 'to try and return with an agreement that will strengthen Israel, an agreement that will be brought for the approval of the people, because the people sent me and gave me a mandate, and only they will decide.' Monday night's no-confidence vote fell short of the absolute majority of 61 to force him to resign.

Barak's game plan is to go over the heads of the politicians. If, as he wishes, he negotiates a compromise peace that ends the conflict with the Palestinians, but leaves Israel strong enough to defend its independence, he will call new elections and take it to the people.

There are signs that Barak may have judged the popular mood better than his tormentors and detractors. An opinion poll published in *Yediot Aharonot* on Monday found 52 per cent supporting his decision to go to the summit, with 45 per cent thinking he should have stayed home. Asked whether the prime minister still had a mandate to make concessions to the Palestinians, 53 per cent said yes, 44 per cent no.

Another survey, Tel Aviv University's 'Peace Index', found 61 per cent of Jewish voters still supporting the Israeli-Palestinian negotiations, with varying degrees of enthusiasm. Now all Barak has to do is convince Yasser Arafat.

After the failure of the summit
Los Angeles Jewish Journal, July 28, 2000

Camp David is dead, long live Camp David. Yasser Arafat flew home yesterday (Wednesday) from the abortive Maryland summit to an orchestrated hero's welcome as the historic leader who steadfastly refused to surrender Palestinian priorities. Ehud Barak followed in his slipstream, projecting himself as the brave Israeli warrior who had been ready to pay 'a heavy price' for peace, but 'not any price'.

Yet, like partners in a Catholic marriage, they are stuck with each other. They can't go backwards. Seven years after the Oslo breakthrough, the Middle East has moved on. Israelis, of right as well as left, no longer delude themselves that they can rule three million Arabs and remain a democracy. The Palestinians recognise that they couldn't win an all-out national liberation struggle.

Nor can either side stand still. The sliver of real estate between the Mediterranean and the Jordan is an unstable patchwork of sovereign and semi-sovereign areas that makes sense only as a transitional phase to a more viable configuration. And the clock is ticking towards the end of the Oslo interim period – and to Arafat's threatened unilateral declaration of a Palestinian state on September 13.

'The process is not over,' said the strategic analyst Yossi Alpher, a former special adviser to Barak. 'It is hard to think that Barak will simply say I'm finished dealing with the peace process. They're going to have to get back to talking.'

What, though, would they talk about? 'They closed some gaps,' Alpher insisted. 'They made some progress, on security and territory. On Jerusalem, what we witnessed was the slaughtering of sacred cows. Barak initiated a public debate, far beyond anything we have known before, on what there is about Jerusalem that is important to us.

'Perhaps they might now consider a partial agreement. It is conceivable that Arafat felt he had to make a tough stand, but that he can be more flexible next time. We'll be back to business some time, maybe sooner rather than later. And Oslo remains the only frame of reference.'

Barak's announcement at the end of the summit that all bets were off ('Nothing is agreed until everything is agreed') convinces no one. 'The mere fact,' commented the liberal daily *Ha'aretz*, 'that the core issues of the Israeli-Palestinian conflict were discussed is a turning point from which there is no return. The era of sloganeering is over.'

The political commentator Nahum Barnea wrote in the mass-circulation *Yediot Aharonot*: 'What happened at Camp David was not a funeral, nor was it a two-week stand that is now over.' The Israeli right is preparing, nonetheless, to deliver its eulogy – on the 1993 Oslo peace formula, if not, heaven forbid, on peace itself.

The Likud opposition leader, Ariel Sharon, said he was willing to discuss joining a national-unity government under Barak. 'If he invites me,' he said, 'I will meet him. The ball is in the prime minister's court. It depends what he decides to do.'

On the messianic settler fringe, Rabbi Benny Elon held out a poisoned chalice. 'The only peace that will result from Camp David,' predicted the far-right National Union MP, 'will be peace among Jews, who will unite now to protect Jerusalem against the joint enemy.'

The right, in other words, is ready to join forces with Barak, provided the prime minister repudiates all the compromises he dangled at Camp David: withdrawal from most of the territory still occupied in the West Bank and Gaza Strip; transfer of some isolated settlers to blocks that would become part of Israel; a token return, under the guise of family reunion, of some Palestinian refugees to Israel proper; a measure of shared control in Jerusalem. But there is no sign that Barak is backtracking.

Dovish Knesset members, from Barak's One Israel, Meretz and the Centre Party, are already signalling that they would refuse to join a coalition which would write 'finis' to any chance of moving towards peace. Barak would find himself, like an Israeli Ramsay MacDonald, a Labour prime minister heading a Conservative government. In Israel's polarised political culture, wall-to-wall coalitions can say 'No', they can't say 'Yes'. They can make war, they can't make peace.

'I don't see how Barak can set up a unity government,' said Yossi Alpher, 'since it is clear to Sharon what his points of departure are in negotiations with the Palestinians and the Syrians, and these are not acceptable to him. If Barak went for the Sharon option, he would be slamming the door in Yasser Arafat's face, slamming the door in Bashar Assad's face. Only if the assessment shifts to very strong expectations of a violent confrontation with the Palestinians, would it look like more of an option.'

It remains easier to forecast what Barak won't do than what he will, or can. The Camp David failure takes some of the immediate heat off the prime minister. The opposition will be less eager to press no-confidence votes. In any case, the Knesset goes into summer recess next week, which will give Barak a three-month respite.

Assuming he does not rush into the arms of the Likud, he will find it equally hard to reconstruct the broad-based coalition that disintegrated on the eve of the Maryland summit. The pro-settler National Religious Party and Natan Sharansky's Russian immigrant Yisrael B'aliyah remain adamantly opposed to territorial compromise. The Sephardi ultra-Orthodox Shas pulled out as soon as Barak announced that he was ready to talk turkey with Arafat.

The only alternative, in that case, would be a 'secular' coalition, embracing One Israel, the left-liberal Meretz, Tommy Lapid's militantly anti-religious Shinui, the Arab parties and an assortment of floating legislators. But Barak knew, before he went to Camp David that he would not be able to rely on the loyalty of these parties or of maverick MPs within them.

Logic points, therefore, to elections within a year, perhaps even sooner. Barak will try to call them on his terms, as the strong leader who brought the boys home from Lebanon and advanced the peace process, rather than be forced to go to the nation as a lame duck. But even then, under Israel's discredited two-tier electoral system in which the people vote separately for prime minister and Knesset, there is no guarantee that he will emerge with a more congenial legislature.

On the edge of the abyss

Maclean's, October 23, 2000

The dream of bringing peace to the Middle East faded when two Israeli soldiers made a wrong turn and ended up in the Palestinian town of Ramallah. They were arrested, but as rumours of their seizure spread, a mob of Palestinians surged towards the police station where they were being held. About ten men broke in and stabbed the two soldiers to death before throwing their bodies into the streets where they were battered with iron bars while other Palestinians joyfully shook their fists in the air. The Israelis responded with fury. Helicopter gunships fired rockets into Ramallah and at Palestinian Authority chairman Yasser Arafat's headquarters in nearby Gaza City. 'The peace process is dead,' said Israeli communications minister Binyamin Ben-Eliezer as plumes of black smoke rose over Ramallah. 'Arafat's clear desire is for war.'

The deaths of the soldiers in Ramallah on October 12 and Israel's strong response added urgency to the UN attempts to arrange an emergency summit meeting in the Egyptian Red Sea resort of Sharm-el-Sheikh that would bring an end to the violence. After two weeks of bloodshed, nearly 100 people were dead and 3,000 wounded, the vast majority of them Palestinians. As the body count mounted under the Israeli barrage, the rush to war seemed to accelerate again when an explosives-laden rubber raft piloted by suicide bombers rammed a US guided-missile destroyer and exploded in the Yemeni port of Aden, killing 17 US sailors and injuring 38. Authorities believe two obscure terrorist groups may have launched the attack in retaliation over US support for Israel. The killing of the Israeli soldiers and the attack on the American ship also created new complications for international efforts led by UN Secretary-General Kofi Annan to end the growing violence. And the insecurity only increased with the weekend hijacking of a London-bound Saudi airliner over Egypt. 'The peace process in its present form doesn't appear to have a chance,' said Israel's acting foreign minister Shlomo Ben-Ami.

The current clashes erupted on September 28, following a visit by Israel's right-wing opposition leader, Ariel Sharon, to a holy site in Jerusalem that is sacred to both Jews and Muslims. Sharon, who was surrounded by security guards, made the trip to demonstrate that Israel has no intention of ever relinquishing control of any part of the city in a peace deal with the Palestinians. The Jews revere it as the Temple Mount, where Solomon built his House of the Lord. To the Muslims, it is the Haram al Sharif, the setting of their third-holiest mosque after those of Mecca and Medina. Most Israelis admit that Sharon's visit was the spark that ignited the violence. Increasingly, however, Israelis of the left as well as the right accuse Arafat of seizing on the incident as a pretext for reviving the intifada uprising. The main difference between the 1987-1993 clashes and the current violence is that the Palestinian side now has guns as well as rocks and petrol bombs to fight with.

With the violence spreading from the West Bank and Gaza into Israel's own Arab towns and villages, many people across the region seemed to be giving up all hope the Oslo accord, which launched the Middle East peace process seven years ago, would ever bear fruit. Maurice Singer, the 55-year-old manager of a job recruitment agency in the town of Ra'anana, north of Tel Aviv, once supported the peace process. But he spoke for thousands of Israelis when he said he now has grave doubts. 'The Arab policy is to let us take an inch, then grab a mile,' said Singer, a father of three grown children. 'Every time the Arabs have a minor victory, it becomes a major victory for them. It just spurs them on.'

The view from the Palestinian side has also hardened. Jihad al Wazir, a Palestinian in his mid-30s who runs an international trade centre in Gaza, said the world, and Israel, underestimated the anger, frustration and helplessness of ordinary Palestinians as Jewish settlements kept expanding in the occupied territories and the Arabs saw no real gains from the peace process. Al Wazir's father, known as Abu Jihad, was one of Arafat's deputies, in charge of the armed struggle in the occupied West Bank and Gaza Strip. He was assassinated by Israeli commandos in Tunis in 1988. His widow, Umm Jihad, is now a minister in Arafat's administration. 'They saw the silence of the Palestinian people as acquiescence and not the eye of the storm,' Jihad al Wazir said. 'Today, we are seeing the beginning of the storm. It ushers in the end of the Oslo cycle.'

The Israelis continue to believe that they made important concessions that should have led down the road to peace – not war. Among them: sharing control of the administration of Jerusalem. 'This government,' said Ben-Ami, the acting foreign minister, 'has gone to the outer limits of the capacity of any Israeli government to reach a reasonable compromise with the Palestinians. And then we get this outburst of violence.' He accused Arafat of orchestrating the violence to win over the sympathy of the international community, adding: 'This cynical attempt to lubricate the improvement of an international image with the blood of Palestinians is tragic.'

According to Palestinian legislator Hanan Ashrawi, the impasse might be impossible to bridge. 'The situation is critical,' she said. 'I think Israel should withdraw from our towns and villages, then say: Let's talk and come to arrangements. Then it might be possible to scale things down. So long as they are there, it's impossible.'

But Prime Minister, Ehud Barak shows no sign of pulling Israeli troops out of the occupied territories – even as Arafat vowed to continue the fight. He emerged belligerent and unhurt after the Israeli attack near his headquarters and visited the wounded in a Gaza hospital. The Palestinian people, he said, will 'continue their march to Jerusalem, the capital of the Palestinian independent state.'

While Israel stepped up its military campaign, there were calls for Barak to form an emergency national-unity government. The advocates of a unity government include communications minister Ben-Eliezer, a retired general and former West Bank commander, along with right-wingers like Sharon, whose Likud party says it will serve under Barak only if he abandons the Oslo peace accords. Sharon, who was the mastermind of Israel's 1982 invasion of Lebanon, is widely hated by Palestinians, and many analysts believe his presence in the government would hurt future peace talks.

The hardening on both sides undermined Annan's efforts to broker a truce. Arafat wanted a broad international inquiry into the cause of the strife. Barak and US President Bill Clinton, however, favoured a smaller summit, chaired by the United States. After meeting with Arafat on Friday, Annan said he expected a US-led summit to be convened within 48 hours at Sharm-el-Sheikh. On Saturday, Arafat dropped his demand for an international inquiry into the fighting and agreed to attend the summit, scheduled to be held on Monday.

The ramming of the USS Cole, one of the world's most advanced warships, in Aden appeared designed to test US resolve to bring peace to the area. The Cole, with a crew of 300, was in port for refuelling when the explosion ripped a hole 12 by 12 metres in the side of the 8,600-tonne ship. Two previously unknown terrorist groups, the Islamic Deterrence Forces and Mohammed's Army later took credit for the blast, while Clinton vowed to find and punish those responsible. And he said the deaths would not deter US peace efforts. 'If their intention was to deter us from our mission of promoting peace and security in the Middle East,' said Clinton, 'they will fail utterly.'

Powerful players in the Arab community, however, including Sheikh Ahmed Yassin, the founder and spiritual leader of the Hamas Islamic Resistance, vowed to fight on regardless of whether a ceasefire is reached. 'You are living on occupied land that you stole,' the wheelchair-bound Muslim cleric said, addressing the people of Israel. 'You are living on land whose homes you destroyed and whose sons were killed. You have no future in this region.'

To further complicate matters, Annan is trying to negotiate a prisoner exchange between Israel and the Lebanese Hezbollah guerrillas, who abducted three Israeli soldiers from a border post last weekend. If the soldiers are killed, analysts predict, Israel could widen the conflict by once again invading south Lebanon, a region Israel invaded in 1982, and finally retreated from in May.

The escalating violence has, meanwhile, undermined the peace movement in Israel. 'Even people like me, who have worked for peace at the grassroots, have doubts now about the trustworthiness of their Palestinian friends,' said Janet Aviad, a veteran leader of the Peace Now movement. 'Everyone has been shocked by the expressions of hatred on both sides.' She remains convinced, though, that Israelis and Palestinians will have to resume the peace negotiations eventually. But even peace campaigners acknowledge that their dream of a new Middle East is slipping away. Aviad, an American-born sociologist, suggests that politicians would have to 'separate these two peoples as much as possible, to place them on an equal footing and hope that we will transcend the hostility.'

But transcending hostility seems almost impossible in a settlement like Shilo, in the Palestinian-controlled area between Ramallah and Nablus. It is also home to Israeli settlers like Shner Katz, a black-bearded teacher in his 40s who has lived in Shilo with his wife and children for 10 years. 'It's very hard,' he said following a funeral for Rabbi Hillel Lieberman, a 37-year-old, New York City-born rabbi whose bullet-riddled body was found last week in a cave near Nablus. 'We've been stoned. We're being shot at all the time. We don't know how much longer we can stand such a situation.' Did that mean he was preparing to pull out? 'Never,' he vowed. 'Only our dead bodies will leave this place. This is our country, this is our home.'

Nothing to go back to

Sunday Statesman, Calcutta, November 12, 2000

After six weeks of violence that has killed at least 176 Palestinians and a dozen Israelis, both sides are now pursuing a policy of 'talk and shoot'.

The Palestinian leader, Yasser Arafat, reiterated after meeting President Bill Clinton in Washington on Thursday that he was still committed to negotiating a peace agreement. The Israeli Prime Minister, Ehud Barak, will say the same when he follows him to the White House on Sunday.

Yet both of their forces are systematically firing live ammunition to kill and intimidate. The Palestinians are making less use of young rioters hurling rocks and petrol bombs at Israeli roadblocks. Instead, the Tanzim, the militia of Mr Arafat's Fatah movement, are deploying machine guns and automatic rifles against troops and Jewish settlers. Palestinians now talk of a 'war of liberation', rather than a spontaneous popular revolt.

On Thursday, Israel went over to the offensive. One of its helicopter gunships fired a rocket at a Tanzim truck in Beit Sahur, a Christian Arab suburb of Bethlehem, killing a 37-year-old regional militia commander, Hussein Abayat, and two women who happened to be passing by. A Palestinian intelligence officer, Khaled Shalahat, was among eight others wounded in the attack.

Israel blamed Abayat, a flamboyant figure who had been photographed brandishing a light machine gun, for the deaths of three Israeli soldiers and the nightly harassment of the Jerusalem settler suburb of Gilo. Thursday's message was clear and explicit: 'We will no longer simply respond to Palestinian attacks. And our intelligence knows where to find you.'

Mr Arafat, who has twice promised to order a ceasefire and twice failed to deliver, is using force to strengthen his bargaining hand. What Mr Barak offered him at the Camp David summit in July satisfied neither the Palestinian leader nor his disenchanted constituency, though the Israelis paraded their concessions as unprecedentedly generous.

The Palestinians want unequivocal sovereignty over the Arab districts of East Jerusalem, including most of the old, walled city and the elevated courtyard which is holy to Muslims as the site of the Al Aqsa mosque and to the Jews as the Temple Mount. They want to rid themselves of most, if not all, of the West Bank and Gaza settlements. And they want a right of return for refugees of the 1948 war.

Mr Arafat is refusing to let Mr Barak write the script for him. Urged at Camp David to 'take it or leave it', he packed his bags. He despairs of negotiating the kind of compromise he can sell to the Palestinian masses, at home and in the refugee camps of Lebanon, Jordan and Syria. He is channelling the popular frustration in the twin hopes of forcing Mr Barak to be more forthcoming and of internationalising the conflict.

The Israeli prime minister, for his part, is refusing to be coerced into more concessions. He continues to insist that the century-long conflict must be resolved between the two embattled peoples. And, after seeing his soldiers taunted for six weeks of Intifada Mark 2, he is (in a memorable phrase coined by a British rugby bruiser) getting the retaliation in first. Mr Barak knows he cannot impose a deal by force, but is determined not to let his diplomacy be eroded by Palestinian violence.

Neither leader expects early results from the latest Washington visits. The West Asian mayhem has yet to run its course. And, even before the embarrassingly deadlocked United States presidential elections, Mr Clinton was a lame duck with diminishing power to persuade or cajole.

Yet neither Mr Arafat nor Mr Barak dares to write off the peace process that began in Oslo seven years ago. There is nothing to go back to. The Palestinian leadership is not going to return to exile. Israel is not going to reconquer the main cities of the West Bank and Gaza Strip. The current patchwork of populations offers no basis for a permanent arrangement, let alone for a viable Palestinian state.

Ironically, the Palestinians, with their poignantly higher body count, have won the war for international public opinion, but foreign governments (including that of Mr Arafat's old patron, India) are reluctant to condemn Israel or to intervene. Even the Arab League refrained from calling for sanctions or threatening to send troops to save the Palestinians. The United Nations is in no mood to deploy peacekeepers without Israel's agreement.

The intifada has, however, had an unexpected impact on Israeli opinion. They would like to get the conflict over and done with. A poll, published this weekend in the mass-circulation *Ma'ariv*, logged 66 per cent in favour of continuing the peace process with the Palestinians, a rise of 7 per cent on the week before. Asked how they would vote if a final agreement was put to a referendum, 59 per cent said for, 32 per cent against. The 'yes' vote was up 10 per cent.

If Mr Arafat can foster a similar conflict weariness in the Palestinian street – and rebuild a measure of trust among Israelis – that could still be fertile ground for an accommodation, if not yet a reconciliation.

Chapter 13 – 2001-02

Analysis on eve of election win

The Statesman, Calcutta, January 30, 2001

New Yorkers used to say that a conservative was a liberal who'd been mugged. That's exactly how Ehud Barak felt this week. That's exactly how the Israeli voters felt.

Short of a miracle, they are about to elect Ariel Sharon prime minister next Tuesday. A survey published in *Ma'ariv* a week before polling day showed the Likud challenger still 20 points clear of the battered incumbent. Yet the same poll found that if the race were between Sharon and the former Labour premier Shimon Peres, it would be neck and neck.

Israelis have not suddenly discovered that the 72-year-old Sharon is a statesman who can deliver an elusive peace. Nor have they forgotten the right-wing Likud contender's chequered past. They are voting against Barak, who went for a final settlement of the Israeli-Palestinian conflict and failed. More to the point, they are voting against Yasser Arafat.

Although they have not turned overnight into warmongers, Israelis no longer believe that the Palestinians are ready for peaceful coexistence, an Arab state alongside a Jewish state. If the four-month intifada had not killed their faith, Arafat's brutal performance at the World Economic Forum in Davos last Sunday dealt the coup de grace.

Addressing the world's most influential audience of opinion-makers and decision-makers, Arafat delivered a prepared diatribe, directed in Arabic at his constituency back home and in the refugee camps in Lebanon, Jordan and Syria.

'The current government of Israel,' he told the Davos forum, 'has waged for the past four months a savage and barbaric war, as well as a blatant and fascist military aggression against our Palestinian people. Particularly against the Palestinian children.' For good measure, he accused the Israeli army of bombarding Palestinian towns with shells tipped with depleted uranium (a charge categorically denied by Israel and for which there is no evidence).

It was hard to fathom that barely 24 hours earlier, high-level Israeli and Palestinian peace negotiators had issued a joint declaration that they had 'never been closer' to an agreement. Once the Israeli election was out of the way, said foreign minister Shlomo Ben-Ami and Arafat's deputy, Ahmed Qurei, their six days of talks in the Egyptian resort of Taba had set the stage for ending the conflict.

Israeli commentators were sceptical, even before Arafat went on his Swiss rampage. Shalom Yerushalmi, writing in *Ma'ariv*, called it 'a waste of time and effort'. Taba was, he suggested, little more than a brazen attempt to salvage Barak's campaign. Shimon Shiffer concluded bleakly in *Yediot Aharonot*: 'Not a thing was accomplished.'

Arafat's harangue proved how right they were. It was a speech frothing with implacable hatred. Whatever he committed himself to in the Oslo accords seven years ago; this was not a national leader who had reconciled himself to half a state in half his homeland. Even the dwindling band of Israelis who wanted to believe he was merely playing to the gallery would be reluctant to bet their all on him now.

There are Arab, as well as Jewish, observers who suspect that Arafat never intended to come to terms. What he always wanted, a veteran Palestinian journalist assured me this week, was to establish a base – and an army – on Palestinian soil, then continue the struggle.

Even if that is an exaggeration, Arafat is simply not prepared to lead from the front, with all the personal and political risks that would entail. Above all, he is not going to tell the 3.5 million refugees of the 1948 'catastrophe' that they can come home to Palestine, but not to Jaffa and Acre, Lod and Ramleh, and the countless pastoral villages inside Israel that no longer exist.

Abdullah Horani, who returned from exile with Arafat in 1994, wrote him an open letter last week. 'Tell the Israelis,' he urged, 'that Jerusalem is part of the problem, but the refugees are the entire problem, that Jerusalem is part of the homeland, while the refugees are the homeland itself. We have a contract with you, under which you guaranteed to get our rights back. You must keep to the terms of the contract, or pay the penalty for breaching it.'

Barry Rubin, a *Jerusalem Post* West Asia columnist, asked a leading Palestinian how he could justify to his children turning down a chance for peace. The man replied: 'It will be difficult, but we Palestinians have a lot of patience.' When Rubin asked another Palestinian how he could say there was no difference between Barak and Sharon, he replied: 'Since neither will give us everything we want, they are the same.'

The futility of the intifada
Los Angeles Jewish Journal, March 30, 2001

Yasser Arafat is floundering. Six months into the new intifada, he has achieved nothing for his people. More and more openly, Palestinians are questioning whether their suffering is worthwhile. The world is in no hurry to intervene. Arab leaders, gathered in Jordan this week, were long on sympathy, short on substance, military or financial.

Ariel Sharon, for his part, is striving to reconcile his twin images of 'Mr Security' and 'Mr Pragmatic Leader' who has put his adventurist past behind him and cherishes his rapport with the new man in the White House. The Palestinians are not making it easy for him.

The intifada is all tactics and no strategy. Marwan Barghouti, the mainstream Fatah commander calling the shots on the West Bank, announced one day that he wanted a popular uprising, with the masses taking to the streets in peaceful protest, then declared the next day that the armed confrontation would continue.

The bombers and the gunmen interpreted this as a license to go on targeting Jews. Israeli commentators suspected Arafat was trying to provoke the hawkish prime minister to order drastic reprisals, which would rally support for the Palestinian cause – at the Amman summit and among Israeli Arabs, who are staging their annual 'Land Day' demonstrations this Friday.

The attacks plumbed new depths in Hebron on Monday, when a Palestinian sniper shot dead a 10-month-old baby, Shalhevet Pass, as she was being wheeled by her parents through the West Bank city's Jewish neighbourhood. The same night, a police disposal crew defused a bomb placed outside a falafel bar in Petah Tikva, near Tel Aviv. On Tuesday, a car bomb went off in Jerusalem's Talpiot shopping district. Then a suicide bomber struck at a bus stop across town near the Jewish suburb of French Hill. A total of 35 were hurt in the two operations.

Wednesday dawned with another atrocity, this time on the Israeli side of the border between Kfar Sava and the West Bank town of Qalqilya. A second suicide bomber blew himself up among a bunch of teenage boys waiting outside the 'Mifgash Hashalom' ('Meeting Place of Peace') gas station for a ride to a West Bank yeshiva. Two of the students were killed on the spot, four others were wounded. One was in critical condition, another required extensive eye surgery. Both were riddled with iron nails that had been packed into the bomb strapped to the terrorist's chest. The Islamic nationalist movement, Hamas, acknowledged responsibility for both suicide raids and announced that it had seven more bombers ready to sacrifice themselves.

Sharon, projecting a new, statesmanlike image, was reluctant to be provoked. The last thing he wanted was to revive memories of Arik Sharon, the 1950s Special Forces commander who killed Palestinian civilians wholesale in reprisal raids, or the defence minister who allowed Lebanese Christian militiamen to massacre refugees in Sabra and Shatilla three decades later.

Having promised his voters to restore their sense of security, however, Sharon could not wait too long. In particular, his own nationalist constituency was losing patience. Avigdor Lieberman, the hard-right infrastructure minister, said: 'The state must provide security for its citizens everywhere, and Israel must act with determination against the terrorism which is afflicting us.' Noam Arnon, a spokesman for the Hebron settlers, said of the baby girl's killers: 'We have to annihilate these monsters.' Shalhevet's young parents refused to bury her until the army retook the hillside from which the sniper fired.

Alex Fishman, a sober military analyst, wrote in *Yediot Aharonot* on Tuesday: 'It is true that revenge is no substitute for policy. Decisions on the national level must not be made with the gut. But it is inconceivable that the murder of a baby in cold blood be left hanging in the air with no response. A murder like this must have a price.'

Whatever that price turns out to be, the violence is cutting the ground from under Sharon's quest for a 'long-term interim agreement'. Arafat could not swallow the permanent solution to the conflict offered by the former Prime Minister, Ehud Barak, at Camp David last summer. But nor, it seems, can he contemplate anything less.

Sharon will not be able to play the benign grandfather much longer, but a more vigorous response will risk straining the alliance with Labour's Shimon Peres and thus the stability of his national-unity coalition. Nor will he have the free hand he enjoyed when Israel's first Prime Minister, David Ben-Gurion, unleashed him on retaliation raids against Arab villagers half a century ago. CNN's cameras will be there before him.

With bombings turning into a daily ordeal, Sharon was forced on Wednesday to abandon his 'business as usual' pose. His aides announced immediately after the Kfar Sava suicide attack that he would not call the inner security cabinet into session. The prime minister's declared policy was to convene it only once every two weeks. Before the morning was out, however, Sharon backtracked. His ministers insisted that they had to be heard. It was too much of an emergency to be left to one man.

The prime minister was determined not to be trapped into a showy strike, like the tank or helicopter hits employed by Barak when the chips were down, or reconquering Palestinian towns or villages. His aides say he prefers pinpoint blows, for which read assassinations, against the men behind the bombers. The idea is to pick them off one by one, over weeks or even months. The question remains whether this will be enough, to reassure Israelis or to deter the terrorists.

Arafat's tactics are making Sharon squirm, but they solve nothing for the Palestinians. Israel's Labour defence minister, Binyamin Ben-Eliezer, began lifting the economic siege. He was repaid with bombs, mortars and sniper fire. The roadblocks will have to stay. There will be no early relief for the one million Palestinians living below the poverty line. There will be no jobs, in Israel or the Palestinian territories, for the 250,000 unemployed.

Despite Arafat's claim that he is still pursuing the 'peace of the brave', the Amman summit did nothing to convince Israelis or comfort hungry Palestinians. While the United States vetoed a United Nations resolution in New York calling for an international force to 'protect' Palestinian civilians, Bashar Assad, Syria's supposedly westernised young president, sounded no different from his brutal father. He denounced Israel as a society 'more racist than the Nazis'. Ze'ev, *Ha'aretz*'s veteran cartoonist, summed it up with the image of the week: a beaming Arafat launching a verbal dove of peace polka-dotted with black bombs.

Barenboim plays Wagner

The Independent, July 8, 2001

It was meant to be the 'not Wagner' concert: Daniel Barenboim, the pride of Israeli music-lovers, conducting his Berlin orchestra, the Staatskapelle, on the last night of this year's Israel Festival. Little did we know.

The festival had originally announced that the orchestra would appear with Placido Domingo and play extracts from *Die Walkurie*. The very idea was denounced by Holocaust survivors and other Israelis, who have not forgiven Wagner, 'Hitler's favourite composer', for being a notorious (and well-documented) Jew-hater.

Israeli MPs beseeched the festival organisers to think again. So did the minister of culture, Matan Vilnai. He didn't want to limit artistic freedom, you understand, but this was, after all, *the* Israel Festival, a state occasion. Barenboim, who launched his musical career as a child prodigy in Tel Aviv, got the message. Under protest, he agreed to change the program.

So, on Saturday night in the Jerusalem International Convention Center, 2,000 of us sat down to a rich, disciplined performance of Schumann's *Fourth Symphony* by one of the world's great orchestras, followed by an exuberant concert version of Stravinsky's *Rite of Spring*. When the Diaghilev ballet premiered the *Rite* in Paris in 1914, the audience went wild, some in anger, some in frenzy. The unshockable Israelis took it in their collective stride.

The drama came later. It was planned and choreographed. Barenboim, who has been trying to break the unofficial Israeli taboo on Wagner for years, manipulated the audience like he manipulates an orchestra. He knew exactly what he wanted. He worked, subtly but firmly, to achieve it.

Israeli concert-goers expect encores. Barenboim gave us one, Tchaikovsky's *Waltz of the Flowers*. It was familiar and soothing after the pagan brass and percussion of the Stravinsky. We were relaxed, enjoying ourselves, and ready for more.

Then, after the applause had died, Barenboim turned to the audience. Speaking quietly, in Hebrew, without a microphone, he said he was talking to us man to man (and woman). He reminded us why he had cancelled the Wagner. But now, he went on, the official concert was over. If we really wanted to hear Wagner, they would play it as his 'personal encore'. Nothing to do with the festival, nothing to do with the orchestra. If not, the musicians would pack up and go home without fuss.

The vast majority of the audience applauded enthusiastically. Yes please, maestro. A handful walked out, perhaps in silent protest, perhaps because they had to relieve the baby-sitter (it was after 11). Half a dozen objected. 'It's a disgrace,' the widow of an eminent rabbi shouted. 'It's the music of the concentration camps,' an elderly man bellowed. Others yelled back: 'If you don't want to hear it, go home. You've had your money's worth.'

The dialogue continued for half an hour. Barenboim never raised his voice. At one point, the conductor invited a persistent heckler to come on stage and 'discuss this like cultured people'. The man, forty something in a white shirt and small black kippa, declined and went on shouting. Another protested in English. 'Shut up,' someone retorted.

One man did go forward, faced the audience and said: 'I was against playing Wagner in the festival, but now I've heard the maestro and I understand that he's talking about playing outside the state event. Now I'm in favour.' More applause.

A man sitting in front of me took out his mobile phone and I heard him saying: 'You'd better send a crew straight away.' I thought he was a television executive, but he turned out to be an off-duty police superintendent. 'I told them to send reinforcements in case hooligans attack him,' he told me later. Happily, it wasn't necessary.

Finally, Barenboim signalled the orchestra and waited, baton-poised, for silence. As they began to play a love song from *Tristan und Isolde*, fewer than a dozen objectors walked out, slamming doors and stamping feet.

The rest of us sat enthralled through 10 minutes of wrenching, lyrical tenderness, the antithesis of the Teutonic bombast that turns some Jews (and not only Jews) off Wagner. You could hardly hear anyone breathe, let alone cough.

At the end, the audience gave Barenboim and the Staatskapelle a standing ovation. A middle-aged woman in a long, pastel-pale dress plucked a rose from a window box at the edge of the stage and presented it to the conductor. Barenboim accepted it with tears in his eyes.

This wasn't the first time Wagner had been played in Israel. A provincial orchestra in Rishon Letzion broke the 50-year barrier a few months ago. But this was Jerusalem, the Israel Festival (disclaimers notwithstanding). It was Daniel Barenboim, a Jewish Israeli cultural icon, and a German ensemble that was the court orchestra of Prussian emperors and East German commissars. Can *The Ring* be far behind?

Palestinian economy and infrastructure being destroyed

The Statesman, Calcutta, August 14, 2001

In the villages of the beleaguered West Bank and Gaza Strip, Christian relief workers report that 40 per cent of Palestinian babies are being born blind, deaf or anaemic. These deficiencies, they say, are not new, but they have been exacerbated by the armed confrontation with Israel that broke out 10 months ago and has all but destroyed the Palestinian infrastructure.

'People are not drinking water,' says Elena Alibi, a Costa Rican field worker with the International Orthodox Christian Charities. 'To buy water is very expensive and the quality is bad. They are not eating meat. They have gone back to traditional ways of cooking, with lots of lentils. Every day they are reducing their diet. At the same time, many small industries and farms have been destroyed by the Israeli army to create buffer zones. People are very desperate.'

Palestinians at all levels are paying a heavy price for their intifada uprising. Israel responded by closing the invisible border and often by blockading Palestinian communities. People can't get to work. They can't obtain raw materials or market their products.

The Palestinians call it collective punishment. The Israelis say they are protecting their own citizens against suicide bombers, like the one who killed 15 Israelis and tourists in a Jerusalem pizza parlour on Thursday. More than 150 Israelis have been killed, more than 580 Palestinians, since the end of last September.

According to United Nations estimates, the Palestinian economy has suffered at least $2 billion in direct losses. Gross domestic product is down by as much as 50 per cent. Unemployment tops 40 per cent this summer, with about 300,000 out of work. In Bethlehem, the birthplace of Jesus which lives or dies on tourism, the rate is as high as 60 per cent.

The Palestinian Bureau of Statistics has logged 68 per cent of families living below the poverty line, defined as $400 a month for a household with six children. That is three times as many as there were a year ago.

Public servants are lucky if they get even a fraction of their salaries. The 300 teachers at Al Quds University in East Jerusalem have not been paid for five months. Bethlehem's 180 municipal employees received half-pay in June and July. There is no money left for August.

Investment in the West Bank and Gaza, much of it by expatriate Palestinians, has dried up. The value of securities traded on the Nablus stock exchange has declined by 84 per cent. Foreign development aid, running at $525 million in 1999, fell to $369 million in 2000 and below $50 million in the first half of 2001. The Jericho casino, which earned millions of (mostly Israeli) dollars for public and private Palestinian coffers, has mothballed its roulette wheels and slot machines.

Construction, which fuelled a mini-boom on hopes of peace in the late 1990s, is faltering. Building plans for next year have been halved. 'This will have an impact on employment for years to come,' says Khaled Islaih, a United Nations economist. 'Confidence has collapsed. Investors will think twice about risking their money here again.'

In Bethlehem, local and overseas Palestinians put $12 million into building a new bus terminal that opened in time for Christmas, 1999, and Pope John Paul's millennium pilgrimage a few months later. Hundreds of tour buses trundled in every day. The investors had an operating franchise for 15 years. The signs were that they would get their money back in half that period, from parking fees and from the shops, restaurants and two cinemas built into the project.

All that collapsed with the intifada. Bethlehem is a ghost town with guns. The few pilgrims who brave Israeli and Palestinian barricades on the road from Jerusalem come alone. The bus terminal is shabby and deserted.

The ambitious new Jacir Palace hotel, in which the Inter-Continental chain invested $54 million, has closed. Other hotels are empty, tourist shops and restaurants shuttered. Light industries that depend on tourism – olive wood carving, mother of pearl work, embroidery and glassware – have ceased production.

Annual per capita income for the city's 28,000 Muslim and Christian residents has dropped by two-thirds, from $1,800 to $600. Bethlehem's textile factories, manufacturing towels and underwear for the Israeli and Palestinian markets, have gone over to a three-day week.

Ironically, they have been hit not only by the Israeli siege, but by globalisation. 'We can't compete with low wages and production costs in China, India and Turkey, let alone Jordan or Egypt,' confides one factory-owner. 'Our wages, electricity and water charges are similar to Israel's.'

In the run-up to the millennium, foreign governments donated $70 million to furbish Bethlehem's infrastructure. Manger Square was paved and landscaped, roads widened. A visitors' centre was erected on the site of an abandoned police station. The private sector, again mostly expatriate Palestinians, added $100 million.

'Now,' says the Catholic mayor, Hanna Nasser, 'none of them are even approaching us. They are not getting any return on their investment. This year, we haven't issued one single building permit. Nobody wants to build because they don't know the future.'

If Thursday's Jerusalem bombing is any guide, the future remains bleak. For the Palestinian economy and for the Israelis.

The bomb next door

Maclean's, September 17, 2001

First we heard the explosion, a tearing, echoing thunderclap that shattered three of our windows and blew in a door. Then we heard the screams and smelled the cordite. We live in a 19th-century house on the Street of the Prophets in the centre of West Jerusalem. We are used to big bangs. Since May, there have been four bombings within three minutes walk of our home. But the one last week, in the road between our neighbours, the French international school and a hospital, Bikur Holim, was nearer than any we'd known before.

We feared the worst. On August 9, a Palestinian suicide bomber had killed 15 Israelis and tourists, including six children, in the

Sbarro pizza parlour just around the corner. Was this another massacre? A police patrol, we soon learnt, had spotted a suspicious-looking man, disguised as an orthodox Jew with a black skullcap and a backpack. When they challenged him, he smiled, reached into his bag and blew himself up.

The screams came from the French school, housed in St Joseph's convent. The blast had decapitated the bomber, flinging his head over a 2.5m high stone wall to a playground where dozens of horrified children were waiting for morning classes to begin. Some were still arriving. Pierre Weill, a French radio correspondent, was delivering his daughter. His car was strewn with the bomber's blood.

Luckily, no one besides the bomber was killed. The only Israeli seriously injured was Natan Sandaka, one of the two alert policemen. Another 20 people were treated for shock, burns and lesser wounds. The bomber was provisionally identified as Raid Barghouti, a 26-year-old Islamic militant from the West Bank village of Aboud. Police sappers retrieved steel screws and jagged fragments of blackened canvas in the yard outside our front door, all that remained of his backpack and its lethal contents. They had been hurled 50m by the blast.

Although the month was barely a week old, the Israeli media were already dubbing it Black September. Four other bombs went off in Jerusalem suburbs the day before the Street of the Prophets suicide interrupted our breakfast. We feel as if we are living under a volcano. Still, somehow we have adjusted. 'It won't happen to us,' we say, even though we know it might. The drama becomes part of the fabric of your life, the familiarity muffling the shock. When a bomb goes off, people phone friends and family to check that they're OK. I call it 'counting your friends'.

Bridget still shops in Maheneh Yehuda market, although her fishmonger, Nissim, lost an arm in a suicide bombing in July, 1997, and two passers-by were killed by a car bomb there last November. She walked past the Sbarro pizza parlour, where we often take our grandchildren, an hour before the August blast. 'This is our city,' she says. 'Many Arabs still shop in our corner grocery store and visit their families in the Jewish hospital opposite our house. If they can carry on as normal, so can I. I'm not going to change the way I live.'

There are many variations on the 'life goes on' refrain. Regine Rimon, who owns Cafe Rimon, a popular fast food restaurant off the Ben-Yehuda pedestrian mall, has seen her business slide 35 per cent from last summer, in part because of the decline in tourism. She remains in equal measures fatalistic and defiant. 'We're not afraid,' she says,'but we're worried. We have to go on all the same. These are hard times, but we're used to hard times.' Her way of coping? She has posted two black-uniformed muscle men, armed with revolvers and two-way radios, outside her cafe with orders not to let in anyone who looks suspicious. 'Even if someone blows himself up,' she explained as if she were recommending the day's special, 'there will be fewer casualties.'

Many Israelis, it seems, have a short trauma span. They soon put an atrocity like the pizza parlour bombing behind them. 'If something like that had happened in Toronto,' says Reuven Gal, a former chief psychologist of the Israel Defence Forces, 'it would have had a devastating impact. People would have panicked because it's so extreme, so unusual. In Israel, it has become almost part of people's lives. People are more cautious, but they don't stop living.'

As if to prove his point, hundreds of families flocked recently to the Sultan's Pool, an outdoor auditorium just outside the Old City walls, for the annual Jerusalem arts and crafts fair. Every inch of parking space in nearby Mamila Road was filled. A multi-storey car park raised its rates from eight shekels to 20, and still did a roaring trade. Nevertheless, Gal detects a weakening of resilience. 'There's an accumulated fatigue and hopelessness,' he explains. 'People are less and less convinced that any approach will resolve this conflict. That diminishes their strength and their stubbornness.'

When we first moved to Jerusalem in the '70s, bombings were not as frequent. Suicide bombers or car bombs were almost unheard of. In the first intifada (1987 to 1993) the trouble was mostly in Arab

East Jerusalem. We cut back on visits there and avoided driving through Arab neighbourhoods.

After the Oslo agreement in 1993, we hoped all that was history. We started shopping again in the Arab gift shops. I took a then six-year-old granddaughter for a walk atop the walls of the Old City, then we walked through the Muslim Quarter en route to the Western Wall. There seemed nothing to fear. But I wouldn't take her younger siblings on the same trek today.

Of course, many East Jerusalem Palestinians are just as cautious about where they venture. They comprise about one third of the city's population of 717,000, and many of them have jobs in Israeli shops, restaurants, offices and building sites. The glazier a government agency sent to repair our bomb-shattered windows last week was an Arab.

Most, in fact, have not joined the current intifada. Still, Ali Qleibo, a painter and anthropologist who teaches at East Jerusalem's Al Quds University, says his students complain about being constantly humiliated at army checkpoints. As for himself, Qleibo says it's impossible to visit friends on the West Bank or drive to a holiday home he owns in Jericho.

Without tourists, his favourite Old City cafes and markets are empty. Qleibo is also reluctant to take his wife and young daughter across town. 'I'd be ashamed to go shopping in West Jerusalem,' he says, 'when my people are being killed.' And he has stopped going to the movies there. 'If I go to a cinema and a bomb goes off,' he explained, 'I'll be seen as an Arab. I'll be the first one to be attacked.'

Yet the holy city has not lost its faith. Painters and plumbers, joiners and tilers, Iraelis and Palestinians, were working around the clock to rebuild the shattered Sbarro pizza parlour in time for its scheduled reopening this week. An improvised sign proclaims: 'The Sbarro chain loves Jerusalem.'

So we get by. But these are days neither Jews nor Arabs in Jerusalem will forget in a hurry.

Profile of Sharon

Sunday Business Post, Dublin, December 9, 2001

According to a conspiracy theory running around the Israeli peace camp, Yasser Arafat deliberately destroyed Ehud Barak's political career because, in return for a viable Palestinian state, the Labour prime minister insisted at Camp David in July, 2000, that he announce the end of the century-old conflict between their two peoples. Arafat couldn't do it, say the disenchanted doves. He would have had to tell the four million refugees of the 1948 war that they were not going home to dozens of demolished or expropriated towns and villages inside what is now Israel. He would have killed the dream he, more than anyone, had fostered.

Arafat preferred, it is suggested, to create a crisis which would bring Ariel Sharon to power. Then Sharon, the old warrior with more Arab blood on his hands than any other Israeli, would run true to form. Sooner or later, by accident or design, he would preside over a massacre of Palestinian civilians. And the world would finally compel Israel to evacuate the occupied West Bank and Gaza Strip. Arafat would get his state without having to sign off on the conflict.

'Sharon,' reflected one of the conspiracy theorists has been a great disappointment to Arafat.' That was before Sharon launched his warplanes, helicopter gunships and tanks on last week's blitzkrieg. The Israeli Left now frets that he may yet prove Arafat correct.

Perhaps we are about to see the 'real' Sharon of Palestinian nightmares. But if his performance as prime minister over the past nine months is any guide, the demonisers could still be disappointed.

At 73, the portly, white-haired, ever-smiling old war-horse is no more of a dove today than when, as a young colonel, he led his commandos on a reprisal raid into the Palestinian village of Qibya in 1953. They blew up 45 houses in revenge for the murder of a Jewish woman and her two children. They killed 69 villagers, half of them women and children. 'I believe in exactly the same things I believed in before,' he assured a recent Israeli interviewer.

Sharon, a farm boy who now squires it over a ranch in the Negev desert, still believes in an absolute Jewish right to the whole of their ancient homeland. If he has to compromise with the Palestinians, it will be a matter of politics, not justice. During his election campaign a year ago, the right-wing Likud candidate published his 'peace plan'. His only concession was that he would not reconquer the Palestinian cities Israel handed to Arafat after the 1993 Oslo peace agreement.

A Sharon government, he said, would cede no more territory, evacuate no Jewish settlements, and keep the whole of Jerusalem. Though he would establish no new settlements, he would expand existing ones. And, if the Palestinians acquiesced, he would be kind enough to recognise their state on 42 per cent of the West Bank and Gaza Strip. Barak had offered 95 per cent.

Nothing Prime Minister Sharon has said or done since he took office in March has deviated a centimetre from last year's blueprint. Yet, whether or not he has disappointed Yasser Arafat, he has surprised his critics. The bull stayed out of the china shop. He did not repeat the kind of mistake he made on September 28, 2000, when his high-profile visit to the Temple Mount, a Jerusalem site uniquely sacred to Jews and Muslims, sparked the intifada uprising.

In his three decades in Israel's multi-party politics, Sharon witnessed prime minister after prime minister hamstrung by self-interested coalition partners. His two immediate predecessors, Barak and Binyamin Netanyahu, watched their parliamentary majorities evaporate as soon as they tried to do something radical. They were demeaned and, ultimately, humiliated.

Sharon was determined not to fall into that trap. He had waited too long for supreme office. Too long for his chance to skewer the 'petty enemies' who had refused to promote him to chief-of-staff in the seventies and hounded him out of the defence ministry a decade later.

So he built a 'unity' coalition, so unprecedentedly large that even the odd defection would not bring him down. It is no accident that in the televised press conference he gave last Monday before ordering his armed forces into action, Sharon repeatedly stressed the imperative of preserving national unity.

The presence of Labour worthies like foreign minister Shimon Peres, a Nobel Peace Prize laureate, and defence minister Binyamin Ben-Eliezer in his team divided the dovish opposition and earned him credit abroad. He was, and perhaps still is, prepared to temper his aggressive instincts to keep them there. He cracked down hard on the Palestinians when he felt it necessary, but within limits. He chose Israel's targets. Most of them were military.

'The government I head,' he said in last Monday's broadcast, 'is a national-unity government. We are now in a time of emergency, and in such times a government which represents the entire public of Israel is of supreme importance.'

Until last week, that meant keeping lines open to the Palestinian Authority, although Sharon himself refused to meet or shake hands with its leader. Peres had to be convinced that there was still a chance of a negotiated peace. Sharon did not repudiate Oslo, though he averted difficult choices (and, his critics say, prolonged the violence) by refusing to negotiate 'under fire'. He had to appease the Right as well as the Left.

However, even last week his government did not brand the PA a bunch of terrorists, but rather 'an entity that supports terrorism'. That may prove to be a distinction without a difference. If so, Peres and his Labour colleagues will either quit or forfeit whatever remains of their credibility – and of their value to Sharon.

But Sharon's new face is more than mere calculation. 'The biggest change,' said one of his associates, 'is that he's learnt to count to 10 before taking a decision.' After his election, Sharon described the process: 'First I wait until evening, when I drive back to the farm and have a long way to think. Then I visit the sheep and cows. Then I go to sleep. The next morning, I visit the sheep and cows again. And only then do I decide what to do.'

He has also learnt a kind of charm, even if he seems sometimes to be trying too hard. The bonhomie disarms even sceptical political commentators like Hemi Shalev, who gushed after interviewing him for the tabloid daily *Ma'ariv*: 'Sharon is one of the nicest prime ministers we have ever had. He is full of humour, sharp sarcastic wit and amusing anecdotes.' His wife, Lily, who died two years ago, is credited with softening the edges – a task now embraced by his son, confidant and universal fixer, Omri.

It wasn't always thus. Sharon was born to Russian Zionist immigrants in Kfar Malal, a smallholders' cooperative north of Tel Aviv. His parents, Shmuel and Vera, were the village awkward squad, anti-socialists in a community of socialists, snobs who built fences to separate them from other, more gregarious pioneers.

As Yossi Klein Halevi wrote in the *Jerusalem Report* magazine. 'Relations were so contentious that in his will Shmuel forbade eulogies at his funeral from any neighbours. When Vera discovered that the village had allotted a burial plot to Shmuel beside the grave of a long-time opponent, she stopped the proceedings until an alternative spot was found.'

The young Sharon grew up in bristling isolation. He learnt to paint and to play the violin; he learnt to farm and to fight. But he made few friends among the village children. 'I wondered,' he wrote wistfully in *Warrior*, his 1989 autobiography, 'what their homes were like inside.'

He joined the Haganah, the precursor of the Israeli army, in 1945 when he was 17. As a platoon commander in Israel's 1948 War of Independence, he made his mark as a fighter and inspirational leader. Five years later, he was appointed to command Unit 101, a flamboyant cross-border force set up to retaliate for guerrilla raids on Israeli villages. It was Unit 101 that laid waste Qibya.

In 1954 Sharon's commandos were merged with the paratroops, and he was appointed to the joint command. The paras took up where 101 left off, striking at targets in Jordan, Syria and Egypt. Sharon operated with little respect for orders or chain of command. He did as he saw fit, leaving the army brass and the politicians to pick up the pieces.

The Israeli author Uzi Benziman wrote in *Sharon: An Israeli Caesar*, his critical 1985 biography: 'As was the case at Qibya, many of these missions took on the most unexpected proportions, surprising both the government and the army, which had authorised them.'

In the 1956 Suez war, Sharon violated orders and sent his paras into the Mitla Pass deep in the Sinai desert. It ended disastrously, with 38 Israelis dead, but Sharon's reputation remained unblemished. Years later middle-aged men boasted that they had 'fought with Arik in the Mitla'. The chief-of-staff, Moshe Dayan, another wilful maverick, wrote afterwards that he would never punish an officer for going beyond his orders.

By the time the 1967 Six-Day War broke out, Sharon was a major-general and commander of an armoured division. He revealed a new strategic talent when he orchestrated huge, set-piece battles.

As chief of Southern Command in the late 1960s, Sharon ruthlessly demolished thousands of homes in the seething Gaza refugee camps to open roads for anti-terror patrols. He achieved his aim. The number of sabotage attacks dropped dramatically. But in the process, hundreds of young men were deported to Lebanon and Jordan. Political leaders and 600 relatives of suspected terrorists were herded into camps in the Israeli-occupied Sinai desert.

When he realised that he was not going to be promoted chief-of-staff, Sharon resigned his commission and entered politics. Rather than serve a modest apprenticeship, he welded four right-wing parties into the Likud. One awed admirer confided: 'He raped four political parties.'

Sharon reinforced his reputation as a bulldozer who gets things done. After the Likud's Menachem Begin won the 1977 election, Sharon masterminded the expansion of Jewish settlements in the Arab hill country of the West Bank. Nevertheless, it was the same Sharon who persuaded Begin to relinquish the town of Yamit and other Sinai settlements in exchange for a peace treaty with Egypt – and Sharon who vigorously evacuated them.

He was, and remains, a schemer who makes his own rules, a leader without doubts. He showed both sides of his personality in the 1973 Yom Kippur War, when he was called up as a reserve divisional commander. He quarrelled constantly with his fellow generals, but it was Sharon, his head romantically bandaged, who planned and executed the strike across the Suez Canal that turned the tide for Israel.

As defence minister in 1982, Sharon drove the Palestine Liberation Organisation out of Lebanon. In September that year, he sent Israel's Lebanese Christian allies, the Phalangists, into Beirut's Sabra and Shatilla refugee camps, ostensibly to clean out residual pockets of Palestinian fighters. The militiamen, thirsting for revenge after the assassination of their leader, Bashir Gemayel, massacred up to 800 refugees, including women, children and old people.

An Israeli commission, headed by chief justice Yitzhak Kahan, censured Sharon for 'having disregarded the danger of acts of vengeance and bloodshed by the Phalangists against the population of the refugee camps.' At first Sharon refused to resign, but Begin persuaded him. Nineteen years later, Sabra and Shatilla have returned to haunt him. After Belgium enacted legislation to try other people's war criminals, survivors of the massacre are seeking to have him indicted.

With a less brazen politician, the Lebanon war might have drawn a controversial line under his career. The tanks were supposed to stop after clearing Palestinian gunmen from a 40-kilometre-deep strip across Israel's northern border. Instead, they rolled on to the gates of Beirut and joined battle with the Syrian garrison in Eastern Lebanon. Sharon had always planned it that way.

Prime Minister Begin's son, Benny, testified to a Tel Aviv court in 1996 that Sharon deceived his late father, who believed Israel was engaged in a limited operation. Yitzhak Berman, who resigned as Begin's energy minister in protest at the expansion of the war aims, claimed in the liberal daily *Ha'aretz* a year ago that the defence minister told the cabinet four times that the invasion would halt after 40 kilometres.

'Begin believed in him,' Berman explained. 'The nation was induced to shut its eyes.'

Is history about to repeat itself?

A Palestinian peace movement?

Jewish Chronicle, February 15, 2002

It sounds confused, if not downright contrary. Most Arabs in the West Bank and Gaza Strip applaud violence against Israelis, yet they are eager for a ceasefire and for their political leaders to get back to the negotiating table.

The latest opinion poll, conducted by the Ramallah-based Dr Khalil Shikaki, registered 58 per cent of Palestinians supporting violence against civilians, while an overwhelming 90 per cent supported attacks on soldiers. But at the same time 60 per cent backed calls for a ceasefire, a ten per cent increase on six months earlier, and as many as 70 per cent wanted a return to negotiations.

It is easy to write them off as muddled, even devious, thinkers: showing their 'true', bellicose colours in answering one question, then luring well-meaning Israelis into a trap by showing their soft side in answering another. Yet there is a logic to their double-talk.

Mainstream Palestinians, from the leadership to the grassroots, recognise that they cannot drive the Jews into the sea, however much they might like to. Israel is there to stay, and somehow, some time, they have to find a way to live alongside it. Only the Islamic fanatics, who remain a small minority when it comes to voting intentions, are ready to fight to the death for the whole of Palestine from the Jordan to the Mediterranean.

There is a debate going on, however muted it is in the smoke and cordite of the war of attrition that calls itself an intifada. But the primary differences are over tactics, the efficacy of violence, not the ethics of it.

'I believe that this conflict will never be resolved by force,' said Father Raed Abusahlia, a Christian advocate of non-violent resistance. 'We are losing support all over the world by using violent resistance. Non-violent resistance is a stronger weapon against the occupation.'

Like Israeli peaceniks, Palestinian doves are not pacifists. Even someone like Father Raed, the 35-year-old chancellor of the Latin Patriarchate in Jerusalem, scarcely pauses to condemn suicide or car bombers for killing innocent people. He is a proud Palestinian, born in a village near Jenin, and he wants to get the Israelis off his back. For the purpose of this debate, violence is wrong because it is counter-productive.

Similarly a network of Palestinian non-governmental organisations, which gladly cooperate with the conscience-stricken Jews of Rabbis for Human Rights, the Committee Against Home Demolitions, or Gush Shalom, orchestrated the viciously anti-Zionist campaign that hijacked the United Nations conference against racism in Durban last September. They may work with Israelis, but they love them not.

Among the political elite, Sari Nusseibeh, the Palestine Liberation Organisation's chief representative in Jerusalem, is the most outspoken champion of a compromise peace. 'Violence leads nowhere,' he told foreign correspondents. 'Neither Israel nor the Palestinians are able to impose their will. Violence breeds more violence.'

Nusseibeh, an Oxford-educated philosophy professor who traces his family's roots to a general in the army of the Caliph Omar which conquered Jerusalem in 637, is the only Palestinian leader who has said openly what many of them think. Asked by a *Ha'aretz* interviewer in December whether Yasser Arafat erred when he rejected Ehud Barak's peace proposals at Camp David in July, 2000, Nusseibeh replied unequivocally: 'Yes. That was a major missed opportunity. If it had been me, I would have told Barak: OK, let's sign.'

Well-placed Palestinians report that Mahmoud Abbas (aka Abu Mazen), Arafat's number two, has spoken 'very harshly' behind closed doors against the strategy of violence, whether his audience was Arafat himself or Al Fatah's hot-headed young guard like the Tanzim militia chieftain Marwan Barghouti. Having burned his fingers in the late 90s by drafting a framework for peace with Yossi Beilin, which the Israelis publicised prematurely, Abu Mazen hesitates to go public.

Ahmed Qurei (Abu Ala), the speaker of the Palestinian legislative council and third man in Arafat's political pantheon, is thought to share Abu Mazen's view, but is more cautious even in private. His track record, however, speaks for itself. He was the Palestinians' chief negotiator at Oslo in 1993 – and before and after Camp David seven years later.

He continues to negotiate with Shimon Peres, another Oslo veteran. He is a tough bargainer. He won't sell Palestinian interests short, but no one who has dealt with him doubts his sincerity.

Surprisingly, perhaps, Arafat's two principal security commanders – Mohammed Dahlan in Gaza and Jibril Rajoub on the West Bank – are also counted in this pragmatic Palestinian 'peace camp'. According to informed Palestinians, Dahlan was one of three members of Arafat's Camp David team who urged him to accept what Barak was offering, then build on it.

Secular leaders like these are seeking a modus vivendi with Israel because they want their Palestinian state, when it comes, to be part of the modern world. They fear an Iranian-style Islamic theocracy; they reject the obscurantism of Hamas and Islamic Jihad. And they are keen to get on with building a 21st-century nation. But, as Danny Rubinstein, a Palestinian affairs analyst for *Ha'aretz*, put it this week, they want Arafat to sign the deal. He alone, they believe, can sell it to the Palestinian street. So talk of a palace revolution is fantasy.

With a Kalashnikov in every home and the rule of law more brittle than ever, it is not easy for those who oppose militarism to find a platform. But some have done so: academics like the Gaza psychiatrist Eyad Sarraj, the Bir Zeit University political scientist Salah Abdul Jawad, the journalists Tawfiq Abu Bakr and Daoud Kuttab.

The controlled Palestinian press is nervous about printing their opinions, which could bring the censor or worse on the editor's head. One dissenter, whose article was rejected by the East Jerusalem daily, *Al Quds*, posted it on the Internet. When the paper's editor saw that no harm ensued and everyone was talking about it, he printed the article anyway. Khalil Shikaki, pollster and political science professor, frequently uses Radio Monte Carlo's Arabic service, widely listened to across the Middle East, to advocate non-violent resistance.

They are a kind of resistance within the resistance. But they all, politicians and professors, have one thing in common. They won't buy 'peace at any price'. They acknowledge that the Palestinians will have to make concessions, but they demand equal, if not more, sacrifice from Israel as the dominant power that holds 78 per cent of 1948 Palestine, even without the West Bank and Gaza Strip.

Sari Nusseibeh spelled it out more starkly (for the Palestinians and the Israelis) than anyone. The Palestinians, he said, had to recognise that the plight of the four million (his figure) refugees must be solved within the borders of a Palestinian state. It was futile to demand that Israel take them back. That was, he said, a 'deal-breaker'.

The other side of the equation, however, was an Israeli withdrawal to the armistice lines that existed as de facto borders before the Six-Day War of June, 1967. The settlements must go, and that included the Jewish suburbs built in the Arab side of Jerusalem. 'Palestinians,' Nusseibeh said, 'will not accept a state in the West Bank and Gaza Strip that is itself another Israel, with its resources and borders controlled by Israel.'

Nusseibeh is still out on a limb, publicly at least, on the refugees' right of return. Arafat wrote in an op-ed article in the *New York Times* earlier this month that Israel's demographic concerns – a Jewish state with a Jewish majority – had to be taken into account, though as always he left himself room for manoeuvre. Jerusalem, the other Camp David sticking point, is still intractable.

The outlook remains bleak, for Arabs and Jews, doves and hawks. Yet as the Hebrew novelist Amos Oz, the most articulate of Israeli peace campaigners, argues, the great achievement of the past two years of hope and despair is that everyone on both sides now knows the price to be paid if they want peace.

Shattered dreams in Israel's war for peace

Sunday Business Post, Dublin, March 10, 2002

Shimon Peres, an indefatigable peacemaker, phoned Yasser Arafat in his beleaguered Ramallah headquarters on Wednesday night. The Israeli foreign minister was trying yet again to persuade his fellow Nobel peace prize winner to reduce the violence. Suddenly, the Palestinian leader yelled down the line: 'Ya Shimon, the planes are bombing me!'

An air force helicopter had rocketed a security building barely 20 metres from Arafat's office. 'You speak to me of peace,' Arafat fumed, 'and the gunships bomb us. I hear the missiles. I cannot talk to you after such a bombing about initiatives to restore calm. Let's talk another time.' The foreign minister mumbled that he was sorry. He would try to end the raid.

Israel has stopped talking about containing an intifada, a popular uprising, and started making war. More than 30 Israelis and more than 80 Palestinians have met a violent end in the past week. But Peres told a group of foreign correspondents earlier that day that he was not giving up. 'There are no shattered dreams,' he said, 'only shattered dreamers. And I am not a shattered dreamer. Without a dream you become blind, you don't know where to go. As long as there is the slightest chance of achieving a ceasefire, I shall work as hard as I may to realise the dream.'

Peres argued that if only Israeli and Palestinian negotiators could sketch a better future, a ceasefire and return to diplomacy would still be possible. He believed a blueprint he has worked out with Ahmed Qurei, the speaker of the Palestinian parliament, offered that prospect.

The 78-year-old foreign minister is sounding like a tragic King Lear, raging against the storm. Ariel Sharon's ungainly, six-party coalition stretches from Peres's Labour, which seeks to trade land for peace, to the tiny, far-right National Union, which wants to expel the Arabs across the river to Jordan. Ministers find it impossible to make strategic decisions.

As the Palestinians step up their terror campaign in the occupied territories and Israeli cities, the only response they can agree on is to hit back harder – with tanks, F-16 warplanes, helicopter gunships and commandos. Peres and defence minister Binyamin Ben-Eliezer, now Labour's elected leader, try to draw lines so that the door to negotiations is not slammed forever. But their resistance is being eroded day-by-day.

Sharon, another veteran, who celebrated his 74th birthday last month, is setting the pace. The burly right-wing Likud leader still thinks like the blunt, rampaging general he once was. 'It's either

318

them or us,' the prime minister told a table of Israeli political correspondents in the parliamentary cafeteria last Monday. 'We are at war and our backs are against the wall. I don't expect the Palestinian Authority to halt terrorism. They are terrorism. Arafat is the father of all terrorism.'

Yet Sharon was careful not to write off the political option. 'I want to conduct negotiations,' he said, 'but we cannot do that until the Palestinians are hit very hard. They thought that by raising the level of terror, they could achieve more than on the diplomatic track. Now they will have to endure many harsh blows until they see that they were mistaken.'

Without naming names, Peres took the prime minister to task. 'There are some people who are saying let's have a war, then we shall have peace,' he said. 'We have had wars. What do we want? To win another time, to occupy another time, what for? And what will happen after the next war? We don't need a war to make peace. We need peace to prevent a war.'

The United States, which has been increasingly sympathetic to Israel since it launched its own, post-September 11 war on terror, shared Peres's alarm. 'Prime Minister Sharon has to take a hard look at his policies to see whether they will work,' secretary of state Colin Powell told congressmen in Washington. 'If you declare war on the Palestinians and think you can solve the problem by seeing how many Palestinians can be killed, I don't know if that leads us anywhere.'

Sharon's bureau responded: 'The war that Israel finds itself in was forced on us by the Palestinian Authority and its chairman following the Camp David summit in July, 2000. Israel never declared war on the Palestinians. Israel is returning fire against the terrorist organisations in the framework of its right of self-defence. He who initiated the war has the power to stop it, but he continues to prefer the terrorist war.'

The sense that the violence of the past 18 months was forced on Israel is shared across Israel's political spectrum – and by Bill Clinton and senior members of his former American peace team. At Camp David, as they see it, the then Labour prime minister Ehud

Barak offered the Palestinians the basis of a viable state in the whole of Gaza and all but a narrow strip of the West Bank. He was ready to compromise on the thorny questions of Jerusalem and the Palestinian refugees. Arafat turned him down.

'There was a leader,' Gilead Sher, Barak's chief negotiator, said, 'who, when he should have taken an historic decision, screwed up and backed off. He took the wrong road at the historic crossroads. Arafat tried to reach a better deal by the use of force, rather than continuing to negotiate a settlement.' According to Sher, the Palestinian leadership did not know how to climb down from historic 'narratives and positions' – the calamitous defeat of 1948, the demand for a right of return for millions of refugees – and get to the level of 'interests and practical arrangements'.

Benny Morris, a left-wing Israeli historian whose 1987 book, *The Birth of the Palestinian Refugee Problem*, forced his countrymen to acknowledge their own role in that exodus, goes further. In the late eighties, during the first intifada, Morris went to prison rather than serve as a reservist on the West Bank. Now, like many in the peace camp, he is bitterly disappointed in the Palestinians in general and Arafat in particular. 'They are unwilling to accept a Jewish state on their land,' he said. 'They don't recognise the legitimacy of Zionism, and they don't care about the Jewish connection to the land.'

Asked if he would serve on the West Bank if he were called up again, the 53-year-old Morris said he probably would. 'The last intifada,' he explained, 'was a struggle for liberation from occupation. They didn't talk about the right of return, which is a formula for the demographic destruction of the Jewish state. They didn't use atrocious terrorism as a means of undermining Israel. They threw stones at soldiers to end the occupation. That was something I could sympathise with.'

Arafat losing support as Palestinians speak out

Sunday Business Post, Dublin, July 14, 2002

In the reoccupied West Bank town of Hebron, an activist in Yasser Arafat's Al Fatah, a graduate of Israeli prisons, lamented the other day: 'I gave up my dream of the whole of Palestine for the sake of the Oslo accord. And what did I get? Corruption, no democracy, security services abusing and blackmailing our people. And now I'm getting Israeli soldiers invading my town and the Palestinian Authority is doing nothing to protect me.'

The middle-aged Palestinian was talking privately, among friends, but such criticism is being voiced more and more openly. And dissenters are no longer afraid to point a finger at Arafat and to challenge his decisions in the streets of the West Bank and Gaza Strip.

Khalil Shikaki, a Palestinian political analyst, told me: 'Arafat has been weakened. He has not been able to control the street, not been able to control the violence and not been able to demonstrate leadership.'

Arafat, who will be 73 next month, remains a national symbol. Aspiring successors, like the former Gaza security chief Mohammed Dahlan, are biding their time. But the chairman is no longer feared.

Israeli tanks have prevented him leaving his Ramallah compound for the past eight months. No American diplomats (and a diminishing number of others) talk to him. His Palestinian Authority has ceased to function. He doesn't have policemen to direct the traffic, let alone resist the Israeli invasion. His disgruntled subjects are having their say.

Muawiya al-Masri, a member of the Palestinian legislative council, recently accused Arafat of diverting millions of dollars of foreign aid to bolster his own power. Hossam Khader, another Palestinian legislator, protested that the wives and children of 50 senior leaders – including Suha Arafat, who lives in Paris with her daughter – left the Palestinian territories and 'settled with their millions of dollars in Europe and Arab countries' when the intifada erupted in September, 2000.

Hundreds of Palestinian security men marched through Ramallah and Hebron early this month against Arafat's dismissal of their commander, Jibril Rajoub, and refused to serve under his designated successor. Such a rebellion would have been unthinkable a year ago. So would a demonstration in Gaza by 3,000 unemployed workers, who complained that the leadership had waxed rich at the expense of the people.

Many Palestinians, who endured three decades of Israeli occupation, are starting to blame Arafat and other 'outsiders' who returned from exile after the 1993 Oslo accords for failing to understand what makes Israel tick. 'They should have known that when you send people to blow themselves up in cafes and bars, it won't force Israelis to book the next flight out,' said a veteran Palestinian journalist. 'Israel was created to achieve security for the Jews. The moment you carry a gun or a bomb, that's the red line.'

Ordinary Palestinians have sobered up and lowered their expectations. It is no accident that the current Israeli incursions, unlike those three months ago, have met little armed resistance. It is not just that there are fewer weapons or fighters around, but also that people are focusing more on feeding their families than on killing Israelis.

Arafat has announced a 100-day reform program, culminating in elections next January. But Palestinian sceptics see it as a familiar exercise in survival rather than a readiness for change. 'He is trying to resist American and domestic pressure to remove him,' Khalil Shikaki argued. 'He fears reform because he doesn't want to give up power.'

That power is already seeping out of Arafat's hands. He tried and failed to marginalise two of the most credible younger-generation Fatah leaders, Mohammed Dahlan and Jibril Rajoub, both of whom have now been promoted within the security hierarchy. Rajoub, in particular, showed that he continued to command the loyalty of his 6,000-man Preventive Security Force and their families, despite the fact that he surrendered his besieged West Bank headquarters to Israeli troops in April.

Where, then, do Yasser Arafat and his unhappy people go from here? The Americans, backed by Egypt and Jordan, the two Arab states which signed peace treaties with Israel, are looking beyond the January elections in which Arafat is unlikely to face a serious challenge. They think of a collective leadership, with Arafat's supreme role as president of the Palestinian Authority and chairman of the Palestine Liberation Organisation divided between a figurehead president, an executive prime minister and a PLO chairman drawn from the diaspora.

That is not how Arafat wants to walk into the sunset. The question is whether he is now so weakened that he will have no choice.

Chapter 14 – 2003-05

Abu Mazen, the first Palestinian prime minister

Jewish Chronicle, March 14, 2002

The imminent election of Mahmoud Abbas, better known as Abu Mazen, as the first Palestinian prime minister could be the best thing that has happened to his stricken people since they launched their intifada two and a half years ago.

Abu Mazen's strength is that he is a major political figure with roots in the Palestine Liberation Organisation and the mainstream Fatah movement reaching back to the 1950s. He has been Yasser Arafat's deputy since the political centre of gravity moved back to the West Bank and Gaza after the 1993 Oslo accords, but he is no yes-man. He is both a patriot and a pragmatist.

As one of the architects of the Oslo breakthrough, the 68-year-old grandfather remains committed to a two-state solution. He kept lines open to Israel. He was one of the first Palestinian leaders to preach that the militarisation of the intifada was a major error for which his people were paying a heavy price. And he did it not in an op-ed article in the *Guardian*, but in the lions' den of the Gaza refugee camps.

According to a transcript leaked last November to the London-based Arabic daily paper, *Al Hayat*, Abu Mazen told grassroots leaders there that the resort to arms had led to the 'complete destruction' of what was built after Oslo. 'Our people are in a situation of loss, starvation and suffering,' he said.

The reason, he argued, was that the intifada deviated from its natural course. 'We are talking about a military battle, not a popular uprising expressing popular rage, to which no one can be opposed. Every day all the West Bank cities are subject to operations of destruction because of the Israeli exploitation of operations that I think are neither necessary nor effective.'

In what reads like a manifesto for his new government, Abu Mazen contended that the Palestinians would not be able to achieve

324

their goals by force. 'Killing,' he insisted, 'is not our hobby.' He emphasised that he was not saying stop the intifada, but he was saying stop the needless shedding of blood.

As a refugee whose family fled the Galilee town of Safed during the 1948 war, Abu Mazen still espoused a 'right of return' for the hundreds of thousands of Palestinians stuck in camps in Lebanon, Syria and Jordan – a taboo for Israelis of all political stripes. But he maintained that the numbers and terms could be determined by negotiation.

Last week, Abu Mazen responded to sniping by radical elements in Fatah and gave his blessing to attacks on Israeli soldiers and settlers in the West Bank and Gaza Strip. Once he is in office, Israelis will judge on performance whether that was a tactical move to shore up his power base (like the secular Moscow University PhD's recent pilgrimage to Mecca), or a strategic shift.

So far, they are giving him the benefit of the doubt. While acknowledging that Abu Mazen was 'no unblemished saint,' columnist Hemi Shalev wrote in the tabloid daily *Ma'ariv*: 'The appointment heralds the beginning of a process in which Palestinian society sobers up from the illusion of victory in the intifada. It also is likely to cause many Israelis to believe again in the possible existence of a Palestinian partner.'

Yossi Beilin, the apostle of Oslo, said: 'Abu Mazen has neither hatred nor admiration for Israel. He recognises it as a fact, as something with which an arrangement must be reached – for want of a better alternative. His appointment creates an opportunity, perhaps the last one, to reach an historic agreement with the secular and nationalist group in the Palestinian leadership.'

Arafat was reluctant to cede Abu Mazen a share of the power he wielded as the symbol of the Palestinian revolution: a leader bruised and humiliated, but still immune to frontal challenge. In the end he bent under international pressure. The president will continue to control the security forces and any peace negotiations with Israel, but the prime minister will hire and fire ministers.

Both Israeli and Palestinian analysts expect Abu Mazen to build on the bridgehead the premiership will provide. 'He is the right man in the right place,' said Hatem Abdel Kader, a West Bank Fatah official. 'We're keeping our fingers crossed for him.'

Pragmatic younger leaders like the former Gaza and West Bank security chiefs Mohammed Dahlan and Jibril Rajoub, marginalised by Arafat, are nudging their way back to centre stage. Abu Mazen pledged to continue finance minister Salam Fayyad's anti-corruption drive.

The first Palestinian prime minister enjoys the backing of the United States, Europe and the United Nations – without being their puppet. Israel welcomed his appointment, but was careful not to appear too enthusiastic. Such support is essential if Abu Mazen is to achieve results, but so are his authenticity and his independence.

Sharon breaks a 36-year taboo

Jewish Chronicle, May 30, 2003

Ariel Sharon this week shattered one of the most staunchly defended taboos of Israeli diplomacy. The day after persuading his cabinet to endorse the international road map for Middle East peace, he incensed his right-wing constituency by calling the Israeli presence in the West Bank and Gaza Strip an 'occupation'.

At most, Israel has always insisted that the territories were 'disputed'. Menachem Begin, the first Likud prime minister, said two days after winning the 1977 election: 'These are not occupied territories. These are liberated territories. A Jew has every right to settle these liberated territories of the Jewish land.'

Twenty-six years later, Mr Sharon, the fourth Likud prime minister, said on Monday: 'I think the idea that it is possible to continue keeping 3.5 million Palestinians under occupation – yes, it is occupation, you might not like the word, but what is happening is occupation – is bad for Israel and bad for the Palestinians and bad for the Israeli economy. Controlling 3.5 million Palestinians cannot go on for ever.'

The National Religious Party's Shaul Yahalom protested: 'What happened to you, Ariel Sharon? Statements like the one you made are a shock from which it is impossible to recover.'

For the Israeli right, the shock began on Sunday when the cabinet voted 12-7 with four abstentions to accept the road map drafted by the United States, European Union, Russia and the United Nations. The three-stage plan calls for the establishment of a Palestinian state by the end of 2005. In the first stage, the Palestinian government is required to prevent all terrorist activity, while Israel has to freeze settlement building and evacuate illegal outposts.

Israel has registered 14 reservations, which ministers said were 'red lines' in future negotiations. The Bush administration promised to address the reservations 'fully and seriously', but did not endorse them. Secretary of state Colin Powell insisted that the road map had to be accepted in full.

On Sunday, Israel complied, but added a proviso: it would never accept that Palestinian refugees had a right to return to the homes in Israel from which they fled or were driven in 1948. However, ministers dropped their demand that the Palestinians renounce this 'right' as a condition for returning to the negotiating table.

Mr Sharon was due to meet his Palestinian opposite number, Mahmoud Abbas, towards the end of this week. President George Bush is expected to convene a broader Middle East summit in early June, probably in the Jordanian port city of Aqaba.

In an interview with the daily paper, *Ha'aretz*, Mr Abbas said: 'This is an historic opportunity to return to a track of normality. We are saying to the Israelis, 'Follow the map and don't waste time haggling over details.' We must get into the implementation phase. It is vital the two peoples feel something is changing on the ground.'

Where and who are the Jewish settlers?
Jewish Chronicle, August 1, 2003

Conventional wisdom has it that there are two types of Jewish settlement in the West Bank and Gaza Strip: 'ideological' and 'quality of life'. The ideologues wanted to 'redeem' the ancient homeland for the Jewish people. The quality of life folk wanted a nice house with clean air at a price they could afford, thanks to government incentives.

Efrat, a red-roofed township of about 1,700 modern Orthodox families 15 minutes' drive along the Hebron road from Jerusalem, combines the two. It takes its name from the biblical site, near Bethlehem, where Rachel died and was buried after giving birth to Benjamin.

David Kahn, a 47-year-old ex-Wall Street lawyer who moved there with his London-born wife in 1993, explained why they chose Efrat and are bringing up their four children there: 'We were looking for a community that reflected our personalities – a modern Orthodox, vibrant Jewish community in a suburban setting that had a mix of English-speaking and veteran Israeli population. Also housing prices were significantly lower than in Jerusalem. You get more for your money.'

If that sounds like an estate agent's pitch, he added: 'To be in this stretch of the biblical woods, where you walk ancient history when you step out of the door, was very appealing to us. I believe strongly that Jews have as much right to live in this area as the Palestinians do.'

His wife, Nicci Green-Kahn, a 41-year-old family doctor from Edgware, added that she had never worried about the safety of their two boys and two girls aged 12 to six. 'They have a more secure, happy childhood than most kids in northwest London. My niece wasn't allowed to go out and post a letter until she was about 10 in northwest London. My kids go to school on the bus by themselves from the age of six.'

The pastoral dream held up, give or take a couple of land disputes with the Palestinian neighbours, until the second intifada broke out three years ago. Since then, snipers have shot dead four Efrat motorists on the Jerusalem road and two suicide bombers have blown themselves up outside a clinic and a supermarket. The road, which bypasses Bethlehem, has since been protected with concrete walls.

And now, like the other 220,000-plus Jews in 146 settlements and dozens of unauthorised outposts all over the West Bank and Gaza, the people of Efrat are waiting to see how serious Ariel Sharon is about negotiating a Palestinian state and making the 'painful sacrifices' for peace he keeps touting.

So far the fourth Likud prime minister has done no more than remove a few outposts – many of them empty or housing a couple of token families – established by the settlers to put down a marker for future expansion. As soon as the soldiers leave, the settlers move back.

Mr Sharon, once the patron of the settlement enterprise, recently broke a taboo and labelled the territories 'occupied'. Menachem Begin, the first Likud prime minister, called them 'liberated'. Mr Sharon said Israel could not go on ruling 3.5million Palestinians. He hinted at evacuating settlements and sites sacred to the Jews. The settlers, the first to take his words at face value, are bracing for a moment of truth.

Yet their anxiety is on hold. They doubt whether the Palestinians, from Yasser Arafat and Prime Minister Mahmoud Abbas down, are reconciled to the existence of a Jewish state alongside them. They expect the international 'road map' to fail, just like Oslo. In any case, they parade good reasons, historic, theological, strategic, why they think their particular community will be spared.

Still, they are brooding. It could happen. The outcome, however, might not be the cataclysmic civil 'war of the Jews' some have predicted.

A survey commissioned this summer by the Peace Now movement found that 90 per cent of the settlers would not break the law if they were ordered to evacuate their homes. Of these, 36 per cent would go quietly, 54 per cent would resist within the boundaries of the law. The other 10 per cent might break the law, with a minority of 1 per cent ready to use violence against soldiers sent to evict them. A growing majority (74 per cent) thinks the state should compensate the evacuees and allow them to choose between relocation inside the pre-1967 border and in other areas of the West Bank and Gaza.

Settlement leaders agree that most people would stay within the law, if the worst came to the worst. 'There would be a lot of pushing and shoving, but not more,' said Bob Lang, a spokesman for the Yesha Council of Jewish Settlements. 'People would say: If you want me out, drag me out. Unfortunately a few fists might be thrown. But the vast majority are loyal citizens.'

In Hebron, where 500 militant Jews live amid 100,000 hostile Arabs, David Wilder, a father of seven, said: 'If soldiers came in and they picked me up and they carried me out, there wouldn't be much I could do about it. But nobody's going to leave here voluntarily under any circumstances. If you ask me do I think there'd be violence or bloodshed, my answer's no, but I can't speak for people coming from outside.'

Outside or inside, Hebron and some other radical settlements have a record of violence – against Arabs and against Israeli security forces. The prospect cannot be discounted. The 'Jewish underground' of the early eighties, which booby-trapped the cars of Palestinian mayors, shot Arab students in the Hebron Islamic University and plotted to blow up Jerusalem's Al Aqsa mosque, was a product of the settlement movement.

Baruch Goldstein, the American-born doctor who massacred 29 Muslims at prayer in the Tomb of the Patriarchs in 1994, came from nearby Kiryat Arba. His grave there was turned into a shrine and a park is named after Meir Kahane, whose Kach party was outlawed as racist by the Knesset. A settler rabbi edited a widely distributed book in praise of Goldstein entitled *Baruch Hagever*, which translates both as 'Blessed is the Man' and 'Baruch the Hero'. Other settler rabbis have instructed their soldier students to refuse any order to uproot Jewish communities.

In Hebron last July, angry settlers returning from a terror victim's funeral clashed with police and shot dead a 14-year-old Palestinian girl on the balcony of her home. Three months later hundreds of youngsters, reared in the ideological hothouse of settlement schools, battled with soldiers and police sent to evacuate the Gilad Farm outpost. Twelve policemen and 10 settlers were injured. Three of the policemen were hit on the head with stones.

Further north in the same month, settlers from Yitzhar, south of Nablus, repeatedly harassed, stoned and shot at Palestinian villagers harvesting olives. When a group of Israeli human rights campaigners went to help the farmers, the *Jerusalem Post* reported, the settlers fired warning shots at them too. It was not exactly the law-abiding image the Yesha council projects.

Despite the climate of violence, which has killed about 820 Israelis and three times as many Palestinians, the settler population is growing. In 1977, when Menachem Begin came to power, 12,000 Jews lived in the West Bank and Gaza. A decade later, when the first intifada broke out, it had risen to 60,000.

The early settlements were built by Labour governments, most of them along what were seen as Israel's future strategic borders (Gush Etzion, the Jordan Valley and Gaza's Gush Katif). Mr Begin, energetically supported by Mr Sharon, changed all that. To prevent any 'repartition', he deliberately sowed settlements among the Arab towns and villages of the West Bank hill country. When Mr Begin was asked how he would like to be remembered, he replied: 'As the man who set the borders of the Land of Israel for all time.'

At the end of last year, according to figures released in late July by the Central Bureau of Statistics, the settler population stood at 220,200. Of these, 212,900 lived on the West Bank and 7,300 in Gaza. The rate of growth in 2002 reached 5.7 per cent, compared with 5 per cent a year earlier. That still leaves the settler community a tiny proportion of Israel's 5.4 million Jews, which perhaps explains why a steady majority of Israelis tell the pollsters they would cede the settlements for peace.

Besides, most of the growth is not in the ideological sector, but in new overspill towns built to house young strictly Orthodox families from overcrowded, high-cost Jerusalem. Two of these, Betar Illit and Modi'in Illit (also known as Kiryat Sefer), both just across the 'Green Line' border, accounted for half of the entire population increase in the settlements.

Modi'in Illit, between Jerusalem and Tel Aviv, grew by nearly 15 per cent last year and now houses 22,000. Betar Illit, west of Bethlehem, grew by 17 per cent to 20,000. A whole new neighbourhood is currently rising there. Most of the building workers are West Bank Arabs, who need the money. As you drive there, you still see Palestinian peasants riding on mules and donkeys, elderly couples gathering wild grains by the roadside.

In contrast to their television image, not all of the settlers are religious. Nor is the settlement enterprise an Anglo-American bunion on the toe of sabra Israel.

According to Bob Lang, the Yesha spokesman, 65 per cent of settlers are secular. Most of those live in commuter towns like Ariel and Ma'aleh Adumim, whose residents don't think of themselves as settlers at all. They might fight for their villas, but not for Yesha (a Hebrew acronym for Judea, Samaria and Gaza). Even in Kiryat Arba, on its ridge above Hebron, 40 per cent are secular, mostly poor Russian and Ethiopian immigrants. Nonetheless, the 35-65 ratio of religious to secular in the settlements is 10 per cent higher than Israel's national average.

The settler leadership is almost exclusively veteran Israeli. All the mayors are sabras - even Eitan Golan in largely English-speaking Efrat. So are the heads of the Gush Emunim settlement campaign and Ze'ev Hever, who spearheads their expansion plans through the Amana subsidiary. The Americans, like Mr Lang, are the ones who talk to the foreign media.

For all that, the settlements have proved a magnet for American, British and French immigrants. 'Anglos who are making aliyah these days are coming for ideological reasons,' Mr Lang explained. 'Yesha is more attractive to them than downtown Tel Aviv. A high proportion of these immigrants are coming to Yesha because that's where they want to be.'

In the opposite direction, there has been a discreet haemorrhaging from some of the more exposed or less successful settlements during the intifada. The Yesha council recently advertised for people to move to Ganim and Kadim, two isolated quality of life villages near Jenin. Mr Lang acknowledged that some people have been leaving, as they have from Immanuel, a strictly Orthodox town which has suffered two fatal bus attacks. Unlike Betar Illit, Immanuel, southwest of Nablus, is remote from the centres of yeshivah life and has been badly managed.

Yair Oppenheimer, the Peace Now spokesman, reported that they received 80 phone calls in the last year from settlers seeking financial assistance to leave. That's not, he said, Peace Now's job, but it is lobbying for the Government to compensate those who want to get out and can't sell or let their homes. Some are moving back to Tel Aviv or Haifa, but keeping their settlement residence to safeguard their tax benefits – and their compensation if Mr Sharon confounds the sceptics and pays the price for peace.

'Is Sharon going to act in a serious way against the settlers?' Mr Oppenheimer asked. 'Will he first dismantle the outposts, then freeze settlement construction? Or is it all a public relations exercise? Is he still the settlers' ally?'

For Israelis on both sides of the Green Line, the jury is still out.

Impact of Sharon's breakthrough – Olmert urges pullback

Jewish Chronicle, December 12, 2003

'Welcome to the club,' Labour MK Dalia Itzik mocked Ehud Olmert this week after Likud's deputy prime minister stunned right wingers by arguing that Israel had to evacuate most of the West Bank and Gaza Strip if it was to remain a Jewish and democratic state, free from fear and regaining world respect.

In fact, Mr Olmert's dramatic shift went beyond the broad two-state solution Labour had advocated since signing the Oslo accords a decade ago. In an interview last Friday with *Yediot Ahronot*, the former Jerusalem mayor called for a unilateral pullback to a border determined by demography.

Despairing of a negotiated peace with the Palestinian Authority, he contended that Israel had to act now in its own interest.

He declined to specify where the new border would be, but said it would leave Israel's population 80 per cent Jewish and 20 per cent Arab. That is the present breakdown within the pre-1967 Green Line. He envisaged large settlement blocks remaining under Israeli rule, but the uprooting of many isolated ones.

Israeli commentators were divided this week on whether the deputy premier was speaking for himself, or as a stalking horse for

Prime Minister Ariel Sharon, who has hinted at 'painful concessions' and is expected to unveil his own plan soon. Mr Sharon told MKs on Tuesday that it would be 'complex, difficult and controversial'. It might include unilateral steps, he added, under which 'communities might be moved to improve our security situation'.

The Yesha settlers' council immediately accused the prime minister of preparing to 'transfer' Jews from their homes in the Land of Israel. It was, they protested, neither moral nor legal. 'It is against Zionism and gives a prize to terror.'

Some pundits also saw the Olmert interview as his first shot in a succession struggle for Likud leader. The deputy premier dismissed such speculation and denied that he had discussed his initiative with Mr Sharon. 'I am too tormented by this matter to play a political game,' he said. 'We are getting close to the moment when Israel will have to make a strategic decision.'

He warned: 'We are approaching a point where more and more Palestinians will say: There is no place for two states between the Jordan and the sea. All we want is the right to vote.

'The day they get it, we will lose everything. It is hard for us to convince the world that we are right when they perpetrate terrorism. It will be all the more so when there is only one demand – a right to vote.'

Mr Olmert signalled his change of heart at the beginning of this month when he spoke on the government's behalf at a graveside ceremony marking the 30th anniversary of David Ben-Gurion's death.

He cited as an example of courageous leadership a 1949 speech in which the first prime minister justified partition. 'Let's say we can conquer all the western Land of Israel militarily, which I am sure we could,' Ben-Gurion said. 'Then what? We will make one state, but that state will want to be democratic.

'There will be general elections, and we will be in the minority. When the question arose of having the entire land without a Jewish state, or a Jewish state without the entire land, we chose a Jewish state without the entire land.'

The fiercest opposition at the time came from Menachem Begin's Herut, in which Mr Olmert's father, Mordechai, was soon to serve as a Knesset member. His son was raised on Ze'ev Jabotinsky's dream of a Jewish state on 'both banks of the Jordan'.

Despite his roots, Mr Olmert, now 58, has always been a pragmatist with a mind of his own. Politics was about doing, not dogma.

As a Herut student leader in 1966, he rebelled against Begin's leadership. 'Up to now,' he said, 'Begin has led the movement as an opposition to the ruling regime, but he has not succeeded in leading it to rule. He must accept the consequences and resign.'

Under Yitzhak Shamir's Likud administration in the late eighties, he held secret talks with Faisal Husseini, an East Jerusalem Palestinian leader, at a time when contact with the PLO was against the law. He abstained when Mr Shamir appointed Rechavam Ze'evi, an advocate of 'transferring' Arabs, to his government.

During the 1998 elections, he infuriated the Likud by praising Ehud Barak's commitment to the unity of Jerusalem. The TV clip became a centrepiece in the Labour challenger's successful campaign to oust Binyamin Netanyahu.

It was no slip of the tongue. The elegant, Havana cigar-chomping Ehud Olmert chooses his words and knows what he's doing.

After Arafat, end of an era in the Middle East

Jewish Chronicle, Weekly Review, November 12, 2004

Yasser Arafat, particularly in his later years, lived his own myth. When one British interviewer was impertinent enough to ask him a challenging question, he puffed with anger and retorted: 'Don't you know who you're talking to? I am General Yasser Arafat.' The journalist got the message, but never the answer. That wasn't the name of the game.

Arafat reigned like a mafia godfather. As a national icon, the man who gave the Palestinians their identity, he divided and ruled. He refused to delegate, on either the political or the security front. No payment was made without his signature. Only the most trusted aides knew where he banked the movement's money. His hit men punished anyone who dared to criticise him in public. Nabil Amr, a dissident former minister, was shot this summer and had to have a leg amputated.

If Arafat didn't order specific terrorist operations, he dictated the strategy of struggle. The bombers and the gunmen knew which would enjoy his blessing. He lied without scruple, as he did to Jack Straw and other western statesmen over the Karin-A arms ship, captured by Israel in January, 2002.

Lacking a son, he groomed no heir. As a result he leaves behind a dangerous void – for the Palestinians and for the Israelis. This week's soap opera confrontation between Arafat's estranged wife Suha and the caretaker leadership could prove a trailer for a far more sinister power struggle.

'We're looking at a potentially revolutionary situation,' warns Yossi Alpher, a strategic analyst and joint editor of *Bitterlemons*, an Israeli-Palestinian Internet journal. 'It's impossible with any degree of accuracy or objectivity to assess what's going to happen. There's simply no precedent for an orderly transfer of power among the Palestinians. Arafat's only the second national leader they've ever had, and between him and the first, Haj Amin al Husseini, there was a 20-year hiatus.

'There are so many potential new dynamics and new power players,' Alpher adds. 'It can go from an orderly transfer to the elders of Fatah, which is what ostensibly we are seeing right now, all the way to a Somalia-like situation and a thousand different gradations in between – coup d'etat, power-sharing, war lords, anarchy.'

Khalil Shikaki, a Palestinian political scientist, expects the short-term transfer of power to go smoothly, if only because Arafat was dying in hospital and not by violence. But he believes the transitional leadership will soon face serious challenges.

'The next six months will be very critical,' he predicts. 'Hamas and Islamic Jihad will not challenge the transfer of power in the immediate future. But if no date is set for elections, if there is more division and fragmentation because the old guard fails to forge a coalition with the young guard, if the transitional leadership tries to enforce a ceasefire in the absence of an Israeli restraint on its use of force, then both Hamas and the young guard will very quickly challenge its control and legitimacy. They will direct their force at the Israelis in order to dispirit and show as impotent the transitional leadership.'

Arafat's interim successor looks like being Mahmoud Abbas, a former prime minister, who currently serves as general secretary of the Palestine Liberation Organisation. He has frequently denounced what he calls the militarisation of the intifada.

'Abu Mazen's real test,' Roni Shaked, an Israeli commentator on Palestinian affairs, wrote in the *Yediot Achronot* daily paper, 'will lie in his ability to impose law and order and ultimately bring about a state of calm.' Amid the prevailing uncertainty, it is a tall order, especially for a 69-year-old without charisma or popular following.

On the optimistic scenario, a more pragmatic Palestinian leadership could present Ariel Sharon with fresh options. The Israeli prime minister insists that Arafat's demise will not change the timetable of his planned evacuation of the Gaza Strip and the northern West Bank. But if he had a partner after all, it could make the disengagement more orderly and less fraught with danger.

It would be easier to pull out both the army and the 8,000 Jewish settlers if the operation were coordinated with the Palestinians. If that happened, the veteran military commentator Ze'ev Schiff suggested in *Ha'aretz*, disengagement would take on a new character.

'If the Palestinians make sure the settlements are evacuated in peace and quiet, they will avoid a lot of fire and destruction,' he wrote. 'Israel might even agree to international agencies entering the strip before the evacuation.'

Schiff detected a renewed readiness in Israel's security establishment to discuss the evacuation of Arab cities, transferring territory to the Palestinians and widening their freedom of movement. But he stressed: 'It's all on condition that the Palestinian side starts taking action against terror. The assessment is that a new and determined Palestinian leadership can promise there won't be

Qassam rockets fired from the Gaza Strip. Quiet in Gaza would also put an end to Israeli military activity there.'

Eventually, with Britain and the United States attempting to revive the international roadmap for peace, the next step could be negotiations for a comprehensive solution of the kind that Arafat rejected at Camp David in 2000. 'It is now time,' says Gilead Sher, who headed the Israeli negotiating team there under Ehud Barak's premiership, 'for the sane and moderate Palestinians to overcome Arafat's legacy and give up some of their aspirations in return for a viable state.'

First, however, Abu Mazen and Prime Minister Ahmed Qureia (Abu Ala) have to establish their authority and legitimacy. It won't happen overnight. And further evacuations weren't what Ariel Sharon had in mind when he spawned disengagement as a way to keep most of the West Bank in Israeli hands.

IDF abuse incidents shock Israeli public

Jewish Chronicle, December 3, 2004

A series of Israeli media reports alleging abuse or cruelty by soldiers was this week threatening a crisis of public confidence in how the army was fighting Palestinian terror. The *Ha'aretz* newspaper quoted an army general as saying that the rules of engagement in the Gaza Strip 'bordered on war crimes'.

The incidents under scrutiny include the case of an IDF company commander being prosecuted for allegedly emptying the magazine of his automatic into the body of a severely wounded 13-year-old Palestinian schoolgirl, Imam al Hamas, who strayed too close to a fortified observation post near Rafah in the Gaza Strip.

Military police are investigating reports that soldiers at a checkpoint in the Jordan Valley tampered with the body parts of a suicide bomber, stuck his head on a concrete barrier, put a cigarette in his mouth, then photographed each other with their 'trophies'.

The army is taking disciplinary action against two marksmen who fired live ammunition at rioters trying to tear down the West Bank security fence near the village of Mashka, severely injuring an Israeli protester, Gil Na'amaty.

A series of disturbing reports in the Israeli media over the past two weeks is threatening a crisis of public confidence in how the army is fighting Palestinian terror.

A military tape recording, made at the time of Imam al Hamas' shooting and broadcast by Channel 2 television, included the company commander stating that he had 'verified the kill', a term used for finishing off a wounded enemy who might still pose a danger. The tape showed that his soldiers kept firing at the girl, even after they had identified her as 'about 10 years old'.

Noam Hayut, a reserve lieutenant, wrote on the Ynet Website this week that he taught his soldiers that it was forbidden to shoot an injured and helpless soldier who had been 'removed from the cycle of war'.

How then, he asked, could a company commander have emptied an entire magazine into the girl's body? 'The answer is simple,' he replied. 'It happens when you link the kill-verification-procedure to the reality in which anything goes in the territories and the culture of "all the Palestinians are either terrorists or support terror".'

The army has a code of conduct, updated last year, on how to make ethical decisions in a new kind of war, where armies do not face armies, where the two sides fight by different rules. The high command draws lines, but the soldiers in the field don't always follow them.

Asa Kasher, professor of professional ethics at Tel Aviv University and an academic adviser to the national defence college, told the *JC* that the formal standards demanded by the IDF of its troops were very high. The problem, he acknowledged, was in the performance.

'Whereas the more professional senior officers are aware of how to move from one type of engagement to a completely different one, the younger ones, those who are hardly professional, don't know the difference between what they may do and what they may not.'

Before an officer or a sergeant was appointed to command a checkpoint, he said, he was instructed on 'what are the commands, what are the regulations, what are the principles that should be applied there.'

Professor Kasher, who helped draft the code of conduct, admitted that it was not enough. He detected a failure of leadership. 'Eventually some of them don't behave as they should,' he said. 'If a soldier does not perform well, the responsibility is on him or her, but always on the commanders too.'

Partly, he blamed it on the atmosphere of violence prevailing in Israeli society – domestic violence, violence in the schools, aggressive driving on the roads. The professor disputed the widely held view that the occupation corrupts young Israelis.

'People come to the occupation with their values, with their education, with their attitudes,' he argued. 'The occupation provides them with situations and opportunities which they don't encounter elsewhere.

'If a soldier at a checkpoint just enjoys seeing dozens of Palestinians moving one step backwards because he's ordered them to, he finds an outlet for his very low moral standards. Now we see who he is.'

Chapter 15 – 2005-08

Outlook unsettled but improved

Jewish Chronicle, August 19, 2005

A couple of weeks ago Daniella Weiss, one of the more strident of veteran West Bank settler leaders, tried to infiltrate Gush Katif, the main Gaza settlement block which had been sealed by the army.

Soldiers young enough to be her grandchildren were filmed grappling with her as she lay squirming on the ground. Then they arrested her.

It was one of the more telling images of Prime Minister Ariel Sharon's extraordinary revolution. Daniella Weiss, as council chair of the Kedumim settlement, is used to ordering soldiers. They feared her, she didn't fear them.

Thirty-seven years after Rabbi Moshe Levinger took a band of Jewish families to an Arab-owned Hebron hotel to celebrate Pesach and never left, the settlement movement is no longer setting Israel's national agenda. For now at least, their Yesha council is outside the decision-making loop.

What will happen afterwards is uncertain. Mr Sharon says his aim is to make the main West Bank settlement blocks – but not the rest – part of Israel in any future agreement with the Palestinians. Vice-premier Ehud Olmert, who trailed disengagement for his leader two years ago, denied last week that Israel was sacrificing Gaza to keep the West Bank.

In any case, the taboo has been broken. A precedent has been set. For the first time, Israel has voluntarily evacuated settlements inside the ancestral Land of Israel. Its people have been tuned to expect surprises. And at 77, Ariel Sharon will not always be the one who maps their fate.

Over the past year, the prime minister has led from the front and doggedly refused to be deflected from his course – by his own right-wing ministers and rebel MKs, by the supposedly all-powerful Likud central committee, by the doubts of the recently-retired chief-of-staff Moshe Ya'alon, or by the orange hoards of protesters.

Like the founding father, David Ben-Gurion, Mr Sharon is a leader in the prophetic mode. He 'knows' what is good for the people of Israel and, by hook or by crook, he will implement it. It doesn't matter to him that he was the supreme patron of the settlement enterprise. As he said recently, he was 'right' when he ordered the settlers to seize the hilltops, and he is 'right' now when he orders them down again.

Mr Sharon has never explained what changed his mind. But it is not hard to work it out. After Yasser Arafat rejected Ehud Barak's offer of a comprehensive peace at Camp David five years ago, Israel had to take its future into its own hands. All the rest fell into place.

The pragmatic right has recognised that Israel is losing the demographic battle. Independent scholars extrapolated that Arabs would outnumber Jews within two decades between the Jordan and the Mediterranean, and the politicians took it to heart.

Mr Sharon adopted the left's slogan that if Israel retained the West Bank and Gaza, it would cease to be a Jewish democratic state. Either it would have to give the Palestinians the vote, or it would have to suppress them forever by force.

Beyond that, Mr Sharon understood that, in the 21st century, Israel is not 'a people that dwells alone'. If it is to be a light unto the Jews, let alone unto the nations, it has to be accepted as part of the democratic community.

Strategically, Israel needs American aid to maintain its qualitative edge over Arab and Muslim enemies. This is especially so when nuclear non-proliferation is crumbling and oil revenues are soaring. And it needs American and European cooperation in setting the terms of a two-state solution.

Economically, Israel cannot afford a boycott. It is in the forefront of globalisation. That is its chosen route to prosperity. Man does not live by Jaffa oranges alone.

Israel's electronics start-ups are working at the cutting edge with American, Indian and Chinese partners in the civilian and military markets. They need worldwide economies of scale.

342

Polgat makes and sells suits around the world, whatever it says on the label. Delta does the same with socks and underpants. Teva is the biggest international manufacturer of generic pharmaceuticals. If you sit on a moulded plastic garden chair, the odds are it was made by Keter.

And finally, the military price of staying in Gaza has become too high. Mr Sharon's senior adviser, Dov Weisglass, testified that the prime minister was influenced by four former security chiefs, who reflected out loud on the corrupting effect of occupation, and by reserve pilots who announced that they would not bomb Palestinian civilians.

These are the kind of people Mr Sharon respects and listens to. It brought home the growing reluctance among his own kind of Israeli patriots to risk their lives and the lives of their children for Gush Katif. Enough was enough.

Psychological warfare gets a new meaning

Jewish Chronicle, August 26, 2005

With more than a touch of theatre, a Gaza settler protesting his eviction from Neveh Dekalim held his six-year-old daughter rigid by her shoulders, harangued a police inspector and tried repeatedly to force him to take her from him. The officer looked straight through him, without blinking and without saying a word.

In Shirat Hayam, a young resister screaming defiance from the roof of his house begged soldiers for a cigarette. They gave him one, then hauled him down. When women soldiers carted away female religious settlers, who were kicking and yelling abuse, they tried to ensure that their skirts remained modestly in place.

These were no random acts of kindness or indifference. About 50 army psychologists trained thousands of soldiers and police for a year in how to conduct themselves in a battle where, as their commanders constantly reiterated, there was no enemy and no victory.

The slogan was 'Sensitivity and determination'. For six days, in Gaza and the northern West Bank, they showed they had learnt their lessons well. The army and police evacuated thousands of settlers and their hotheaded supporters with unprecedented discipline and restraint.

'Going into people's houses is a very difficult thing to do, no matter what your political views,' Major Yael Ben-Horin, a senior army psychologist, told the *JC* this week. 'We were sure there would be tears. We were sure it would be very difficult, even with a potential of trauma, because of the children, the crying, the pain the settlers really feel. We needed the soldiers to feel that they would be emotionally aroused, but at the same time we wanted them to go on with the mission.'

First, army and police commanders were brought together and taught how to work as a team in the kind of operation for which they had never been trained. Then their men and women were put through intensive preparation. Every lieutenant colonel had his own consultant. A psychologist was assigned to every company.

Instructors showed them video footage of the 1982 evacuation of the Sinai town of Yamit under the peace treaty with Egypt. They also interviewed people who went through that disengagement.

'We spoke with both sides, the settlers and the forces,' Major Ben-Horin explained. 'That was very important. We wanted them to feel empathy for the settlers. We wanted them to hear stories of the people involved, what was difficult for them and what helped them.'

The lessons were reviewed in simulations and workshops. All the potential challenges – the insults, the Holocaust imagery, the spitting and struggling – were played out in advance.

'We taught them that if somebody calls you a Nazi, it's not personal,' Major Ben-Horin said. 'No one is trying to hurt you personally. We didn't tell the soldiers not to answer. We didn't say avoid eye contact.

'What we said was that you need to address people like a representative of the state. Don't go into political issues. Don't get into a fight or an argument. In practice, it differed from person to person. Some found it easier not to answer, others answered.'

Officers were more confident than other ranks about talking to the settlers, the psychologists found. The dialogue, at whatever level, helped.

'When the soldiers answered,' Major Ben-Horin reported, 'a lot of times it calmed the situation down. The settler felt that you were addressing him personally and that you cared about him. Even saying, I know what you feel, I'm in pain as well, was very helpful.'

The touchy-feely tactics provoked some amusement among the chattering classes. A cartoon in the daily paper *Ha'aretz* showed a traffic warden handing out a parking ticket. The victim looked at him and asked: 'Don't I even get a hug?'

But over six historic days, in the tumultuous Gaza Strip and Northern Samaria, the training proved its worth. Now that the disengagement is over, the psychologists are not going to leave the soldiers to their traumas.

'We're not going to make everyone go through therapy,' Major Ben-Horin said, 'but we'll be working with them as a group, about their feelings, how they came through, how they're feeling now.'

Then the soldiers and police can get back to their real jobs of hunting terrorists and catching car thieves.

Sharon's new party, Kadima
Jewish Chronicle, November 22, 2005

Even Ariel Sharon's most fervent admirers admit that he has not always been right. But in a 60-year career in the army and in politics, he has never doubted his own judgement.

He had his failures as well as his triumphs. But whatever Mr Sharon did, he did with absolute conviction that he was acting in the best interests, not just of himself, his unit or his party, but of Israel and the Jewish people. He doesn't confess that he was wrong. What he says is: 'I was right then, and I'm right now.'

Three decades ago, he welded the Likud (the Hebrew word for 'unity') from four right-wing parties. Since 2001 he has led it to two election victories. This week he shattered that unity, launching a new centre party and taking five Likud ministers and at least eight backbenchers with him.

He built settlements and he evacuated settlements. Netzarim, he said barely three years ago, is as much part of Israel as is Tel Aviv. Last August, Netzarim, the most exposed of the Gaza settlements, was bulldozed into the sand.

For decades, he passionately resisted a Palestinian state. Now he is working towards its creation, on his terms: Palestinian independence in exchange for Israeli security. Diehard Likudniks like Uzi Landau, who lacked his ideological flexibility, could never accept that.

For most of his five years as party leader, he preached that they would have to recognise a future Palestinian state. 'It shook the earth of Likud identity,' Eyal Arad, his strategic adviser, said this week. 'The Likud dream of Greater Israel crashed against the walls of reality. What we see today is the logical result of that earthquake.'

By sheer force of personality, Mr Sharon bludgeoned through the Gaza disengagement. It was, he argued, a way to break out of the cycle of bloodshed that was getting Jews and Arabs nowhere. It would ensure that Israel remained a Jewish and democratic state.

The ideologues never forgave him. Every Knesset vote became a cliffhanging nightmare. Three weeks ago, eight Likud rebels stopped him appointing two new ministers. Mr Sharon concluded that they were not going to let him govern, even if he led the Likud to another win at the polls.

Divorce was inevitable, though his confidants acknowledge that it remains a gamble. 'Life in the Likud in its present form,' Mr Sharon said after resigning from the party on Monday, 'has become unbearable.'

On the tactical level, the prime minister has freed himself from the dead weight of old Likud: from its ideological rigidity, from the insatiable demands and dictates of the unelected, 3,000-strong central committee, from jobs for the boys.

On the strategic level, assuming he wins a third term, Mr Sharon is determined to pursue the international roadmap for peace. Instead of what he called the 'failed' formula of land for peace, adviser Arad argued that the roadmap met the real needs of both sides: a national home for the Palestinians in return for 'the total end of the terrorist war against the existence of the State of Israel.' Ultimately, he conceded, it would entail territorial concessions.

At 77, Mr Sharon aims to reshuffle the cards, to present the voters with a third choice between left and right. In the spirit of the first Prime Minister, David Ben-Gurion, he wants to be a manager who puts the security of the state and the welfare of its citizens before dogma.

'The new movement we are establishing,' Mr Sharon said, 'will be a new home for all Israelis who want to act responsibly and faithfully on behalf of the state and to realise the Zionist vision.'

Israel's friends can only hope he's got it right this time.

The second Lebanon war from Haifa

The Independent, July 17, 2006

Yossi Amergi, a 46-year-old mechanic, lay in the emergency ward of Haifa's Rambam hospital yesterday (Sunday), tubes sticking out of his arm, raw skin showing through a thick bandage on his right leg. A few hours earlier eight of his workmates were killed by a rocket that burst through the corrugated iron roof of their railway maintenance depot, sending arc lights crashing, splintering carriage windows and washing the concrete platforms with gore.

He was one of the 28 wounded, five of them seriously, in the worst aerial attack on Israel's third largest city since Saddam Hussein's Scud missiles in 1991. 'I heard a boom,' he recalled. 'My ears were bursting; blood was spurting from my leg. I lost friends, Jews and Arabs who worked together.'

Just as we arrived at the hospital, a siren sounded, the promised one-minute warning of another Hezbollah attack. We took cover under solid-looking concrete steps on the edge of the car park and waited for the boom which never came. Apparently, that rocket landed in the sea.

When we reached the ward on the ninth floor, the stocky Mr Amergi was on his mobile phone, calmly instructing his wife and children to get into the nearest shelter. Earlier he asked them not to visit him. 'I'm more worried about my family than myself,' he said. 'They're better off staying at home.'

Haifa is like that: a phlegmatic Mediterranean port and holiday city of 268,300 people, 90 per cent of them Jewish, 10 per cent Arab, living in what until yesterday had seemed a safe 33 kilometres south of the Lebanese border. They comforted themselves that Katyushas, the primitive Russian-designed rockets Palestinian and Lebanese enemies have launched at border towns and villages for three decades, could not reach that far.

Well now, as the citizens of Haifa and Tiberias, 52 kilometres to the east on the Sea of Galilee, discovered this weekend, they can. Shaul Mofaz, the transport minister and former army commander who visited the railway workshop, accused Syria of supplying Hezbollah with a more sophisticated, longer-range model. It sounded more like a threat than a statement.

Haifa folks were anxious and wary, but not panicking, although the government declared a state of emergency throughout the north. By midday, three hours after the bombing of the railway workshop in a rundown industrial zone below the desirable residences of Mount Carmel, cars and trucks were going about their business. Containers were arriving at the port. Some shops and factories were open, perhaps not as many as on a normal Sunday, which is a working day in these parts. People were walking in the streets, though the city's two universities closed.

Adi Goldberg, a 17-year-old high school student who plays clarinet in the local youth orchestra, confessed that she was scared when she heard the explosion. 'We knew it was possible that a Katyusha would come to Haifa,' she said, 'but we didn't really think it would happen. We don't know what to expect now.'

Yesterday, she stayed at home. 'We have a shelter,' she said. 'We'll hear if the siren goes. After that, it depends how things develop. It's very frustrating. It's the summer holidays and I can't even go to the grocer's.'

Avi Friedman, a 56-year-old high-tech businessman and father of three teen and twenties children, urged his family to stay near a shelter, to listen to the news, but not to panic. For himself, he was more philosophic. Like most male Israelis of his generation, he has served in the army. 'I know what war is like,' he said with a shrug as he filled his car at a petrol station.

He welcomed the opportunity to settle scores once and for all with Hezbollah. 'It's been a long time coming,' he argued. 'I'm extremely proud that my government has decided not to turn the other cheek. Whatever the price for me and my family, we are ready to pay it.'

Not everyone was so gung-ho. Half a dozen Jewish and Arab women stood outside the gates of the wrecked railway depot, holding up placards calling for a ceasefire. 'War will not bring peace,' read one; 'Talk don't fight,' another. A burly worker harangued them. 'I lost friends in there,' he bellowed. 'You don't know what it's like.' One of the women pointed up the hill. 'I live there,' she retorted. 'I know as well as you do.'

Yehezkel Farkash, the side-curled young head of the northern branch of Zaka, the ultra-Orthodox volunteers who retrieve bodies from bombsites and traffic accidents, knows better perhaps than either of them. He was one of the first on the scene after the rocket struck.

'It was one of the worst I've ever witnessed,' he said. 'I hope I'll never see one like it again. You don't expect a major disaster like this in the city of Haifa. We found great devastation, dozens wounded, screaming and shouting. Blood and body parts were everywhere.'

Miri Eisen, a reserve army colonel drafted to serve as government spokeswoman, was on hand to deliver the message. 'The government of Israel is determined that at the end of this war that Hezbollah declared on us, Hezbollah will not be a terrorist organisation, Hezbollah will not be deployed on our northern border,' she said. 'We will not stop until this situation has changed dramatically.'

In Jerusalem, Ehud Olmert, the prime minister, threatened that the rocket attacks on Haifa would have 'far-reaching consequences' for Lebanon. He swore not to surrender to threats from Hezbollah in the north and Hamas in the south. 'We know that many tests yet await us. Our enemies are trying to disrupt life in Israel. They will fail.'

Why Israel must keep on pounding Hezbollah
Jewish Chronicle, July 21, 2006

Long before he was Mr Peace, the architect of Oslo, the prophet of a New Middle East, Shimon Peres was Mr Security. He laid the foundations of Israel's aircraft and military industries. He was the political father of the nuclear research programme. This summer, with Hamas rampant in Gaza and Hezbollah rampant in Lebanon, the elder statesman has reverted to type.

The vice-premier is no longer looking for compromise formulas. He scorns international diplomacy. He is singing from the same hawkish hymn sheet as Prime Minister Ehud Olmert. He is supporting the bombardment of Lebanon to the hilt. He may be a peacenik, but he is no pacifist.

Israel will go on pounding Hezbollah for as long as it takes to bring the Shi'ite militia to its knees, he told the *JC* in an exclusive interview, snatched between official meetings on Wednesday. He expected the war to last weeks, but not months.

The international community, he contended, would not be able to impose a time limit. It had forfeited its leverage by allowing Iran, Hezbollah's principal sponsor, to defy the world over its nuclear ambitions.

'The problem is that world opinion, the United States and the United Nations, does not have much impact on Hezbollah. It's the first time that the international community was left practically without influence because they allowed the Iranians to make a mockery of their own resolutions.

'How can they impose a time limit on Israel if they cannot impose anything upon Hezbollah, if they can neither stop them, nor defend us? We are going to defend ourselves. We don't ask anyone to defend us. When it comes to Hezbollah, they can say whatever they want, unless they can show that they have a real say with them.'

Mr Peres, a Nobel Peace Prize laureate, denied charges that Israel's massive aerial response to Hezbollah's July 5 raid, which killed eight Israeli soldiers and kidnapped two others, was disproportionate.

'Is it proportionate to shoot 1,500 missiles over our villages and towns?' he asked. 'We are extremely careful. We don't try to kill civilians. We are very careful not to destroy Lebanese infrastructure. The one who is destroying the Lebanese people and the Lebanese infrastructure is Hezbollah.

'We are fighting Hezbollah because Hezbollah tried to force Israel to do things by taking hostages and by firing rockets and missiles. We have shown that we can withstand them. We are much stronger than their rockets and their missiles.'

He saw a role for diplomacy, but only after Israel had overcome Hezbollah in the north and Hamas in the south. 'As long as they are alive and shooting, and diplomacy cannot stop it, diplomacy doesn't have a role.'

Earlier on Wednesday, the inner security cabinet set three conditions for a diplomatic solution: the unconditional release of the abducted soldiers, Udi Goldwasser and Eldad Regev; a halt to Hezbollah rocket firing at Israeli targets; and full implementation of UN Security Council resolution 1559, including the disarming of all Lebanese militias, the extension of Lebanese government sovereignty over all its territory and deployment of the Lebanese army along the border with Israel.

Mr Peres dismissed doubts about the Lebanese government's capacity to comply. 'The Lebanese government and the Lebanese army are as strong as much as they decide to be strong,' he insisted. 'The Lebanese army is made up of 50,000 soldiers. Hezbollah, with all its reserves, has perhaps 6,000-7,000 soldiers. But the Lebanese army is not ready to fight. If the government of Lebanon will not govern, what can we do?'

One thing Mr Olmert's ruling coalition is determined not to do is re-conquer Southern Lebanon, which Israel evacuated in 2000. It learnt a bitter lesson after the 1982 invasion and has deliberately limited ground operations this time.

'We are not going to re-occupy Southern Lebanon,' Mr Peres vowed, 'but we will defend our land. We were attacked, and we are defending our land, and that's it. We left there completely, in accordance with a UN resolution. We were praised by the UN itself because of it. So there's no room to talk about occupation.'

Like the prime minister, Mr Peres did not rule out an international peace force of the kind advocated by Britain's Tony Blair, provided it had the strength and the will to prevent Hezbollah resuming its confrontation.

'If it is an international force that can stop the firing of missiles,' he said, 'why not? But then they have to decide that this is their task. If they want to be there just as observers, that won't solve anything.'

Mr Peres rejected outright any exchange of prisoners, though some Israeli commentators believe it will come eventually. 'I see no way that there will be a prisoner exchange,' the vice-premier said. 'Hezbollah entered our land illegally. They captured our soldiers for the sake of negotiation. We are not going to negotiate because of it. We are going to try and release our soldiers by our own strength.'

Two weeks from now, Mr Peres will be 83. Despite a reputation for deviousness, a record of losing elections when they matter most, he is still going strong. He has been written off time and again, but buries his rivals and his detractors. If Amir Peretz defeats him for Labour Party leader, he switches to the new centre party, Kadima, first under Ariel Sharon, then Ehud Olmert. If Tsipi Livni beats him to the foreign ministry, he'll be minister for the development of the Negev and Galilee. If Ms Livni is too busy to talk to the world media or to receive second-tier foreign visitors, the instantly recognisable Shimon is there to charm and glad-hand them.

He is being touted as a possible successor to the scandal-ridden Moshe Katsav, the man who beat him for president six years ago. Mr Peres would be 90 by the time his seven-year term expired. They will have to hand it to him on a platter this time. And if they do, they'd better not expect him to be a figurehead of state. He's not ready for pipe and slippers.

After the war – analysis

Open Democracy, October 17, 2006

Two months after the end of the devastating Lebanon war, Israelis are still scourging themselves for failing to achieve what they thought they were fighting for: the disarming of Hezbollah and the release of the two soldiers whose abduction on 12 July provoked them into battle.

The Lebanese, by contrast, are increasingly blaming the Shi'ite militants for the death and destruction they brought on their country. An unusually apologetic Hassan Nasrallah, Hezbollah's secretary-general, admitted in an interview with the Lebanese NTV on August 27 that he would not have ordered the cross-border operation if he had known the scale of Israel's response.

Fuad Saniora, the Sunni Muslim prime minister, is cautiously beginning to assert his authority. Samir Geagea, a Christian warlord turned political leader, told a Beirut rally on 24 September: 'The majority of the Lebanese people don't feel victory. The majority of the Lebanese people feel that a major catastrophe has befallen them, throwing their present and future up in the air.'

But with tales of incompetence by military commanders and political leaders proliferating daily, Israelis are not convinced by Ehud Olmert's insistence that Israel made significant strategic and political gains. Confidence in the prime minister's centrist Kadima party is collapsing. An opinion poll published in *Yediot Ahronot* on October 12 found that it would win only 15 parliamentary seats if elections were held now, barely half the 29 it captured at the first time of asking in a general election six months earlier. Kadima would come third behind the right-wing opposition Likud and Yisrael Beitenu. Olmert is desperately seeking to expand his coalition to survive the winter, despite a thriving economy and a shekel that is at its highest against the dollar for more than five years.

Yet even the sceptical Israeli media are starting to acknowledge that things are changing across their northern border. The Lebanese army has deployed in the south for the first time in three decades. Twelve thousand government troops were in place by early

October. They were backed by 5,500 soldiers from a beefed-up United Nations peace force, with international naval units patrolling the Mediterranean coast to enforce a UN embargo on the re-supply of Hezbollah arms. Other troops were patrolling the eastern border to stop arms smuggling from Syria. Miri Eisin, Olmert's spokeswoman, told foreign correspondents in Jerusalem on October 4 that no longer-range missiles, the kind that could hit Tel Aviv, had reached Hezbollah since the 14 August ceasefire to replace the arsenal destroyed by the Israeli air force.

Elias Murr, the Lebanese defence minister, claimed to reporters in Beirut on October 10 that the army had confiscated weapons from Hezbollah fighters. He declined to say how many. It seems, however, that his men are not actively searching for Hezbollah arms caches still hidden in Shi'a villages. The government is not disarming Hezbollah. It is content that the movement is complying with an agreement not to display its weapons in public.

Israel estimates that Hezbollah lost 650 combatants in the 33-day war, about 10 per cent of its regular force. Nasrallah's commanders are concentrating on the slow business of rebuilding. For now at least, Southern Lebanon is no longer 'Hezbollahstan'. Armed men are not harassing Israeli border posts. Lebanese and UN troops are even limiting the number of civilian demonstrators allowed to approach the fence.

Nasrallah still boasts of a 'divine victory' over the Zionist enemy, but Hezbollah has lost much of its swagger. It has ceased to dominate Lebanon's fragmented political map. A poll published in the Beirut French language daily *L'Orient-Le Jour* on August 28, two weeks after the ceasefire, found only 33.3 per cent of Lebanese convinced that the war had strengthened Hezbollah. Fifty-one per cent favoured disarming it. Support for disarmament was particularly strong among Hezbollah's perennial foes, the Druze (79 per cent) and Christians (77 per cent), but less so among Sunni Muslims (54 per cent).

An overwhelming majority of Shi'ites (84 per cent) wanted Hezbollah to keep its arms, but the disenchantment has set in there too. Sheikh Ali al-Amin, the respected Shi'a mufti of the southern port city of Tyre, scathingly dismissed Nasrallah's victory talk. In two interviews with the Lebanese LBC television station on August 26 and September 5, the cleric said: 'We suffered more than our enemy. The destruction caused to us was greater than that caused to our enemy. We lost more lives than the enemy... I don't understand how anyone can claim that one side was defeated, without losing lives or suffering destruction, while the other side won, with all this destruction and loss of lives.'

The mufti scorned the rebuilding grants Hezbollah promised thousands of Shi'a families whose homes were demolished by Israeli air strikes and army sappers. 'People are not simple and naïve,' he argued, 'that money will make them forget their wounds, their tragedies, and the loved ones they have lost. Life must go on, but how can anyone forget such pains and all the suffering of becoming displaced?'

The Beirut press, Arabic, French and English, provides a willing platform for Hezbollah's critics. Mona Fayyad, a professor at the Lebanese University, wrote one of the most searing denunciations on August 8 while the war was still raging. Under the heading 'To be a Shi'ite Now...' she wrote in the liberal daily *An Nahar*:

> To be a Shi'ite is to accept that your country be destroyed in front of your eyes – with no surprise – and that it comes tumbling down on your head and that your family be displaced and dispersed, and becomes a refugee at the four corners of the nation and the world, and that you accept standing up to the enemy with no complaints as long as there is a fighter out there with a rocket that he can launch at northern Israel without asking about the why, or about the timing, or about the usefulness of the end result.

Nabih Berri, leader of the more secular Shi'ite Amal party, is distancing himself from Hezbollah. He gave up acting as a proxy for his militant rival in negotiations for a prisoner exchange. In early October Berri, the Speaker of the Lebanese parliament, went to Saudi Arabia to solicit political and financial assistance for his country. Israeli analysts hope it will strengthen democratic, anti-Syrian voices among the Shi'ites, Lebanon's largest community.

Berri is urging Hezbollah to concentrate on charity and welfare. Israelis, who learnt a few lessons of their own this summer, are not banking on it.

The birthday party that captured Israel's heart
The Independent, August 31, 2007

Maria Amin, a chubby-faced Palestinian girl with gleaming brown eyes, celebrated her birthday yesterday like any pampered six year old. Doting aunts decked her out like a princess in a gauzy white chiffon dress, spotted with pink hearts and topped with a toy tiara.

A make-up girl primped her hair, rouged her cheeks and painted her lips. With a pout and a shake of the head, Maria rejected a plain lipstick and demanded a glittery gold one. She insisted on being sprayed with a favourite scent. When the make-up girl held up a mirror, she cooed: 'How pretty!'

But Maria was no ordinary birthday girl. She came to the party in a wheelchair, which she navigates with her chin against a joystick. She was paralysed from the neck down in May last year when the car she was travelling in was caught in an Israeli missile strike on an Islamic Jihad commander in Gaza. Her mother, grandmother and older brother were killed.

She celebrated her birthday with a party in the Israeli Alyn hospital and rehabilitation centre for handicapped children, where she has been hooked up to a respirator for 15 months. She will need it for the rest of her life.

Her father, Hamdi, who is on call 24 hours a day, supervised the festivities. The Israeli army allowed his father, grandfather and sundry cousins to visit from Gaza. The hall, overlooking the Jerusalem forest, was awash with balloons.

Television reporters, who had filmed Maria's story, turned up with their own children, bearing gifts. Arab and Jewish family friends brought presents.

The birthday girl thanked them in her native Arabic and the Hebrew she has picked up from the hospital staff. Hamdi, a 30-year-old former building worker, embraced them in both languages.

356

But the celebrations were overshadowed. The Israeli defence ministry has paid for Maria's rehabilitation at Alyn and for a small flat on the premises for her father and younger brother. Now, however, the ministry says she must move to the Abu Raya Rehabilitation Centre in Ramallah, where it will continue covering their expenses.

The Palestinian doctors say that they cannot provide the care Maria needs. They don't have the equipment; they don't have the trained staff. The Israeli hospital is defying orders and refusing to discharge her. The case will come before the Israeli Supreme Court on September 25.

Dr Shirley Meyer, Alyn's chief executive, said yesterday: 'Maria need not be under my care. My only stipulation is that she has access to a facility that can take care of her medical needs. As long as that doesn't happen, she can't leave. I don't mind where those facilities are in the world.'

Hamdi Amin is a father in limbo. He can't work, even if the Israelis give him a permit. Maria needs him constantly. 'Until the judges decide,' he said, 'I don't know how we'll live or where we'll go. Maria's condition is still very grave. For her it's a matter of life or death. She can't move her arms or legs. She can't breathe on her own. There's nowhere in Gaza or the West Bank that can look after her. How can the defence ministry say the Ramallah hospital has to treat her?'

The family has encountered the worst and the best of Israel. Hamdi declines to blame or to praise. 'I don't care about wars, I don't care about Hamas, I don't care about America,' he explained. 'I grew up in a family where you worked to put food on the table for your children. I believe that the Lord gives and the Lord takes away.'

After their plight was aired in the Hebrew media, a support group of Israeli and Palestinian activists has rallied to the Amin family's side. Dalia Becker, a chain-smoking Israeli matron, said: 'We're Hamdi's second family. Anything he needs, he turns to us. We're paying for the lawyers who will represent Maria at the Supreme

Court. It's hard to believe that once the judges see her, they will send her away.'

Back in Gaza, the undeclared war flares on. Children are still paying a price. An Israeli shell killed two Palestinian boys and a girl near Beit Hanoun on Wednesday. A military spokesman said the troops targeted several Qassam rocket launchers aimed at Israel. It expressed 'sorrow for the cynical use the terror organisations make of the active participation of teenagers in terror attacks.'

The army announced yesterday that it had arrested a 15-year-old Gaza boy on his way to a suicide bombing against Israeli soldiers.

Israel's nightmare: homegrown neo-nazis in the Holy Land

The Independent, October 9, 2007

Rivka Zagaron, a 75-year-old Holocaust survivor, left her home in the Israeli port city of Haifa one September morning for her daily stroll along the beach. Two young men accosted her and shouted: 'Heil Hitler!' One of them kicked her, the other cursed her. When she managed to get away, she saw them beating a street sweeper. 'I never thought,' she said afterwards, 'that in our country I would hear Heil Hitler!'

The attack took place a week after Israelis were stunned by the arrest of eight neo-nazis in the Tel Aviv satellite town of Petah Tikva. Like the old lady, they thought the Jewish state, founded on the ashes of Auschwitz, was immune to that particular virus. But the epidemic continues to spread, prompting questions about Israel's failure to adjust to the multicultural society of Jews and non-Jews it has become.

Last week police arrested two 13-year-old boys on suspicion of daubing swastikas and naked women on the door of a Haifa synagogue. A 19-year-old has been charged with setting fire to a booth where Haifa's religious Jews celebrated the Sukkot festival. In Bnei Brak, a predominantly Orthodox town near Tel-Aviv, others painted Heil Hitler! on a synagogue wall.

According to the police, the Petah Tikva gang met every few days under their leader, Eli Buatinov, the self-styled 'Eli the Nazi', to decide who and where to strike next. Buatinov is quoted as saying he would never have children because his grandfather was half Jewish and he didn't want to father a 'piece of trash with even the smallest percentage of Jewish blood'.

Their arms are tattooed with Nazi and white-power symbols, though they protest their innocence. They are expected to come to trial later this month on charges of assault, illegally possessing weapons and denying the Holocaust.

Members of the cell, aged 16 to 21, are all Russian immigrants. One is Jewish, the rest were admitted to Israel under the Law of Return, which grants automatic citizenship to anyone with at least one Jewish grandparent – the same criterion adopted by the Third Reich for sending Jews to the gas chambers. In the former Soviet Union, their families were defined on their identity cards as ethnic Russians. In Israel, they are outsiders, frustrated and angry. Neo-nazism is a way to hit back where they know it hurts.

One of the gang's alleged victims was Anatoly Levin, a 38-year-old Orthodox Jew with a bushy black beard and black hat who migrated from St Petersburg 12 years ago. He was walking home through a local park late one night after a Talmud study session. Two teenage skinheads mocked him and made anti-Semitic jokes in Russian.

When they started throwing stones, he threw stones back. One of theirs hit his leg. When another struck a passing car, the driver jumped out and the boys ran off. As Levin, a geriatric nurse, continued on his way, the two assailants attacked him again, this time with wooden clubs, and broke his right hand. He says he couldn't escape because of his injured leg. The boys fled when he yelled 'Police!' and people rushed out to see what was going on.

Zalman Gilichenski, a Russian immigrant teacher who runs a help and information line for victims of anti-Semitism, says neo-nazism is widespread in the Jewish state. 'There are groups in many towns. They distribute cassettes and written material. They began with graffiti, and then graduated to beatings.'

The police say there are more individuals than groups. They spray-paint swastikas, vandalise synagogues, taunt recognisably religious Jews and terrorise people who look vulnerable – the homeless, homosexuals, drunks, old people. There is no evidence of a coordinated nationwide movement, no Führer, no Oswald Mosley figure. The Petah Tikva gang was unusually well organised. Israeli neo-nazis have no publications of their own. Two websites were closed a couple of years ago.

The Petah Tikva youths were caught after they made videos of their rampages and posted them on a viciously anti-Semitic Moscow site. One showed them savagely beating a Thai worker in the Tel Aviv bus station. The site, Format 18, said the images had been sent by 'our comrades in Israel'.

The choice was no accident. Russian racism is going global. The Israeli neo-nazis draw their inspiration from the thriving radical right in mother Russia, where Vladimir Putin's interior ministry estimates there are 70,000 white-supremacist skinheads and a poll this summer found that 35 per cent of the population disliked Jews.

Sergei Makarov, a researcher who monitors Russian racism from Jerusalem, argues: 'You can't understand neo-Nazis in Israel if you don't understand the upsurge in neo-nazism in Russia itself. It's nourished by what's going on back home. These people came from there, and they are in touch through the internet.'

Despite the Russians' bitter memories of their 'Great Patriotic War' against Germany, groups there flaunt the Nazi connection. One, the National Socialist Forum, boasts that 80,000 messages have been posted on its website. It claims 1,500 regular participants and 343 visits a day. One of its contributors calls himself 'Dr Goebbels'.

Some groups are reported to hold military training camps. They have headquarters, weapons caches and firing ranges. Neo-nazism is banned, but tolerated. When violators are prosecuted, the sentences tend to be light.

The Russian ultra-nationalists, nostalgic for the glory of the Czars, target migrant workers from the former Soviet Asian republics, as well as Jews. The National Socialist Party of Russia posted a gruesome video clip of its members stabbing and decapitating two 'aliens' from Dagestan and Tajikistan. 'Our party is a fighting avant-garde of the National Socialist struggle,' it bragged.

Another nationalist site, Russkoe Delo ('Russian Cause'), accused the 'Zhids' (Yids) of seeking to dominate the world and of encouraging white women to have sex with black men, who infect them with AIDS. 'The Jews, through their knavish propaganda, infect the minds of white women and inspire them to look at the Niggers with friendliness and benevolence,' it wrote. 'We must protect our women. We must liberate their minds from the Zhid obsession.'

Up to 300,000 of the one million immigrants who flocked to Israel after the collapse of the Soviet Union in 1989 do not identify themselves as Jewish. The families came because the gates were suddenly thrown open and the economic prospects looked brighter in Israel than Russia. Some are the gentile spouses of people with a half-forgotten Jewish grandparent. Others are the children of previous all-gentile marriages, who have no connection to Jewish history or the Jewish religion. Their divorced parent married a Jew. To complicate things further, in Russia ethnicity is defined by the father's origins, in Israel by the mother's. So a child could be a Jew in Russia and a Russian in Israel.

It is estimated that 20-25 per cent of the post-Soviet wave has failed to integrate into Israeli society. Their children came to Israel because their parents brought them. Immigrants account for 42 per cent of all school dropouts, although they are only 11.5 per cent of the total school population. Even those who have been successfully absorbed remember being tormented as 'Stinking Russians' and told to 'Get back to Russia', mostly by working-class North African children of a previous mass immigration.

A recent Hebrew University study found that only one third of Russian immigrant teenagers identified themselves as Israelis. In a society with no binge-booze culture, about 90 per cent of them reported drinking alcohol in the past year. One third said they got drunk at least four times, while 36 per cent admitted using drugs. Almost a third of those who took drugs said they had committed violent acts under the influence.

Marina Solodkin, a Russian member of the Israeli parliament and former deputy minister of immigrant absorption, explains: 'Neo-nazi activity is the way a young generation that has not found itself in Israel protests. They've lost their identity. They are not Jews, they are not Israelis. They are Russians who are not accepted, not in schools, not in the families of other children.'

Eli Zarkhin, an educational counsellor who runs the Israel Association for Immigrant Children, says: 'We're talking about 40,000 children who are not Jewish and identify themselves as not Jewish. It adds one more difficulty. They already have problems in Israel because it's a foreign country, because it has a foreign language, because there are foreign cultural codes, because their parents are busy with their own integration and can't help the children, and because there are no programmes in schools to bring these children closer to Israel.

'There is no Nazi ideology, but there is a lot of anger. We used to see graffiti against the Moroccans. Now we see them against the Jews, who represent for them the Israel that doesn't want to accept them. These teenagers are looking for provocative symbols. They use the swastika because they know it makes Jews angry. It also makes the educational authorities take notice of them. They get attention.'

Zarkhin cites the case of Sasha, whose family settled in the Mediterranean town of Ashkelon when he was eight. 'He feels himself Russian, he grew up as Russian. He had a Russian father and a Russian mother. One day his mother came home and said his father's grandfather was Jewish. So they were allowed to go to Israel. Life there was easier. They could earn more money.'

In Ashkelon, Sasha went to a school where half the children were Russian-speaking and half native Israelis. 'Nobody accepted him,' Zarkhin reports. 'Even the Russian-speaking children didn't want to deal with him because he was a goy. They hit him, they called him names. He has problems with Hebrew. His parents are working. So, more and more he started fighting in school. On one occasion he said: It's a pity Hitler didn't kill you. When we talked to him, he knew nothing about Hitler, except that Hitler killed Jews.'

Israel takes pride in fulfilling its Zionist mission by absorbing more than three million Jews from 100 different countries in Africa,

Asia, Europe and the Americas over the past 60 years. But critics protest that a country whose raison d'etre is to be the state of the Jews has yet to come to terms with multiculturalism – the presence of nearly one and a half million Arab citizens, 20 per cent of the total population, and tens of thousands of Russian non-Jews, as well as long-term migrant workers who care for the aged, till the fields and build the cities.

'Being Jewish,' Eli Zarkhin contends, 'doesn't mean to be against other nations. We have a reality. Israel is not the state of the Jews only. We should take it into account, we should deal with it. The government should do more to make others feel they belong. Maybe a state with a Jewish majority, a state with Jewish values of all people being equal, all people having rights, can work too.' More bluntly, the Arabs demand 'a state of all its citizens'.

Anatoly Gerasimov, another advocate of multiculturalism, is trying to give the ethnic Russians a voice through a new lobby, the Russian Centre of Culture and Information. Gerasimov, a dapper 49-year-old Christian who worked as a nurse, denounces successive Israeli governments for failing to adopt a clear and considered policy on minorities.

'In Israel,' he complains, 'all problems revolve around Jews and their conflict with the Arabs. National minorities have long been cast to the margins of cultural, public and political life. The state refuses to perceive hundreds of thousands of citizens, working in industry, studying in schools and universities, serving in the army as full members of society.

'Every fourth citizen of Israel is non-Jewish, but open any newspaper and you will not see anything about our non-Jewish holidays, about the history of our presence in the Holy Land, or about our communal activities. Last year our Russian community participated in an international youth sports festival in Moscow. Our boys and girls brought gold and silver medals back to Israel. Not a line was written about it in Israeli newspapers. Even Russian-speaking MPs gave them no encouragement.

'Israel has problems with non-Jews? Israel has one greater problem – the absence of a desire to cooperate with us in solving the vital issues of Jews and non-Jews living together in the Holy Land.'

Marina Solodkin, the immigrant MP, says that many of the mixed Russian families came to Israel because they wanted to be one thing or the other. 'If they had Jewish blood, they wanted to be Jewish.' Israel, she protests, has not made it easy for them. The Orthodox rabbis still control the conversion process. They try to impose a pious way of life that is alien to most veteran Israelis, who manage to be both Jewish and secular. Converts are expected to keep the Sabbath and observe kosher dietary laws. Inspectors reserve the right to make random checks that they are not backsliding.

Women are ordered to stop wearing trousers, which are regarded as masculine and thus immodest. Girls are forbidden to join the army, though it is widely accepted that military service offers the best route to integration. The rabbis don't want them hanging out with the opposite sex. 'Not everyone,' Solodkin insists, 'wants to live the strict Orthodox way of life.'

Coalition constraints keep the more liberal Reform rabbis at arm's length. Ehud Olmert, like previous prime ministers, needs the support of at least one Orthodox religious party to stay in office. They fight every effort to recognise Reform Judaism.

So far, anti-Semitic hate crimes are restricted to the young. But some older non-Jewish immigrants quietly share their smouldering resentment at the discrimination and ostracism they have experienced. They seek comfort in old prejudices.

A Russian-language bookshop near Jerusalem's Mahaneh Yehuda market stocks anti-Semitic books and Holocaust denial among its shelves of novels, thrillers, science fiction and DVDs. They are on open display. One, *What we Don't Like About Them*, an anti-Jewish tract by Vasily Shulgin, first published in 1929 and reprinted in 2005, has the exiled Jewish oligarch Boris Berezhovsky on its cover. Another, by Alexei Mukhin, is dedicated to 'Jewish Elites'. It features the familiar smiling face of Chelsea's Roman Abramovich.

Vladimir, the bookshop owner, a mild-mannered intellectual who asks us not to publish his second name, reports a steady demand from older customers. He draws the line at Hitler's *Mein Kampf* and the notorious century-old forgery, *The Protocols of the Elders of Zion*, which purports to map a Jewish takeover of the world. 'As for the rest,' he shrugs, 'I'm in the business of selling books.'

For the 75-80 per cent of Russians who made it, the post-Soviet immigration has been a success story. Most of them were educated people with modern skills. Once they got over the initial difficulties, they found jobs. Israel's orchestras are full of Russian musicians. Russian doctors and nurses man its hospitals. Engineers and mathematicians work in high tech.

Lisa Rubchinsky, a 29-year-old hairdresser who came here alone when she was 18, says: 'At first I felt hatred of Russians in the street, in the market. But I'm a strong person. I know how to defend myself. If you've chosen to come here, try to be part of this country. Don't blame other people.'

She admits it's been easier for her than for some of her friends. Unlike them, she doesn't look Slavic.

No comfort for bereaved parents: reservists talk about the Lebanon war

Jewish Chronicle, February 1, 2008

Before going to war in Lebanon in 2006 Staff Sergeant David Tal's combat engineering platoon had to forage for night vision equipment, a staple of modern warfare. Their own battalion had none in its stores.

'We went round all the bases in Northern Israel,' Mr Tal, who made aliyah from Leeds in 1989, told the *JC* after the Winograd Report was published on Wednesday. 'Eventually we found some. In Lebanon another platoon, which didn't get night vision equipment, panicked when they encountered us in the dark. They shot one of our guys.'

On its first day, Mr Tal's platoon was sent into Lebanon in broad daylight. 'The thinking,' he said, 'was that the enemy would see where we were going, then we'd withdraw and go somewhere else. We got shelled from all directions, then they sent us in again to the same place. When we asked the battalion commander why he'd sent us in like sitting ducks, he replied that he'd never expected anything like that.'

Reservists like Mr Tal, a 37-year-old father who works in a Jerusalem high tech company, are bitter that the army allowed stocks to run down and neglected their training. They blame the politicians for sending them into battle without checking that they were ready for it. Bereaved families share their anger at the way decisions were made.

Both groups were encouraged that Winograd endorsed their criticisms, but were disappointed that it did not urge Ehud Olmert, the last of the war leaders still in office, to resign – and that the prime minister seemed to be brazening it out.

Mr Tal accused Mr Olmert of being too arrogant to take advice during the war and of failing to see what was going on. 'The fact that Olmert wants to disregard the committee that he appointed says more about Olmert than anything else. Somebody who's not prepared to take responsibility for what happened is not somebody who should be leading the country. The ironic thing is that the army has learnt the lessons, while the politicians are refusing to learn the lessons.'

David Einhorn, a bereaved father, vowed: 'We will continue our struggle. There were many failures during the war. Once the report addresses both the political and the military echelons, they both have to take responsibility. The prime minister can't throw the blame on to somebody else. He has to go.'

Mr Einhorn's 22-year-old paratrooper son Yehonatan was killed on the 19th day of the war. Yehonatan, his father recalled, was an observant Jew who loved the Land of Israel. He was doing his national service as a staff sergeant. 'I met him two days before he died. He said he was fighting for his country so that we'd have the kind of country he wanted to live in.'

The Einhorns remain a proud military family. They are not giving up. The 47-year-old father was himself on reserve service in the air force when he heard of Yehonatan's death. Two other sons are also in the army.

'I have two younger sons, aged 15 and 12,' Mr Einhorn boasted. 'Both of them will go to the army. I still do reserve duty. We serve in elite combat units. We will continue to serve the state.'

They just want the state to continue to serve them.

Comment after the attack on the Mercaz Harav Yeshivah

Jewish Chronicle, March 14, 2008

As we often do on Friday lunchtime in Jerusalem, my wife and I went out for a salad and cappuccino in a coffee shop off Jaffa Road. It was the day after a Palestinian gunman from East Jerusalem murdered eight students in the Mercaz Harav Yeshivah, the capital's first major terrorist attack in four years. A memorial service was taking place at the yeshivah, a couple of miles away in the shadow of the new suspension bridge at the northern entrance to town.

In the city centre, three police armoured vehicles were drawn up in Zion Square. But that was the only sign that anything untoward had happened. If anyone felt traumatised, they were keeping it to themselves. No flags flew at half-mast. Israelis were doing their last minute Shabbat shopping. In the Kadosh coffee shop, anyone arriving after 1 o'clock had to wait for a vacant table.

The next day, friends visiting from London asked us to take them for lunch in Abu Ghosh, an Israeli Arab village off the Tel Aviv road. We wondered whether secular Israelis, who flock there every Saturday hunting for bargains and gorging themselves on grilled meat, would be inhibited this week about visiting an Arab village, albeit one with a unique history of coexistence stretching back to 1948.

We needn't have worried. It was as hard as ever to find a parking place on the narrow, hilly main street, with its textile factory shops, humus stalls, restaurants, plant nursery and designer candle-maker. In our restaurant of choice, a Jewish family was celebrating a birthday. Children were playing in the garden.

It is a sad truth that the Mercaz Harav massacre highlighted the fragmented state of Israeli society. Almost all the mourners at the memorial service and the funerals that followed it were drawn from the pro-settler religious Zionist community.

The majority of Israelis outside that camp were not indifferent. The mainstream media covered the atrocity in depth and at length for days afterwards. But it did not impinge on most of their readers' and viewers' lives. As happened at the time of the Gaza disengagement in 2005, the settlers found themselves isolated in their grief and anger.

It was not only the secular Israelis either. I went to buy challahs in Mea She'arim on Friday morning. The walls of the haredi ghetto were plastered with their usual polemical bulletins in Hebrew and Yiddish. But I spotted none mourning the slaughtered yeshivah boys or calling for revenge. They were not 'their' victims.

Israel has become a tribal society. Last November, Beitar Yerushalayim football fans booed when they were asked to observe a minute's silence on the anniversary of Yitzhak Rabin's assassination.

For rank-and-file Beitar supporters, most of them Likud voters of Middle Eastern origin, the murdered prime minister was an Ashkenazi and a leftist who shook hands with Yasser Arafat. Despite Rabin's record as the army's commander-in-chief in the Six-Day War and as an elected national leader, even in death he did not merit their respect.

Perhaps Israel has always been a divided society, riven along political lines. In 1965, Harold Wilson hesitated to send the army to quell white Rhodesia's unilateral declaration of independence because he did not trust British troops to fire on their 'kith and kin'. David Ben-Gurion had no such qualms when he ordered the Israel Defence Forces to sink the Irgun Zvai Leumi arms ship Altalena off Tel Aviv in 1948.

Over the past week, the settlers and their allies have reinforced the divisions by using the yeshivah massacre to advance their political agenda. It was legitimate, but hardly designed to win friends and influence people. Rabbi Ya'acov Shapira, the head of Mercaz Harav, called on Israelis to oust Ehud Olmert's government and continue to settle the land.

The yeshivah was the seedbed of the militant Gush Emunim movement, inspiring the settlement campaign following the 1967 conquest of the West Bank and Gaza Strip. Rabbi Shapira reiterated the religious ruling, issued by one of his predecessors, Rabbi Tzvi Yehuda Kook, that forbade surrendering any of the Promised Land.

When education minister Yuli Tamir paid a condolence call, boisterous yeshivah students heckled her as a 'traitor' and a 'murderer.' Tamir, a Labour MK, was among the founders of Peace Now. When the prime minister's office asked whether he would be welcome, the answer was a resounding no.

Olmert was Ariel Sharon's principal ally in the Gaza disengagement, a champion of a two-state solution whose manifesto in the last election promised to follow suit on part of the West Bank. Despite their anguish, the Mercaz Harav rabbis saw him first and foremost as an enemy, not as a head of government delivering the nation's sympathy.

They cannot complain if they find themselves isolated once again, if and when the crunch comes.

Afterword by Martin Woollacott

Eric Silver lived in the wonderfully named Street of the Prophets in Jerusalem, and the consensus of his friends was that he looked the part. Tall and commanding, and with an always evident confidence in both speech and writing, he was one of the foremost journalistic interpreters of the Israeli scene for British and other English speaking readers for over 30 years, and at the same time a very English presence within the Israeli press corps. If he was not literally prophetic, he was nevertheless an extremely accurate and reliable guide to the complexities of Israeli politics.

He and I worked as foreign correspondents for the *Guardian* in the same era, when the paper was trying, in spite of very limited resources, to expand and improve its foreign coverage. His knowledge of Israeli society was unmatched, and made its contribution to that effort. Eric was always ready to explain and discuss, often prefacing his remarks with a very Yorkshire 'Look,' as in 'Look, you've got to understand two things about Sharon', or 'Look, it's not that simple'. Colleagues who were more critical of Israel sometimes faulted him for bias. But, while his loyalty to Israel was plain, so was his concern about the movement away from the relative certainties of an earlier era to the more right wing and fragmented condition of Israeli politics today, and his anxieties about the shrinking prospects of peace with the Palestinians.

When Eric began as a foreign correspondent, his personal centre left position as a sympathiser with two Labour parties, the British and the Israeli ones, was a relatively easy one to maintain. Later it became more difficult as both Israeli and British politics changed, but Eric persisted in the idea that ultimately these contradictions and conflicts would prove soluble. In the meantime, he saw it as his role to provide the informed reporting that fair-minded people needed if they were to understand the situation. Eric's range was wide and his eye was sharp, and the pieces reprinted in this book illustrate both the rapid and unpredictable way events move in the

Middle Eastern region and the transformation of Israeli political structures.

Eric's interests in both Israel and in politics were foreshadowed during his PPE studies at St Catherine's Oxford, after a Leeds upbringing. He was a member and officer of the Israel Society, and had earlier belonged to the Habonim Zionist youth movement. He liked arguing in coffee shops, a trait still apparent years later in Israel. A college friend has recalled his rather distant attitude to Wittgenstein, whom he regarded as more amusing than enlightening.

After working on provincial papers and on the *Guardian* as a sub-editor, labour reporter, and diarist, Eric became the Jerusalem correspondent of the *Guardian* and the *Observer* in 1972. He went on to India for the two papers in 1983, enjoying his time in the sub-continent, but he had left his heart in Israel. Rather than return to Britain when his time in Delhi came to an end, he chose to exchange the security of a full time job for the exigencies of a freelance existence in Israel. It was a testimony to his abilities that, in a highly competitive field, he never lacked employment.

Eric and Bridget's vaulted and thick walled home in the Street of the Prophets was a haven for Israeli friends and for visitors from outside Israel alike. They set a fine table, and Eric was as generous with his knowledge and his contacts book as was his wife with her superlative chocolate cake. The thick walls came in useful when a suicide bomber blew himself up on the street outside, an incident which underlined a principle Eric often advanced in argument, which was that life in the Middle East was too difficult and dangerous to be seen in black and white terms.

51 - after Yom Kippur
62 - Arab Israelis - neglect
79 - 10yrs after 1967 war
90 - Begin + Deir Yassin (~138?)
98 - Sadat's visit Nov. 1977
101 - decline of Cairo
127 - Begin - right wing vision
— no room for Palestinian nationalism
134 - Israeli withdrawal from Sinai 1982
141 - Begin: land of Israel; invasion of Lebanon
147 - Start of first Intifada Dec 1987
163 - Arafat ready for peace 1989
162 - Shamir 1989
196 - Israeli withdrawal from Gaza 1993
215 - Gaza's independence; Nov 1994
228 - funeral of Yitzhak Rabin after assassination
by Jewish fanatic Nov 1995
230 - Rabin
248 - Netanyahu 1996
278 - Arab frustration with Netanyahu Dec 96
279 - death of King Hussein 1999
283 - Barak's failure at Camp David 2000
286 - conflict sparked by Sharon's visit to Temple Mount
(Oct 2000)
226 - the 2nd intifada March 2001
248 - Birzeit 2001
308 - Sharon Dec 2001
321 - Arafat's plight Dec 2002
324 - Abu Mazen P.M. March 2003

Lightning Source UK Ltd.
Milton Keynes UK
UKOW020701200112

185750UK00002B/36/P

326/7 Int. road map May 2003
334 after Arafat Dec 2004